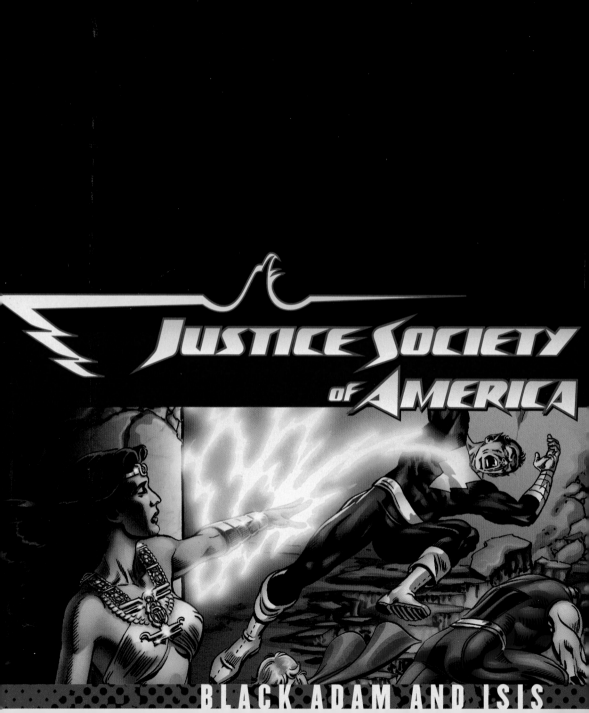

JUSTICE SOCIETY OF AMERICA

BLACK ADAM AND ISIS

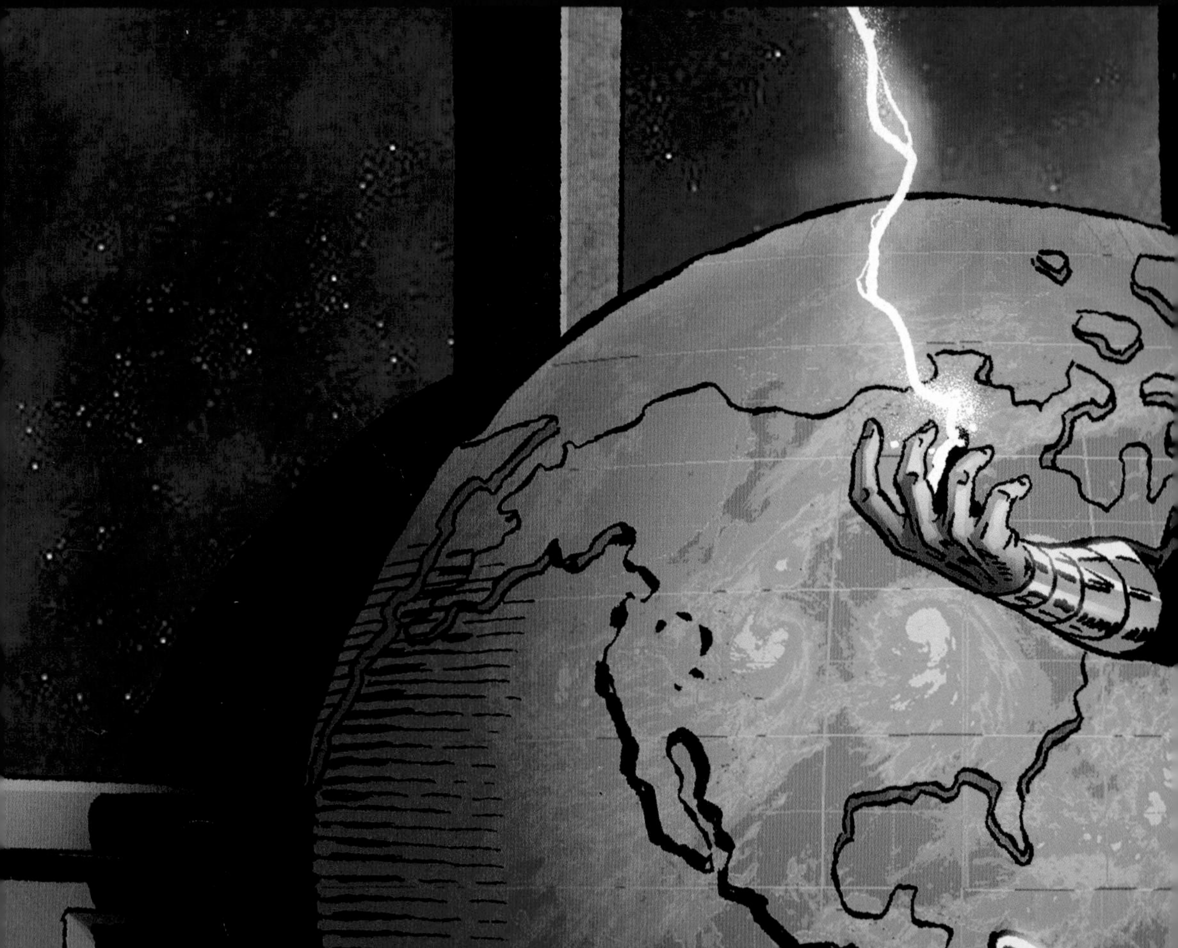

JUSTICE SOCIETY of AMERICA

BLACK ADAM AND ISIS

JSA #23-25
STORY BY **GEOFF JOHNS** & **JERRY ORDWAY** PENCILS **JERRY ORDWAY**
INKS **BOB WIACEK** WITH **JERRY ORDWAY**

JSA #26
WRITER **GEOFF JOHNS** PENCILS **DALE EAGLESHAM** INKS **NATHAN MASSENGILL**

JSA #27 & 28
WRITER AND PENCILS **JERRY ORDWAY** INKER **BOB WIACEK**

ORIGINS & OMENS
WRITER **MATTHEW STURGES** ART **FERNANDO PASARIN**

DAN DIDIO SVP – EXECUTIVE EDITOR **MICHAEL SIGLAIN MIKE CARLIN** EDITORS – ORIGINAL SERIES
GEORG BREWER VP – DESIGN & DC DIRECT CREATIVE **BOB HARRAS** GROUP EDITOR – COLLECTED EDITIONS
ANTON KAWASAKI EDITOR **ROBBIN BROSTERMAN** DESIGN DIRECTOR – BOOKS

DC COMICS
PAUL LEVITZ PRESIDENT & PUBLISHER **RICHARD BRUNING** SVP – CREATIVE DIRECTOR
PATRICK CALDON EVP – FINANCE & OPERATIONS **AMY GENKINS** SVP – BUSINESS & LEGAL AFFAIRS
JIM LEE EDITORIAL DIRECTOR – WILDSTORM **GREGORY NOVECK** SVP – CREATIVE AFFAIRS
STEVE ROTTERDAM SVP – SALES & MARKETING **CHERYL RUBIN** SVP – BRAND MANAGEMENT

COVER BY ALEX ROSS
PUBLICATION DESIGN BY ROBBIE BIEDERMAN

JUSTICE SOCIETY OF AMERICA: BLACK ADAM AND ISIS

DC COMICS, 1700 BROADWAY, NEW YORK, NY 10019. A WARNER BROS. ENTERTAINMENT COMPANY. PRINTED IN USA. FIRST PRINTING. HC ISBN: 978-1-4012-2530-8 SC ISBN: 978-1-4012-2531-5

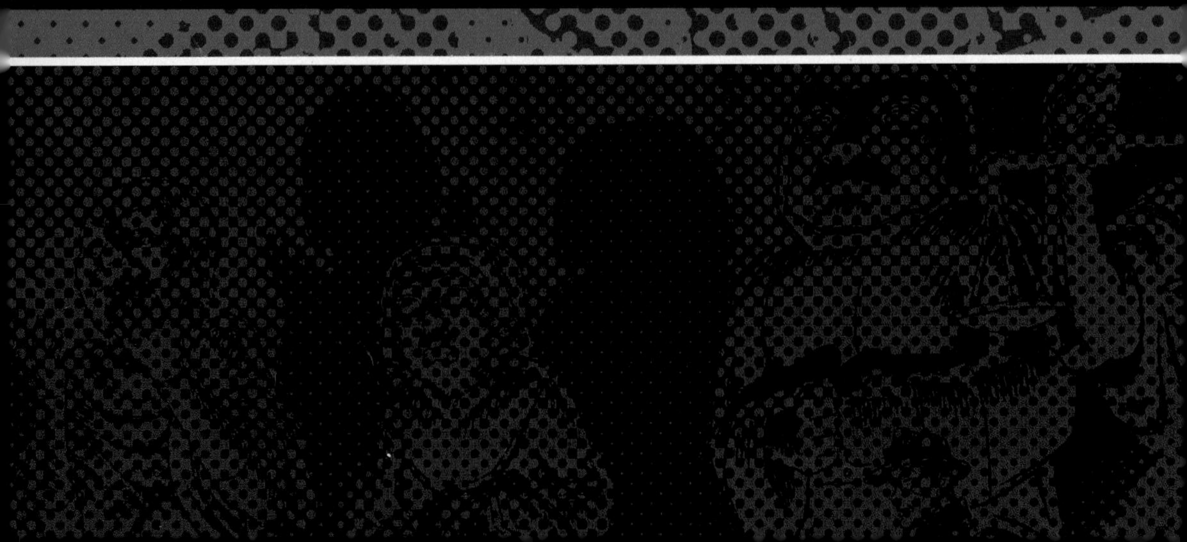

GREEN LANTERN Engineer Alan Scott found a lantern carved from a meteorite known as the Starheart. Fulfilling the lamp's prophecy to grant astonishing power, Scott tapped into the emerald energy and fought injustice as the Green Lantern. His ring can generate a variety of effects and energy constructs, sustained purely by his will.

THE FLASH The first in a long line of super-speedsters, Jay Garrick is capable of running at velocities near the speed of light. A scientist, Garrick has also served as mentor to other speedsters, and to many heroes over several generations.

WILDCAT A former heavyweight boxing champ, Ted Grant, a.k.a. Wildcat, prowls the mean streets defending the helpless. One of the world's foremost hand-to-hand combatants, he has trained many of today's best fighters — including Black Canary, Catwoman, and the Batman himself.

HAWKMAN Originally Prince Khufu of ancient Egypt, the hero who would become known as Hawkman discovered an alien spacecraft from the planet Thanagar, powered by a mysterious antigravity element called Nth metal. The unearthly energies of the metal transformed his soul, and he and his love Princess Chay-Ara were reincarnated over and over for centuries. Currently he is Carter Hall, archaeologist and adventurer.

POWER GIRL Once confused about her origins, Karen Starr now knows she is the cousin of an alternate-Earth Superman — who gave his life in the Infinite Crisis. Her enhanced strength and powers of flight and invulnerability are matched only by her self-confidence in action, which sometimes borders on arrogance.

MR. TERRIFIC Haunted by the death of his wife, Olympic gold medal-winning decathlete Michael Holt was ready to take his own life. Instead, inspired by the Spectre's story of the original Mr. Terrific, he rededicated himself to ensuring fair play among the street youth, using his wealth and technical skills to become the living embodiment of those ideals. He now divides his time between the JSA and the government agency known as Checkmate.

HOURMAN Rick Tyler struggled for a while before accepting his role as the son of the original Hourman. It hasn't been an easy road — he's endured addiction to the Miraclo drug that increases his strength and endurance, and nearly died from a strange disease. Now, after mastering the drug, he uses a special hourglass that enables him to see one hour into the future.

LIBERTY BELLE Jesse Chambers is the daughter of the Golden Age Johnny Quick and Liberty Belle. Originally adopting her father's speed formula, Jesse became the superhero known as Jesse Quick. After a brief period without powers, Jesse has returned — now taking over her mother's role. As the new Liberty Belle, Jesse is an All-American Powerhouse.

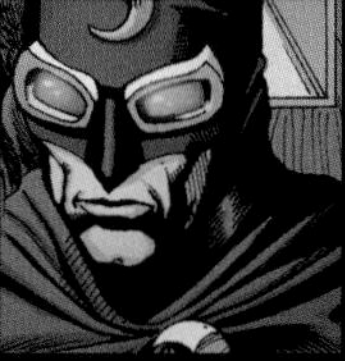

DR. MID-NITE A medical prodigy, Pieter Anton Cross refused to work within the limits of the system. Treating people on his own, he came into contact with a dangerous drug that altered his body chemistry, enabling him to see light in the infrared spectrum. Although he lost his normal sight in a murder attempt disguised as a car accident, his uncanny night vision allows him to protect the weak under the assumed identity of Dr. Mid-Nite.

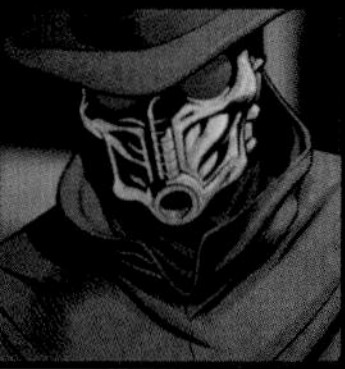

SANDMAN Sandy Hawkins was the ward of original Sandman Wesley Dodds, and he is the nephew of Dodds's lifelong partner, Dian Belmont. After a bizarre accident, Hawkins was able to transform himself into a pure silicon or sand form. Recently, he has been experiencing prophetic dreams. He also carries a gas mask, gas guns and other equipment.

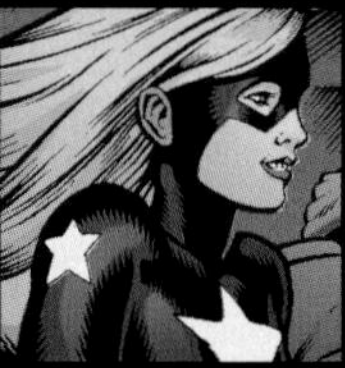

STARGIRL When Courtney Whitmore discovered the cosmic converter belt that had been worn by the JSA's original Star-Spangled Kid (her stepfather, Pat Dugan, was the Kid's sidekick Stripesy), she saw it as an opportunity to cut class and kick some butt. Now called Stargirl, she divides her time between her adventures with the JSA and bickering/teaming up with Pat — who sometimes monitors Courtney from his S.T.R.I.P.E. robot.

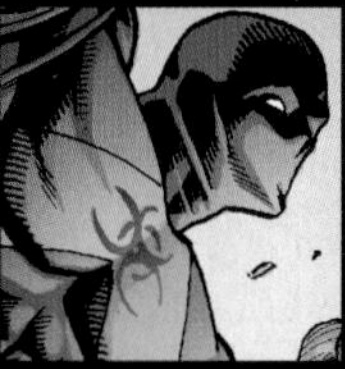

DAMAGE Grant Emerson has had a difficult life. Growing up, he was the victim of an abusive foster father. Then later, after discovering his explosive powers, he accidentally blew up half of downtown Atlanta. Last year, he was almost beaten to death by the super-speed villain known as Zoom. Grant has worn a full-face mask as Damage ever since.

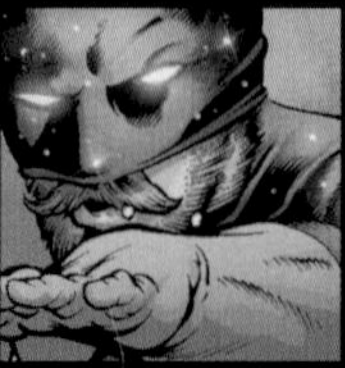

STARMAN A mysterious new Starman recently appeared in Opal City, saving its citizens numerous times. He apparently suffers from some form of schizophrenia, and hears voices in his head. Voluntarily residing in the Sunshine Sanitarium, Starman will occasionally leave and use his gravity-altering powers to fight crime.

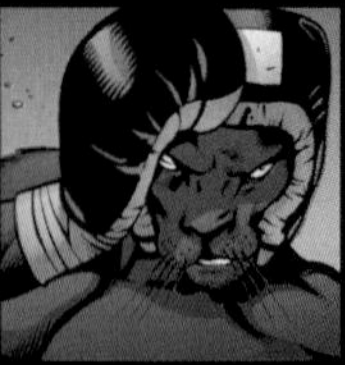

WILDCAT II Tommy Bronson is the newly discovered son of original Wildcat Ted Grant. But it's not quite "like father, like son" here. For one thing, Tom doesn't want to be a fighter like his dad. And second, this new Wildcat has the ability to turn into a feral creature, with enhanced agility and animalistic senses.

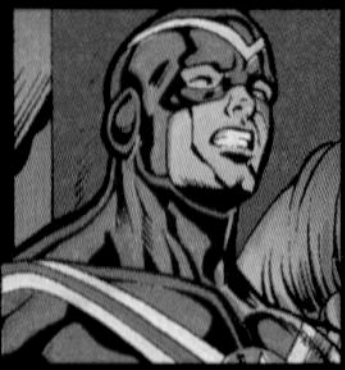

CITIZEN STEEL The grandson of the original Steel, Nathan Heywood is a former football hero who has suffered numerous tragedies. First, an injury and infection required his leg to be amputated. Then, a vicious attack by the Fourth Reich wiped out most of his family. But during the attack, a bizarre incident left him with metal-like skin and superhuman strength.

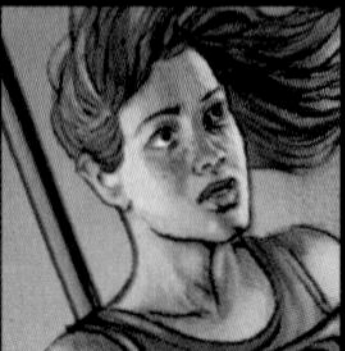

CYCLONE Maxine Hunkel is the granddaughter of the original Red Tornado, Abigail Mathilda "Ma" Hunkel (who is the current custodian of the Justice Society Museum). Maxine grew up idolizing her grandmother's allies in the JSA and still can't believe she's now part of the team. Maxine has the power of wind manipulation and can summon up cyclones and whirlwinds while gliding through the air.

JUSTICE SOCIETY OF AMERICA #23 cover by Alex Ross
Interior art by Jerry Ordway & Bob Wiacek

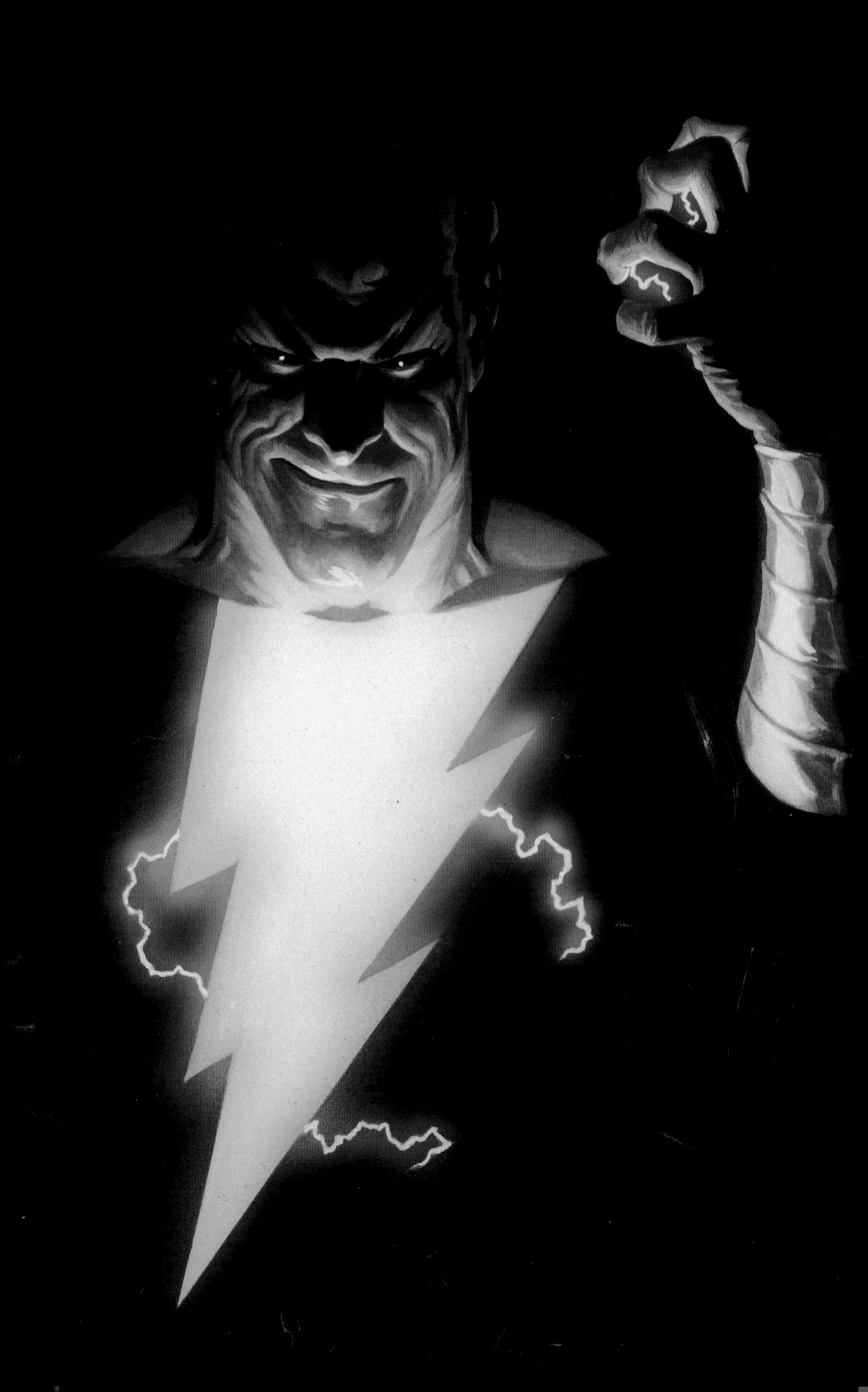

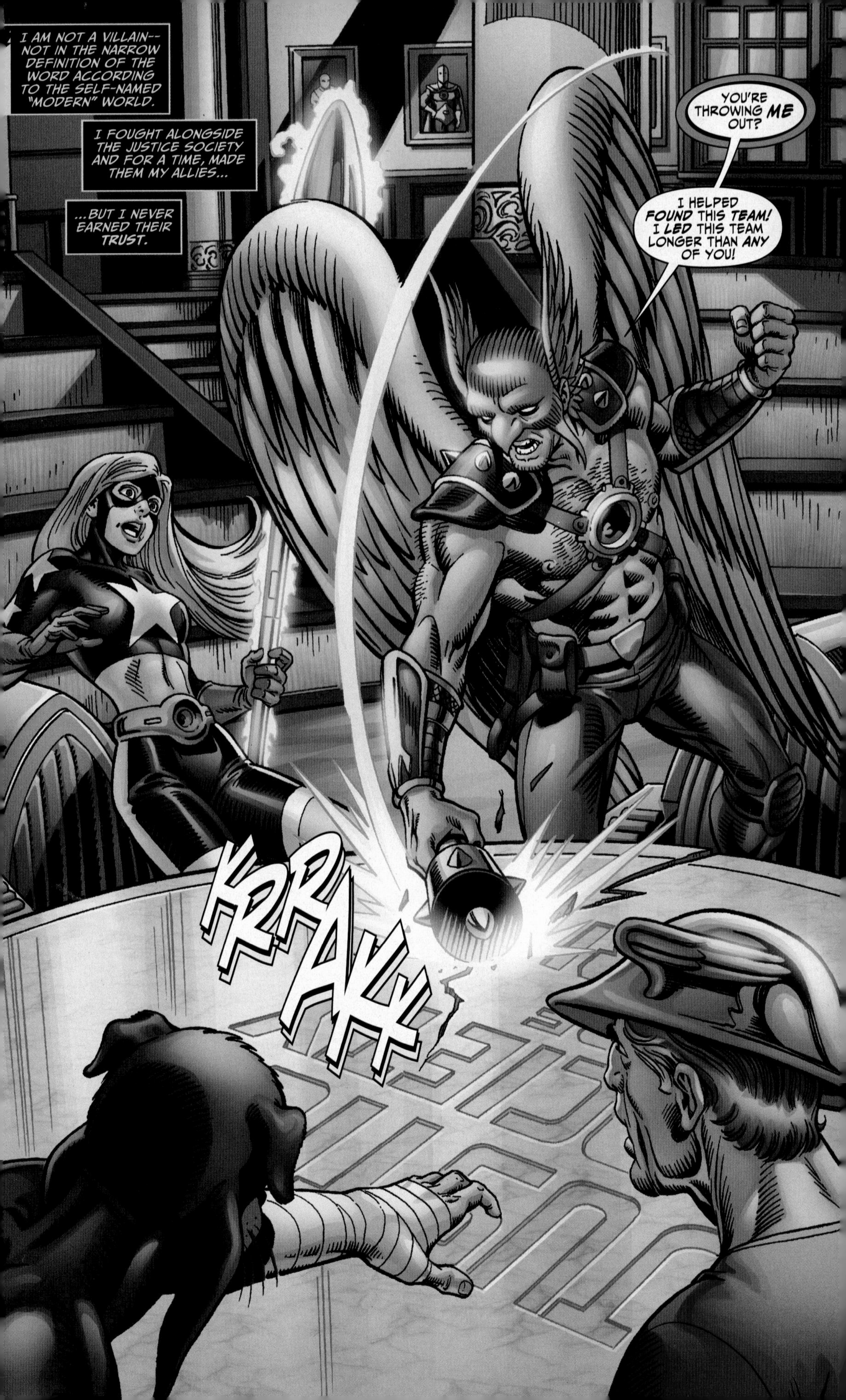
I AM NOT A VILLAIN--NOT IN THE NARROW DEFINITION OF THE WORD ACCORDING TO THE SELF-NAMED "MODERN" WORLD.
I FOUGHT ALONGSIDE THE JUSTICE SOCIETY AND FOR A TIME, MADE THEM MY ALLIES...
...BUT I NEVER EARNED THEIR TRUST.
YOU'RE THROWING ME OUT?
I HELPED FOUND THIS TEAM! I LED THIS TEAM LONGER THAN ANY OF YOU!
KRRAKK

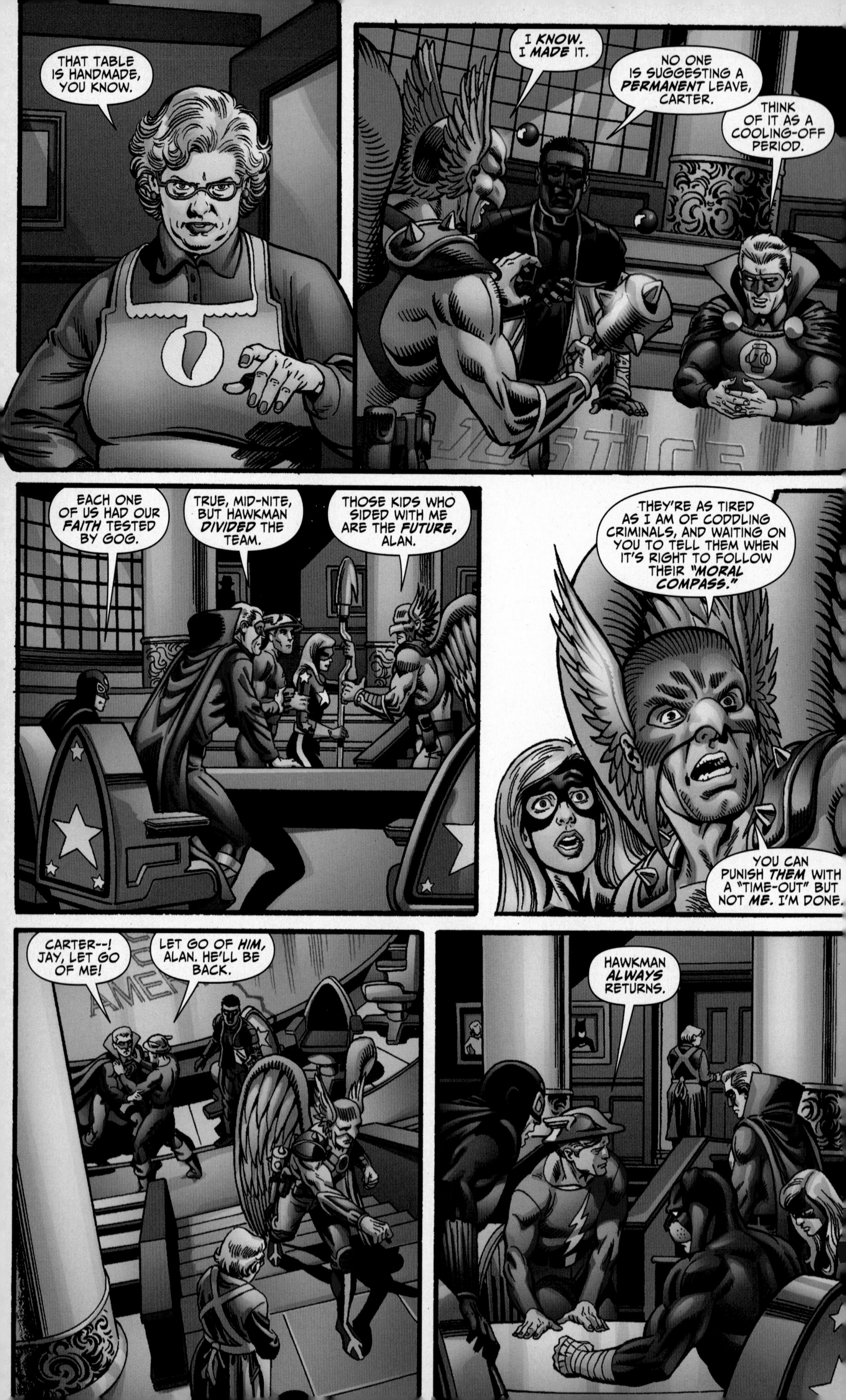
THAT TABLE IS HANDMADE, YOU KNOW.
I KNOW. I MADE IT.
NO ONE IS SUGGESTING A PERMANENT LEAVE, CARTER.
THINK OF IT AS A COOLING-OFF PERIOD.
JUSTICE
EACH ONE OF US HAD OUR FAITH TESTED BY GOG.
TRUE, MID-NITE, BUT HAWKMAN DIVIDED THE TEAM.
THOSE KIDS WHO SIDED WITH ME ARE THE FUTURE, ALAN.
THEY'RE AS TIRED AS I AM OF CODDLING CRIMINALS, AND WAITING ON YOU TO TELL THEM WHEN IT'S RIGHT TO FOLLOW THEIR "MORAL COMPASS."
YOU CAN PUNISH THEM WITH A "TIME-OUT" BUT NOT ME. I'M DONE.
CARTER--! JAY, LET GO OF ME!
LET GO OF HIM, ALAN. HE'LL BE BACK.
HAWKMAN ALWAYS RETURNS.

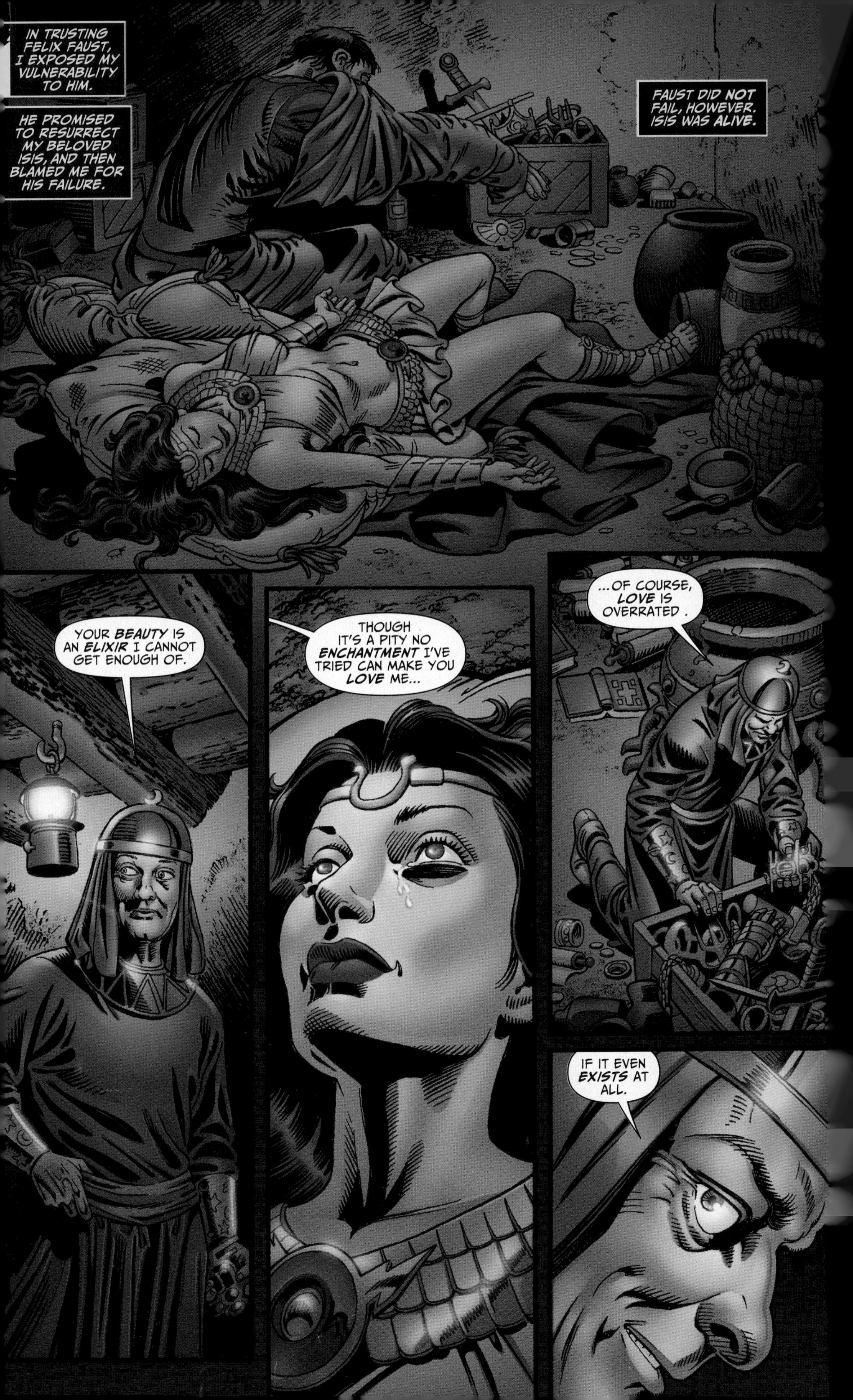
IN TRUSTING FELIX FAUST, I EXPOSED MY VULNERABILITY TO HIM.
HE PROMISED TO RESURRECT MY BELOVED ISIS, AND THEN BLAMED ME FOR HIS FAILURE.
FAUST DID NOT FAIL, HOWEVER. ISIS WAS ALIVE.
YOUR BEAUTY IS AN ELIXIR I CANNOT GET ENOUGH OF.
THOUGH IT'S A PITY NO ENCHANTMENT I'VE TRIED CAN MAKE YOU LOVE ME...
...OF COURSE, LOVE IS OVERRATED.
IF IT EVEN EXISTS AT ALL.

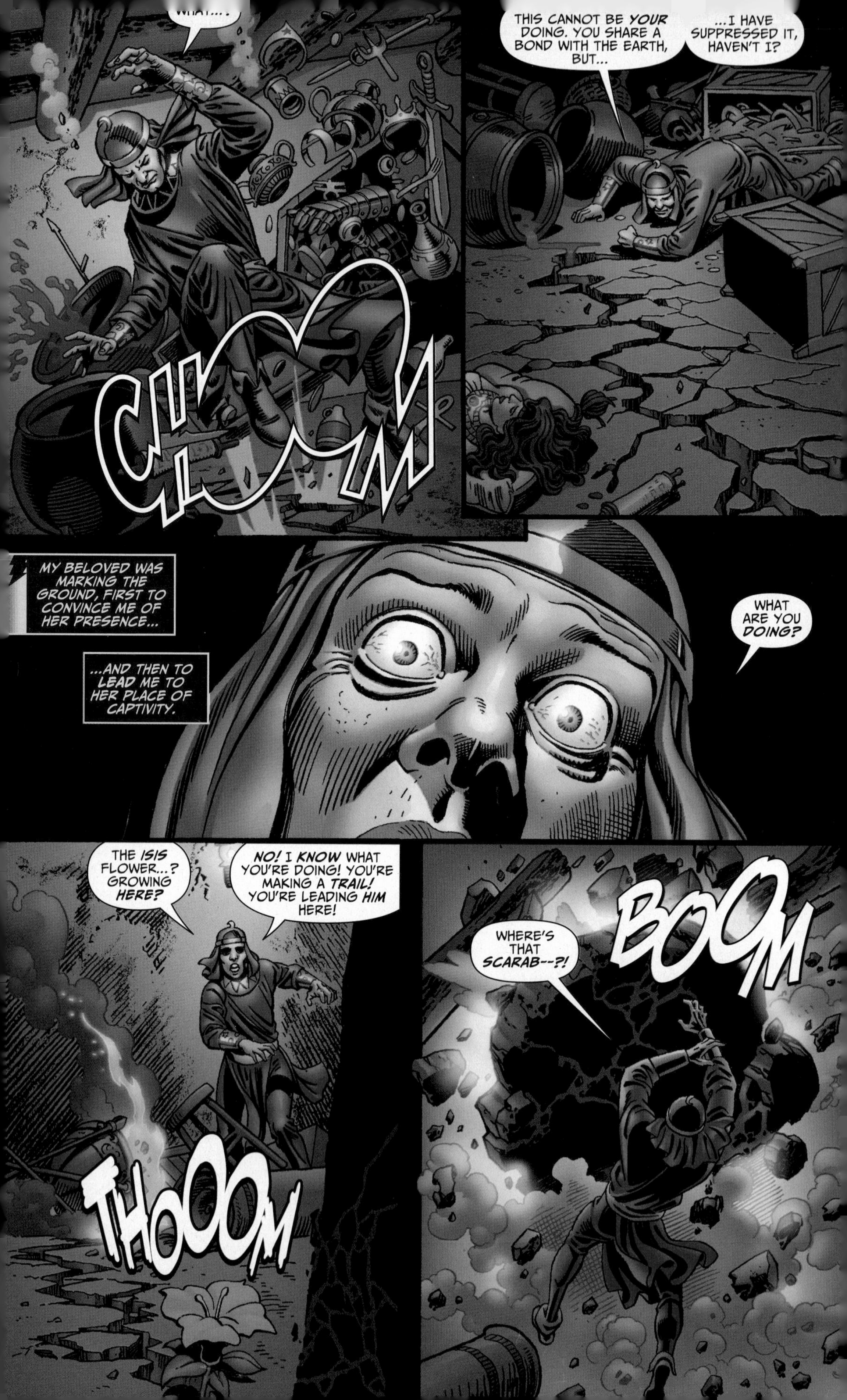

CHOOM
THIS CANNOT BE YOUR DOING. YOU SHARE A BOND WITH THE EARTH, BUT...
...I HAVE SUPPRESSED IT, HAVEN'T I?
MY BELOVED WAS MARKING THE GROUND, FIRST TO CONVINCE ME OF HER PRESENCE...
...AND THEN TO LEAD ME TO HER PLACE OF CAPTIVITY.
WHAT ARE YOU DOING?
THE ISIS FLOWER...? GROWING HERE?
NO! I KNOW WHAT YOU'RE DOING! YOU'RE MAKING A TRAIL! YOU'RE LEADING HIM HERE!
THOOOM
WHERE'S THAT SCARAB--?!
BOOM

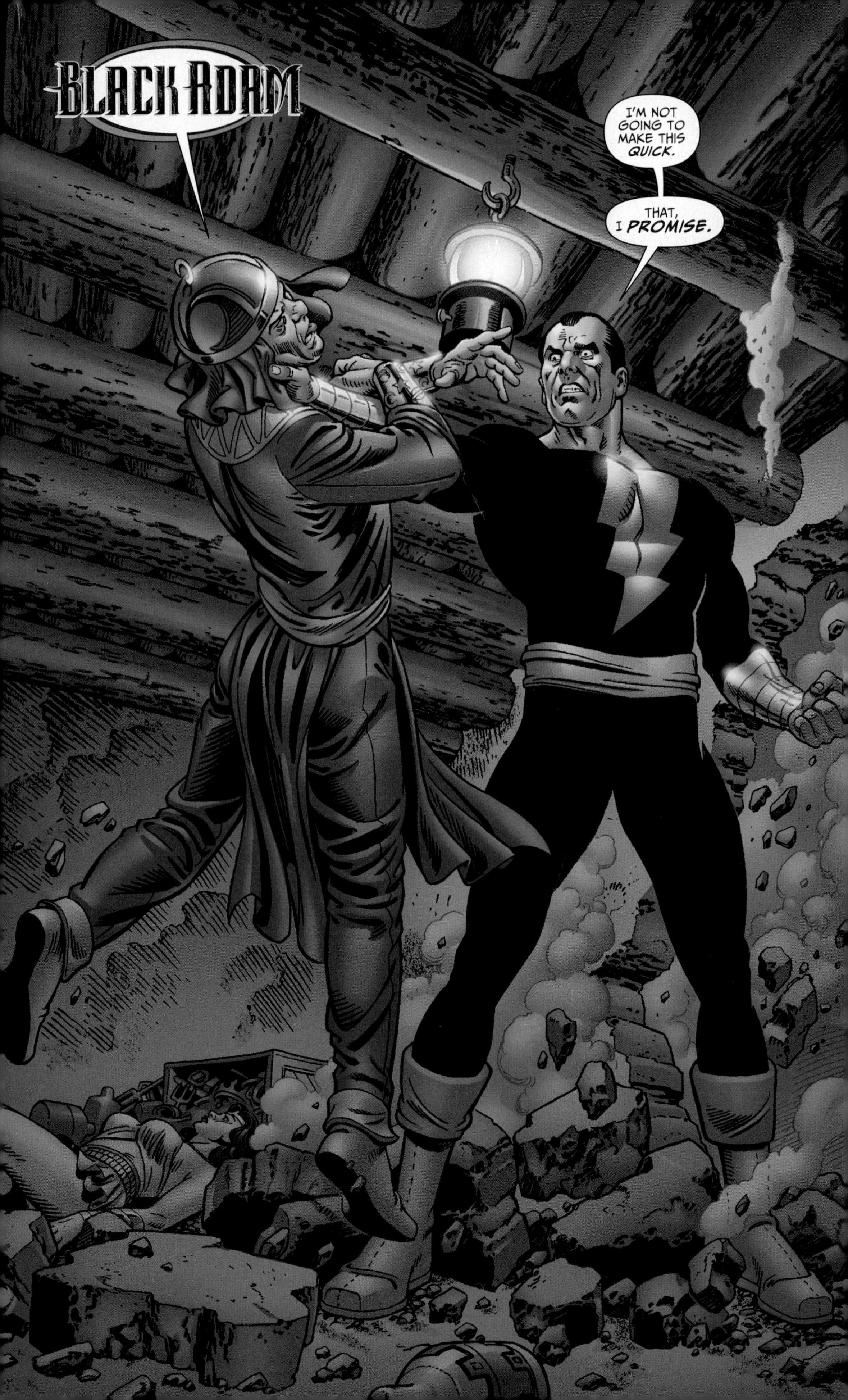
BLACK ADAM
I'M NOT GOING TO MAKE THIS QUICK.
THAT, I PROMISE.

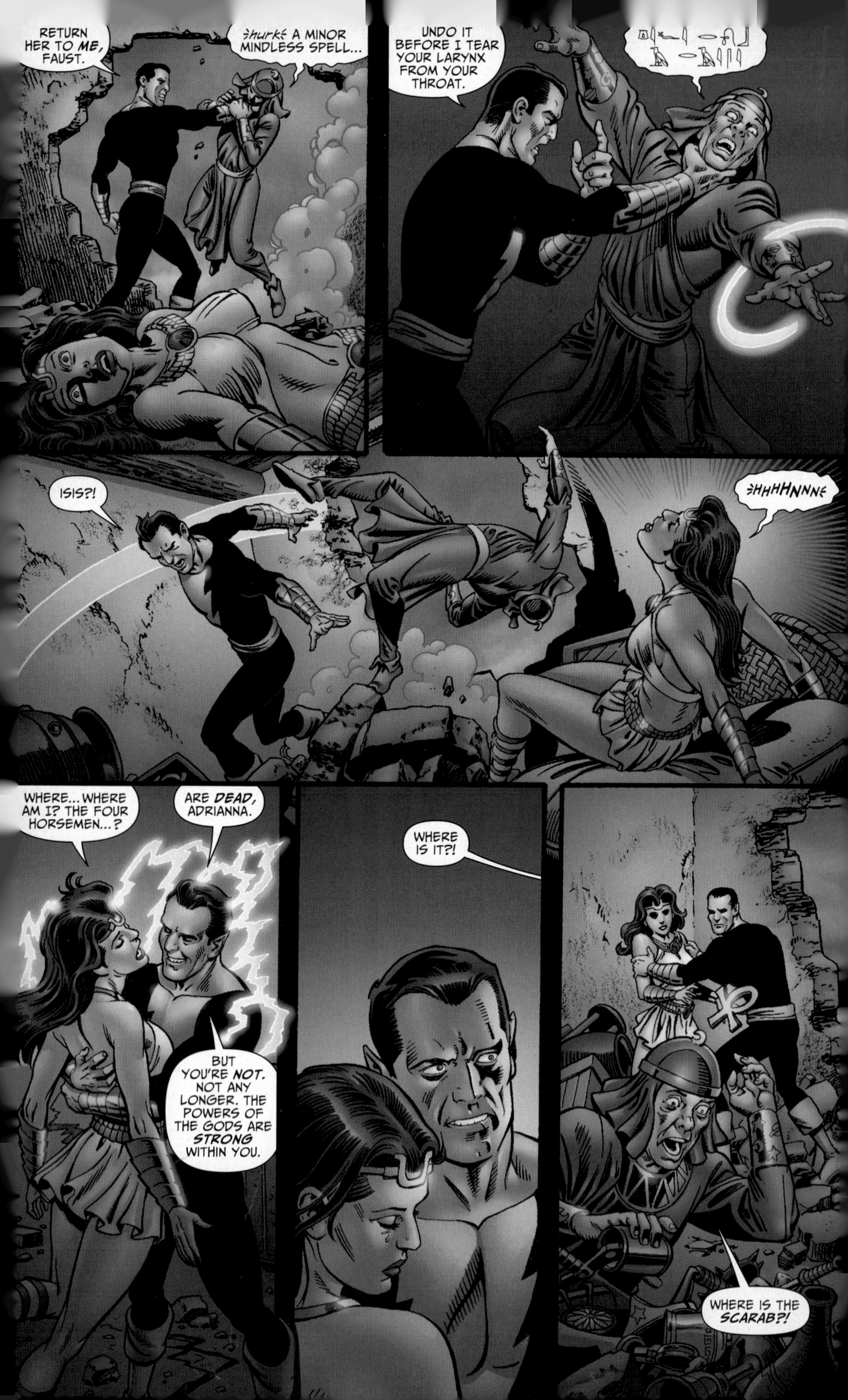
RETURN HER TO ME, FAUST.
hurk A MINOR MINDLESS SPELL...
UNDO IT BEFORE I TEAR YOUR LARYNX FROM YOUR THROAT.
ISIS?!
HHHHNNN
WHERE... WHERE AM I? THE FOUR HORSEMEN...?
ARE DEAD, ADRIANNA.
BUT YOU'RE NOT. NOT ANY LONGER. THE POWERS OF THE GODS ARE STRONG WITHIN YOU.
WHERE IS IT?!
WHERE IS THE SCARAB?!

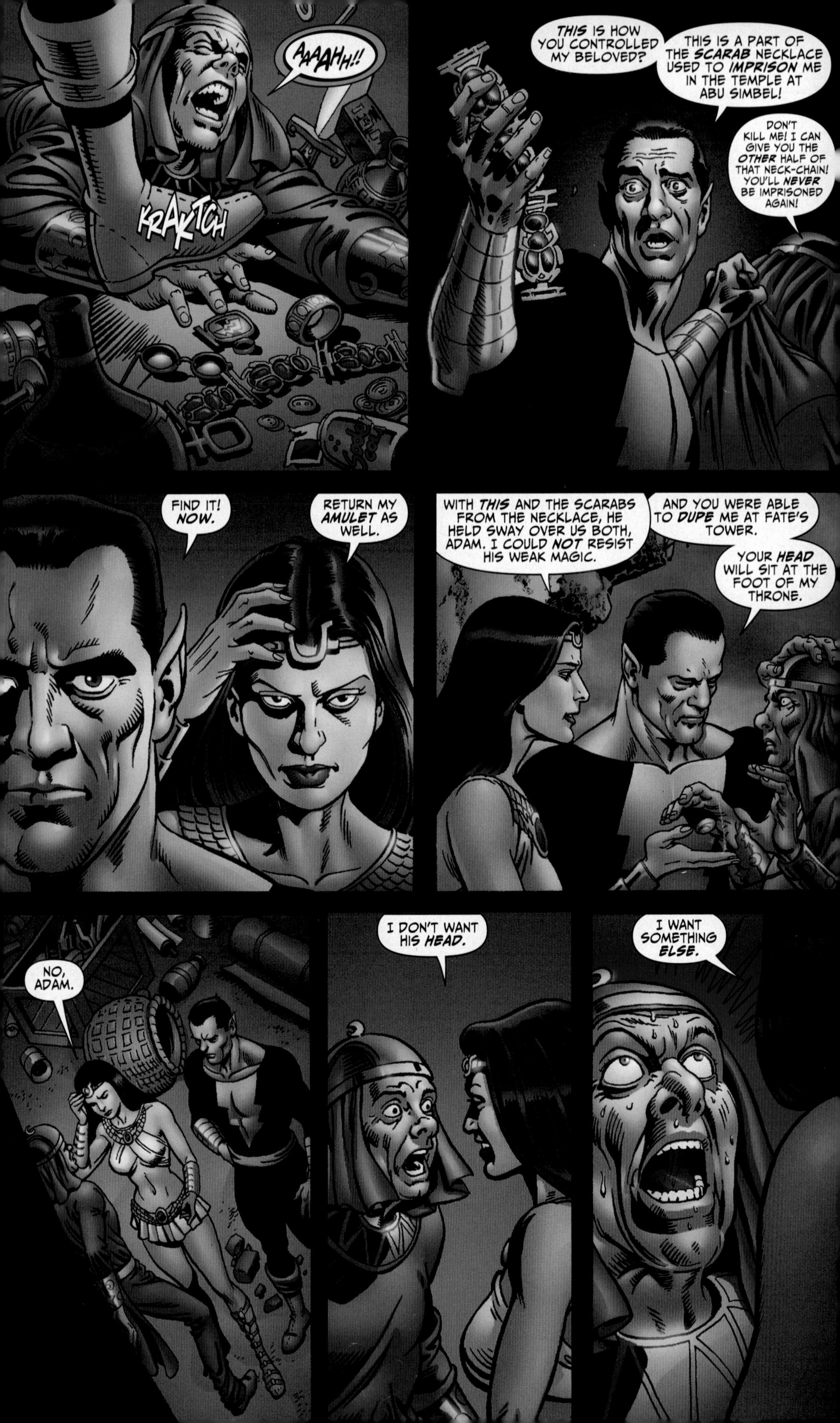

AAAAHH!!
KRAKTCH
THIS IS HOW YOU CONTROLLED MY BELOVED?
THIS IS A PART OF THE SCARAB NECKLACE USED TO IMPRISON ME IN THE TEMPLE AT ABU SIMBEL!
DON'T KILL ME! I CAN GIVE YOU THE OTHER HALF OF THAT NECK-CHAIN! YOU'LL NEVER BE IMPRISONED AGAIN!
FIND IT! NOW.
RETURN MY AMULET AS WELL.
WITH THIS AND THE SCARABS FROM THE NECKLACE, HE HELD SWAY OVER US BOTH, ADAM. I COULD NOT RESIST HIS WEAK MAGIC.
AND YOU WERE ABLE TO DUPE ME AT FATE'S TOWER.
YOUR HEAD WILL SIT AT THE FOOT OF MY THRONE.
NO, ADAM.
I DON'T WANT HIS HEAD.
I WANT SOMETHING ELSE.

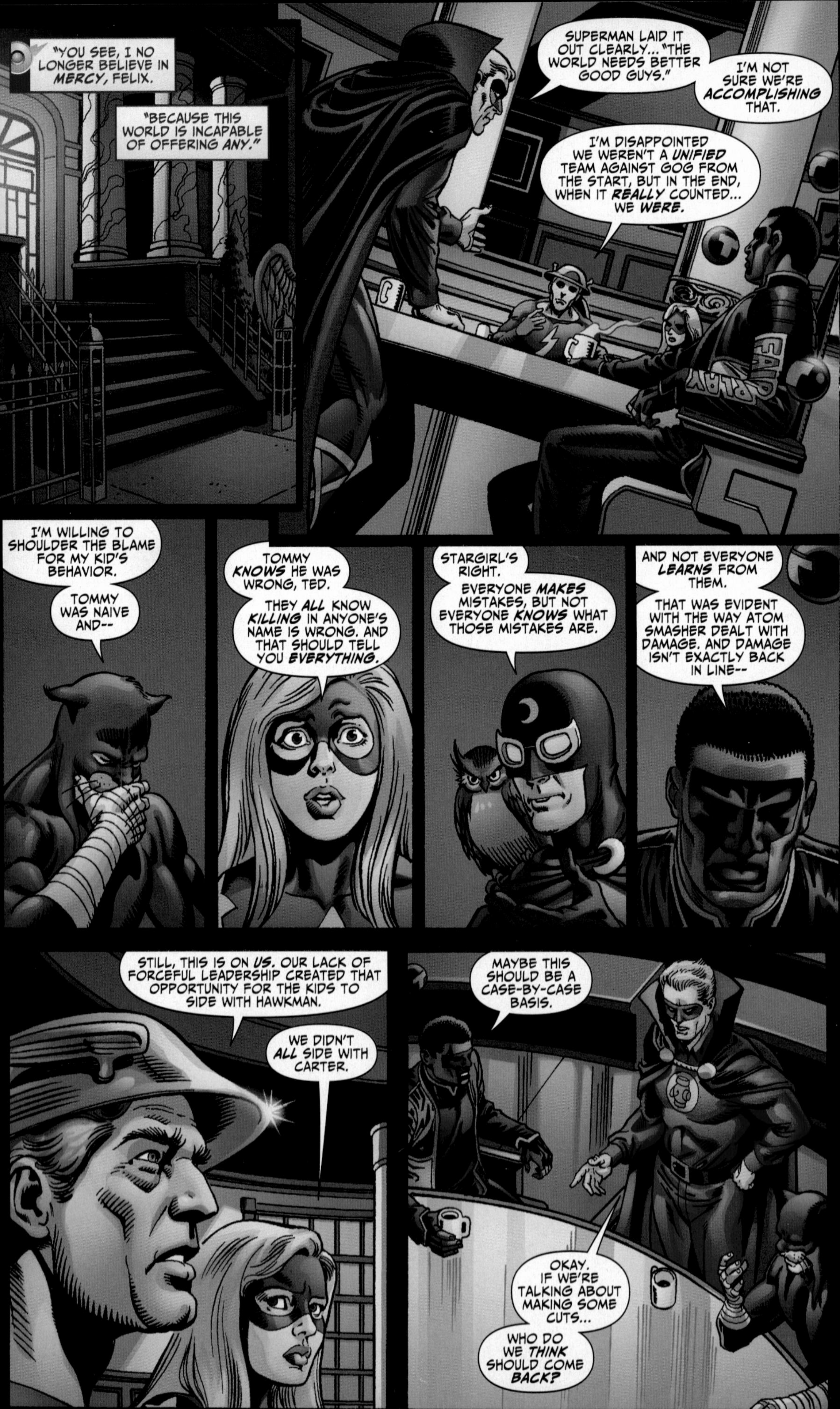
"YOU SEE, I NO LONGER BELIEVE IN MERCY, FELIX.
"BECAUSE THIS WORLD IS INCAPABLE OF OFFERING ANY."
SUPERMAN LAID IT OUT CLEARLY... "THE WORLD NEEDS BETTER GOOD GUYS."
I'M NOT SURE WE'RE ACCOMPLISHING THAT.
I'M DISAPPOINTED WE WEREN'T A UNIFIED TEAM AGAINST GOG FROM THE START, BUT IN THE END, WHEN IT REALLY COUNTED... WE WERE.
FAIRPLAY
I'M WILLING TO SHOULDER THE BLAME FOR MY KID'S BEHAVIOR.
TOMMY WAS NAIVE AND--
TOMMY KNOWS HE WAS WRONG, TED.
THEY ALL KNOW KILLING IN ANYONE'S NAME IS WRONG. AND THAT SHOULD TELL YOU EVERYTHING.
STARGIRL'S RIGHT.
EVERYONE MAKES MISTAKES, BUT NOT EVERYONE KNOWS WHAT THOSE MISTAKES ARE.
AND NOT EVERYONE LEARNS FROM THEM.
THAT WAS EVIDENT WITH THE WAY ATOM SMASHER DEALT WITH DAMAGE. AND DAMAGE ISN'T EXACTLY BACK IN LINE--
STILL, THIS IS ON US. OUR LACK OF FORCEFUL LEADERSHIP CREATED THAT OPPORTUNITY FOR THE KIDS TO SIDE WITH HAWKMAN.
WE DIDN'T ALL SIDE WITH CARTER.
MAYBE THIS SHOULD BE A CASE-BY-CASE BASIS.
OKAY. IF WE'RE TALKING ABOUT MAKING SOME CUTS...
WHO DO WE THINK SHOULD COME BACK?

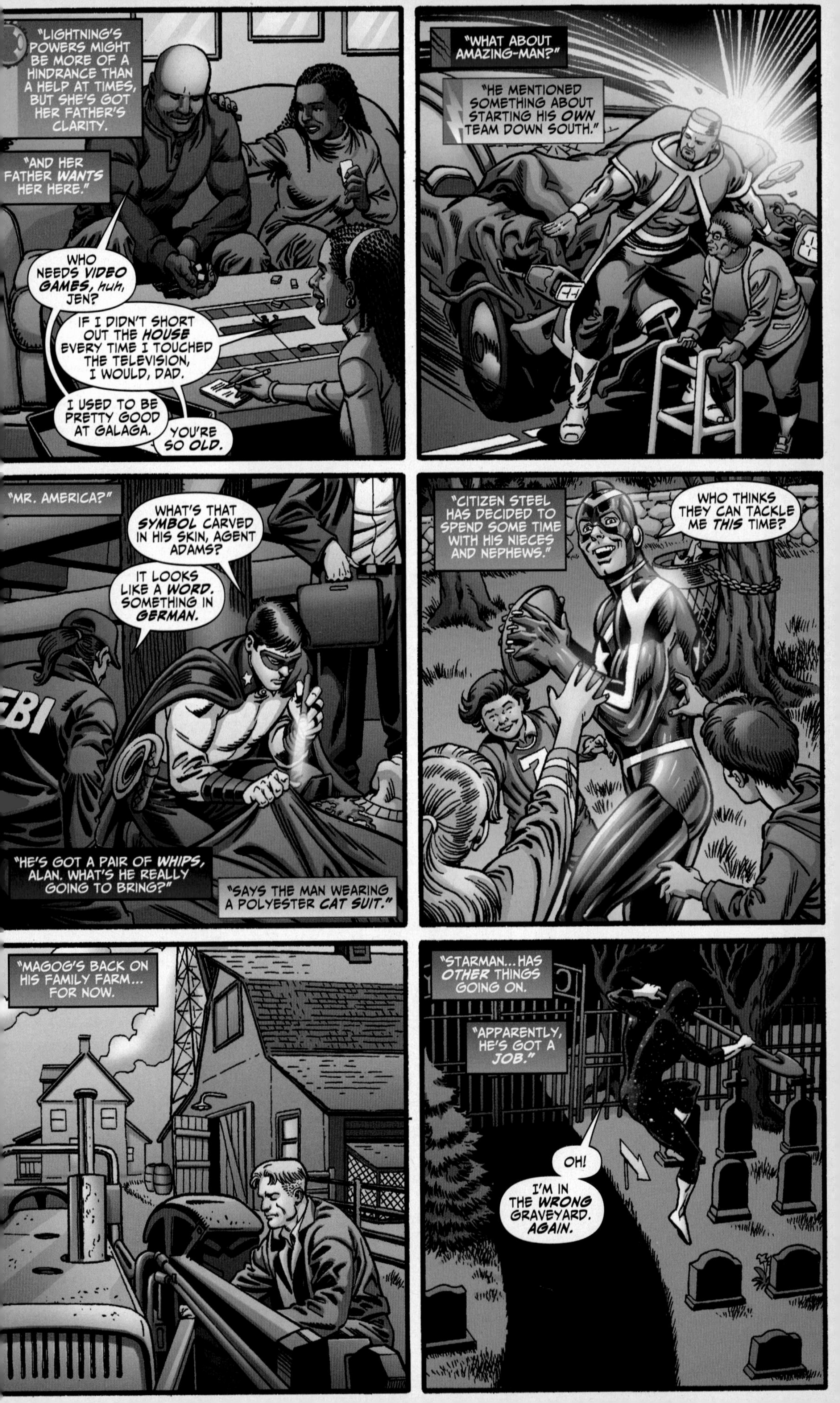
"LIGHTNING'S POWERS MIGHT BE MORE OF A HINDRANCE THAN A HELP AT TIMES, BUT SHE'S GOT HER FATHER'S CLARITY.
"AND HER FATHER WANTS HER HERE."
WHO NEEDS VIDEO GAMES, huh, JEN?
IF I DIDN'T SHORT OUT THE HOUSE EVERY TIME I TOUCHED THE TELEVISION, I WOULD, DAD.
I USED TO BE PRETTY GOOD AT GALAGA.
YOU'RE SO OLD.
"WHAT ABOUT AMAZING-MAN?"
"HE MENTIONED SOMETHING ABOUT STARTING HIS OWN TEAM DOWN SOUTH."
"MR. AMERICA?"
WHAT'S THAT SYMBOL CARVED IN HIS SKIN, AGENT ADAMS?
IT LOOKS LIKE A WORD. SOMETHING IN GERMAN.
FBI
"HE'S GOT A PAIR OF WHIPS, ALAN. WHAT'S HE REALLY GOING TO BRING?"
"SAYS THE MAN WEARING A POLYESTER CAT SUIT."
"CITIZEN STEEL HAS DECIDED TO SPEND SOME TIME WITH HIS NIECES AND NEPHEWS."
WHO THINKS THEY CAN TACKLE ME THIS TIME?
"MAGOG'S BACK ON HIS FAMILY FARM... FOR NOW.
"STARMAN... HAS OTHER THINGS GOING ON.
"APPARENTLY, HE'S GOT A JOB."
OH!
I'M IN THE WRONG GRAVEYARD. AGAIN.

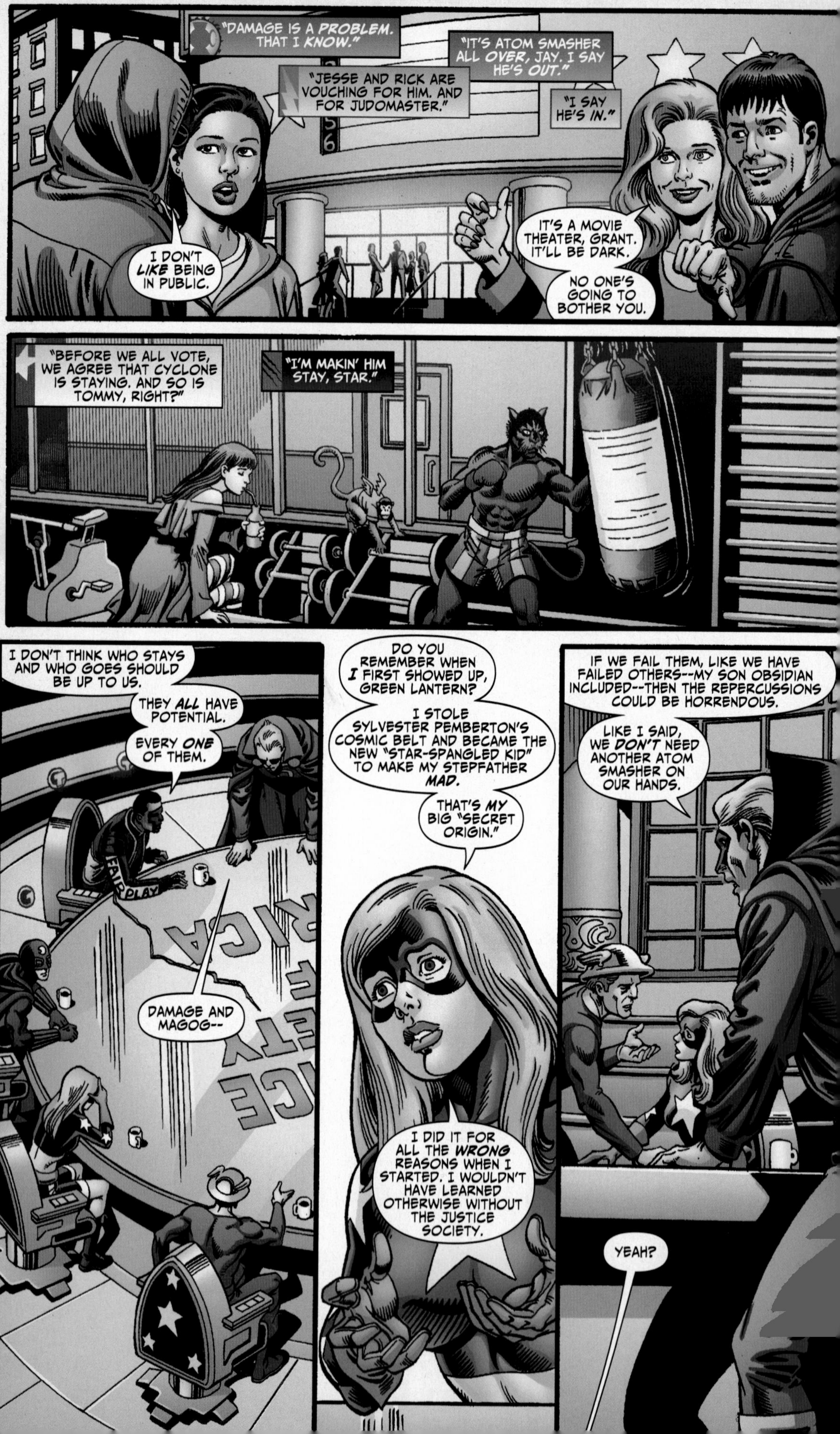
"DAMAGE IS A PROBLEM. THAT I KNOW."
"JESSE AND RICK ARE VOUCHING FOR HIM. AND FOR JUDOMASTER."
"IT'S ATOM SMASHER ALL OVER, JAY. I SAY HE'S OUT."
"I SAY HE'S IN."
I DON'T LIKE BEING IN PUBLIC.
IT'S A MOVIE THEATER, GRANT. IT'LL BE DARK.
NO ONE'S GOING TO BOTHER YOU.
"BEFORE WE ALL VOTE, WE AGREE THAT CYCLONE IS STAYING. AND SO IS TOMMY, RIGHT?"
"I'M MAKIN' HIM STAY, STAR."
I DON'T THINK WHO STAYS AND WHO GOES SHOULD BE UP TO US.
THEY ALL HAVE POTENTIAL.
EVERY ONE OF THEM.
DAMAGE AND MAGOG--
DO YOU REMEMBER WHEN I FIRST SHOWED UP, GREEN LANTERN?
I STOLE SYLVESTER PEMBERTON'S COSMIC BELT AND BECAME THE NEW "STAR-SPANGLED KID" TO MAKE MY STEPFATHER MAD.
THAT'S MY BIG "SECRET ORIGIN."
I DID IT FOR ALL THE WRONG REASONS WHEN I STARTED. I WOULDN'T HAVE LEARNED OTHERWISE WITHOUT THE JUSTICE SOCIETY.
IF WE FAIL THEM, LIKE WE HAVE FAILED OTHERS--MY SON OBSIDIAN INCLUDED--THEN THE REPERCUSSIONS COULD BE HORRENDOUS.
LIKE I SAID, WE DON'T NEED ANOTHER ATOM SMASHER ON OUR HANDS.
YEAH?

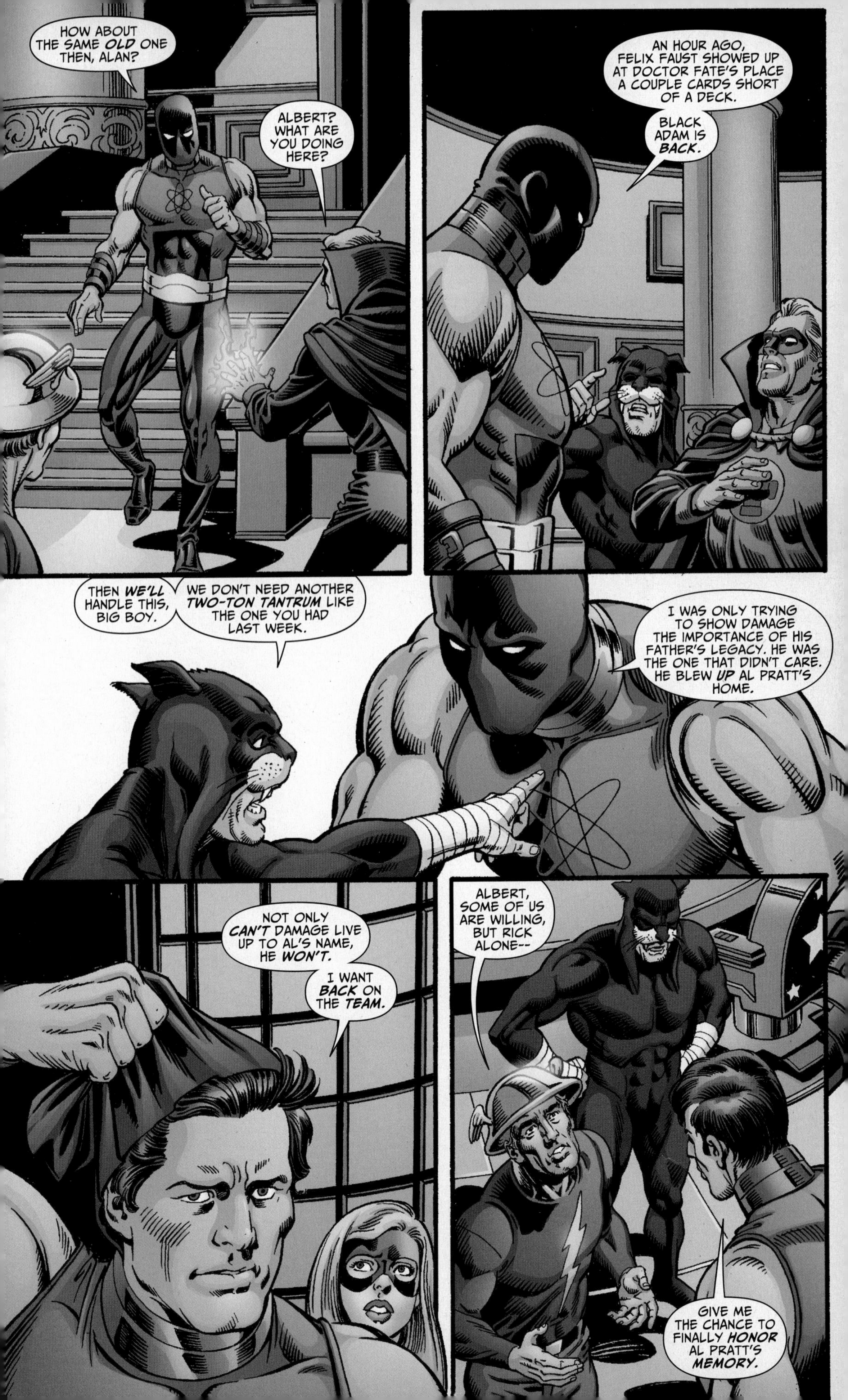
HOW ABOUT THE SAME *OLD* ONE THEN, ALAN?
ALBERT? WHAT ARE YOU DOING HERE?
AN HOUR AGO, FELIX FAUST SHOWED UP AT DOCTOR FATE'S PLACE A COUPLE CARDS SHORT OF A DECK.
BLACK ADAM IS *BACK.*
THEN *WE'LL* HANDLE THIS, BIG BOY.
WE DON'T NEED ANOTHER *TWO-TON TANTRUM* LIKE THE ONE YOU HAD LAST WEEK.
I WAS ONLY TRYING TO SHOW DAMAGE THE IMPORTANCE OF HIS FATHER'S LEGACY. HE WAS THE ONE THAT DIDN'T CARE. HE BLEW *UP* AL PRATT'S HOME.
NOT ONLY *CAN'T* DAMAGE LIVE UP TO AL'S NAME, HE *WON'T.*
I WANT *BACK* ON THE *TEAM.*
ALBERT, SOME OF US ARE WILLING, BUT RICK ALONE--
GIVE ME THE CHANCE TO FINALLY *HONOR* AL PRATT'S *MEMORY.*

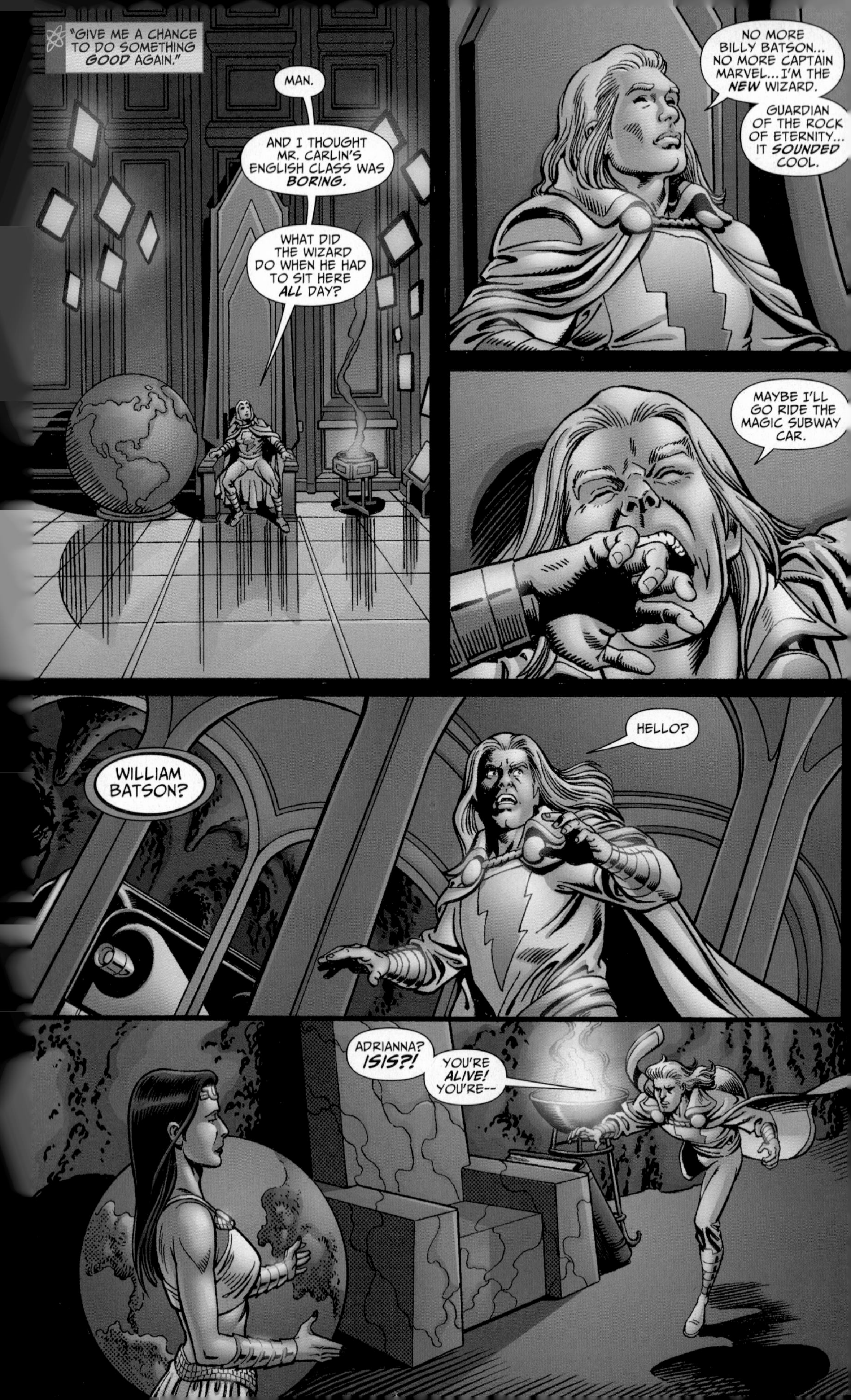
"GIVE ME A CHANCE TO DO SOMETHING GOOD AGAIN."
MAN.
AND I THOUGHT MR. CARLIN'S ENGLISH CLASS WAS BORING.
WHAT DID THE WIZARD DO WHEN HE HAD TO SIT HERE ALL DAY?
NO MORE BILLY BATSON... NO MORE CAPTAIN MARVEL... I'M THE NEW WIZARD.
GUARDIAN OF THE ROCK OF ETERNITY... IT SOUNDED COOL.
MAYBE I'LL GO RIDE THE MAGIC SUBWAY CAR.
HELLO?
WILLIAM BATSON?
ADRIANNA? ISIS?!
YOU'RE ALIVE! YOU'RE--

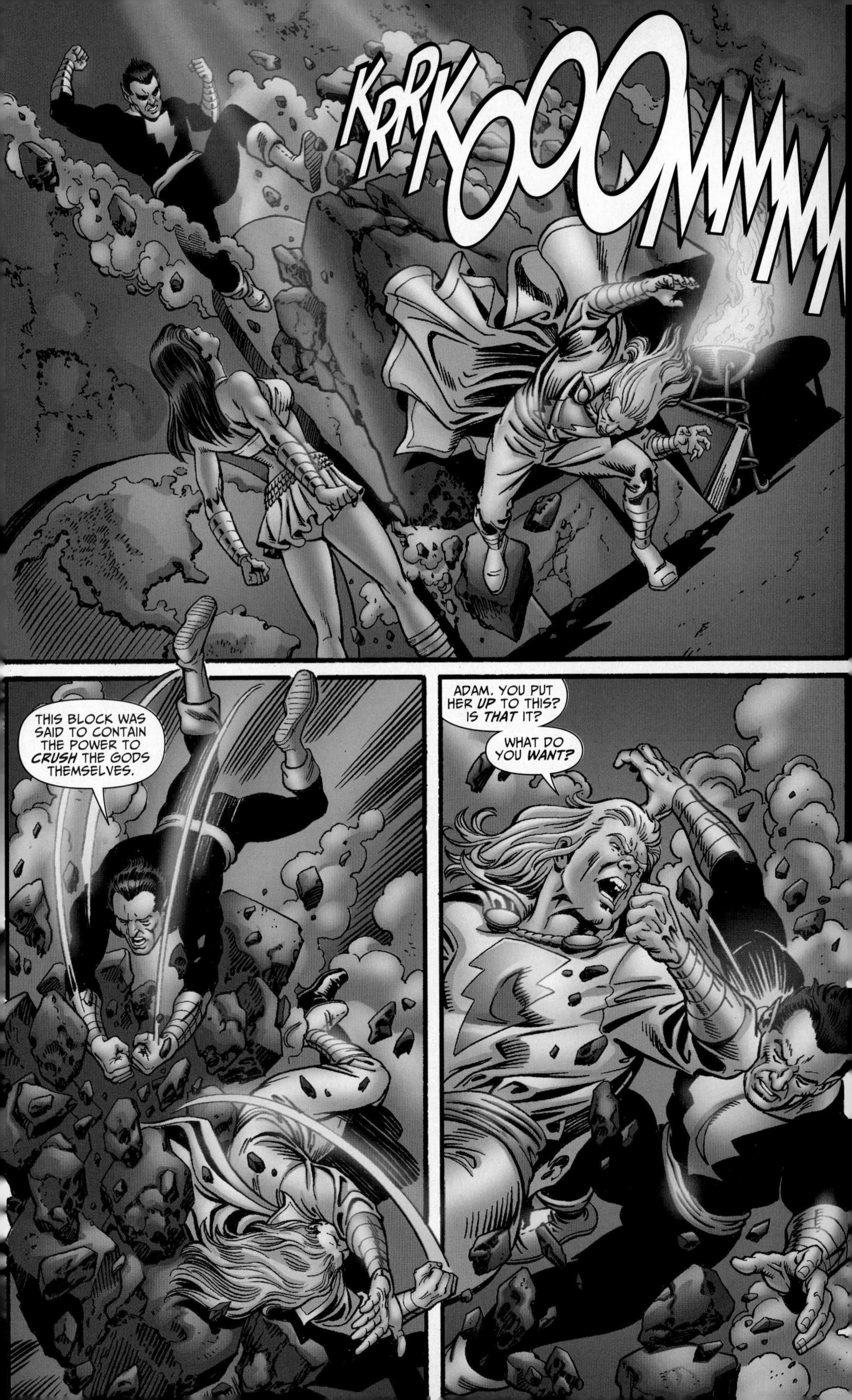
KRRKOOOMMMM
THIS BLOCK WAS SAID TO CONTAIN THE POWER TO CRUSH THE GODS THEMSELVES.
ADAM. YOU PUT HER UP TO THIS? IS THAT IT?
WHAT DO YOU WANT?

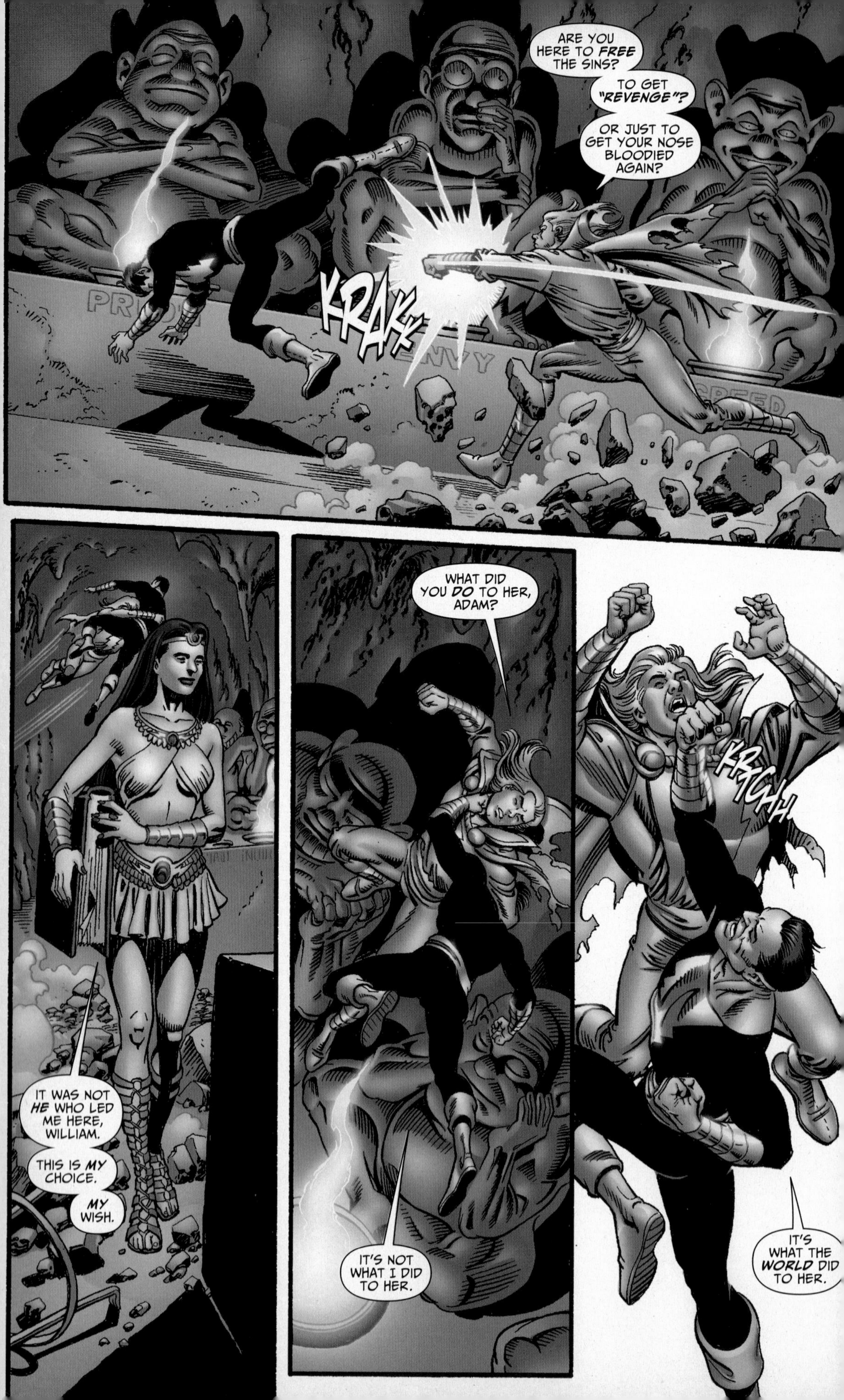
ARE YOU HERE TO FREE THE SINS?
TO GET "REVENGE"?
OR JUST TO GET YOUR NOSE BLOODIED AGAIN?
KRAKK
ENVY
IT WAS NOT HE WHO LED ME HERE, WILLIAM.
THIS IS MY CHOICE.
MY WISH.
WHAT DID YOU DO TO HER, ADAM?
IT'S NOT WHAT I DID TO HER.
KRTCHH
IT'S WHAT THE WORLD DID TO HER.

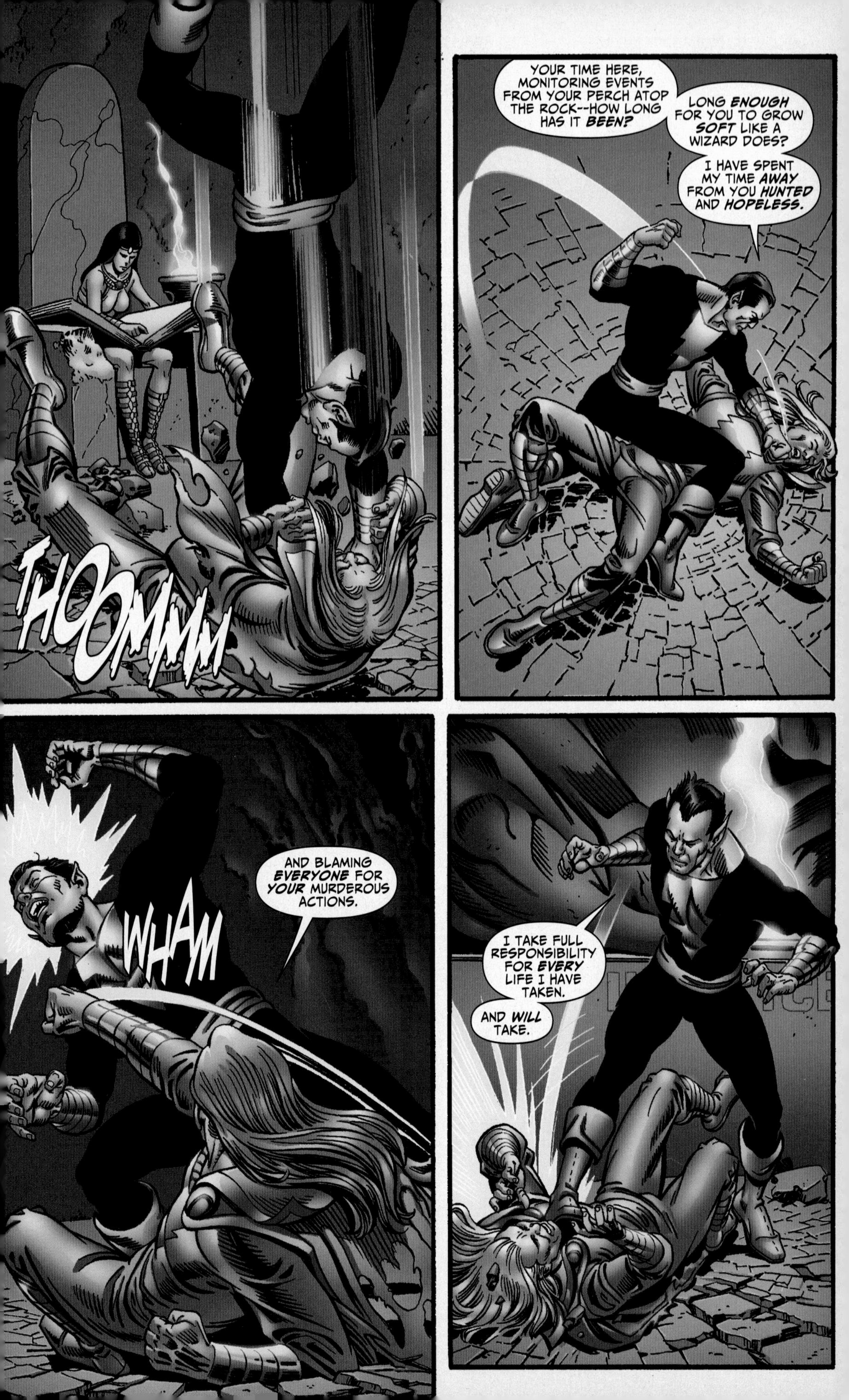
THOOMMM
YOUR TIME HERE, MONITORING EVENTS FROM YOUR PERCH ATOP THE ROCK--HOW LONG HAS IT BEEN?
LONG ENOUGH FOR YOU TO GROW SOFT LIKE A WIZARD DOES?
I HAVE SPENT MY TIME AWAY FROM YOU HUNTED AND HOPELESS.
WHAM
AND BLAMING EVERYONE FOR YOUR MURDEROUS ACTIONS.
I TAKE FULL RESPONSIBILITY FOR EVERY LIFE I HAVE TAKEN.
AND WILL TAKE.

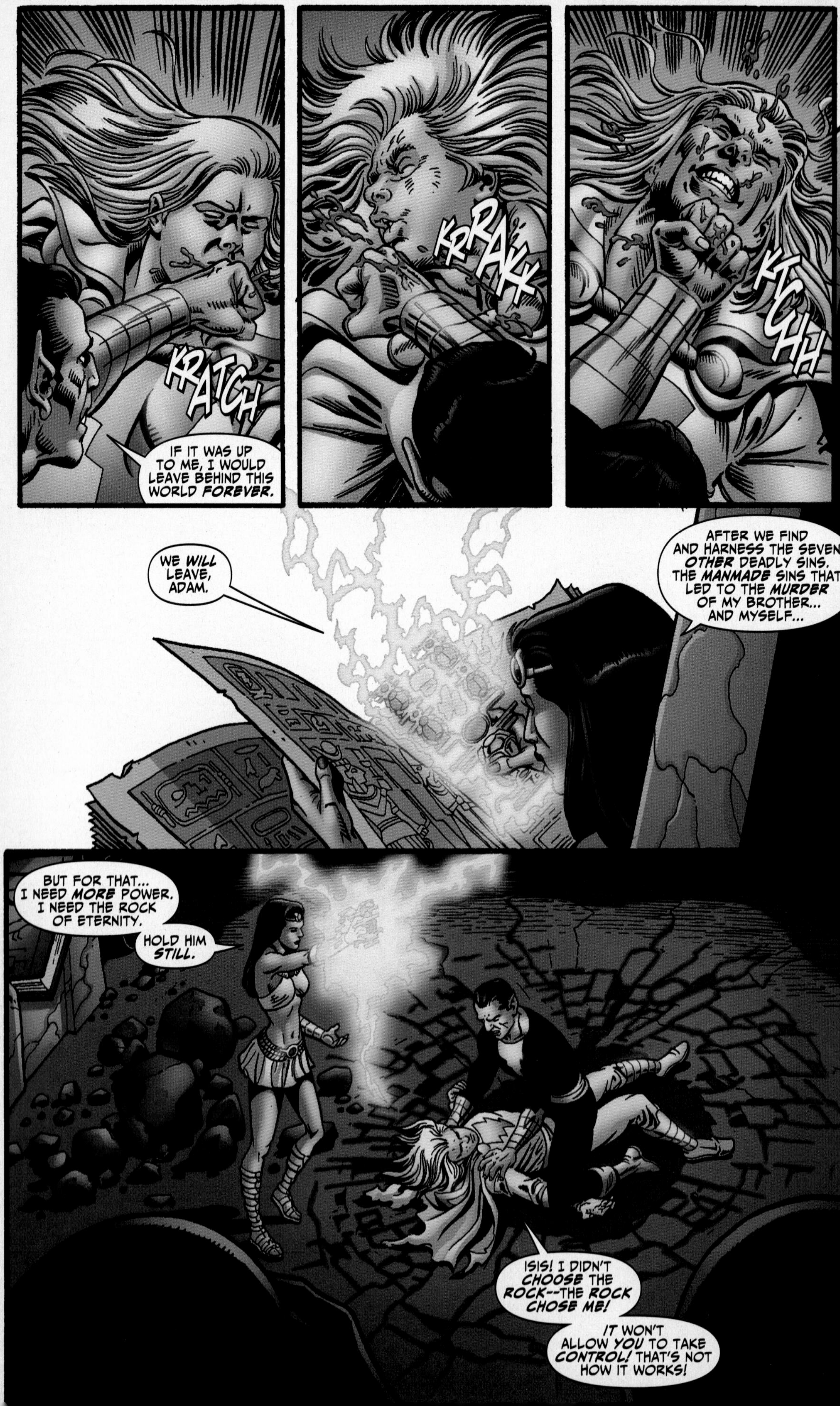
KRATCH
IF IT WAS UP TO ME, I WOULD LEAVE BEHIND THIS WORLD *FOREVER.*
KRRAKK
KTCHH
WE *WILL* LEAVE, ADAM.
AFTER WE FIND AND HARNESS THE SEVEN *OTHER* DEADLY SINS. THE *MANMADE* SINS THAT LED TO THE *MURDER* OF MY BROTHER... AND MYSELF...
BUT FOR THAT... I NEED *MORE* POWER. I NEED THE ROCK OF ETERNITY.
HOLD HIM *STILL.*
ISIS! I DIDN'T *CHOOSE* THE *ROCK*--THE *ROCK* *CHOSE ME!*
IT WON'T ALLOW *YOU* TO TAKE *CONTROL!* THAT'S NOT HOW IT WORKS!

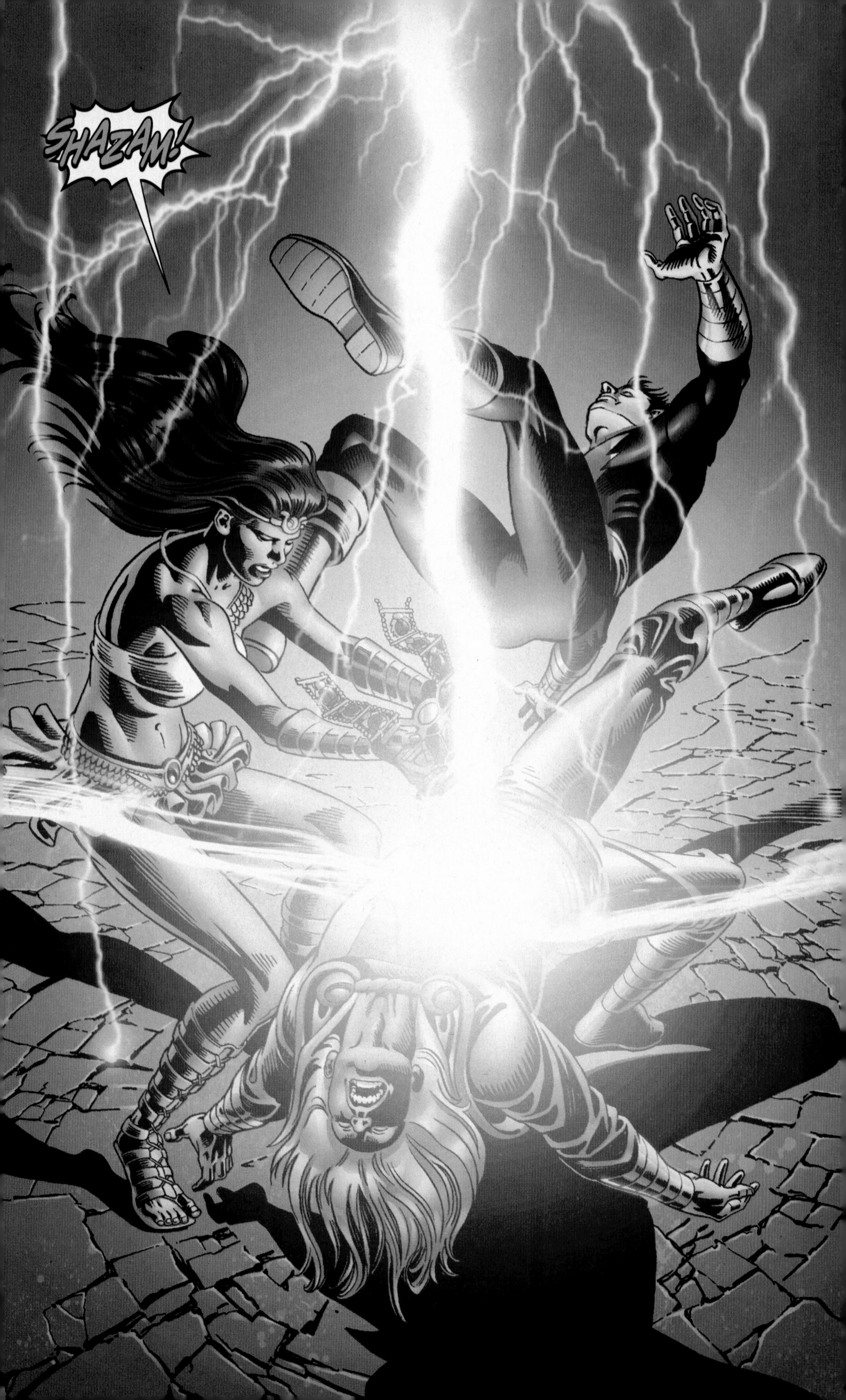
SHAZAM!

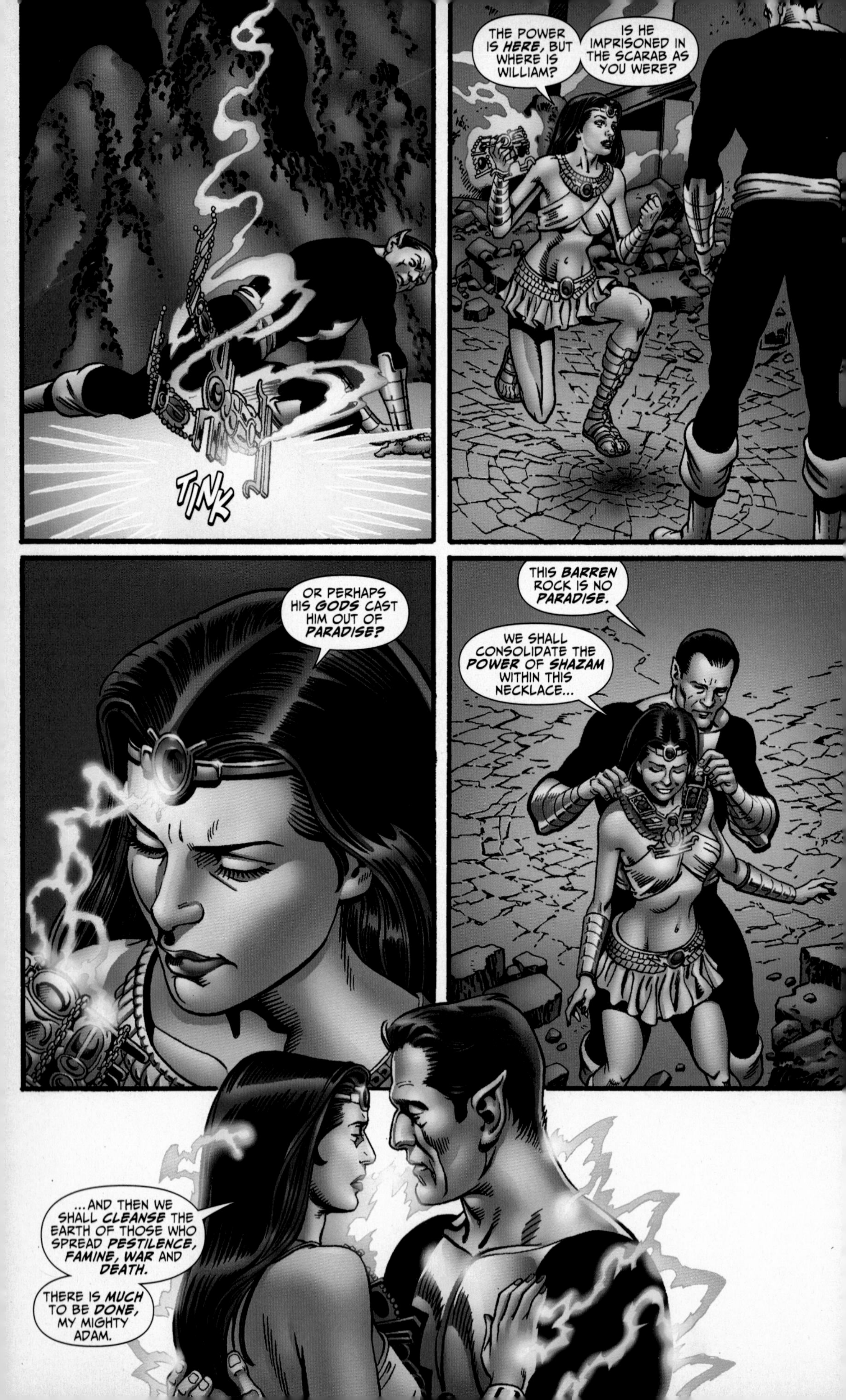
TINK
THE POWER IS HERE, BUT WHERE IS WILLIAM?
IS HE IMPRISONED IN THE SCARAB AS YOU WERE?
OR PERHAPS HIS GODS CAST HIM OUT OF PARADISE?
THIS BARREN ROCK IS NO PARADISE.
WE SHALL CONSOLIDATE THE POWER OF SHAZAM WITHIN THIS NECKLACE...
...AND THEN WE SHALL CLEANSE THE EARTH OF THOSE WHO SPREAD PESTILENCE, FAMINE, WAR AND DEATH.
THERE IS MUCH TO BE DONE, MY MIGHTY ADAM.

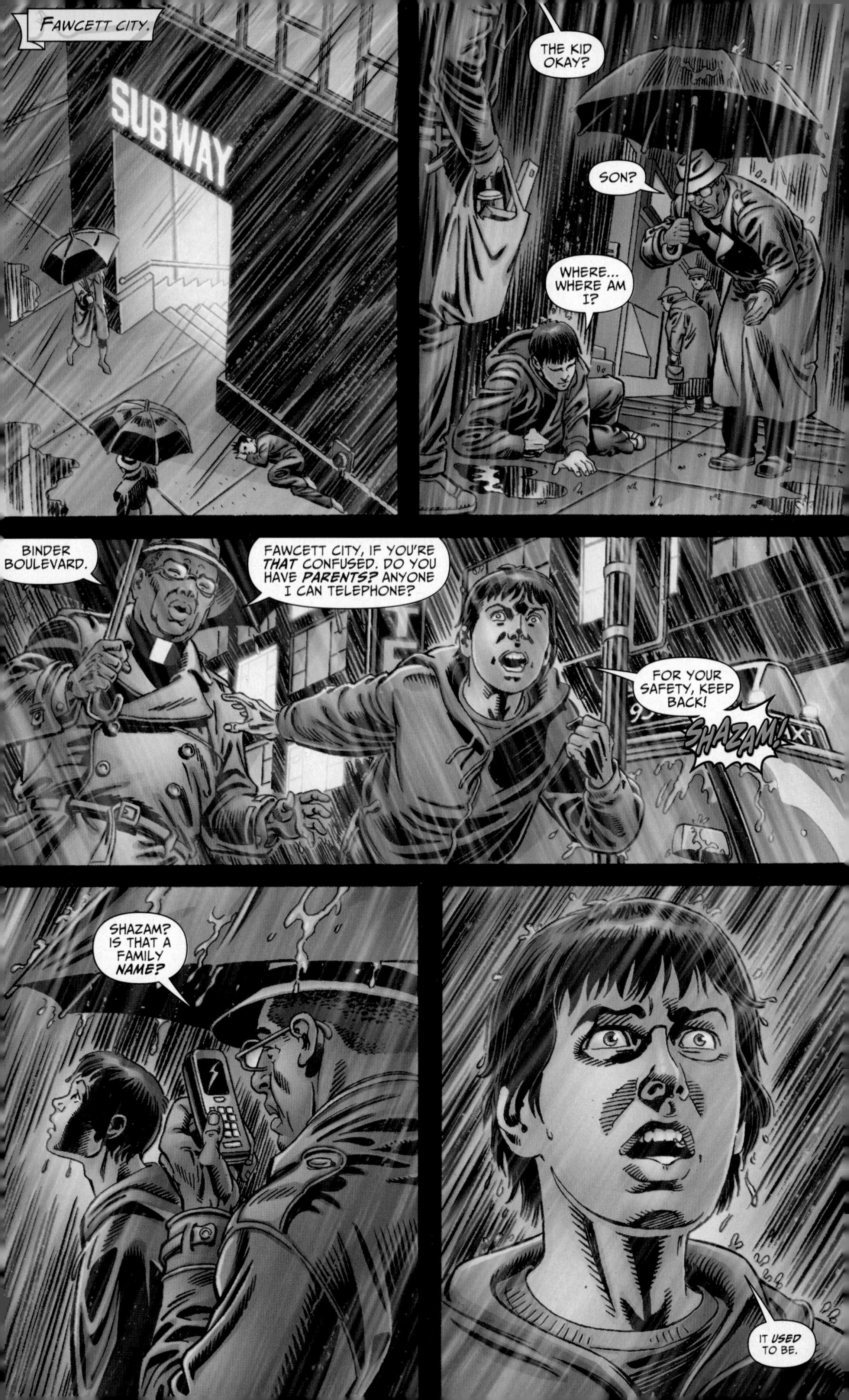
FAWCETT CITY.
SUBWAY
THE KID OKAY?
SON?
WHERE... WHERE AM I?
BINDER BOULEVARD.
FAWCETT CITY, IF YOU'RE THAT CONFUSED. DO YOU HAVE PARENTS? ANYONE I CAN TELEPHONE?
FOR YOUR SAFETY, KEEP BACK!
SHAZAM!
SHAZAM? IS THAT A FAMILY NAME?
IT USED TO BE.

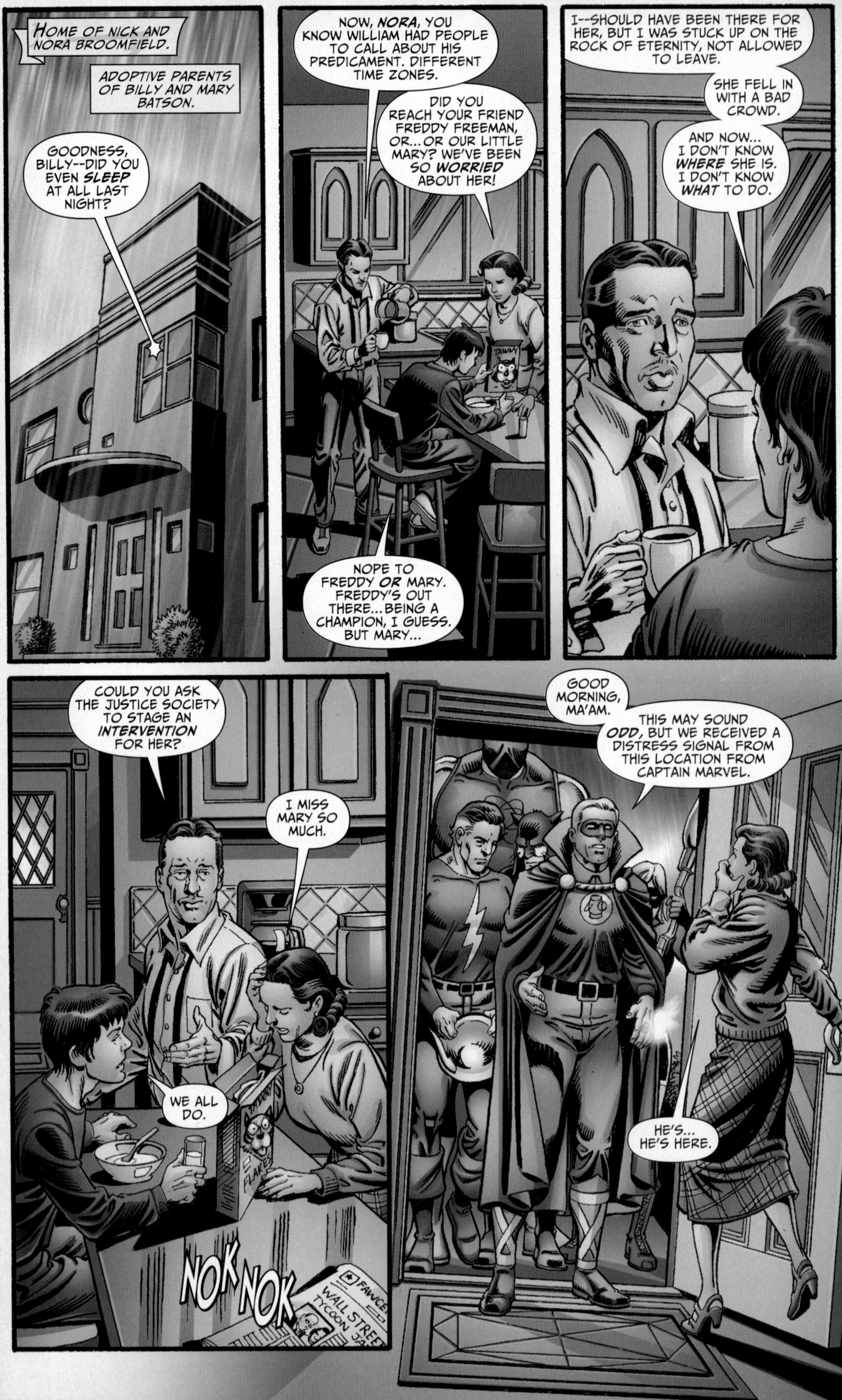
HOME OF NICK AND NORA BROOMFIELD.
ADOPTIVE PARENTS OF BILLY AND MARY BATSON.
GOODNESS, BILLY--DID YOU EVEN SLEEP AT ALL LAST NIGHT?
NOW, NORA, YOU KNOW WILLIAM HAD PEOPLE TO CALL ABOUT HIS PREDICAMENT. DIFFERENT TIME ZONES.
DID YOU REACH YOUR FRIEND FREDDY FREEMAN, OR...OR OUR LITTLE MARY? WE'VE BEEN SO WORRIED ABOUT HER!
NOPE TO FREDDY OR MARY. FREDDY'S OUT THERE...BEING A CHAMPION, I GUESS. BUT MARY...
I--SHOULD HAVE BEEN THERE FOR HER, BUT I WAS STUCK UP ON THE ROCK OF ETERNITY, NOT ALLOWED TO LEAVE.
SHE FELL IN WITH A BAD CROWD.
AND NOW... I DON'T KNOW WHERE SHE IS. I DON'T KNOW WHAT TO DO.
COULD YOU ASK THE JUSTICE SOCIETY TO STAGE AN INTERVENTION FOR HER?
I MISS MARY SO MUCH.
WE ALL DO.
NOK NOK
GOOD MORNING, MA'AM.
THIS MAY SOUND ODD, BUT WE RECEIVED A DISTRESS SIGNAL FROM THIS LOCATION FROM CAPTAIN MARVEL.
HE'S... HE'S HERE.

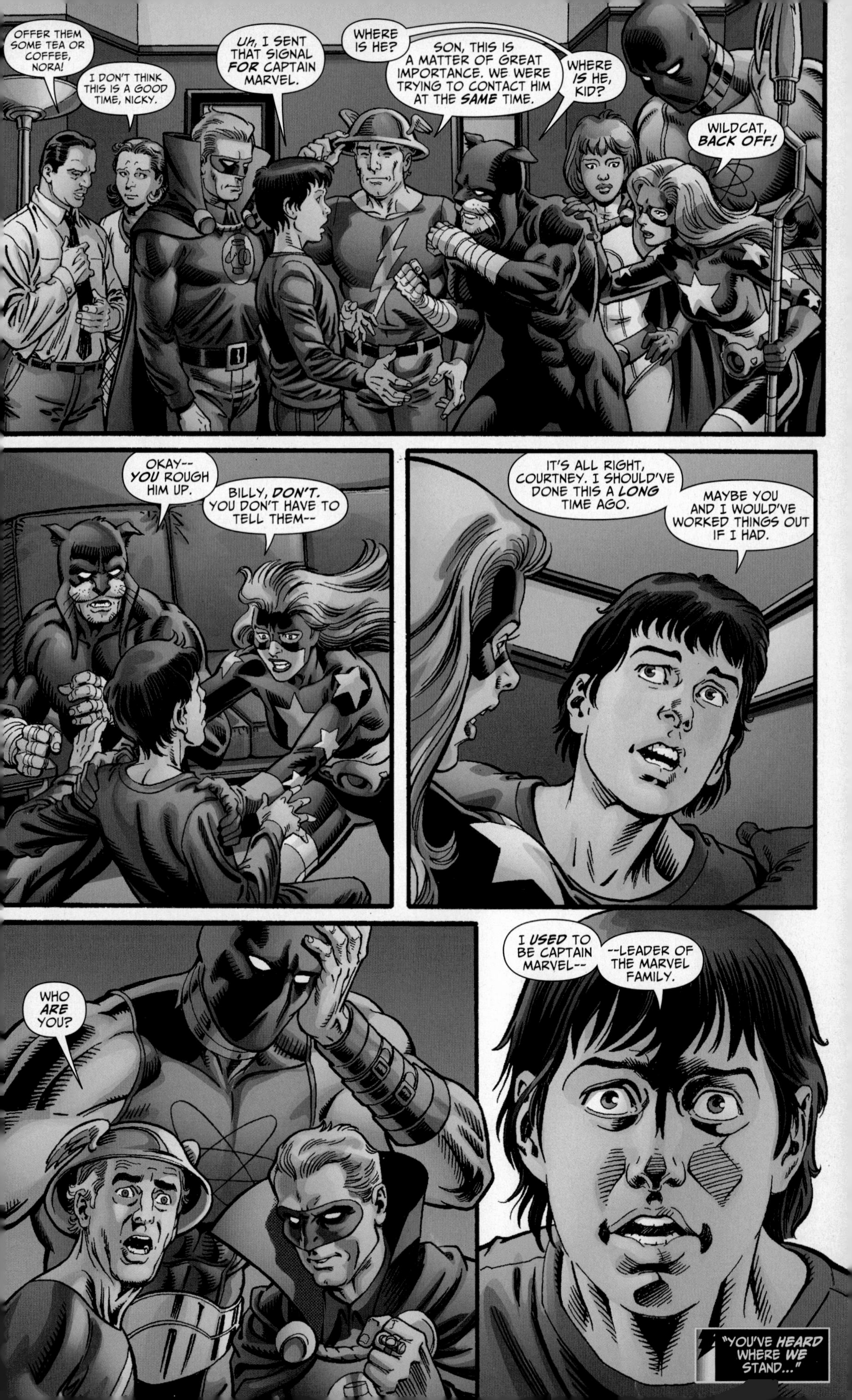
OFFER THEM SOME TEA OR COFFEE, NORA!
I DON'T THINK THIS IS A GOOD TIME, NICKY.
UH, I SENT THAT SIGNAL FOR CAPTAIN MARVEL.
WHERE IS HE?
SON, THIS IS A MATTER OF GREAT IMPORTANCE. WE WERE TRYING TO CONTACT HIM AT THE SAME TIME.
WHERE IS HE, KID?
WILDCAT, BACK OFF!
OKAY-- YOU ROUGH HIM UP.
BILLY, DON'T. YOU DON'T HAVE TO TELL THEM--
IT'S ALL RIGHT, COURTNEY. I SHOULD'VE DONE THIS A LONG TIME AGO.
MAYBE YOU AND I WOULD'VE WORKED THINGS OUT IF I HAD.
WHO ARE YOU?
I USED TO BE CAPTAIN MARVEL--
--LEADER OF THE MARVEL FAMILY.
"YOU'VE HEARD WHERE WE STAND..."

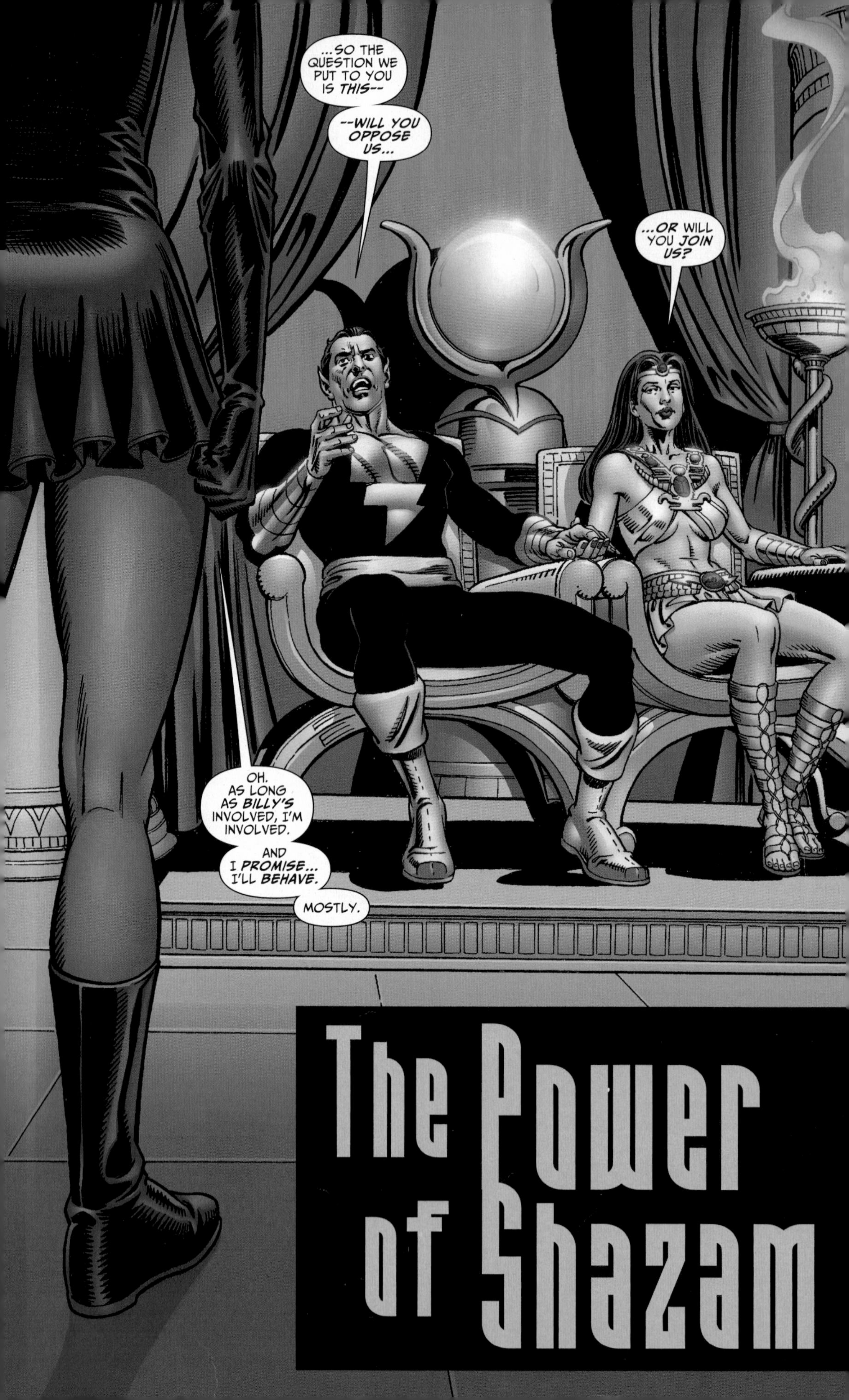
...SO THE QUESTION WE PUT TO YOU IS THIS--
--WILL YOU OPPOSE US...
...OR WILL YOU JOIN US?
OH. AS LONG AS BILLY'S INVOLVED, I'M INVOLVED.
AND I PROMISE... I'LL BEHAVE.
MOSTLY.
The Power of Shazam

JUSTICE SOCIETY OF AMERICA #24 cover A by Alex Ross
Interior art by Jerry Ordway & Bob Wiacek, with Flashback sequence by Ordway

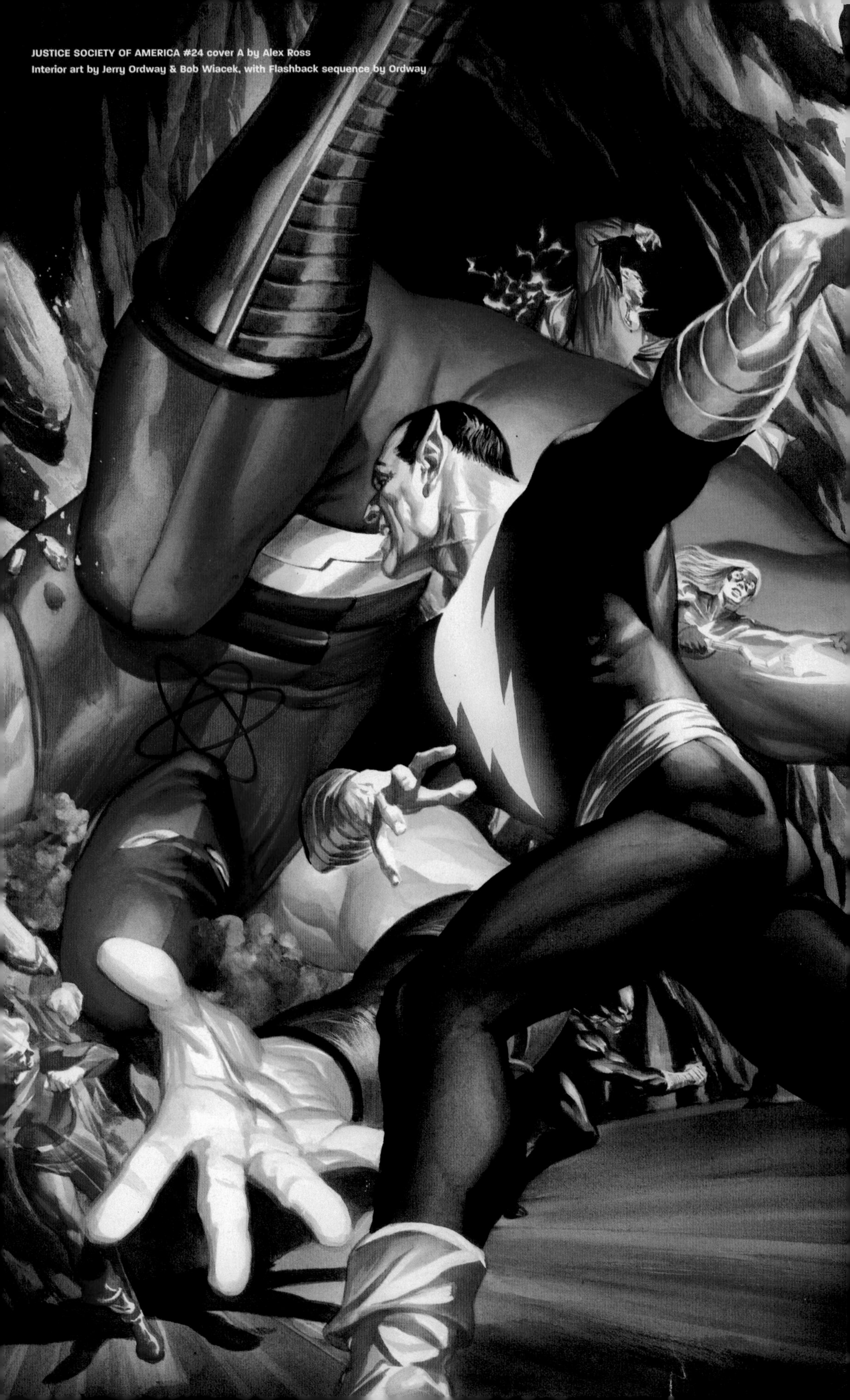

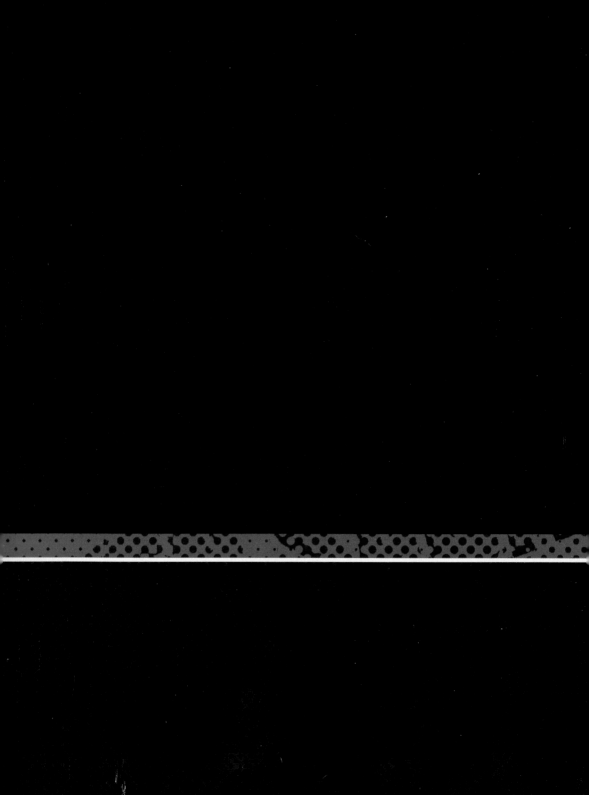

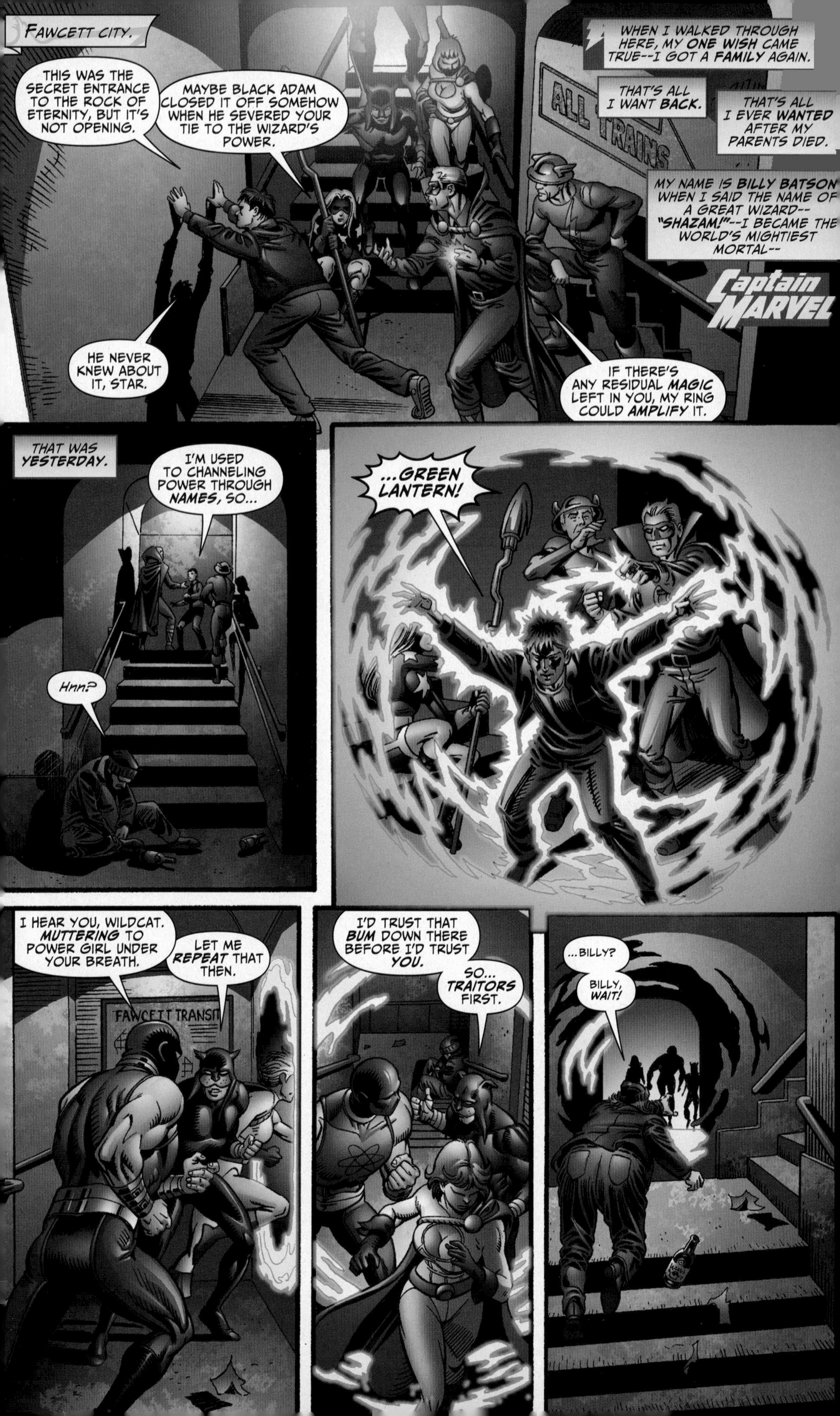
FAWCETT CITY.
THIS WAS THE SECRET ENTRANCE TO THE ROCK OF ETERNITY, BUT IT'S NOT OPENING.
MAYBE BLACK ADAM CLOSED IT OFF SOMEHOW WHEN HE SEVERED YOUR TIE TO THE WIZARD'S POWER.
HE NEVER KNEW ABOUT IT, STAR.
WHEN I WALKED THROUGH HERE, MY ONE WISH CAME TRUE--I GOT A FAMILY AGAIN.
THAT'S ALL I WANT BACK.
THAT'S ALL I EVER WANTED AFTER MY PARENTS DIED.
ALL TRAINS
MY NAME IS BILLY BATSON WHEN I SAID THE NAME OF A GREAT WIZARD-- "SHAZAM!"--I BECAME THE WORLD'S MIGHTIEST MORTAL--
Captain MARVEL
IF THERE'S ANY RESIDUAL MAGIC LEFT IN YOU, MY RING COULD AMPLIFY IT.
THAT WAS YESTERDAY.
I'M USED TO CHANNELING POWER THROUGH NAMES, SO...
Hnn?
...GREEN LANTERN!
I HEAR YOU, WILDCAT. MUTTERING TO POWER GIRL UNDER YOUR BREATH.
LET ME REPEAT THAT THEN.
FAWCETT TRANSIT
I'D TRUST THAT BUM DOWN THERE BEFORE I'D TRUST YOU.
SO... TRAITORS FIRST.
...BILLY?
BILLY, WAIT!

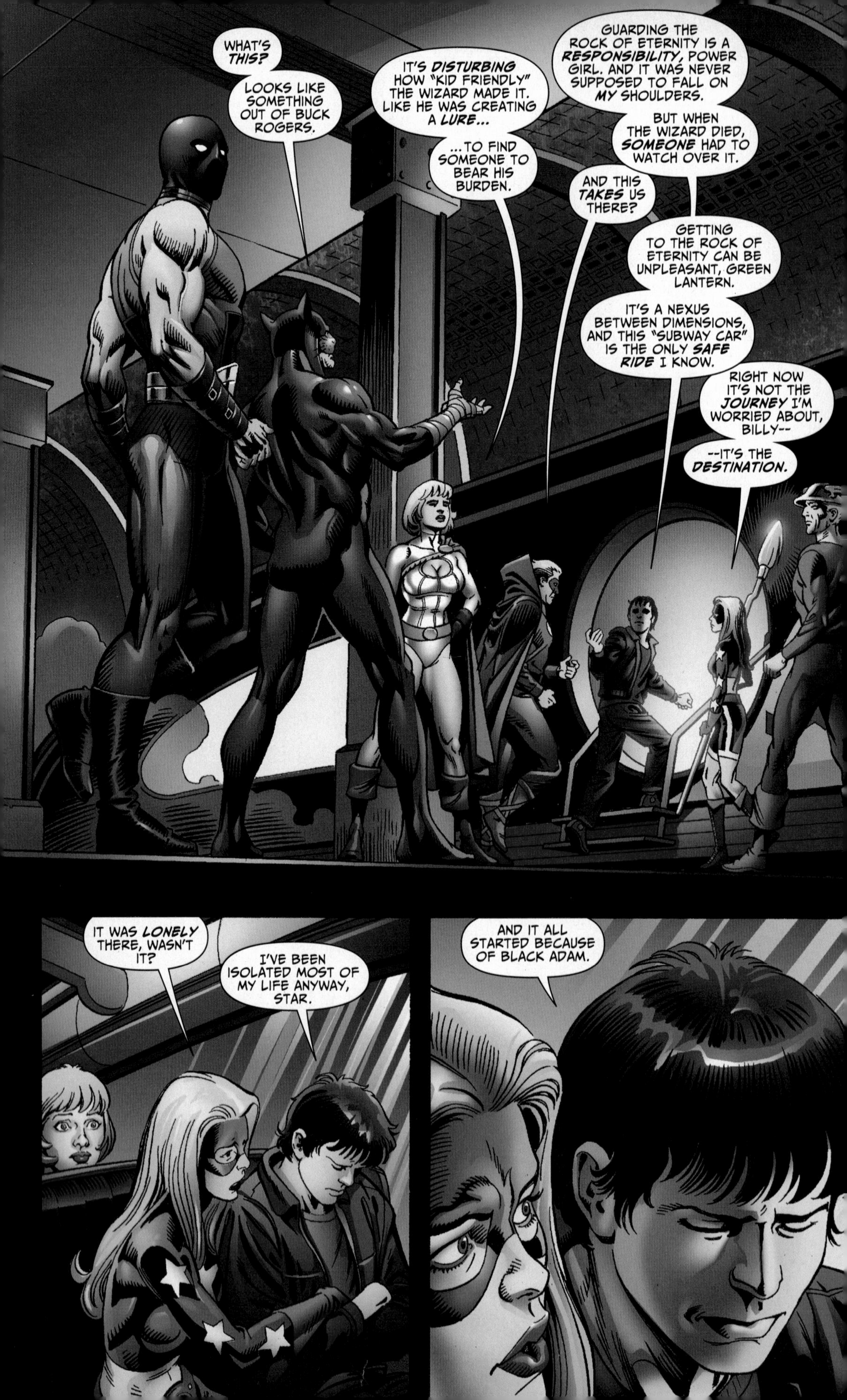
WHAT'S THIS?
LOOKS LIKE SOMETHING OUT OF BUCK ROGERS.
IT'S DISTURBING HOW "KID FRIENDLY" THE WIZARD MADE IT. LIKE HE WAS CREATING A LURE...
...TO FIND SOMEONE TO BEAR HIS BURDEN.
GUARDING THE ROCK OF ETERNITY IS A RESPONSIBILITY, POWER GIRL. AND IT WAS NEVER SUPPOSED TO FALL ON MY SHOULDERS.
BUT WHEN THE WIZARD DIED, SOMEONE HAD TO WATCH OVER IT.
AND THIS TAKES US THERE?
GETTING TO THE ROCK OF ETERNITY CAN BE UNPLEASANT, GREEN LANTERN.
IT'S A NEXUS BETWEEN DIMENSIONS, AND THIS "SUBWAY CAR" IS THE ONLY SAFE RIDE I KNOW.
RIGHT NOW IT'S NOT THE JOURNEY I'M WORRIED ABOUT, BILLY--
--IT'S THE DESTINATION.
IT WAS LONELY THERE, WASN'T IT?
I'VE BEEN ISOLATED MOST OF MY LIFE ANYWAY, STAR.
AND IT ALL STARTED BECAUSE OF BLACK ADAM.

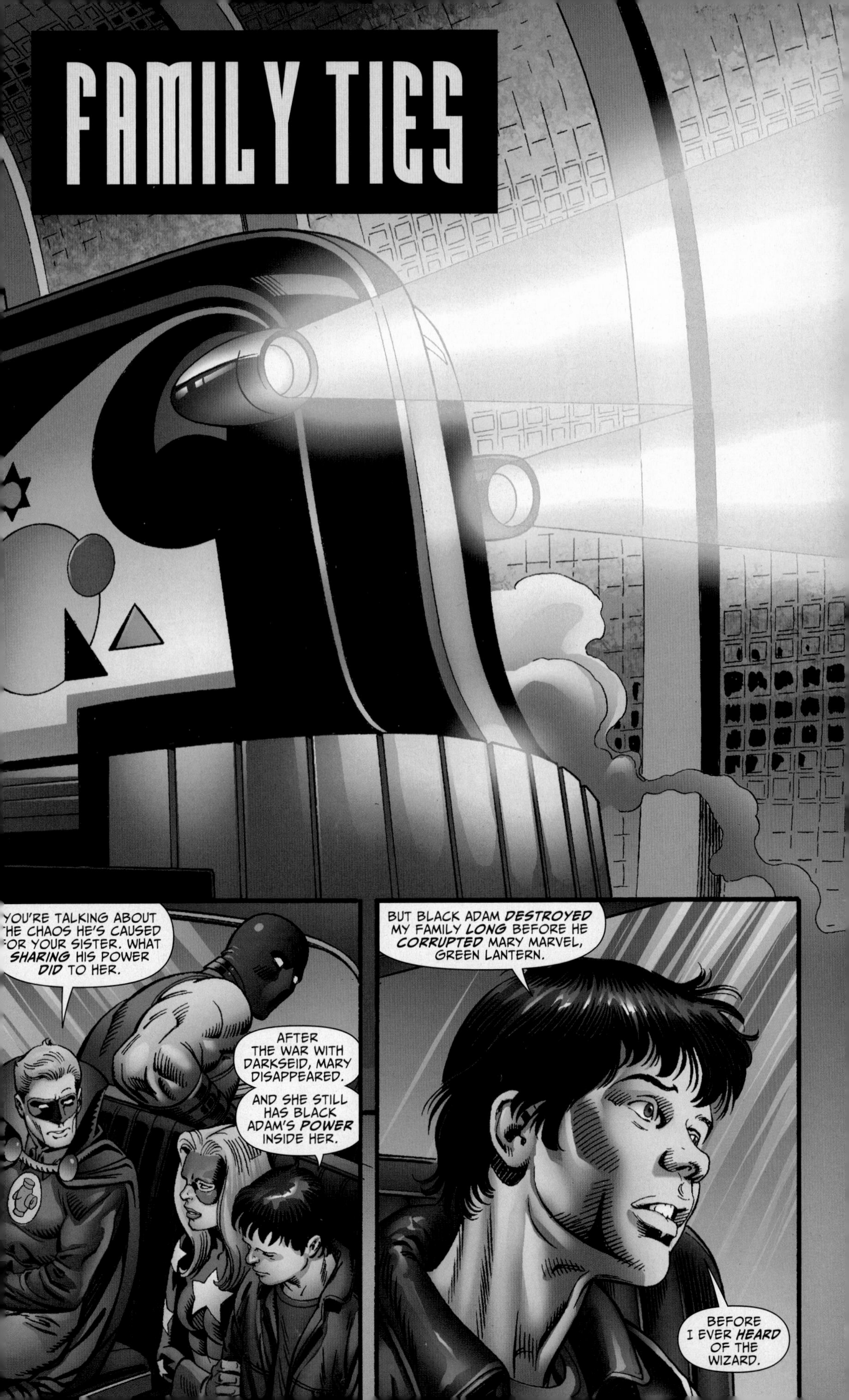
FAMILY TIES
YOU'RE TALKING ABOUT THE CHAOS HE'S CAUSED FOR YOUR SISTER. WHAT SHARING HIS POWER DID TO HER.
AFTER THE WAR WITH DARKSEID, MARY DISAPPEARED.
AND SHE STILL HAS BLACK ADAM'S POWER INSIDE HER.
BUT BLACK ADAM DESTROYED MY FAMILY LONG BEFORE HE CORRUPTED MARY MARVEL, GREEN LANTERN.
BEFORE I EVER HEARD OF THE WIZARD.

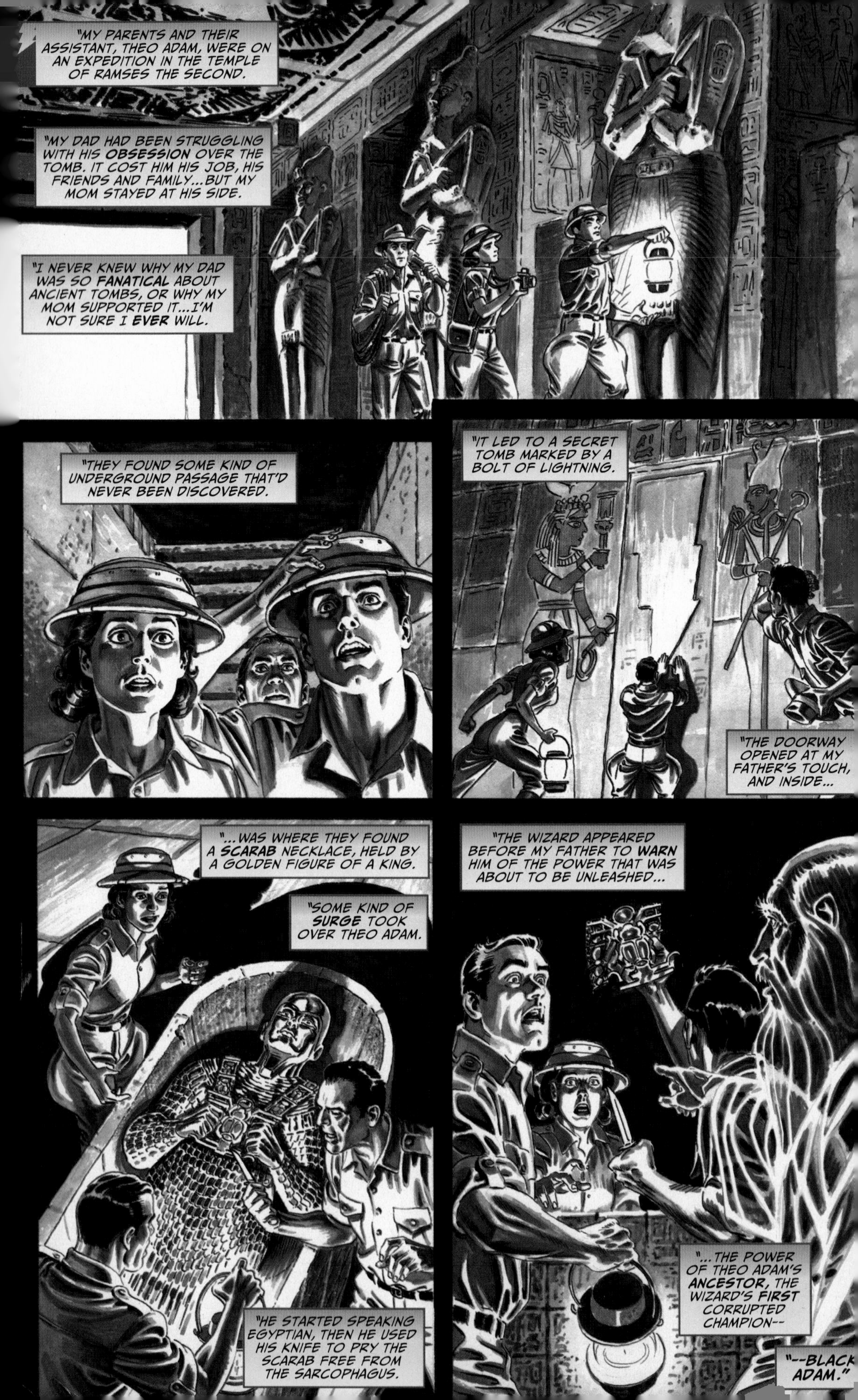
"MY PARENTS AND THEIR ASSISTANT, THEO ADAM, WERE ON AN EXPEDITION IN THE TEMPLE OF RAMSES THE SECOND.
"MY DAD HAD BEEN STRUGGLING WITH HIS OBSESSION OVER THE TOMB. IT COST HIM HIS JOB, HIS FRIENDS AND FAMILY...BUT MY MOM STAYED AT HIS SIDE.
"I NEVER KNEW WHY MY DAD WAS SO FANATICAL ABOUT ANCIENT TOMBS, OR WHY MY MOM SUPPORTED IT...I'M NOT SURE I EVER WILL.
"THEY FOUND SOME KIND OF UNDERGROUND PASSAGE THAT'D NEVER BEEN DISCOVERED.
"IT LED TO A SECRET TOMB MARKED BY A BOLT OF LIGHTNING.
"THE DOORWAY OPENED AT MY FATHER'S TOUCH, AND INSIDE...
"...WAS WHERE THEY FOUND A SCARAB NECKLACE, HELD BY A GOLDEN FIGURE OF A KING.
"SOME KIND OF SURGE TOOK OVER THEO ADAM.
"HE STARTED SPEAKING EGYPTIAN, THEN HE USED HIS KNIFE TO PRY THE SCARAB FREE FROM THE SARCOPHAGUS.
"THE WIZARD APPEARED BEFORE MY FATHER TO WARN HIM OF THE POWER THAT WAS ABOUT TO BE UNLEASHED...
"...THE POWER OF THEO ADAM'S ANCESTOR, THE WIZARD'S FIRST CORRUPTED CHAMPION--
"--BLACK ADAM."

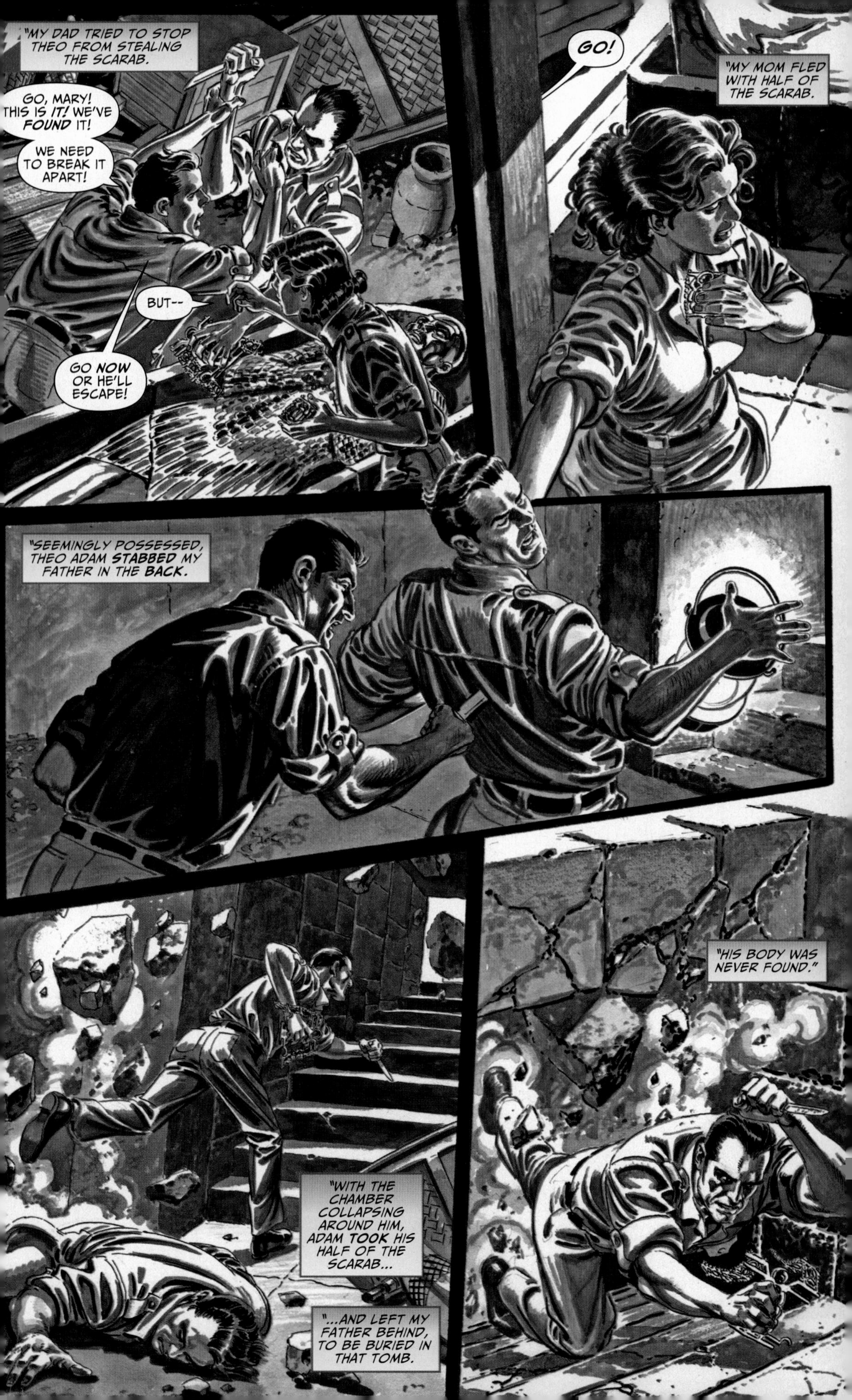
"MY DAD TRIED TO STOP THEO FROM STEALING THE SCARAB.
GO, MARY! THIS IS IT! WE'VE FOUND IT!
WE NEED TO BREAK IT APART!
BUT--
GO NOW OR HE'LL ESCAPE!
GO!
"MY MOM FLED WITH HALF OF THE SCARAB.
"SEEMINGLY POSSESSED, THEO ADAM STABBED MY FATHER IN THE BACK.
"WITH THE CHAMBER COLLAPSING AROUND HIM, ADAM TOOK HIS HALF OF THE SCARAB...
"...AND LEFT MY FATHER BEHIND, TO BE BURIED IN THAT TOMB.
"HIS BODY WAS NEVER FOUND."

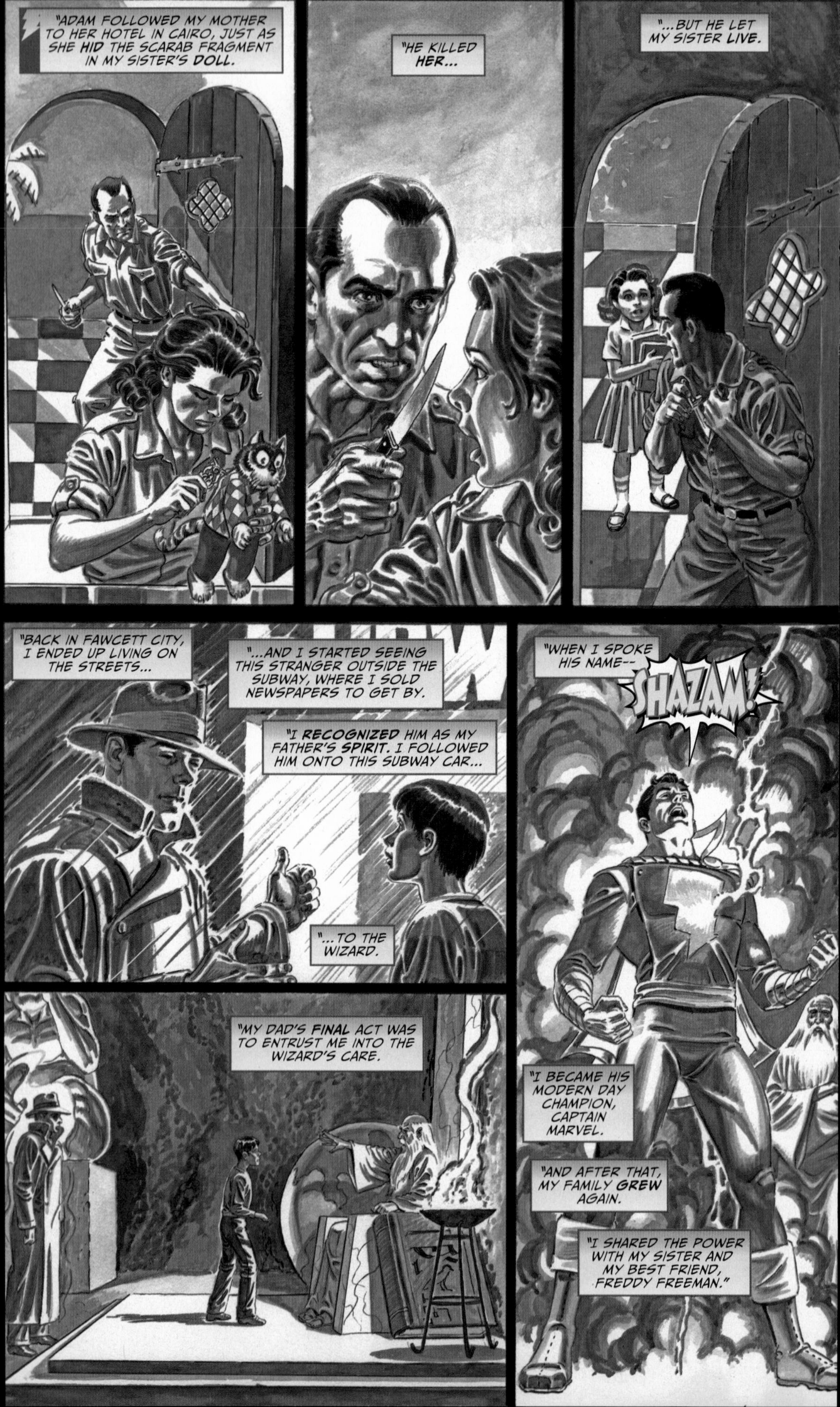
"ADAM FOLLOWED MY MOTHER TO HER HOTEL IN CAIRO, JUST AS SHE HID THE SCARAB FRAGMENT IN MY SISTER'S DOLL.
"HE KILLED HER...
"...BUT HE LET MY SISTER LIVE.
"BACK IN FAWCETT CITY, I ENDED UP LIVING ON THE STREETS...
"...AND I STARTED SEEING THIS STRANGER OUTSIDE THE SUBWAY, WHERE I SOLD NEWSPAPERS TO GET BY.
"I RECOGNIZED HIM AS MY FATHER'S SPIRIT. I FOLLOWED HIM ONTO THIS SUBWAY CAR...
"...TO THE WIZARD.
"MY DAD'S FINAL ACT WAS TO ENTRUST ME INTO THE WIZARD'S CARE.
"WHEN I SPOKE HIS NAME--
SHAZAM!
"I BECAME HIS MODERN DAY CHAMPION, CAPTAIN MARVEL.
"AND AFTER THAT, MY FAMILY GREW AGAIN.
"I SHARED THE POWER WITH MY SISTER AND MY BEST FRIEND, FREDDY FREEMAN."

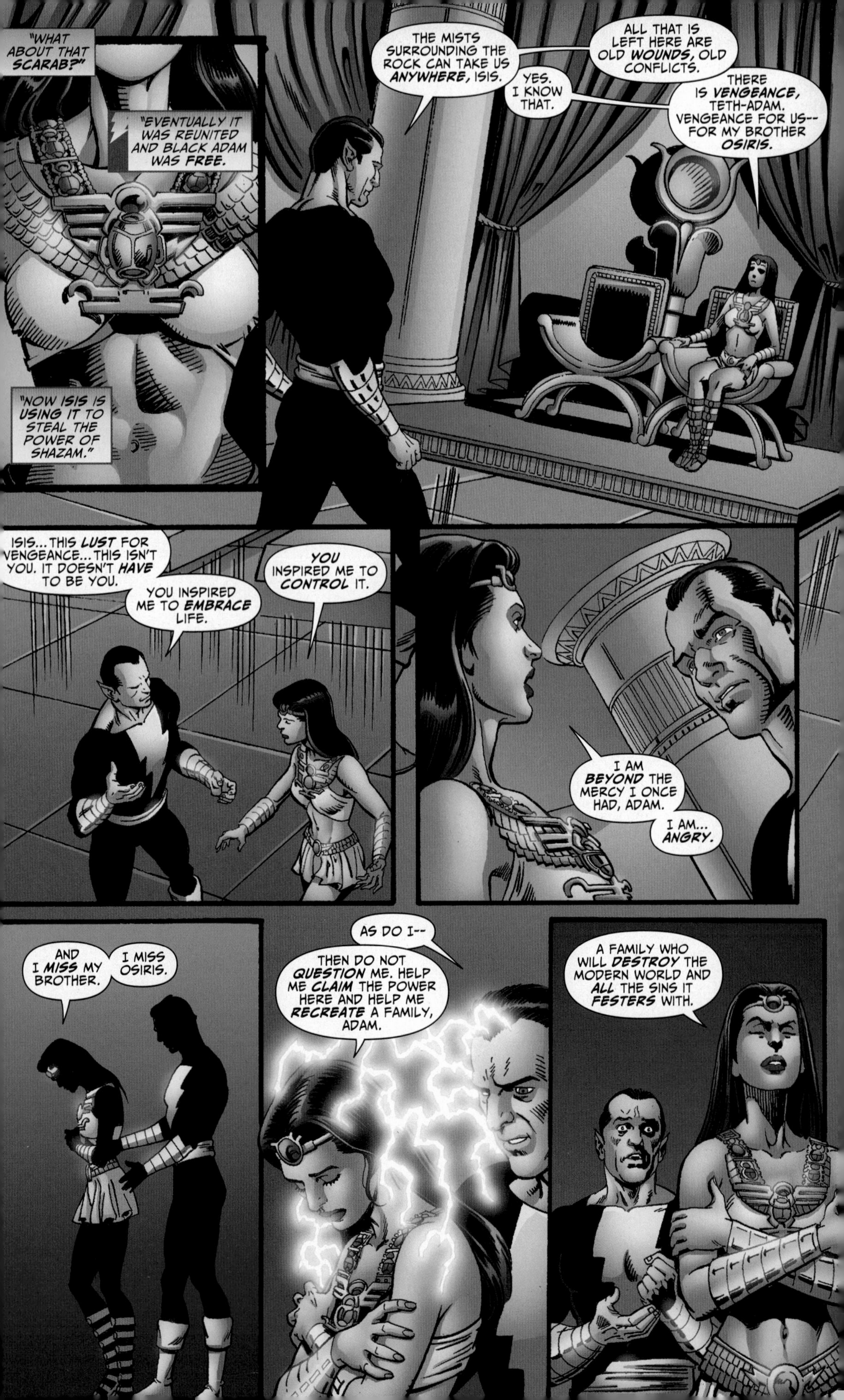
"WHAT ABOUT THAT SCARAB?"
"EVENTUALLY IT WAS REUNITED AND BLACK ADAM WAS FREE.
"NOW ISIS IS USING IT TO STEAL THE POWER OF SHAZAM."
THE MISTS SURROUNDING THE ROCK CAN TAKE US ANYWHERE, ISIS.
ALL THAT IS LEFT HERE ARE OLD WOUNDS, OLD CONFLICTS.
YES. I KNOW THAT.
THERE IS VENGEANCE, TETH-ADAM. VENGEANCE FOR US-- FOR MY BROTHER OSIRIS.
ISIS... THIS LUST FOR VENGEANCE... THIS ISN'T YOU. IT DOESN'T HAVE TO BE YOU.
YOU INSPIRED ME TO EMBRACE LIFE.
YOU INSPIRED ME TO CONTROL IT.
I AM BEYOND THE MERCY I ONCE HAD, ADAM.
I AM... ANGRY.
I MISS OSIRIS.
AND I MISS MY BROTHER.
AS DO I--
THEN DO NOT QUESTION ME. HELP ME CLAIM THE POWER HERE AND HELP ME RECREATE A FAMILY, ADAM.
A FAMILY WHO WILL DESTROY THE MODERN WORLD AND ALL THE SINS IT FESTERS WITH.

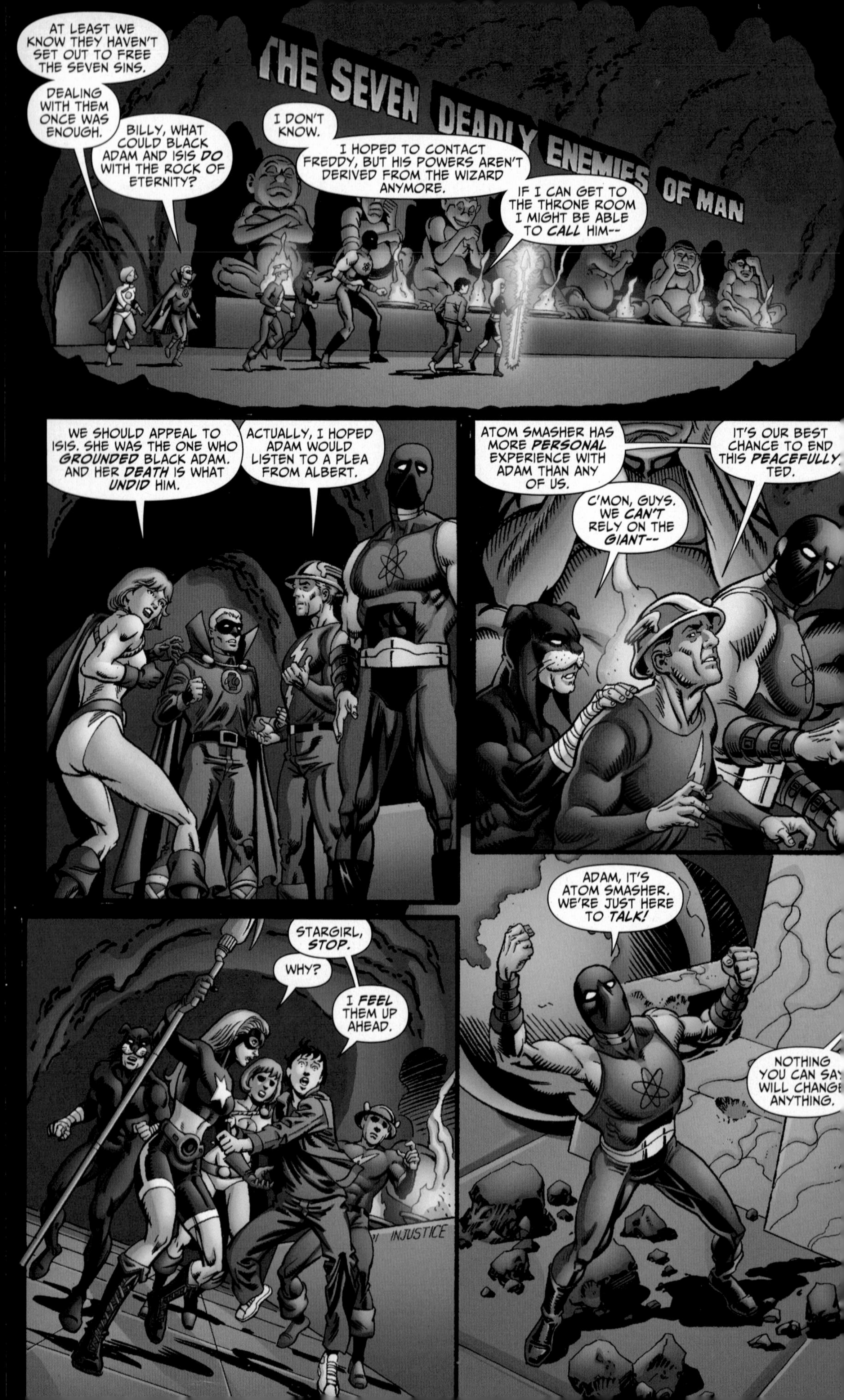

AT LEAST WE KNOW THEY HAVEN'T SET OUT TO FREE THE SEVEN SINS.
DEALING WITH THEM ONCE WAS ENOUGH.
THE SEVEN DEADLY ENEMIES OF MAN
BILLY, WHAT COULD BLACK ADAM AND ISIS DO WITH THE ROCK OF ETERNITY?
I DON'T KNOW.
I HOPED TO CONTACT FREDDY, BUT HIS POWERS AREN'T DERIVED FROM THE WIZARD ANYMORE.
IF I CAN GET TO THE THRONE ROOM I MIGHT BE ABLE TO CALL HIM--
WE SHOULD APPEAL TO ISIS. SHE WAS THE ONE WHO GROUNDED BLACK ADAM. AND HER DEATH IS WHAT UNDID HIM.
ACTUALLY, I HOPED ADAM WOULD LISTEN TO A PLEA FROM ALBERT.
ATOM SMASHER HAS MORE PERSONAL EXPERIENCE WITH ADAM THAN ANY OF US.
IT'S OUR BEST CHANCE TO END THIS PEACEFULLY, TED.
C'MON, GUYS. WE CAN'T RELY ON THE GIANT--
STARGIRL, STOP.
WHY?
I FEEL THEM UP AHEAD.
INJUSTICE
ADAM, IT'S ATOM SMASHER. WE'RE JUST HERE TO TALK!
NOTHING YOU CAN SAY WILL CHANGE ANYTHING.

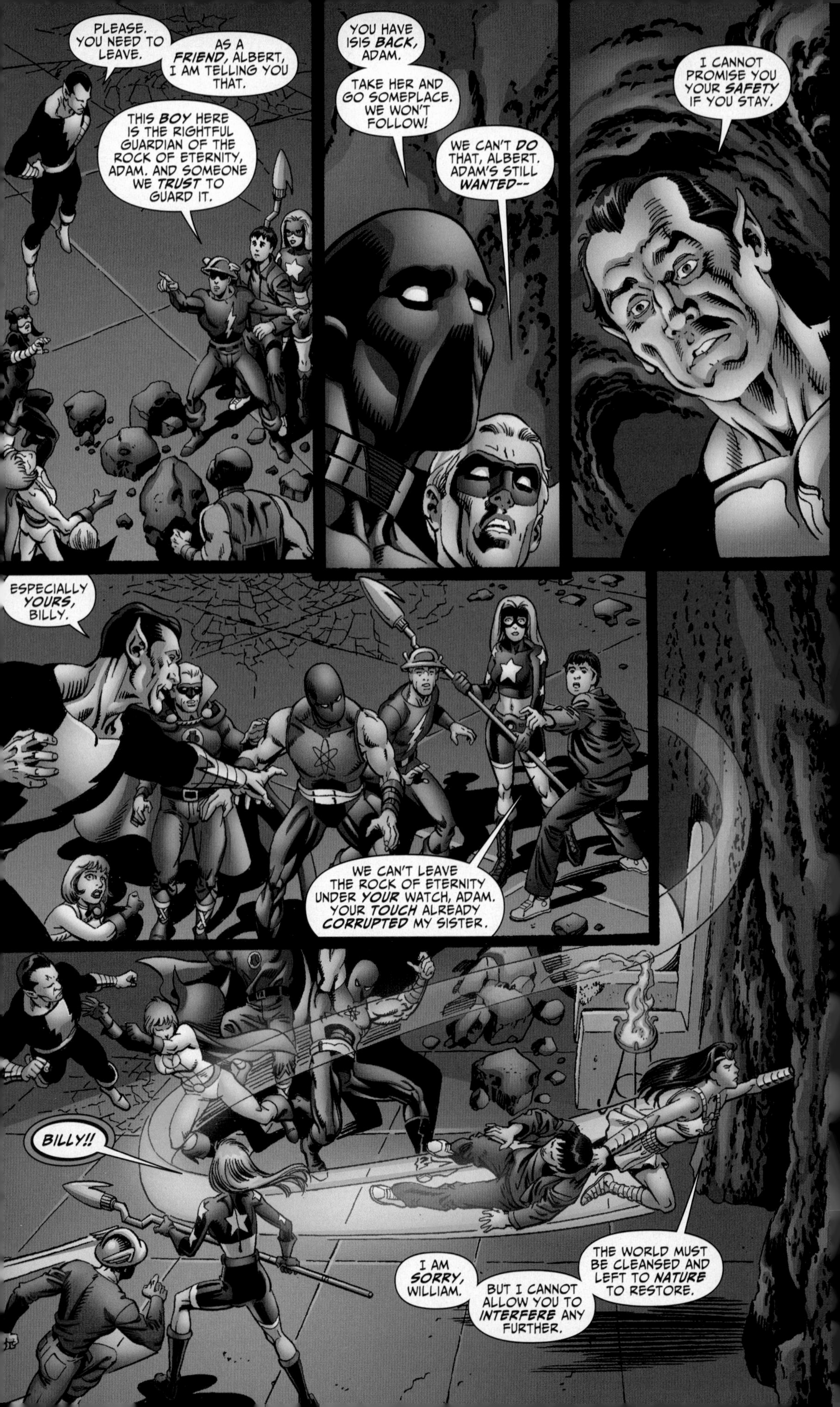

PLEASE. YOU NEED TO LEAVE.
AS A FRIEND, ALBERT, I AM TELLING YOU THAT.
THIS BOY HERE IS THE RIGHTFUL GUARDIAN OF THE ROCK OF ETERNITY, ADAM. AND SOMEONE WE TRUST TO GUARD IT.
YOU HAVE ISIS BACK, ADAM.
TAKE HER AND GO SOMEPLACE. WE WON'T FOLLOW!
WE CAN'T DO THAT, ALBERT. ADAM'S STILL WANTED--
I CANNOT PROMISE YOU YOUR SAFETY IF YOU STAY.
ESPECIALLY YOURS, BILLY.
WE CAN'T LEAVE THE ROCK OF ETERNITY UNDER YOUR WATCH, ADAM. YOUR TOUCH ALREADY CORRUPTED MY SISTER.
BILLY!!
I AM SORRY, WILLIAM.
BUT I CANNOT ALLOW YOU TO INTERFERE ANY FURTHER.
THE WORLD MUST BE CLEANSED AND LEFT TO NATURE TO RESTORE.

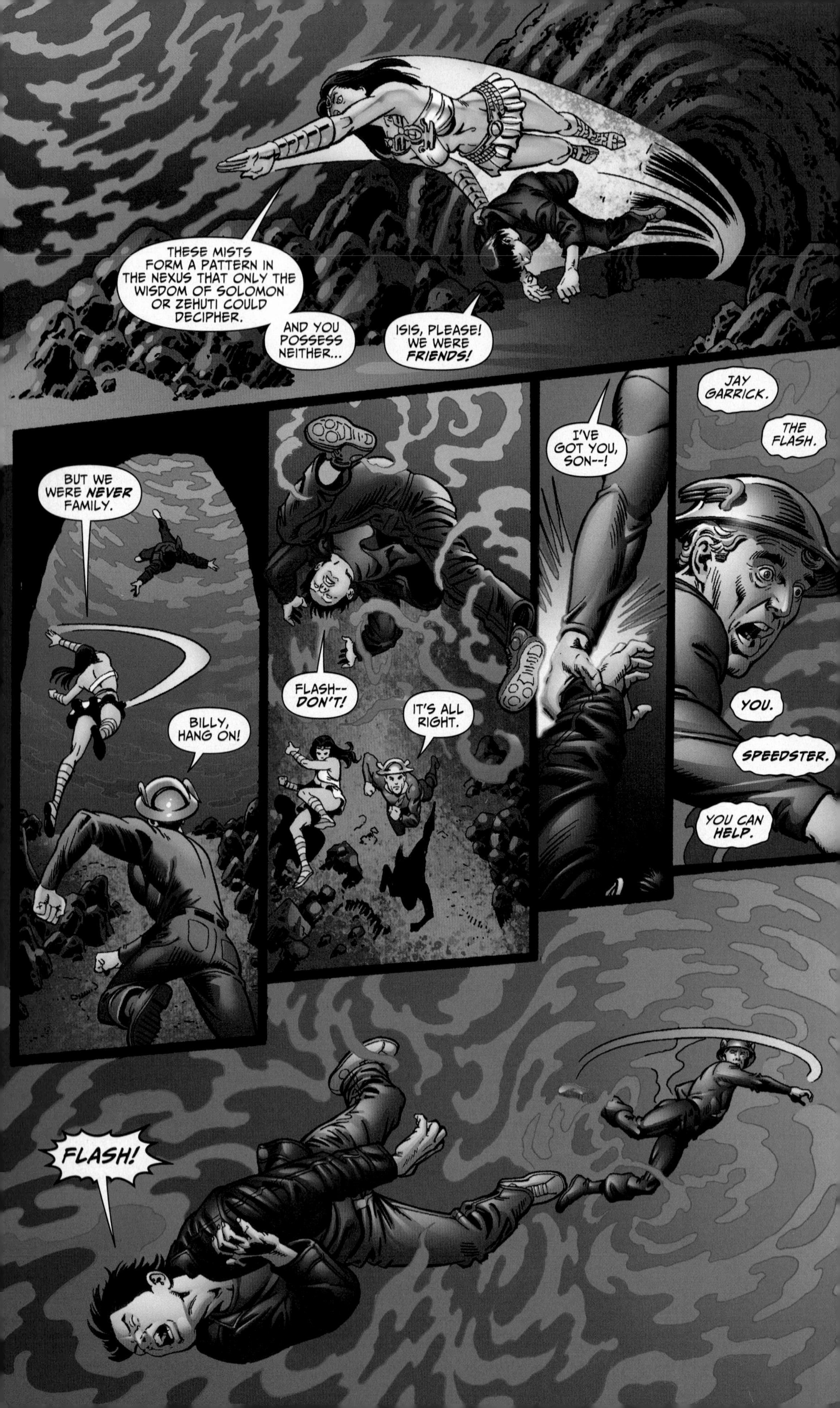

THESE MISTS FORM A PATTERN IN THE NEXUS THAT ONLY THE WISDOM OF SOLOMON OR ZEHUTI COULD DECIPHER.
AND YOU POSSESS NEITHER...
ISIS, PLEASE! WE WERE FRIENDS!
BUT WE WERE NEVER FAMILY.
BILLY, HANG ON!
FLASH-- DON'T!
IT'S ALL RIGHT.
I'VE GOT YOU, SON--!
JAY GARRICK.
THE FLASH.
YOU.
SPEEDSTER.
YOU CAN HELP.
FLASH!

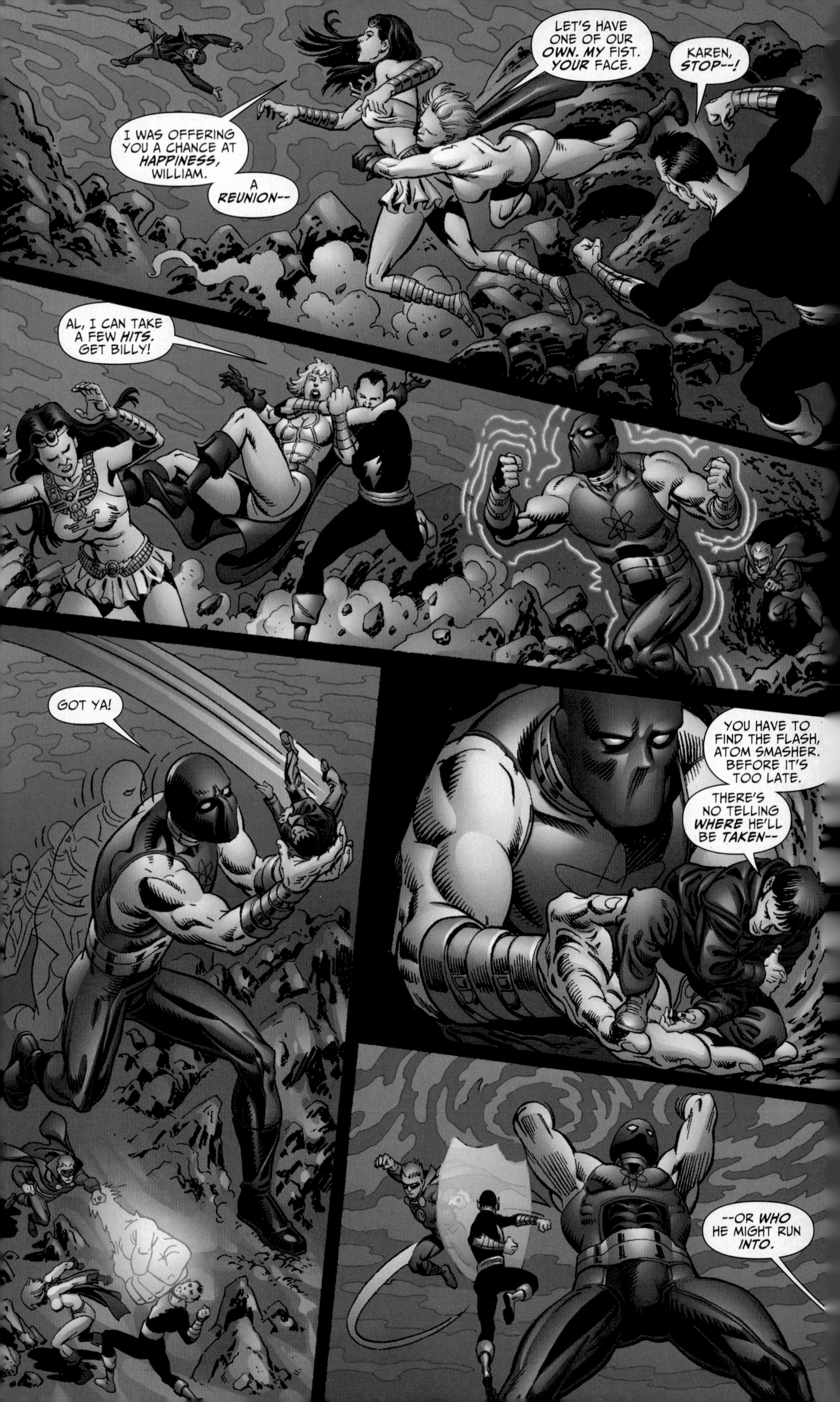
I WAS OFFERING YOU A CHANCE AT HAPPINESS, WILLIAM.
A REUNION--
LET'S HAVE ONE OF OUR OWN. MY FIST. YOUR FACE.
KAREN, STOP--!
AL, I CAN TAKE A FEW HITS. GET BILLY!
GOT YA!
YOU HAVE TO FIND THE FLASH, ATOM SMASHER. BEFORE IT'S TOO LATE.
THERE'S NO TELLING WHERE HE'LL BE TAKEN--
--OR WHO HE MIGHT RUN INTO.

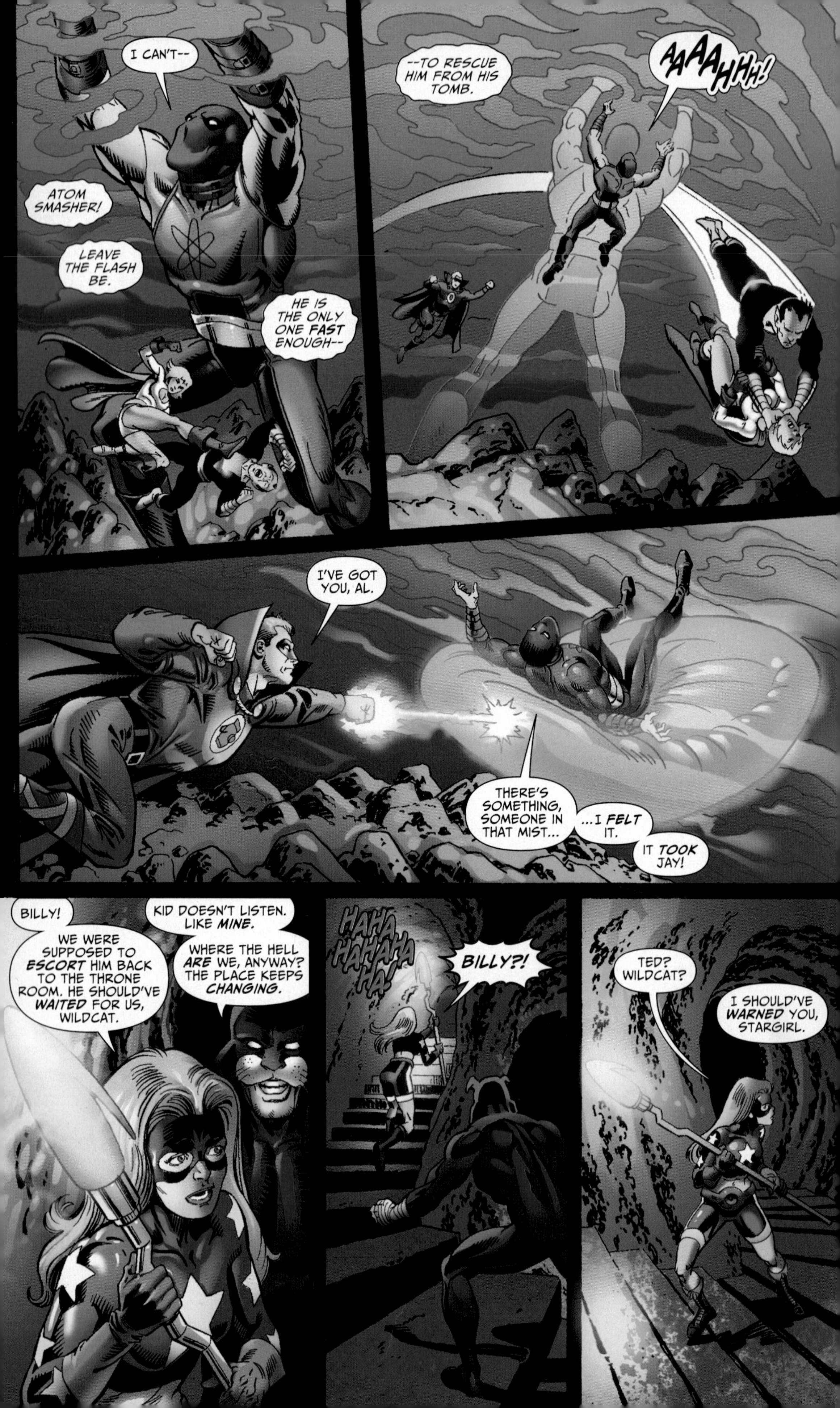

I CAN'T--
ATOM SMASHER!
LEAVE THE FLASH BE.
HE IS THE ONLY ONE FAST ENOUGH--
--TO RESCUE HIM FROM HIS TOMB.
AAAAHHH!
I'VE GOT YOU, AL.
THERE'S SOMETHING, SOMEONE IN THAT MIST...
...I FELT IT.
IT TOOK JAY!
BILLY!
WE WERE SUPPOSED TO ESCORT HIM BACK TO THE THRONE ROOM. HE SHOULD'VE WAITED FOR US, WILDCAT.
KID DOESN'T LISTEN. LIKE MINE.
WHERE THE HELL ARE WE, ANYWAY? THE PLACE KEEPS CHANGING.
HAHAHAHAHAHA!
BILLY?!
TED? WILDCAT?
I SHOULD'VE WARNED YOU, STARGIRL.

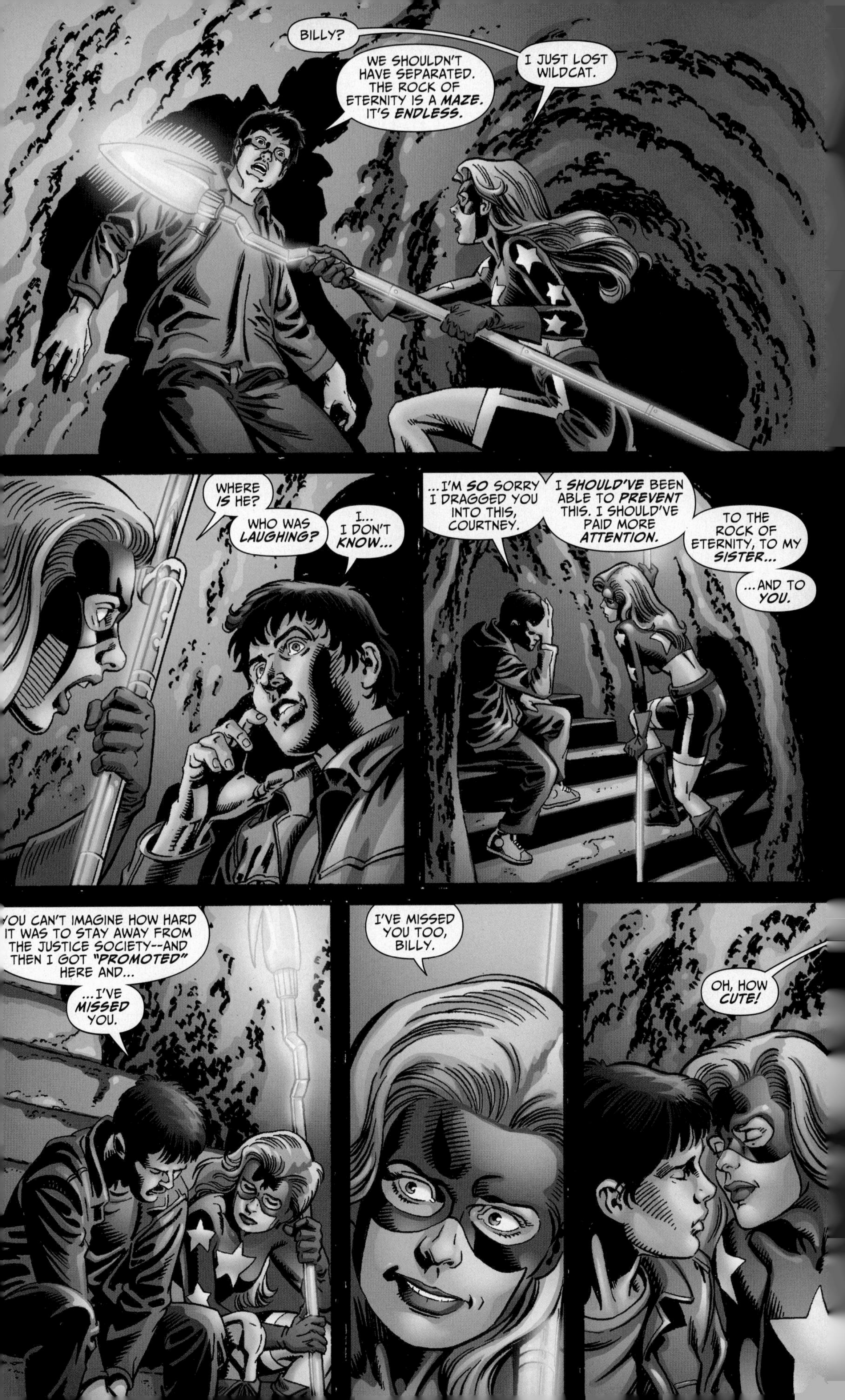
BILLY?
WE SHOULDN'T HAVE SEPARATED. THE ROCK OF ETERNITY IS A MAZE. IT'S ENDLESS.
I JUST LOST WILDCAT.
WHERE IS HE?
WHO WAS LAUGHING?
I... I DON'T KNOW...
...I'M SO SORRY I DRAGGED YOU INTO THIS, COURTNEY.
I SHOULD'VE BEEN ABLE TO PREVENT THIS. I SHOULD'VE PAID MORE ATTENTION.
TO THE ROCK OF ETERNITY, TO MY SISTER...
...AND TO YOU.
YOU CAN'T IMAGINE HOW HARD IT WAS TO STAY AWAY FROM THE JUSTICE SOCIETY--AND THEN I GOT "PROMOTED" HERE AND...
...I'VE MISSED YOU.
I'VE MISSED YOU TOO, BILLY.
OH, HOW CUTE!

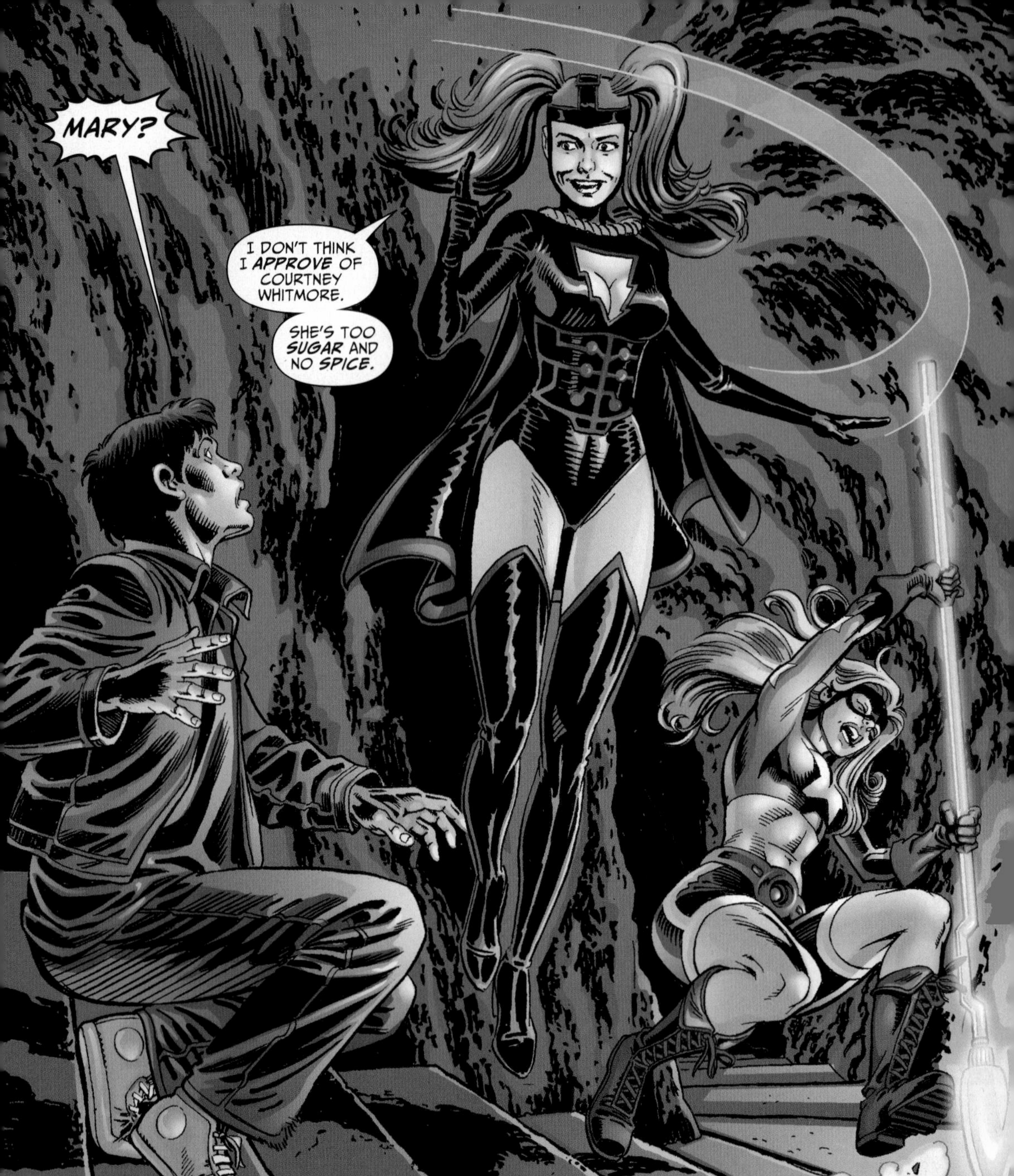
MARY?
I DON'T THINK I APPROVE OF COURTNEY WHITMORE.
SHE'S TOO SUGAR AND NO SPICE.

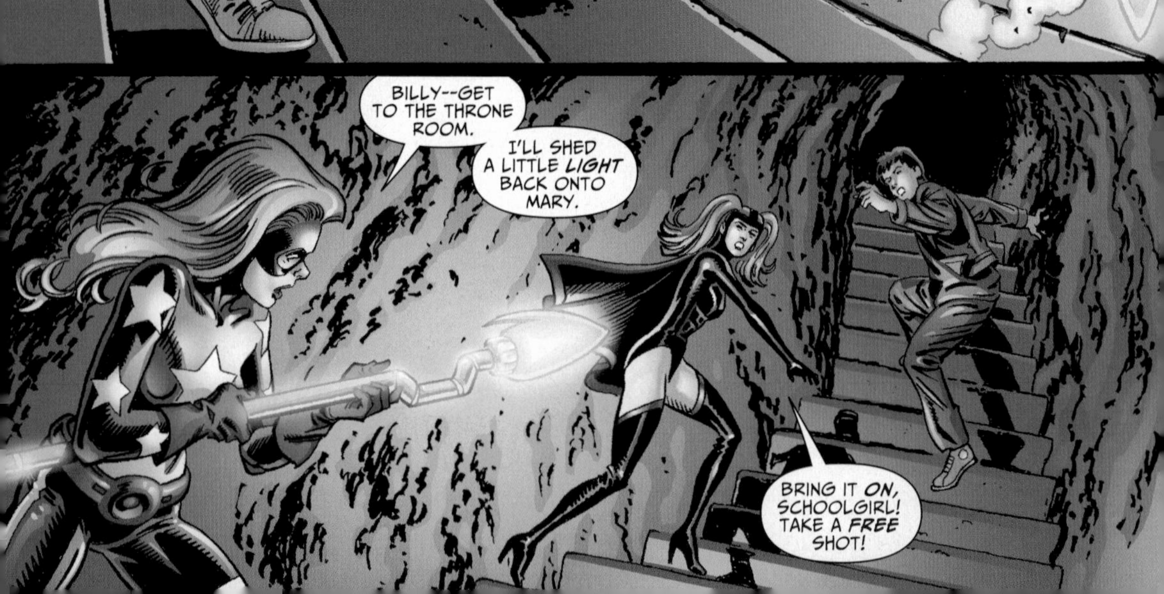
BILLY--GET TO THE THRONE ROOM.
I'LL SHED A LITTLE LIGHT BACK ONTO MARY.
BRING IT ON, SCHOOLGIRL! TAKE A FREE SHOT!

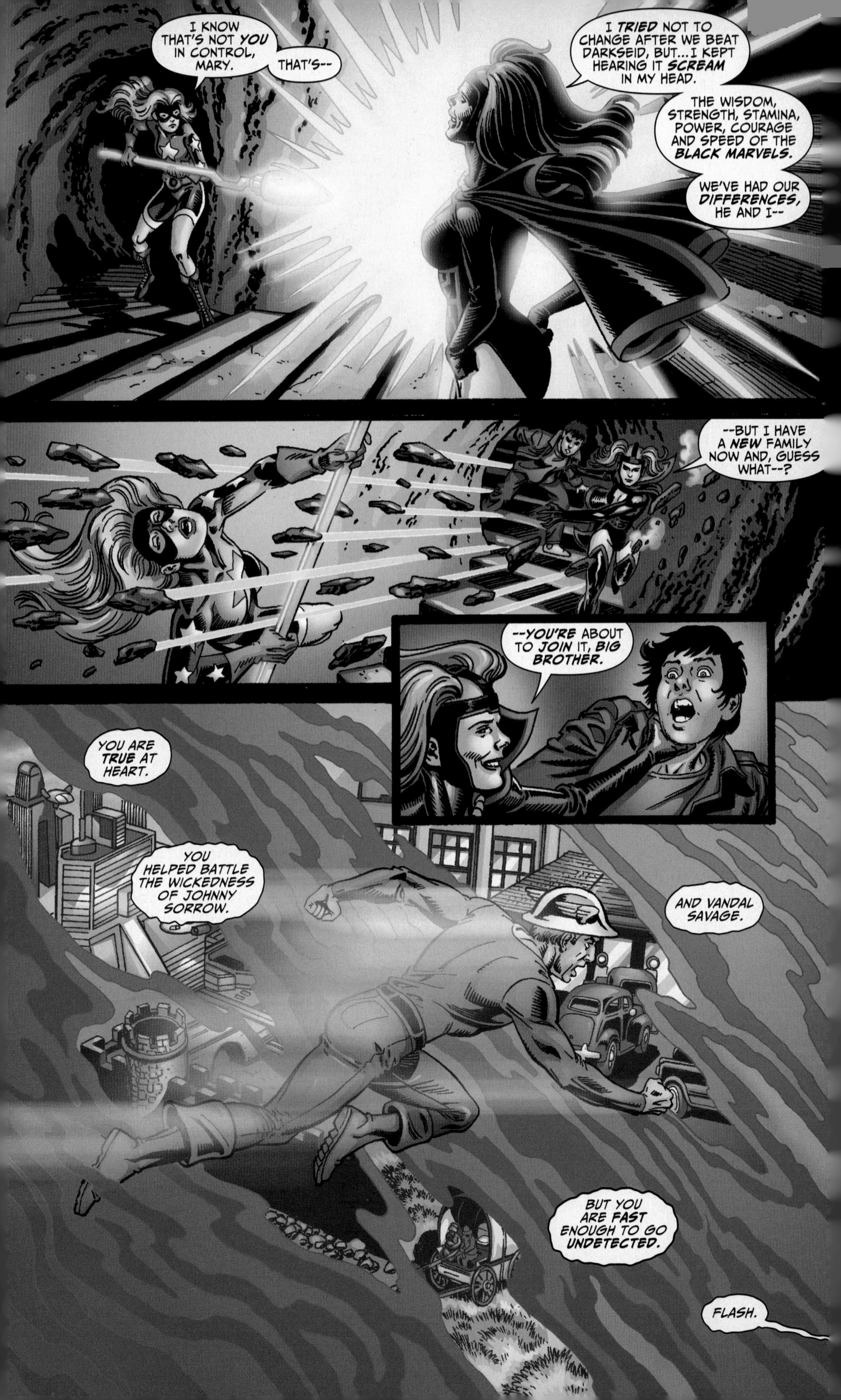

I KNOW THAT'S NOT YOU IN CONTROL, MARY.
THAT'S--
I TRIED NOT TO CHANGE AFTER WE BEAT DARKSEID, BUT...I KEPT HEARING IT SCREAM IN MY HEAD.
THE WISDOM, STRENGTH, STAMINA, POWER, COURAGE AND SPEED OF THE BLACK MARVELS.
WE'VE HAD OUR DIFFERENCES, HE AND I--
--BUT I HAVE A NEW FAMILY NOW AND, GUESS WHAT--?
--YOU'RE ABOUT TO JOIN IT, BIG BROTHER.
YOU ARE TRUE AT HEART.
YOU HELPED BATTLE THE WICKEDNESS OF JOHNNY SORROW.
AND VANDAL SAVAGE.
BUT YOU ARE FAST ENOUGH TO GO UNDETECTED.
FLASH.

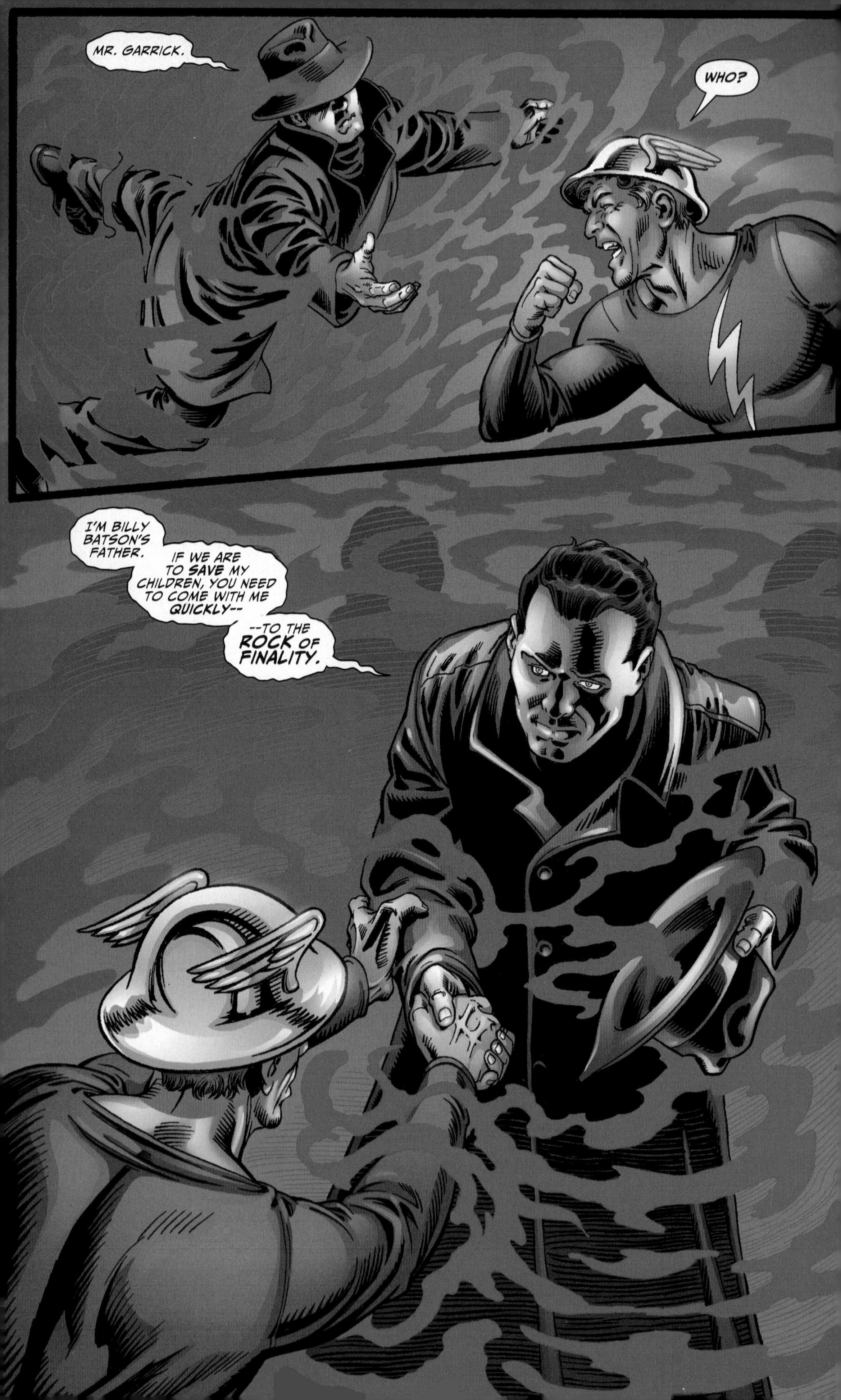
MR. GARRICK.
WHO?
I'M BILLY BATSON'S FATHER.
IF WE ARE TO SAVE MY CHILDREN, YOU NEED TO COME WITH ME QUICKLY--
--TO THE ROCK OF FINALITY.

JUSTICE SOCIETY OF AMERICA #25 cover A by Alex Ross
Interior pencils by Jerry Ordway and inks by Bob Wiacek and Ordway

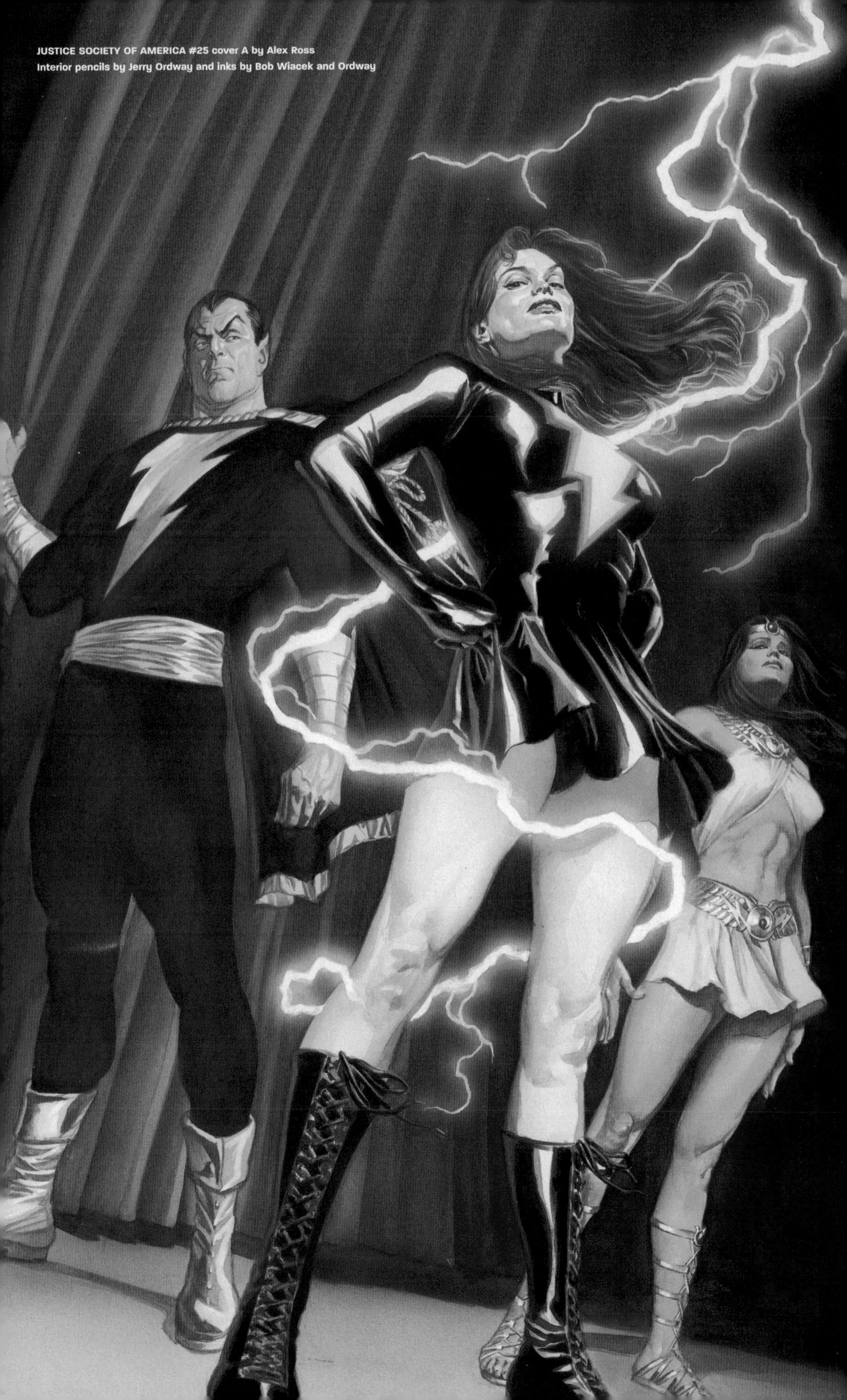

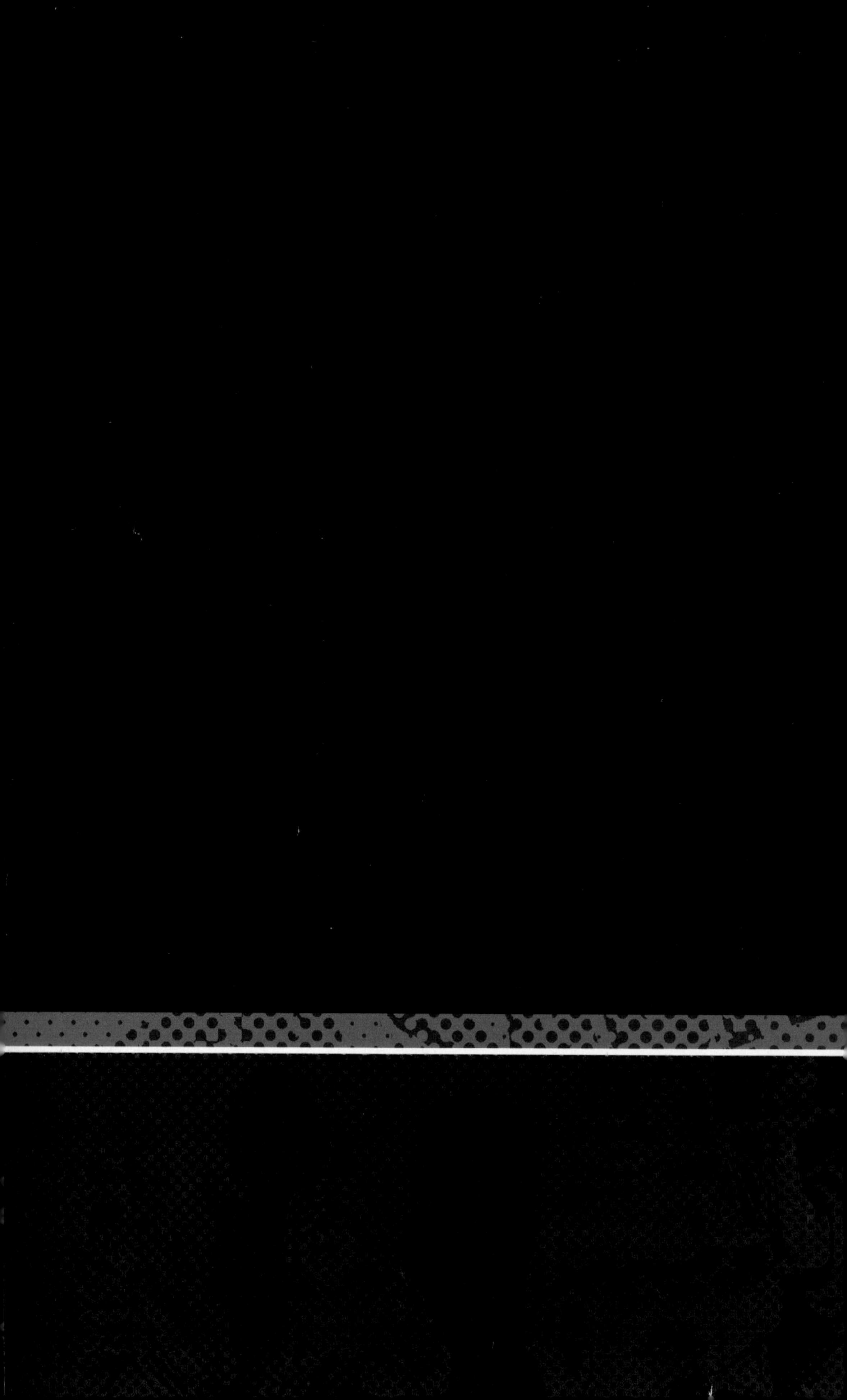

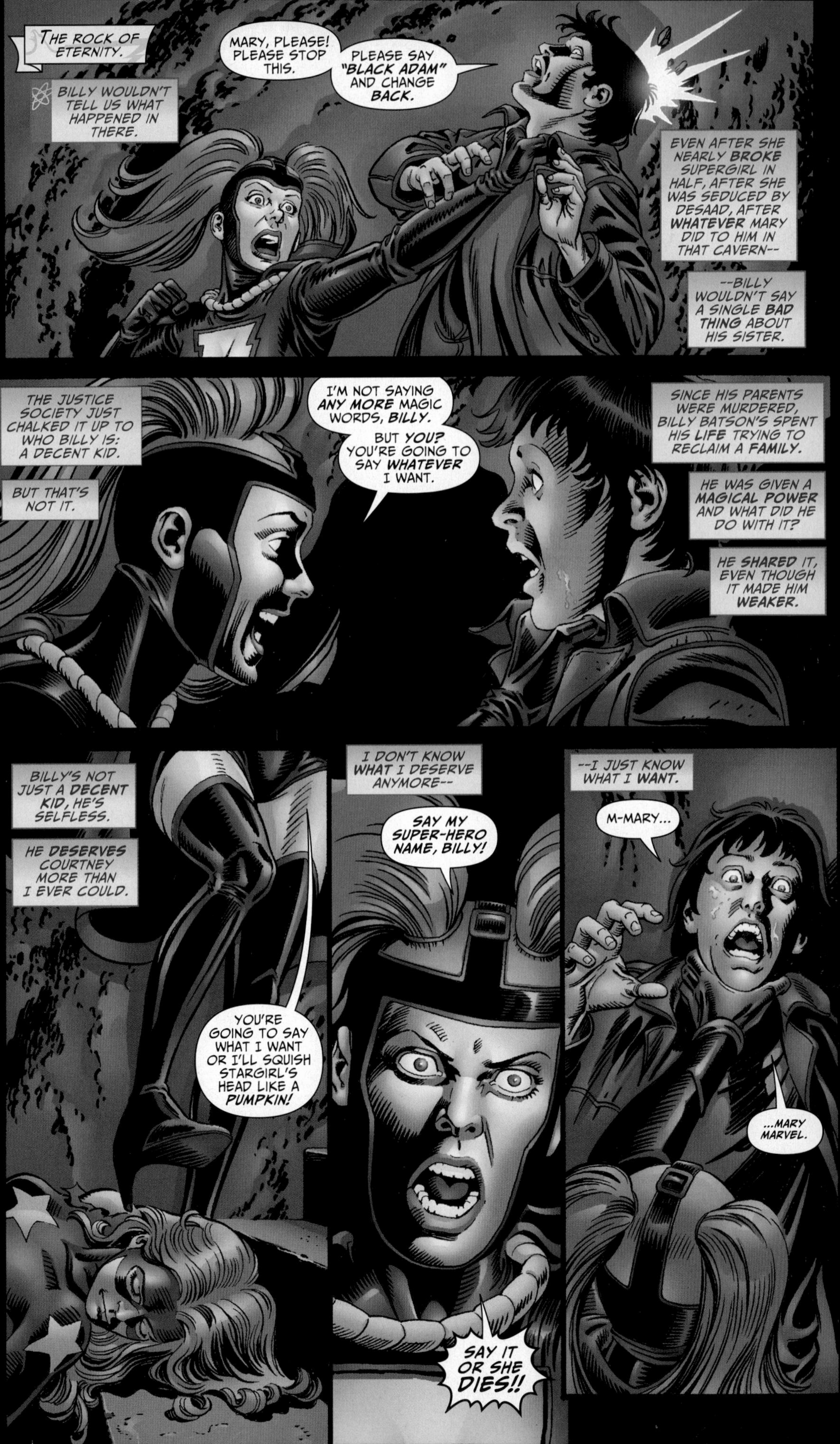
THE ROCK OF ETERNITY.
BILLY WOULDN'T TELL US WHAT HAPPENED IN THERE.
MARY, PLEASE! PLEASE STOP THIS.
PLEASE SAY "BLACK ADAM" AND CHANGE BACK.
EVEN AFTER SHE NEARLY BROKE SUPERGIRL IN HALF, AFTER SHE WAS SEDUCED BY DESAAD, AFTER WHATEVER MARY DID TO HIM IN THAT CAVERN--
--BILLY WOULDN'T SAY A SINGLE BAD THING ABOUT HIS SISTER.
THE JUSTICE SOCIETY JUST CHALKED IT UP TO WHO BILLY IS: A DECENT KID.
BUT THAT'S NOT IT.
I'M NOT SAYING ANY MORE MAGIC WORDS, BILLY.
BUT YOU? YOU'RE GOING TO SAY WHATEVER I WANT.
SINCE HIS PARENTS WERE MURDERED, BILLY BATSON'S SPENT HIS LIFE TRYING TO RECLAIM A FAMILY.
HE WAS GIVEN A MAGICAL POWER AND WHAT DID HE DO WITH IT?
HE SHARED IT, EVEN THOUGH IT MADE HIM WEAKER.
BILLY'S NOT JUST A DECENT KID, HE'S SELFLESS.
HE DESERVES COURTNEY MORE THAN I EVER COULD.
YOU'RE GOING TO SAY WHAT I WANT OR I'LL SQUISH STARGIRL'S HEAD LIKE A PUMPKIN!
I DON'T KNOW WHAT I DESERVE ANYMORE--
SAY MY SUPER-HERO NAME, BILLY!
SAY IT OR SHE DIES!!
--I JUST KNOW WHAT I WANT.
M-MARY...
...MARY MARVEL.

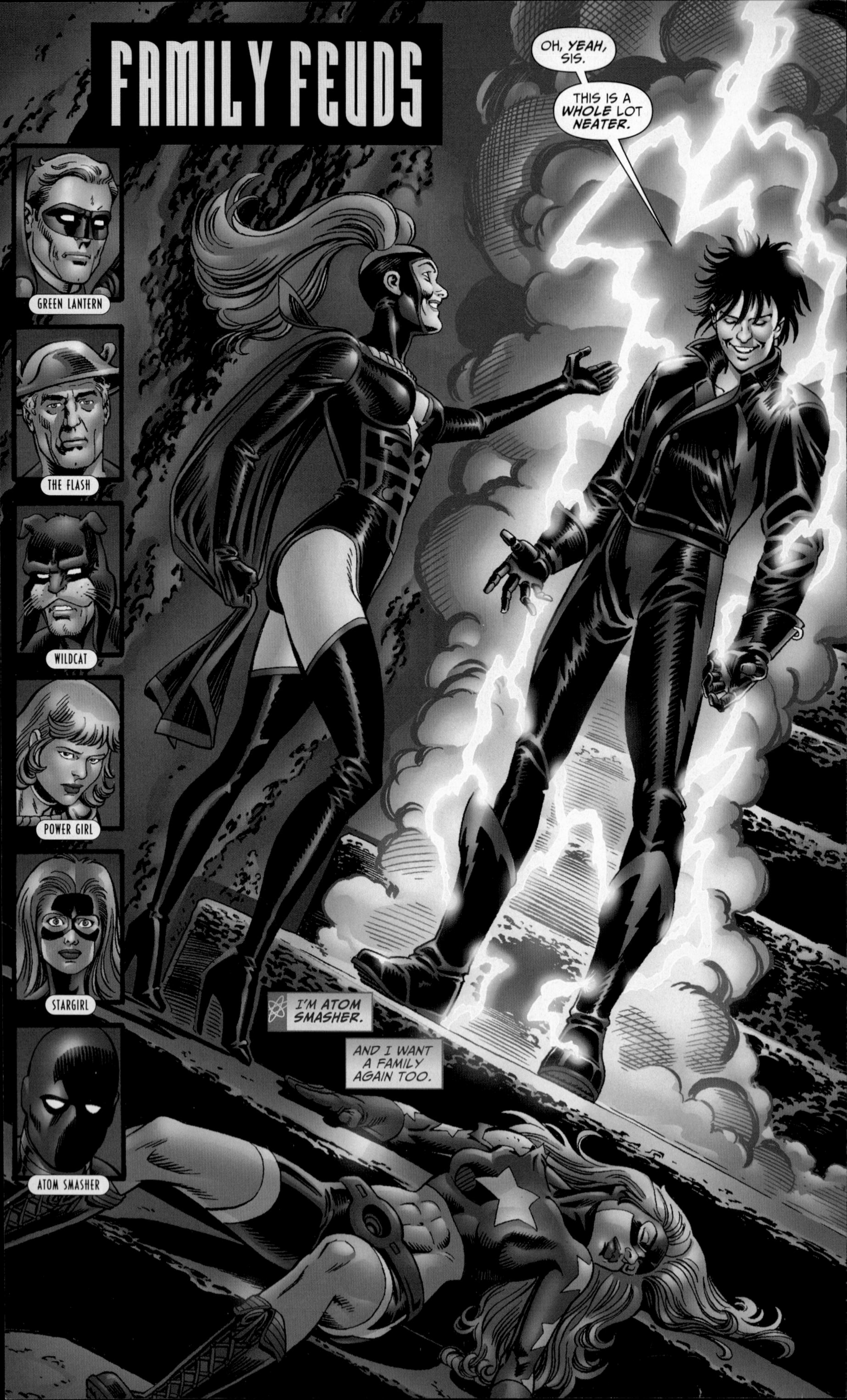
FAMILY FEUDS
GREEN LANTERN
THE FLASH
WILDCAT
POWER GIRL
STARGIRL
ATOM SMASHER
OH, YEAH, SIS.
THIS IS A WHOLE LOT NEATER.
I'M ATOM SMASHER.
AND I WANT A FAMILY AGAIN TOO.

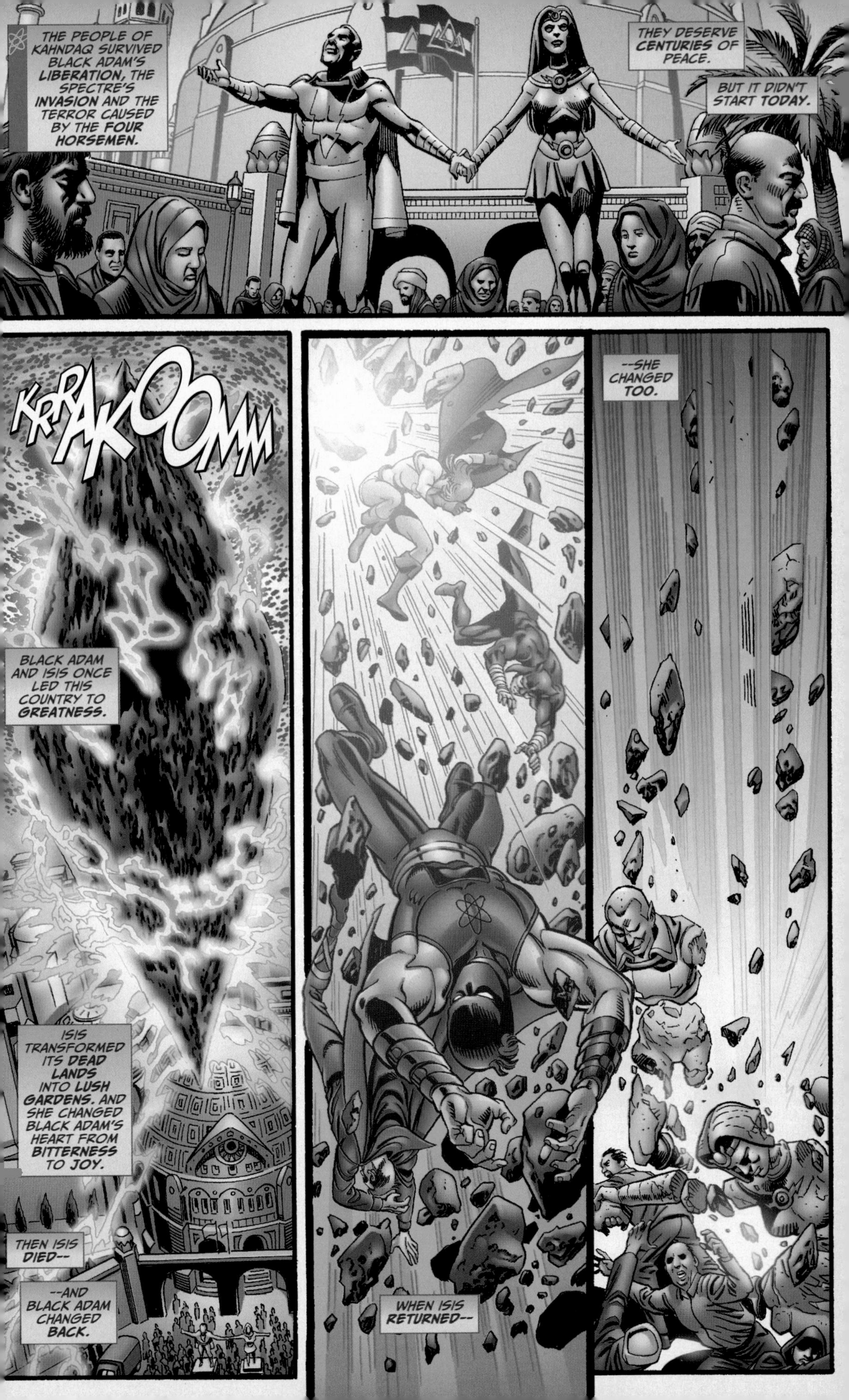
THE PEOPLE OF KAHNDAQ SURVIVED BLACK ADAM'S LIBERATION, THE SPECTRE'S INVASION AND THE TERROR CAUSED BY THE FOUR HORSEMEN.
THEY DESERVE CENTURIES OF PEACE.
BUT IT DIDN'T START TODAY.
KRRAKOOMM
BLACK ADAM AND ISIS ONCE LED THIS COUNTRY TO GREATNESS.
ISIS TRANSFORMED ITS DEAD LANDS INTO LUSH GARDENS. AND SHE CHANGED BLACK ADAM'S HEART FROM BITTERNESS TO JOY.
THEN ISIS DIED--
--AND BLACK ADAM CHANGED BACK.
WHEN ISIS RETURNED--
--SHE CHANGED TOO.

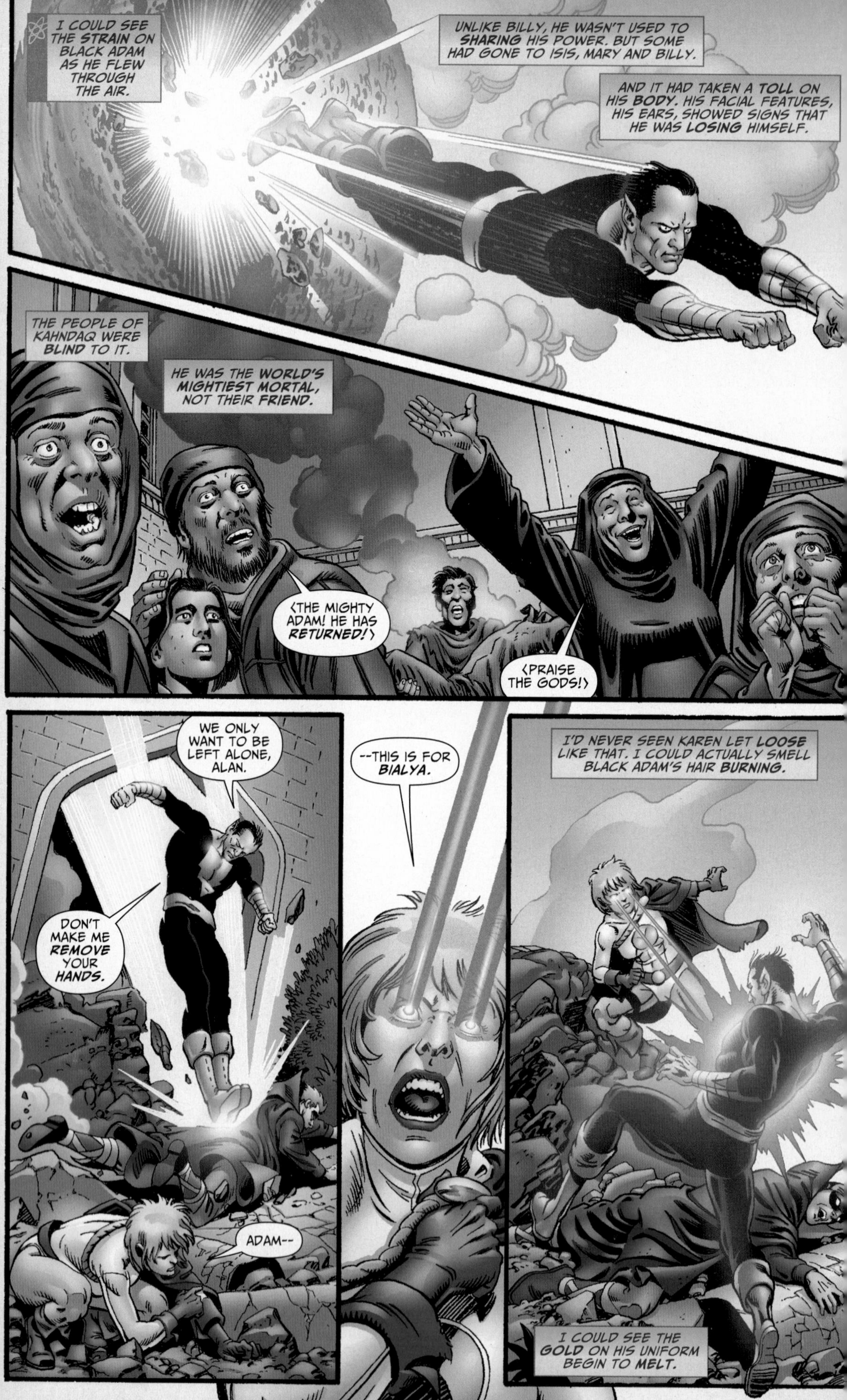
I COULD SEE THE STRAIN ON BLACK ADAM AS HE FLEW THROUGH THE AIR.
UNLIKE BILLY, HE WASN'T USED TO SHARING HIS POWER. BUT SOME HAD GONE TO ISIS, MARY AND BILLY.
AND IT HAD TAKEN A TOLL ON HIS BODY. HIS FACIAL FEATURES, HIS EARS, SHOWED SIGNS THAT HE WAS LOSING HIMSELF.
THE PEOPLE OF KAHNDAQ WERE BLIND TO IT.
HE WAS THE WORLD'S MIGHTIEST MORTAL, NOT THEIR FRIEND.
<THE MIGHTY ADAM! HE HAS RETURNED!>
<PRAISE THE GODS!>
WE ONLY WANT TO BE LEFT ALONE, ALAN.
DON'T MAKE ME REMOVE YOUR HANDS.
ADAM--
--THIS IS FOR BIALYA.
I'D NEVER SEEN KAREN LET LOOSE LIKE THAT. I COULD ACTUALLY SMELL BLACK ADAM'S HAIR BURNING.
I COULD SEE THE GOLD ON HIS UNIFORM BEGIN TO MELT.

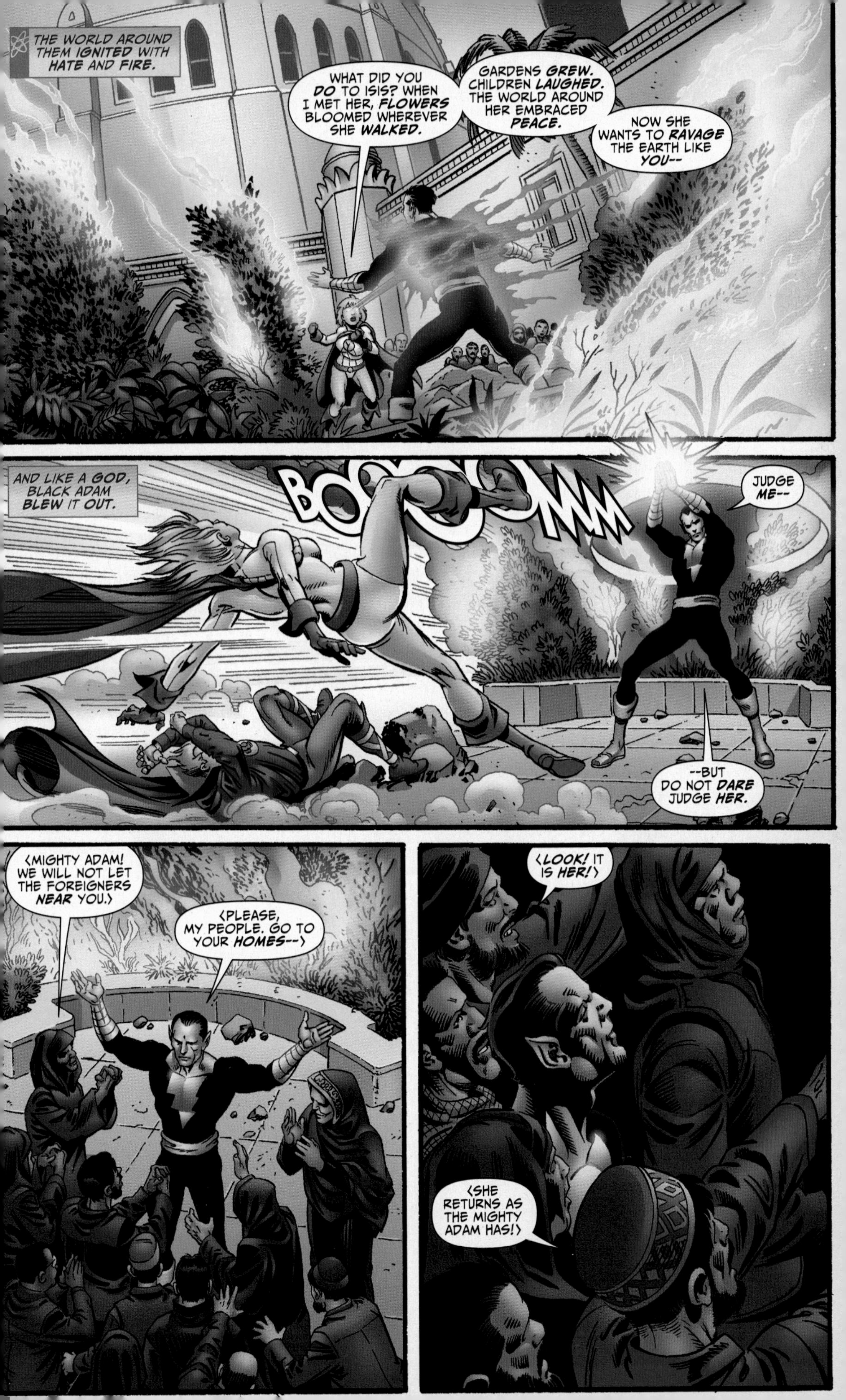

THE WORLD AROUND THEM IGNITED WITH HATE AND FIRE.
WHAT DID YOU DO TO ISIS? WHEN I MET HER, FLOWERS BLOOMED WHEREVER SHE WALKED.
GARDENS GREW. CHILDREN LAUGHED. THE WORLD AROUND HER EMBRACED PEACE.
NOW SHE WANTS TO RAVAGE THE EARTH LIKE YOU--
AND LIKE A GOD, BLACK ADAM BLEW IT OUT.
JUDGE ME--
--BUT DO NOT DARE JUDGE HER.
<MIGHTY ADAM! WE WILL NOT LET THE FOREIGNERS NEAR YOU.>
<PLEASE, MY PEOPLE. GO TO YOUR HOMES-->
<LOOK! IT IS HER!>
<SHE RETURNS AS THE MIGHTY ADAM HAS!>

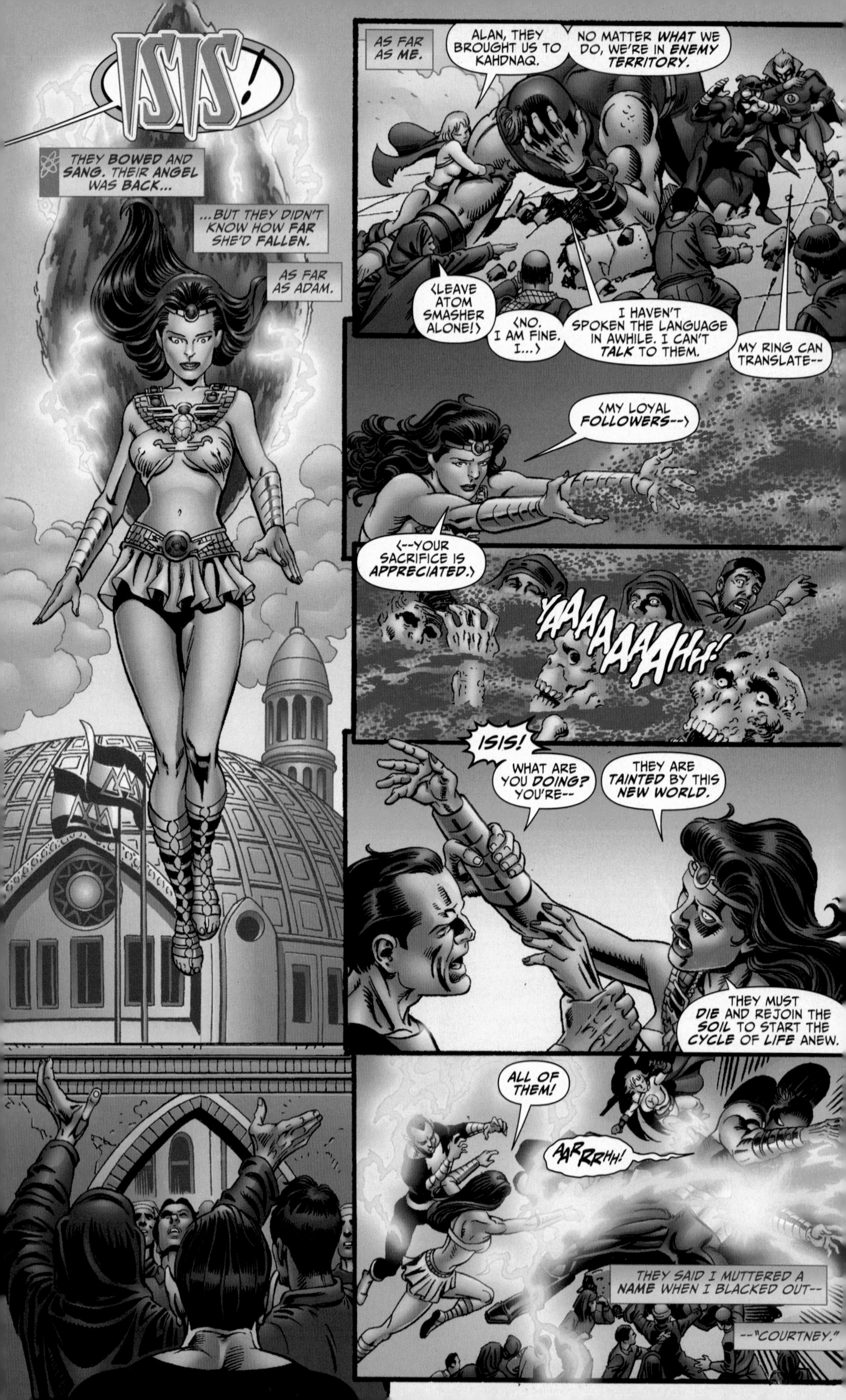
ISIS!
THEY BOWED AND SANG. THEIR ANGEL WAS BACK...
...BUT THEY DIDN'T KNOW HOW FAR SHE'D FALLEN.
AS FAR AS ADAM.
AS FAR AS ME.
ALAN, THEY BROUGHT US TO KAHDNAQ.
NO MATTER WHAT WE DO, WE'RE IN ENEMY TERRITORY.
‹LEAVE ATOM SMASHER ALONE!›
‹NO. I AM FINE. I...›
I HAVEN'T SPOKEN THE LANGUAGE IN AWHILE. I CAN'T TALK TO THEM.
MY RING CAN TRANSLATE--
‹MY LOYAL FOLLOWERS--›
‹--YOUR SACRIFICE IS APPRECIATED.›
YAAAAAAAAHH!
ISIS!
WHAT ARE YOU DOING? YOU'RE--
THEY ARE TAINTED BY THIS NEW WORLD.
THEY MUST DIE AND REJOIN THE SOIL TO START THE CYCLE OF LIFE ANEW.
ALL OF THEM!
AARRRHH!
THEY SAID I MUTTERED A NAME WHEN I BLACKED OUT--
--"COURTNEY."

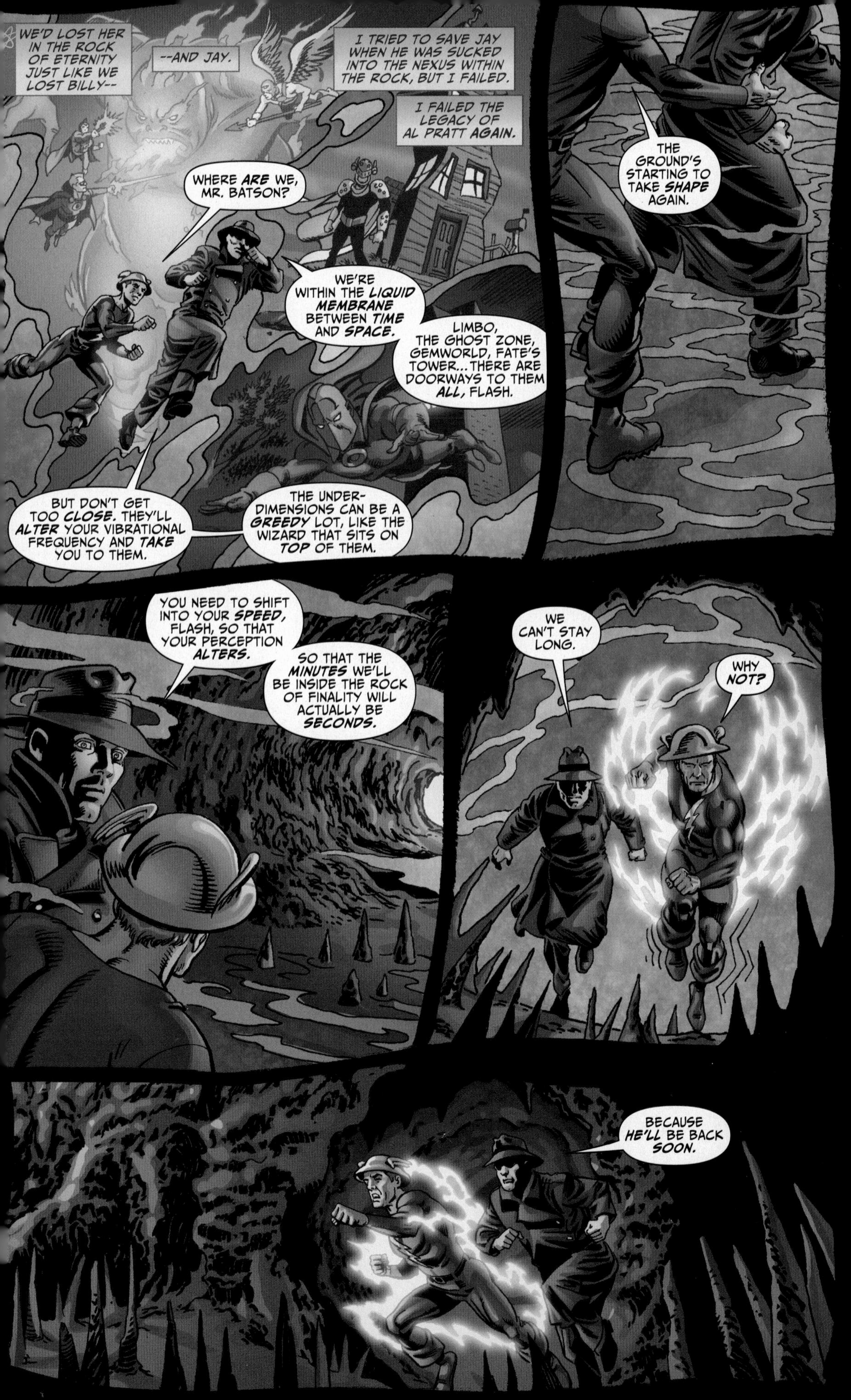
WE'D LOST HER IN THE ROCK OF ETERNITY JUST LIKE WE LOST BILLY--
--AND JAY.
I TRIED TO SAVE JAY WHEN HE WAS SUCKED INTO THE NEXUS WITHIN THE ROCK, BUT I FAILED.
I FAILED THE LEGACY OF AL PRATT AGAIN.
WHERE ARE WE, MR. BATSON?
WE'RE WITHIN THE LIQUID MEMBRANE BETWEEN TIME AND SPACE.
LIMBO, THE GHOST ZONE, GEMWORLD, FATE'S TOWER... THERE ARE DOORWAYS TO THEM ALL, FLASH.
BUT DON'T GET TOO CLOSE. THEY'LL ALTER YOUR VIBRATIONAL FREQUENCY AND TAKE YOU TO THEM.
THE UNDER-DIMENSIONS CAN BE A GREEDY LOT, LIKE THE WIZARD THAT SITS ON TOP OF THEM.
THE GROUND'S STARTING TO TAKE SHAPE AGAIN.
YOU NEED TO SHIFT INTO YOUR SPEED, FLASH, SO THAT YOUR PERCEPTION ALTERS.
SO THAT THE MINUTES WE'LL BE INSIDE THE ROCK OF FINALITY WILL ACTUALLY BE SECONDS.
WE CAN'T STAY LONG.
WHY NOT?
BECAUSE HE'LL BE BACK SOON.

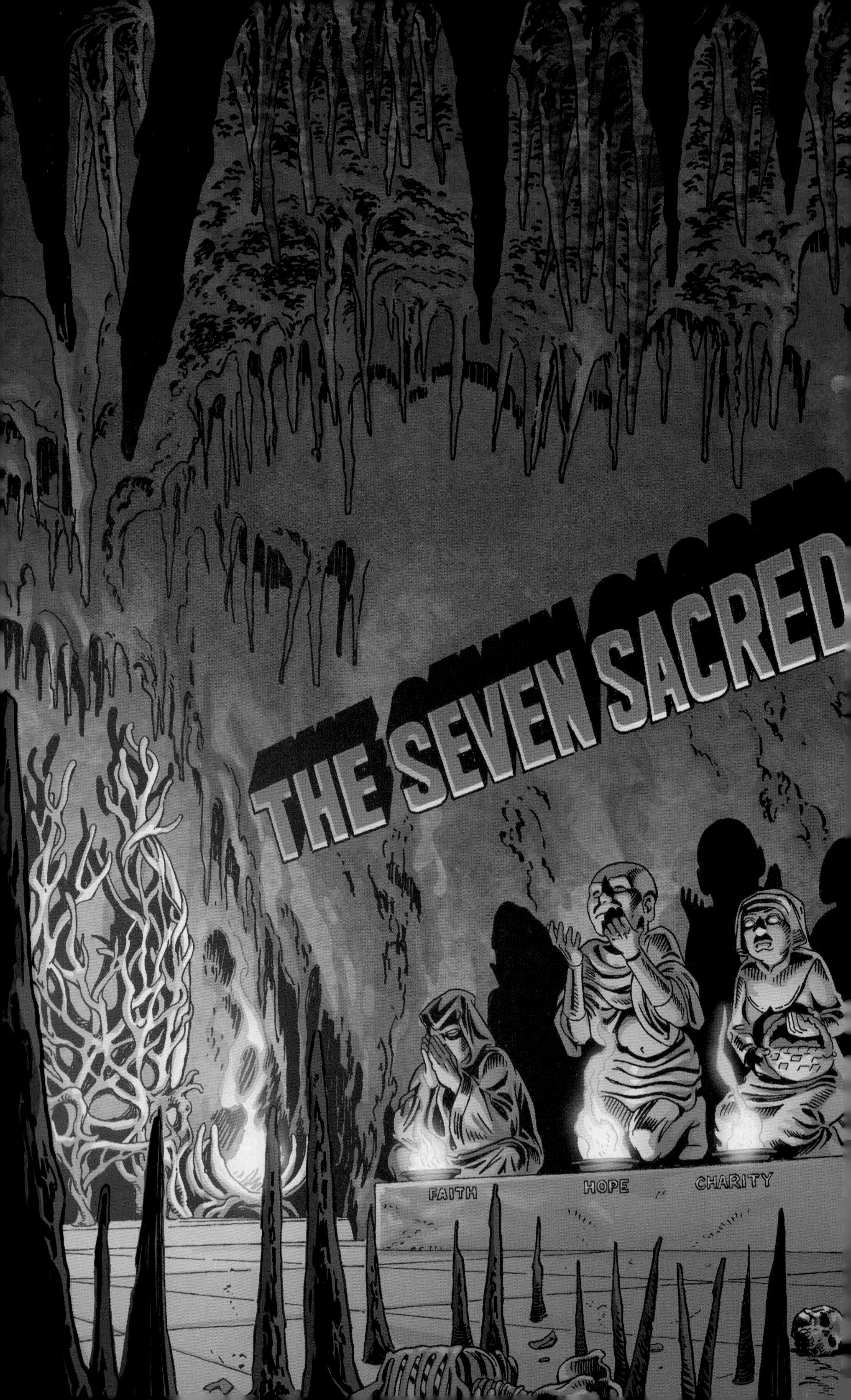
THE SEVEN SACRED
FAITH
HOPE
CHARITY

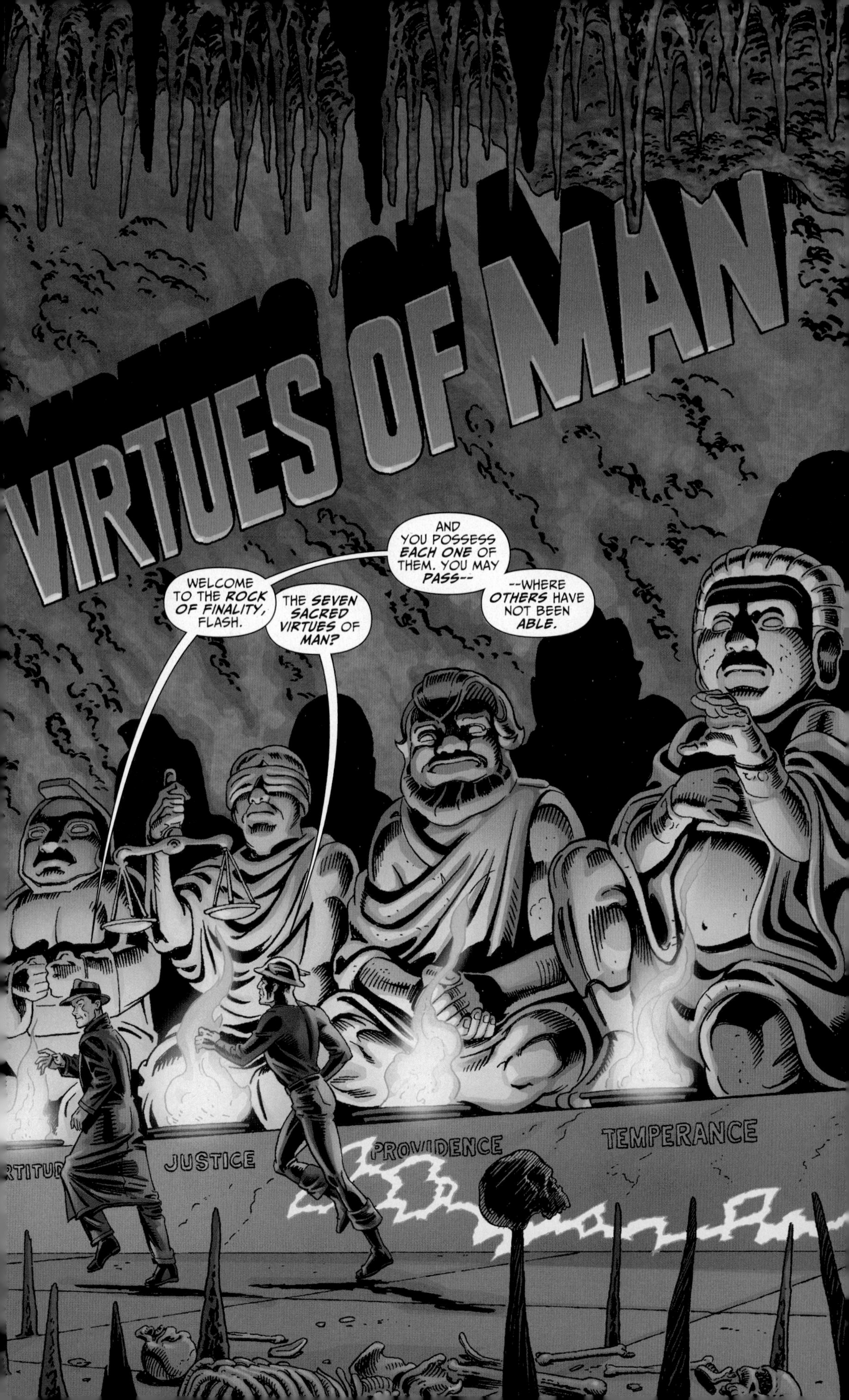
VIRTUES OF MAN
WELCOME TO THE ROCK OF FINALITY, FLASH.
THE SEVEN SACRED VIRTUES OF MAN?
AND YOU POSSESS EACH ONE OF THEM. YOU MAY PASS--
--WHERE OTHERS HAVE NOT BEEN ABLE.
RTITUD
JUSTICE
PROVIDENCE
TEMPERANCE

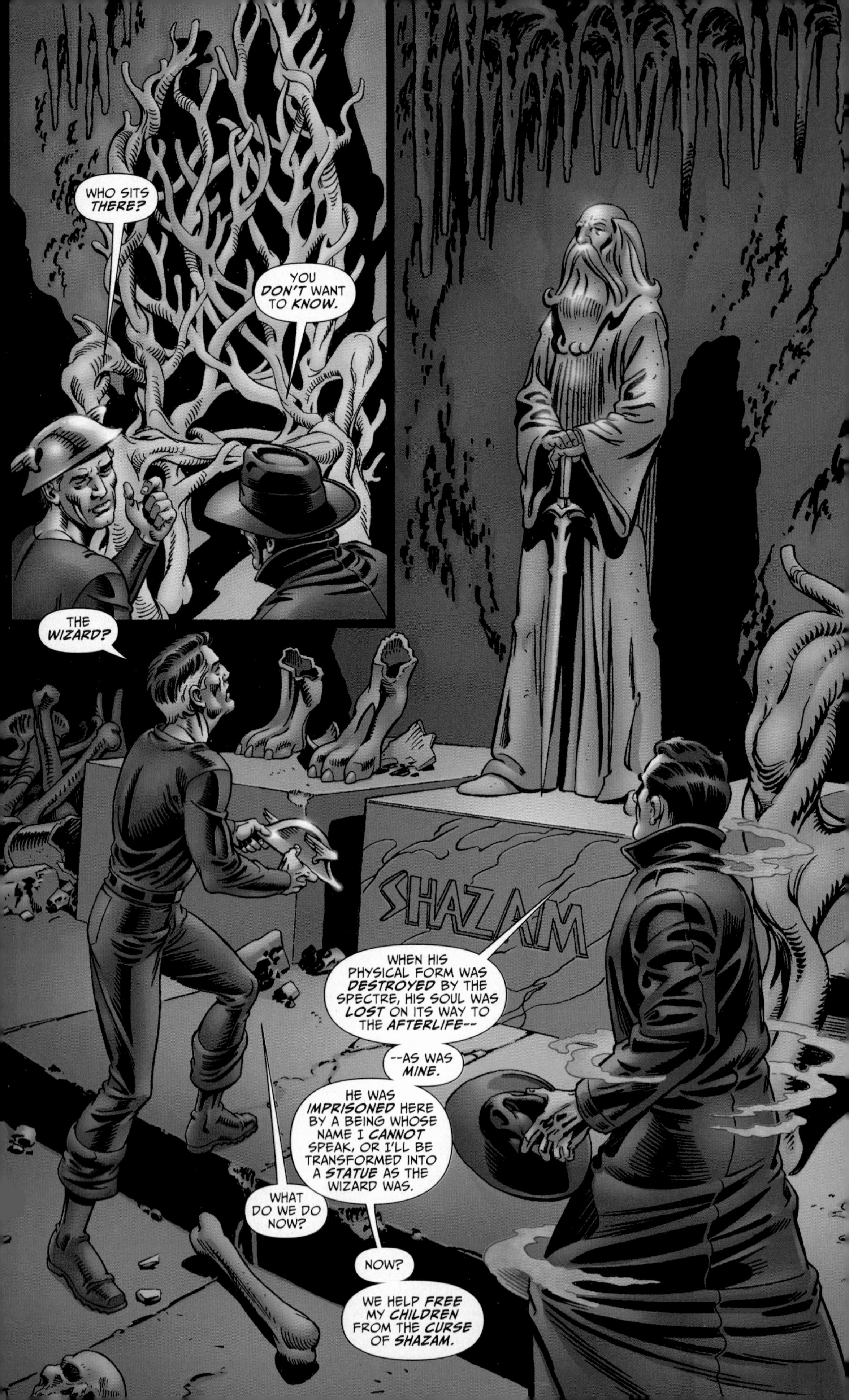
WHO SITS THERE?
YOU DON'T WANT TO KNOW.
THE WIZARD?
SHAZAM
WHEN HIS PHYSICAL FORM WAS DESTROYED BY THE SPECTRE, HIS SOUL WAS LOST ON ITS WAY TO THE AFTERLIFE--
--AS WAS MINE.
HE WAS IMPRISONED HERE BY A BEING WHOSE NAME I CANNOT SPEAK, OR I'LL BE TRANSFORMED INTO A STATUE AS THE WIZARD WAS.
WHAT DO WE DO NOW?
NOW?
WE HELP FREE MY CHILDREN FROM THE CURSE OF SHAZAM.

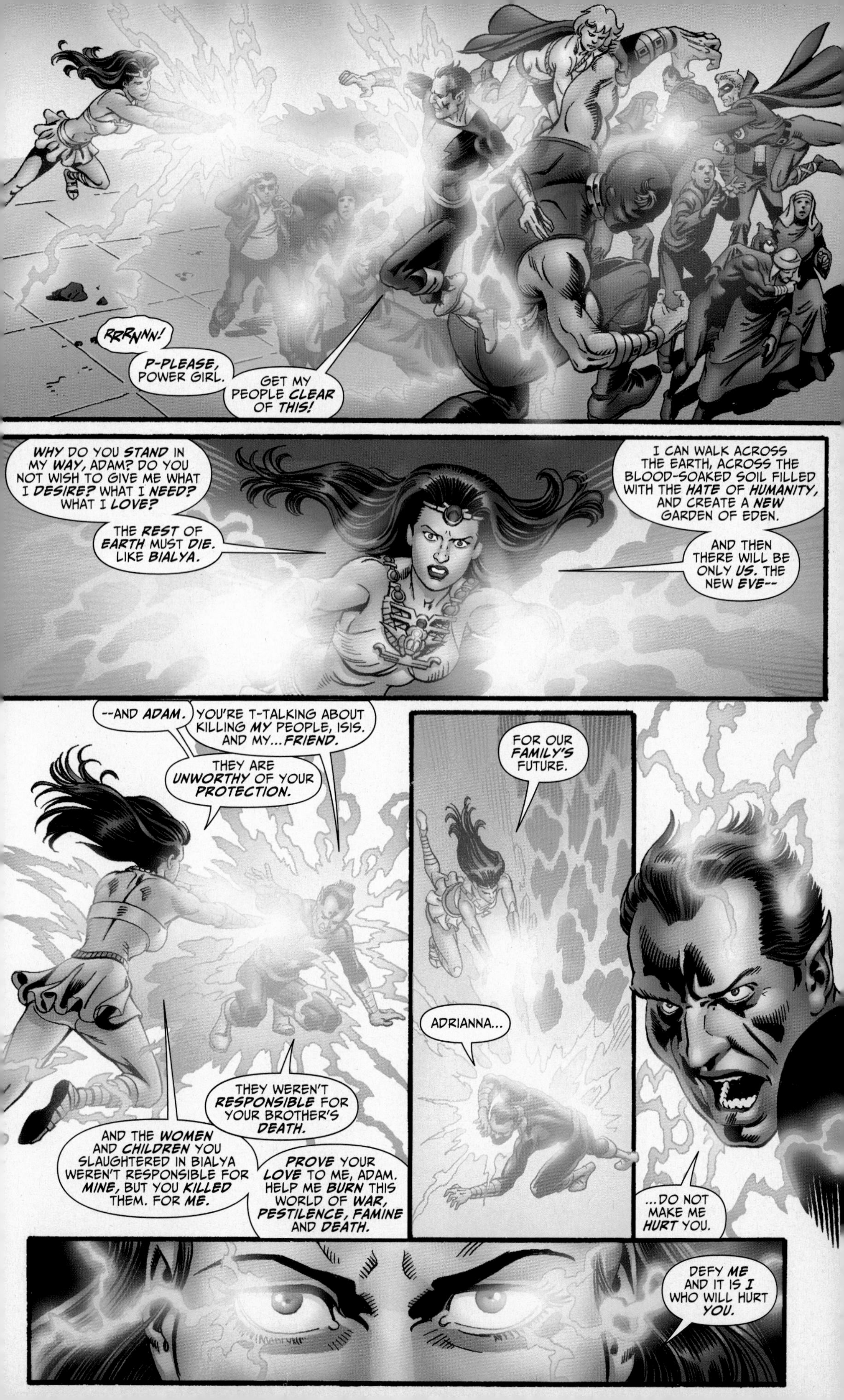
RRRNNN!
P-PLEASE, POWER GIRL.
GET MY PEOPLE CLEAR OF THIS!
WHY DO YOU STAND IN MY WAY, ADAM? DO YOU NOT WISH TO GIVE ME WHAT I DESIRE? WHAT I NEED? WHAT I LOVE?
THE REST OF EARTH MUST DIE. LIKE BIALYA.
I CAN WALK ACROSS THE EARTH, ACROSS THE BLOOD-SOAKED SOIL FILLED WITH THE HATE OF HUMANITY, AND CREATE A NEW GARDEN OF EDEN.
AND THEN THERE WILL BE ONLY US. THE NEW EVE--
--AND ADAM.
YOU'RE T-TALKING ABOUT KILLING MY PEOPLE, ISIS. AND MY... FRIEND.
THEY ARE UNWORTHY OF YOUR PROTECTION.
THEY WEREN'T RESPONSIBLE FOR YOUR BROTHER'S DEATH.
AND THE WOMEN AND CHILDREN YOU SLAUGHTERED IN BIALYA WEREN'T RESPONSIBLE FOR MINE, BUT YOU KILLED THEM. FOR ME.
PROVE YOUR LOVE TO ME, ADAM. HELP ME BURN THIS WORLD OF WAR, PESTILENCE, FAMINE AND DEATH.
FOR OUR FAMILY'S FUTURE.
ADRIANNA...
...DO NOT MAKE ME HURT YOU.
DEFY ME AND IT IS I WHO WILL HURT YOU.

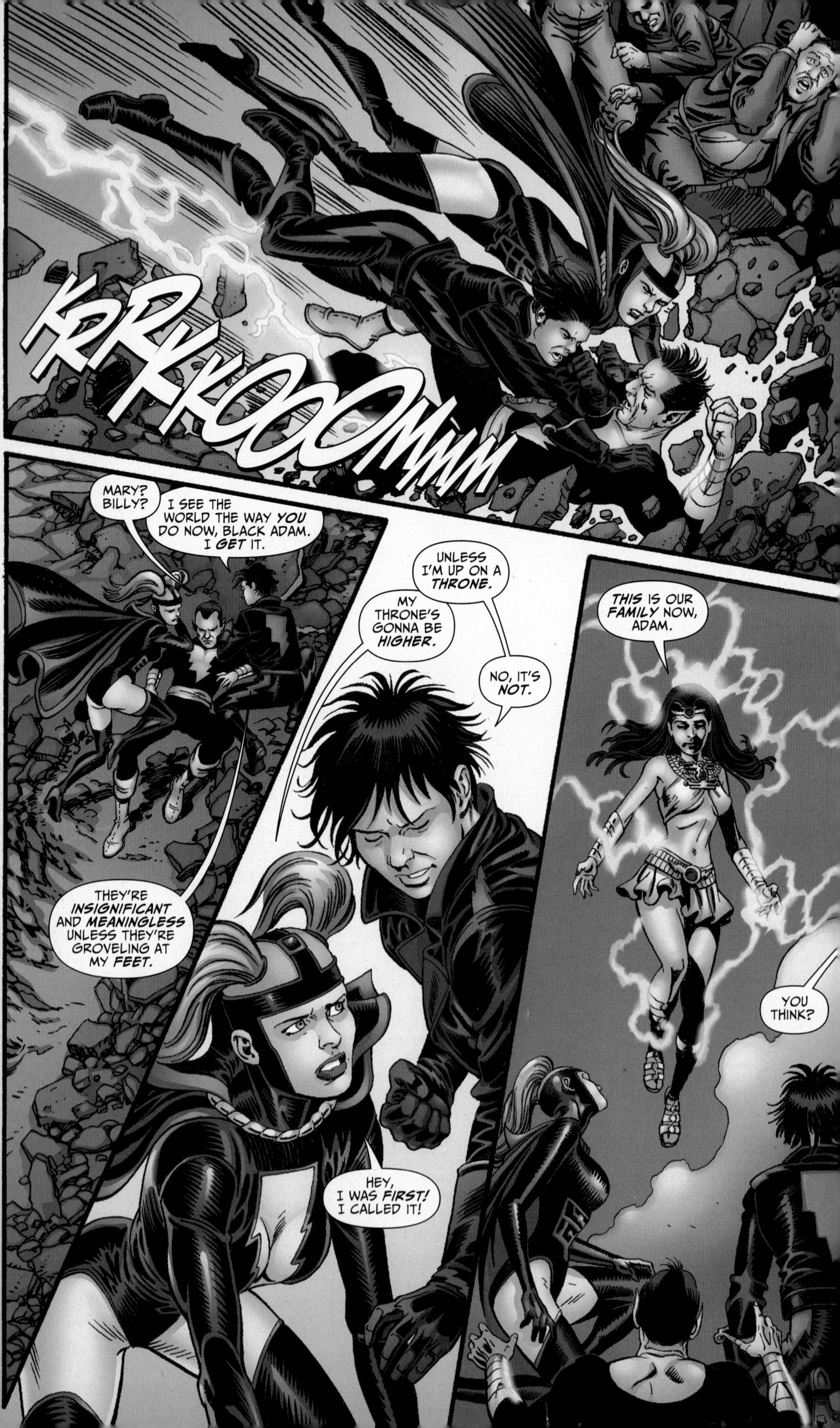
KRRKKOOOMMM
MARY? BILLY?
I SEE THE WORLD THE WAY YOU DO NOW, BLACK ADAM. I GET IT.
THEY'RE INSIGNIFICANT AND MEANINGLESS UNLESS THEY'RE GROVELING AT MY FEET.
UNLESS I'M UP ON A THRONE.
MY THRONE'S GONNA BE HIGHER.
NO, IT'S NOT.
HEY, I WAS FIRST! I CALLED IT!
THIS IS OUR FAMILY NOW, ADAM.
YOU THINK?

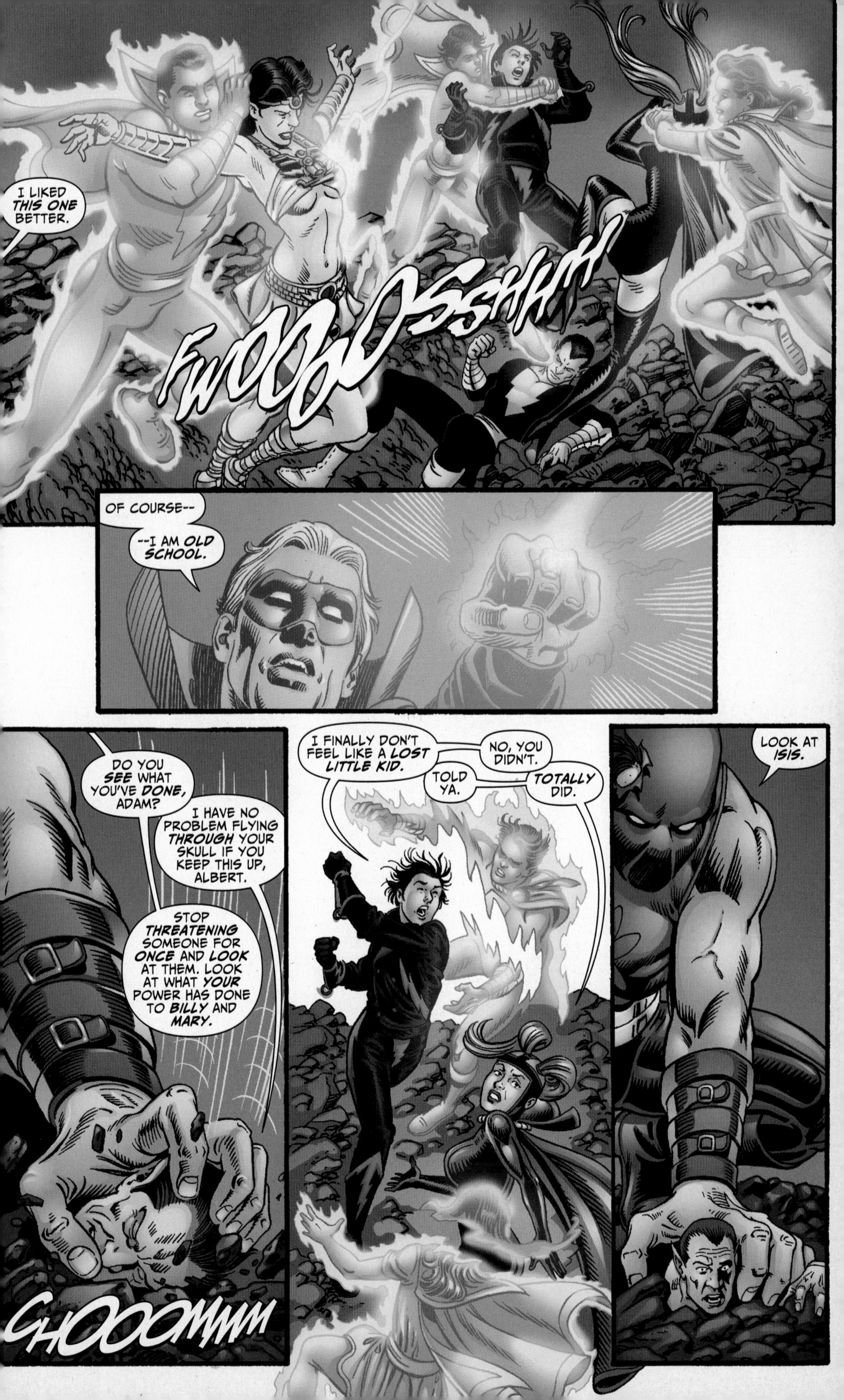
I LIKED THIS ONE BETTER.
FWOOOOSSHHH
OF COURSE--
--I AM OLD SCHOOL.
DO YOU SEE WHAT YOU'VE DONE, ADAM?
I HAVE NO PROBLEM FLYING THROUGH YOUR SKULL IF YOU KEEP THIS UP, ALBERT.
STOP THREATENING SOMEONE FOR ONCE AND LOOK AT THEM. LOOK AT WHAT YOUR POWER HAS DONE TO BILLY AND MARY.
CHOOOMMM
I FINALLY DON'T FEEL LIKE A LOST LITTLE KID.
NO, YOU DIDN'T.
TOLD YA.
TOTALLY DID.
LOOK AT ISIS.

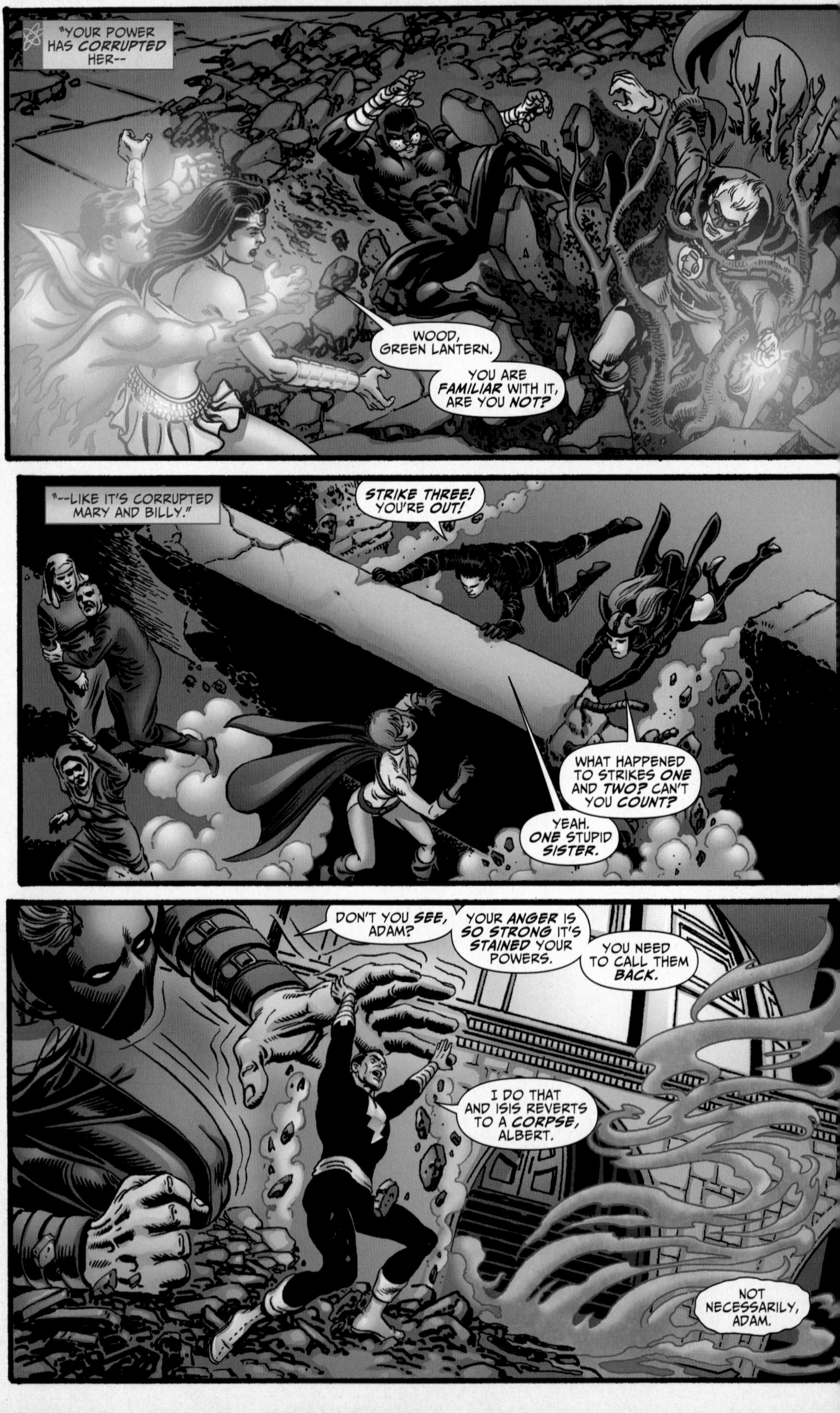
"YOUR POWER HAS CORRUPTED HER--
WOOD, GREEN LANTERN.
YOU ARE FAMILIAR WITH IT, ARE YOU NOT?
"--LIKE IT'S CORRUPTED MARY AND BILLY."
STRIKE THREE! YOU'RE OUT!
WHAT HAPPENED TO STRIKES ONE AND TWO? CAN'T YOU COUNT?
YEAH. ONE STUPID SISTER.
DON'T YOU SEE, ADAM?
YOUR ANGER IS SO STRONG IT'S STAINED YOUR POWERS.
YOU NEED TO CALL THEM BACK.
I DO THAT AND ISIS REVERTS TO A CORPSE, ALBERT.
NOT NECESSARILY, ADAM.

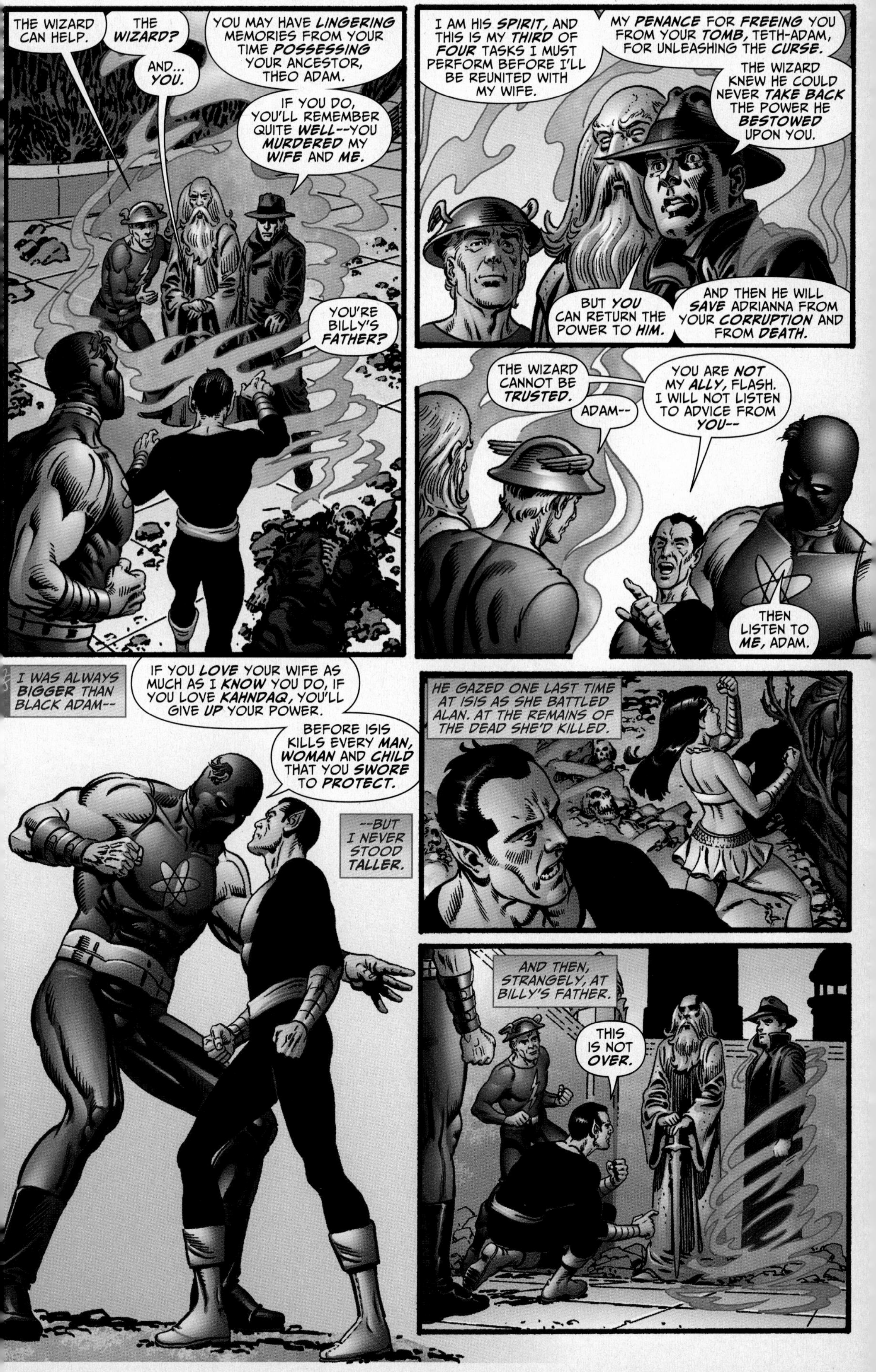

THE WIZARD CAN HELP.
THE WIZARD?
AND... YOU.
YOU MAY HAVE LINGERING MEMORIES FROM YOUR TIME POSSESSING YOUR ANCESTOR, THEO ADAM.
IF YOU DO, YOU'LL REMEMBER QUITE WELL--YOU MURDERED MY WIFE AND ME.
YOU'RE BILLY'S FATHER?
I AM HIS SPIRIT, AND THIS IS MY THIRD OF FOUR TASKS I MUST PERFORM BEFORE I'LL BE REUNITED WITH MY WIFE.
MY PENANCE FOR FREEING YOU FROM YOUR TOMB, TETH-ADAM, FOR UNLEASHING THE CURSE.
THE WIZARD KNEW HE COULD NEVER TAKE BACK THE POWER HE BESTOWED UPON YOU.
BUT YOU CAN RETURN THE POWER TO HIM.
AND THEN HE WILL SAVE ADRIANNA FROM YOUR CORRUPTION AND FROM DEATH.
THE WIZARD CANNOT BE TRUSTED.
ADAM--
YOU ARE NOT MY ALLY, FLASH. I WILL NOT LISTEN TO ADVICE FROM YOU--
THEN LISTEN TO ME, ADAM.
I WAS ALWAYS BIGGER THAN BLACK ADAM--
IF YOU LOVE YOUR WIFE AS MUCH AS I KNOW YOU DO, IF YOU LOVE KAHNDAQ, YOU'LL GIVE UP YOUR POWER.
BEFORE ISIS KILLS EVERY MAN, WOMAN AND CHILD THAT YOU SWORE TO PROTECT.
--BUT I NEVER STOOD TALLER.
HE GAZED ONE LAST TIME AT ISIS AS SHE BATTLED ALAN. AT THE REMAINS OF THE DEAD SHE'D KILLED.
AND THEN, STRANGELY, AT BILLY'S FATHER.
THIS IS NOT OVER.

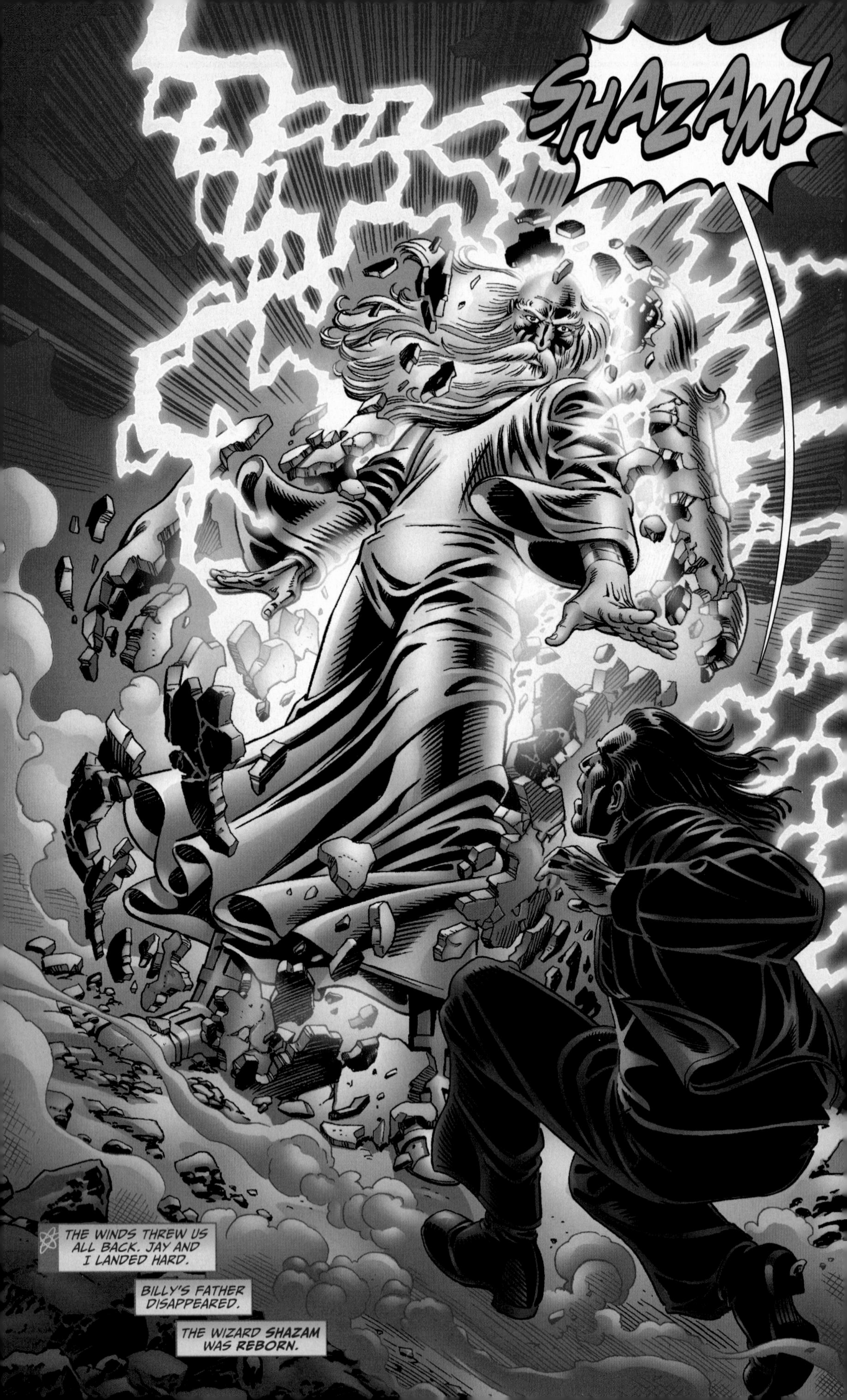
SHAZAM!
THE WINDS THREW US ALL BACK. JAY AND I LANDED HARD.
BILLY'S FATHER DISAPPEARED.
THE WIZARD SHAZAM WAS REBORN.

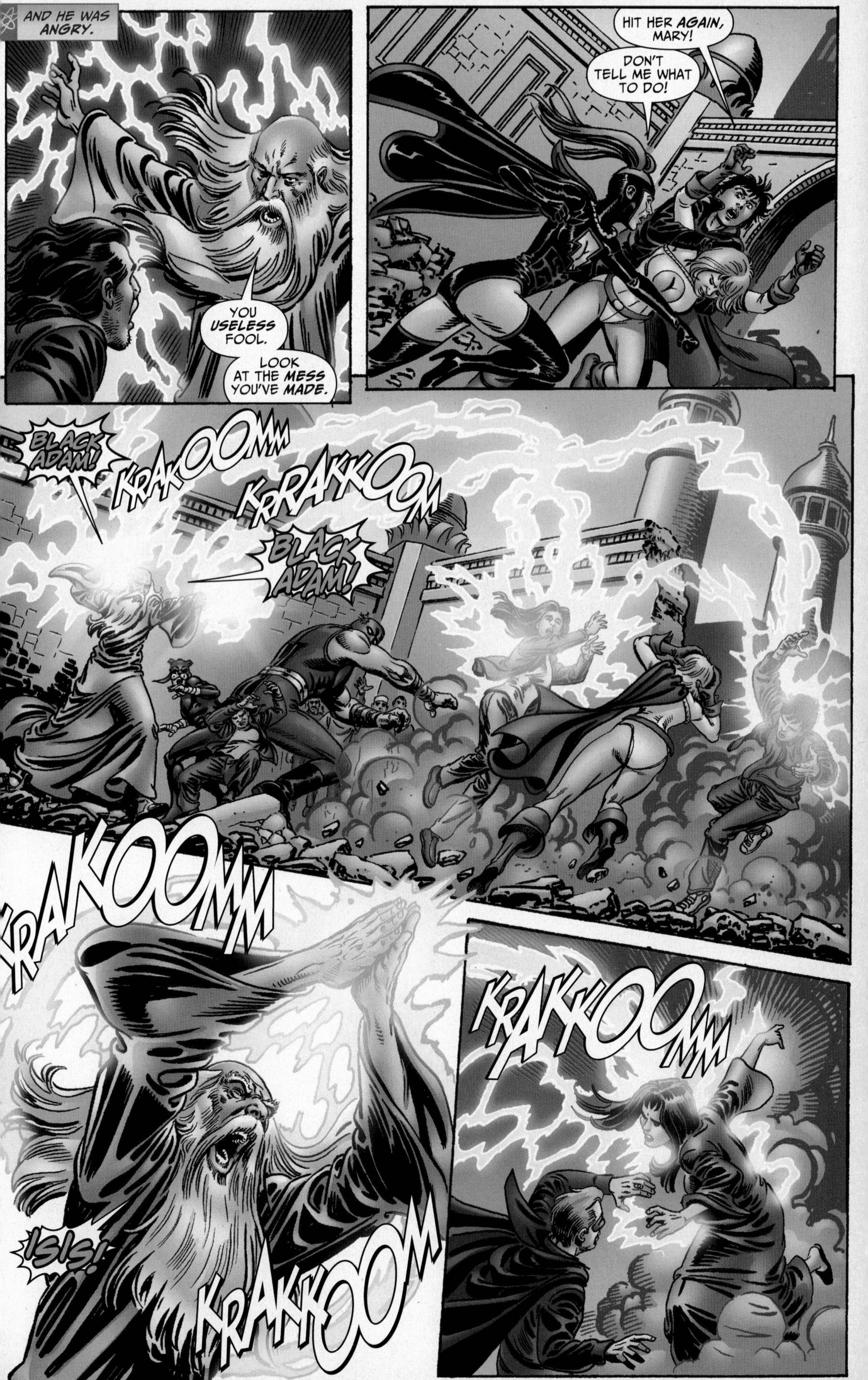
AND HE WAS ANGRY.
YOU USELESS FOOL.
LOOK AT THE MESS YOU'VE MADE.
HIT HER AGAIN, MARY!
DON'T TELL ME WHAT TO DO!
BLACK ADAM!
KRAKOOMM
KRRAKKOOM
BLACK ADAM!
KRAKOOMM
ISIS!
KRAKKOOM
KRAKKOOMM

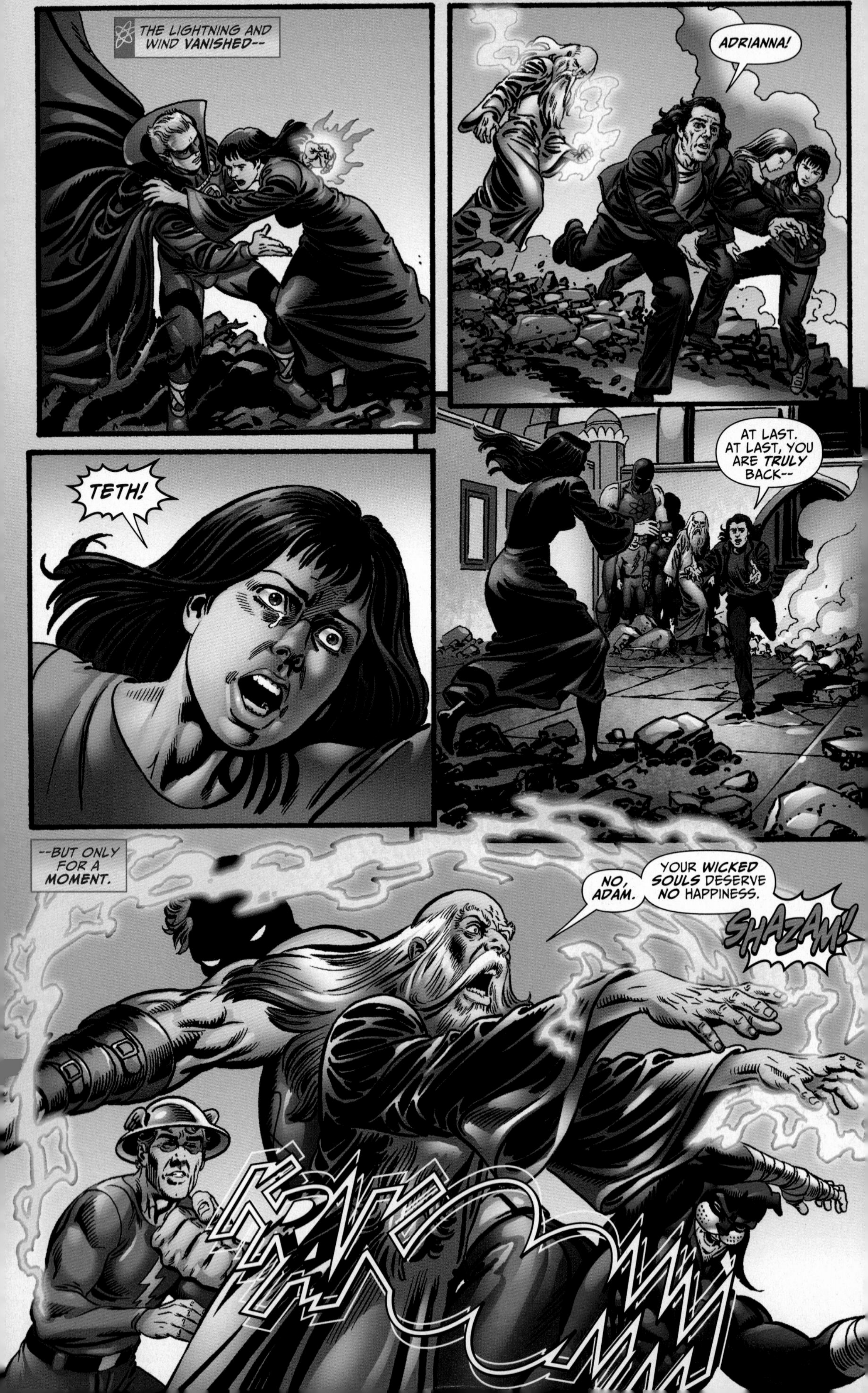
THE LIGHTNING AND WIND VANISHED--
ADRIANNA!
TETH!
AT LAST. AT LAST, YOU ARE TRULY BACK--
--BUT ONLY FOR A MOMENT.
NO, ADAM.
YOUR WICKED SOULS DESERVE NO HAPPINESS.
SHAZAM!
KRAKOOM

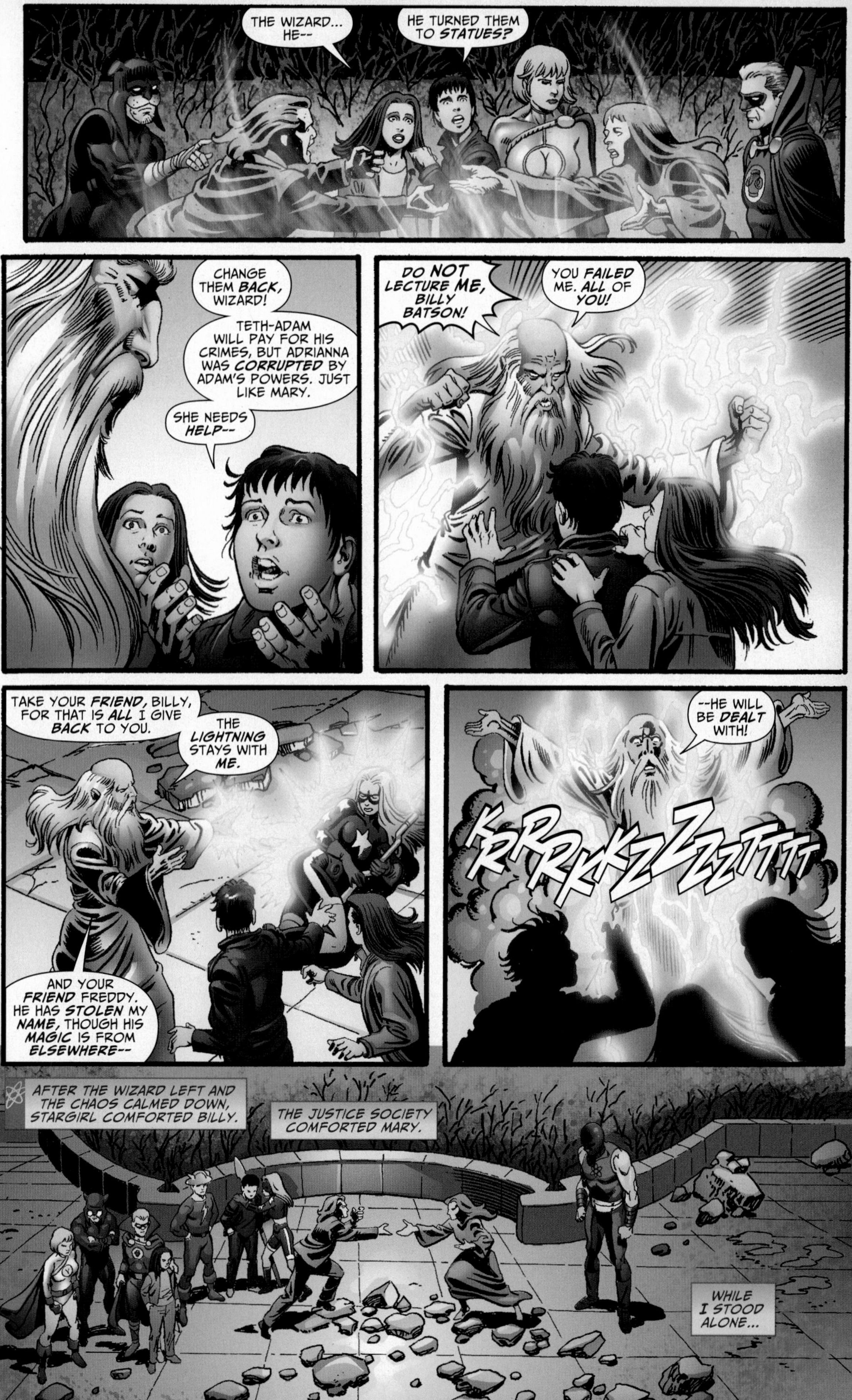
THE WIZARD... HE--
HE TURNED THEM TO STATUES?
CHANGE THEM BACK, WIZARD!
TETH-ADAM WILL PAY FOR HIS CRIMES, BUT ADRIANNA WAS CORRUPTED BY ADAM'S POWERS. JUST LIKE MARY.
SHE NEEDS HELP--
DO NOT LECTURE ME, BILLY BATSON!
YOU FAILED ME. ALL OF YOU!
TAKE YOUR FRIEND, BILLY, FOR THAT IS ALL I GIVE BACK TO YOU.
THE LIGHTNING STAYS WITH ME.
AND YOUR FRIEND FREDDY. HE HAS STOLEN MY NAME, THOUGH HIS MAGIC IS FROM ELSEWHERE--
--HE WILL BE DEALT WITH!
KRRRKKKZZZZZTTTTT
AFTER THE WIZARD LEFT AND THE CHAOS CALMED DOWN, STARGIRL COMFORTED BILLY.
THE JUSTICE SOCIETY COMFORTED MARY.
WHILE I STOOD ALONE...

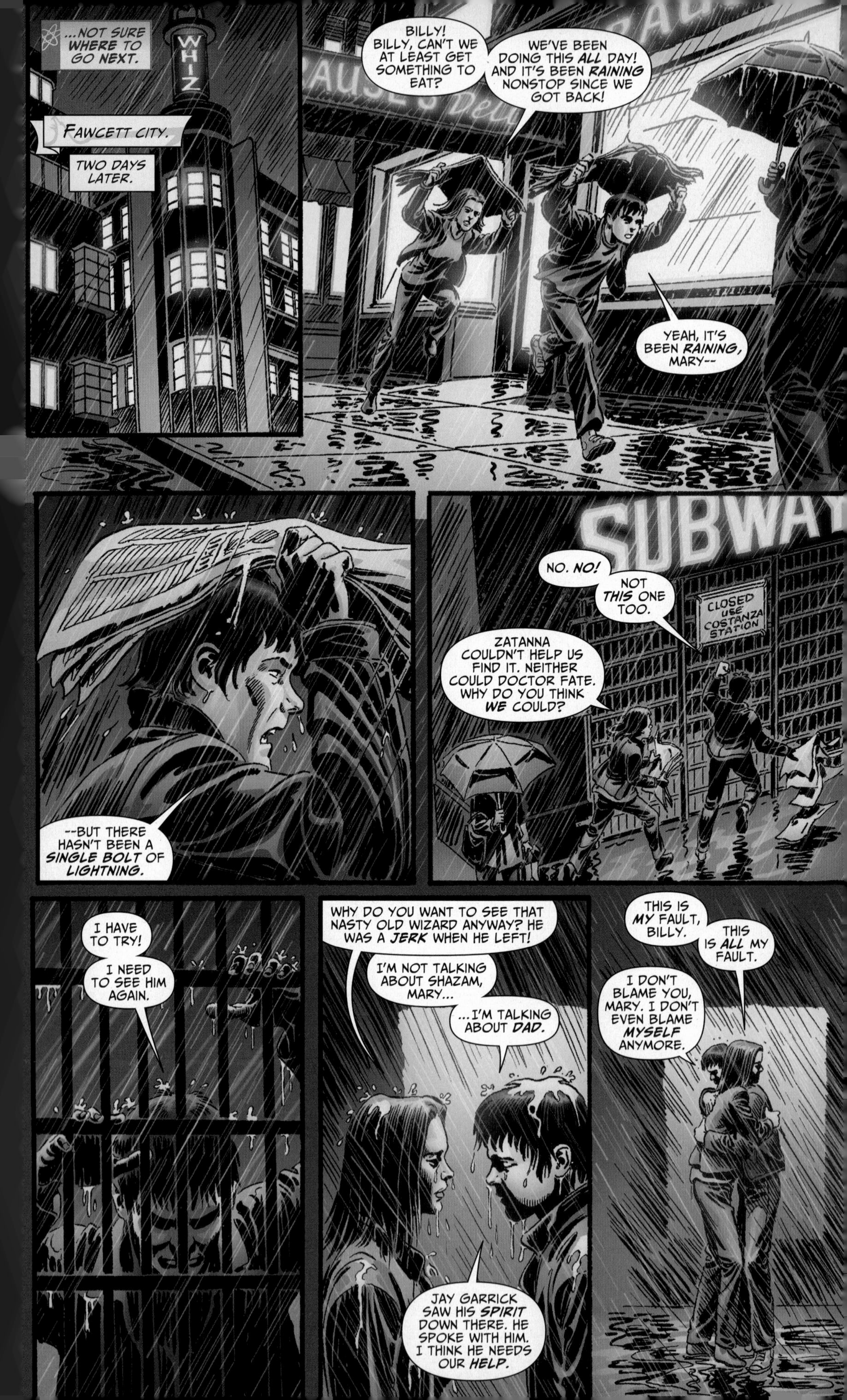

...NOT SURE WHERE TO GO NEXT.
FAWCETT CITY.
TWO DAYS LATER.
WHIZ
BILLY! BILLY, CAN'T WE AT LEAST GET SOMETHING TO EAT?
WE'VE BEEN DOING THIS ALL DAY! AND IT'S BEEN RAINING NONSTOP SINCE WE GOT BACK!
YEAH, IT'S BEEN RAINING, MARY--
--BUT THERE HASN'T BEEN A SINGLE BOLT OF LIGHTNING.
SUBWAY
NO. NO!
NOT THIS ONE TOO.
CLOSED USE COSTANZA STATION
ZATANNA COULDN'T HELP US FIND IT. NEITHER COULD DOCTOR FATE. WHY DO YOU THINK WE COULD?
I HAVE TO TRY!
I NEED TO SEE HIM AGAIN.
WHY DO YOU WANT TO SEE THAT NASTY OLD WIZARD ANYWAY? HE WAS A JERK WHEN HE LEFT!
I'M NOT TALKING ABOUT SHAZAM, MARY...
...I'M TALKING ABOUT DAD.
JAY GARRICK SAW HIS SPIRIT DOWN THERE. HE SPOKE WITH HIM. I THINK HE NEEDS OUR HELP.
THIS IS MY FAULT, BILLY.
THIS IS ALL MY FAULT.
I DON'T BLAME YOU, MARY. I DON'T EVEN BLAME MYSELF ANYMORE.

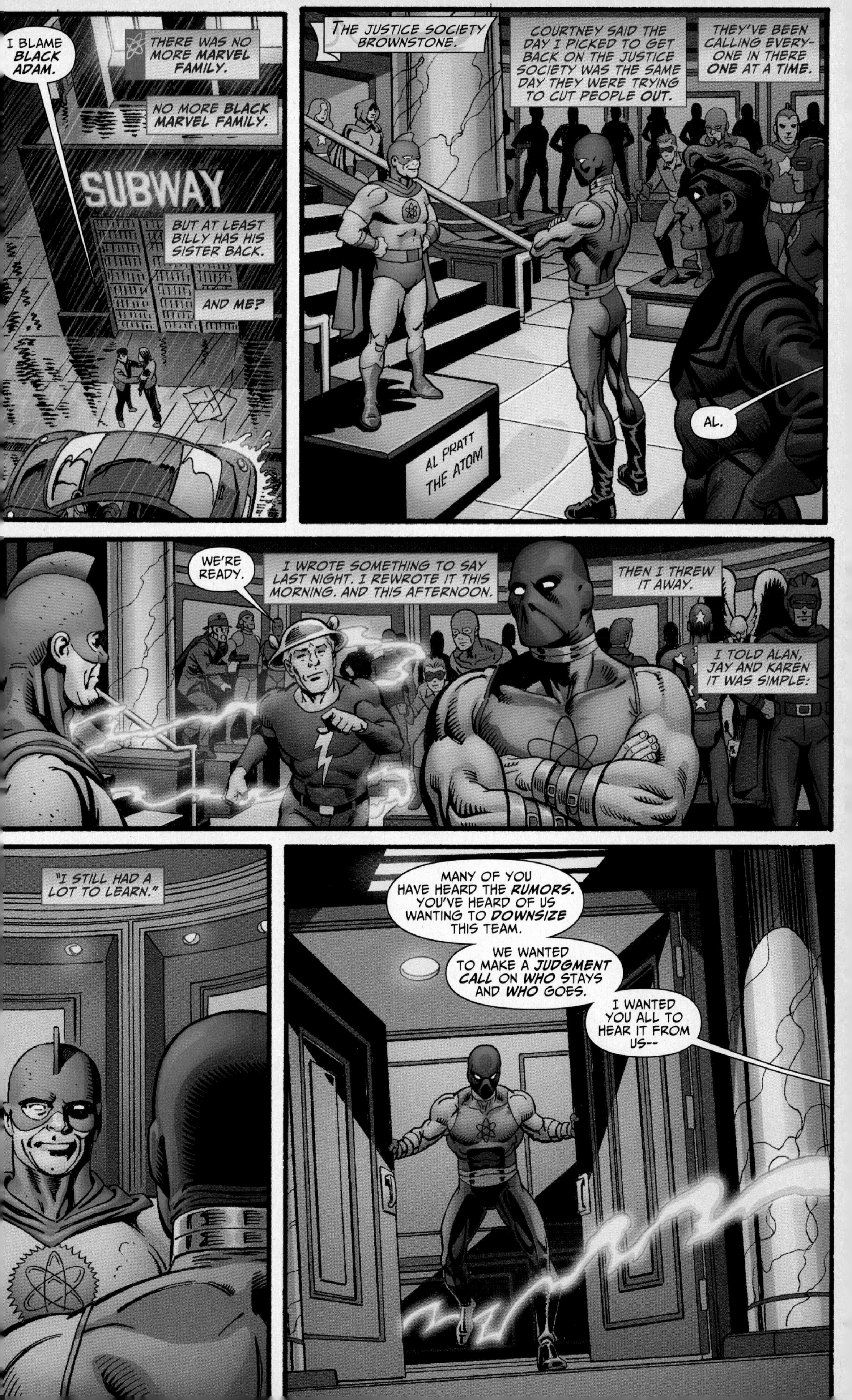
I BLAME BLACK ADAM.
THERE WAS NO MORE MARVEL FAMILY.
NO MORE BLACK MARVEL FAMILY.
SUBWAY
BUT AT LEAST BILLY HAS HIS SISTER BACK.
AND ME?
THE JUSTICE SOCIETY BROWNSTONE.
COURTNEY SAID THE DAY I PICKED TO GET BACK ON THE JUSTICE SOCIETY WAS THE SAME DAY THEY WERE TRYING TO CUT PEOPLE OUT.
THEY'VE BEEN CALLING EVERY-ONE IN THERE ONE AT A TIME.
AL PRATT THE ATOM
AL.
WE'RE READY.
I WROTE SOMETHING TO SAY LAST NIGHT. I REWROTE IT THIS MORNING. AND THIS AFTERNOON.
THEN I THREW IT AWAY.
I TOLD ALAN, JAY AND KAREN IT WAS SIMPLE:
"I STILL HAD A LOT TO LEARN."
MANY OF YOU HAVE HEARD THE RUMORS. YOU'VE HEARD OF US WANTING TO DOWNSIZE THIS TEAM.
WE WANTED TO MAKE A JUDGMENT CALL ON WHO STAYS AND WHO GOES.
I WANTED YOU ALL TO HEAR IT FROM US--

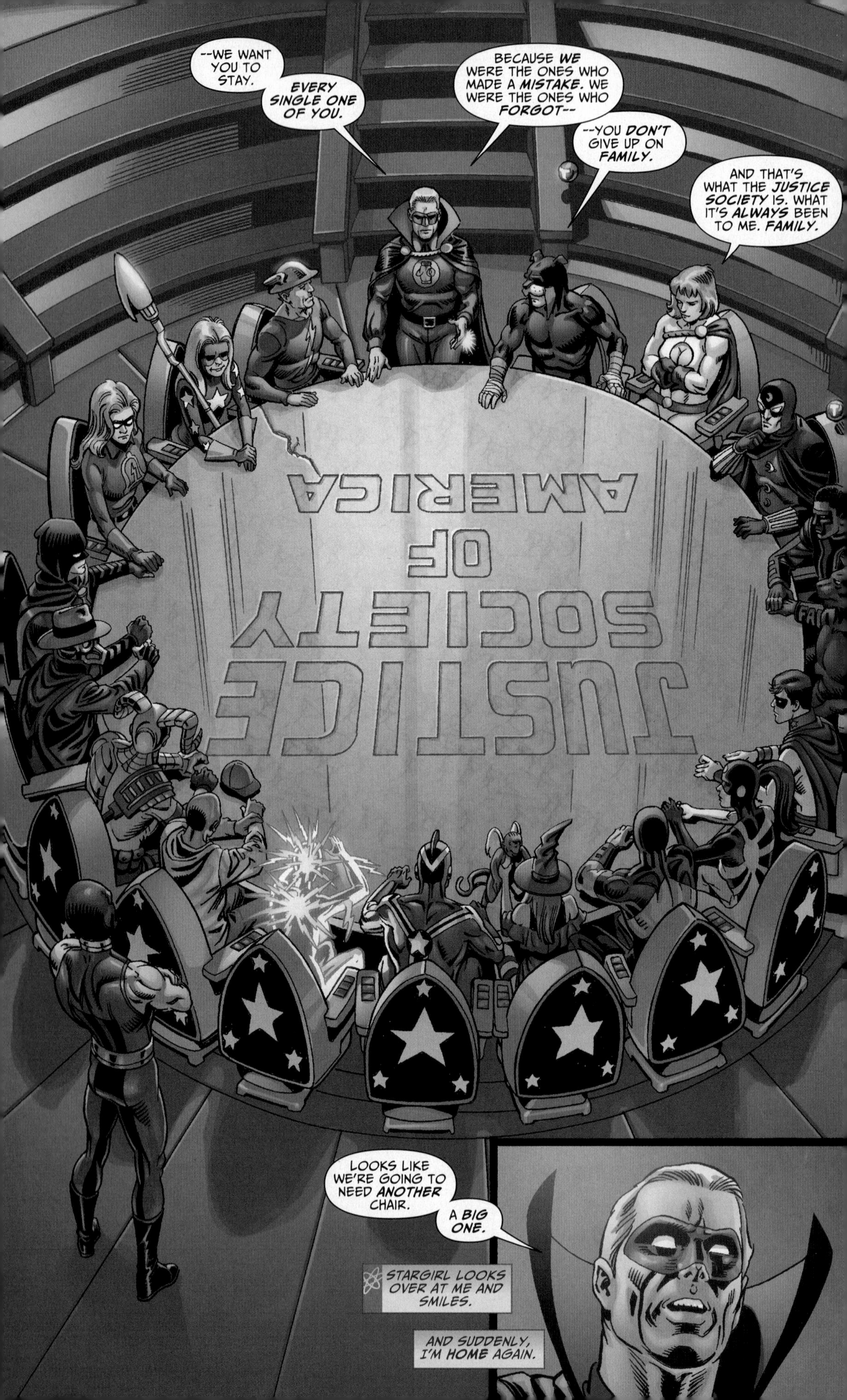
--WE WANT YOU TO STAY.
EVERY SINGLE ONE OF YOU.
BECAUSE WE WERE THE ONES WHO MADE A MISTAKE. WE WERE THE ONES WHO FORGOT--
--YOU DON'T GIVE UP ON FAMILY.
AND THAT'S WHAT THE JUSTICE SOCIETY IS. WHAT IT'S ALWAYS BEEN TO ME. FAMILY.
JUSTICE SOCIETY OF AMERICA
LOOKS LIKE WE'RE GOING TO NEED ANOTHER CHAIR.
A BIG ONE.
STARGIRL LOOKS OVER AT ME AND SMILES.
AND SUDDENLY, I'M HOME AGAIN.

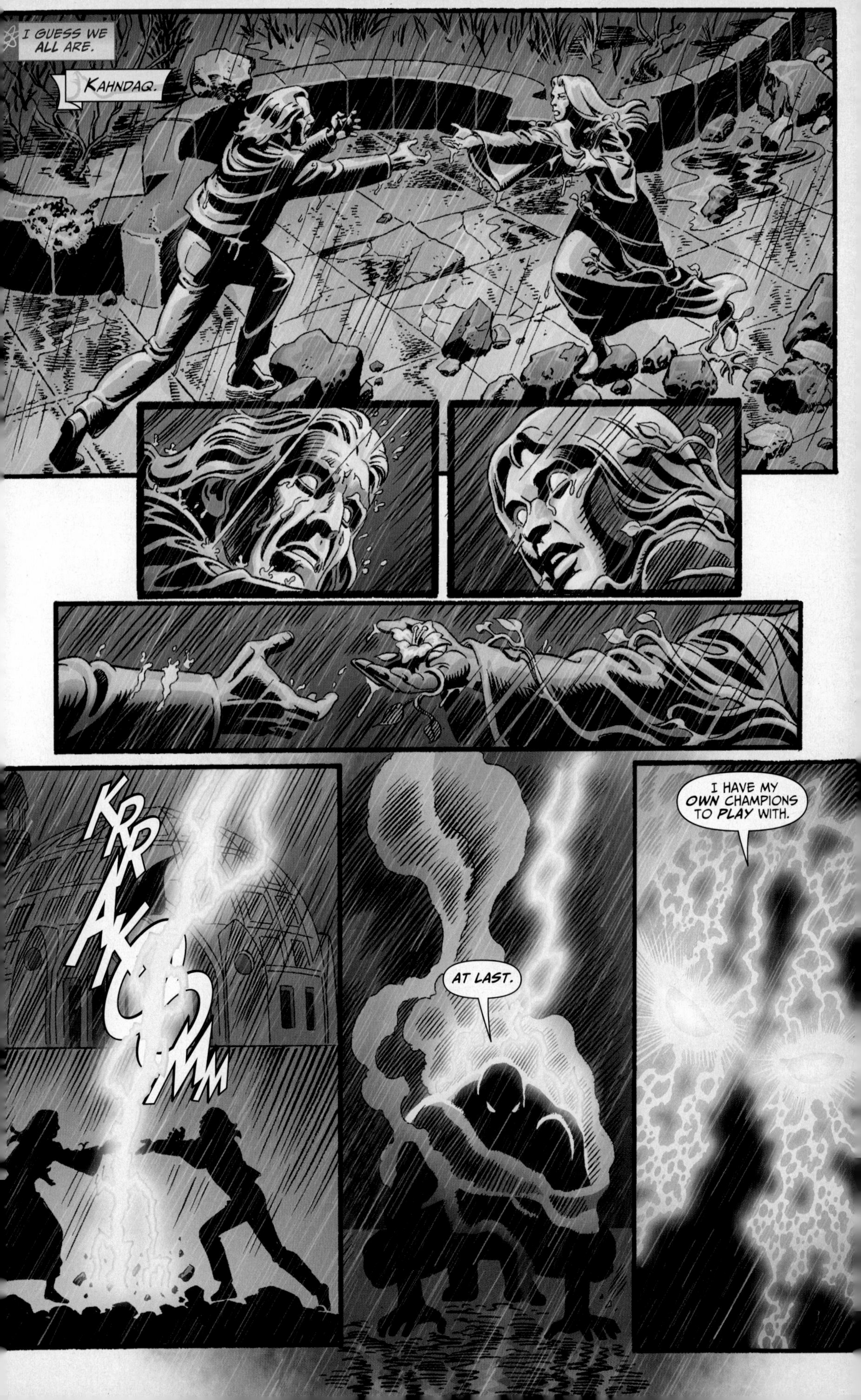
I GUESS WE ALL ARE.
KAHNDAQ.
KRRAKOOM
AT LAST.
I HAVE MY OWN CHAMPIONS TO PLAY WITH.

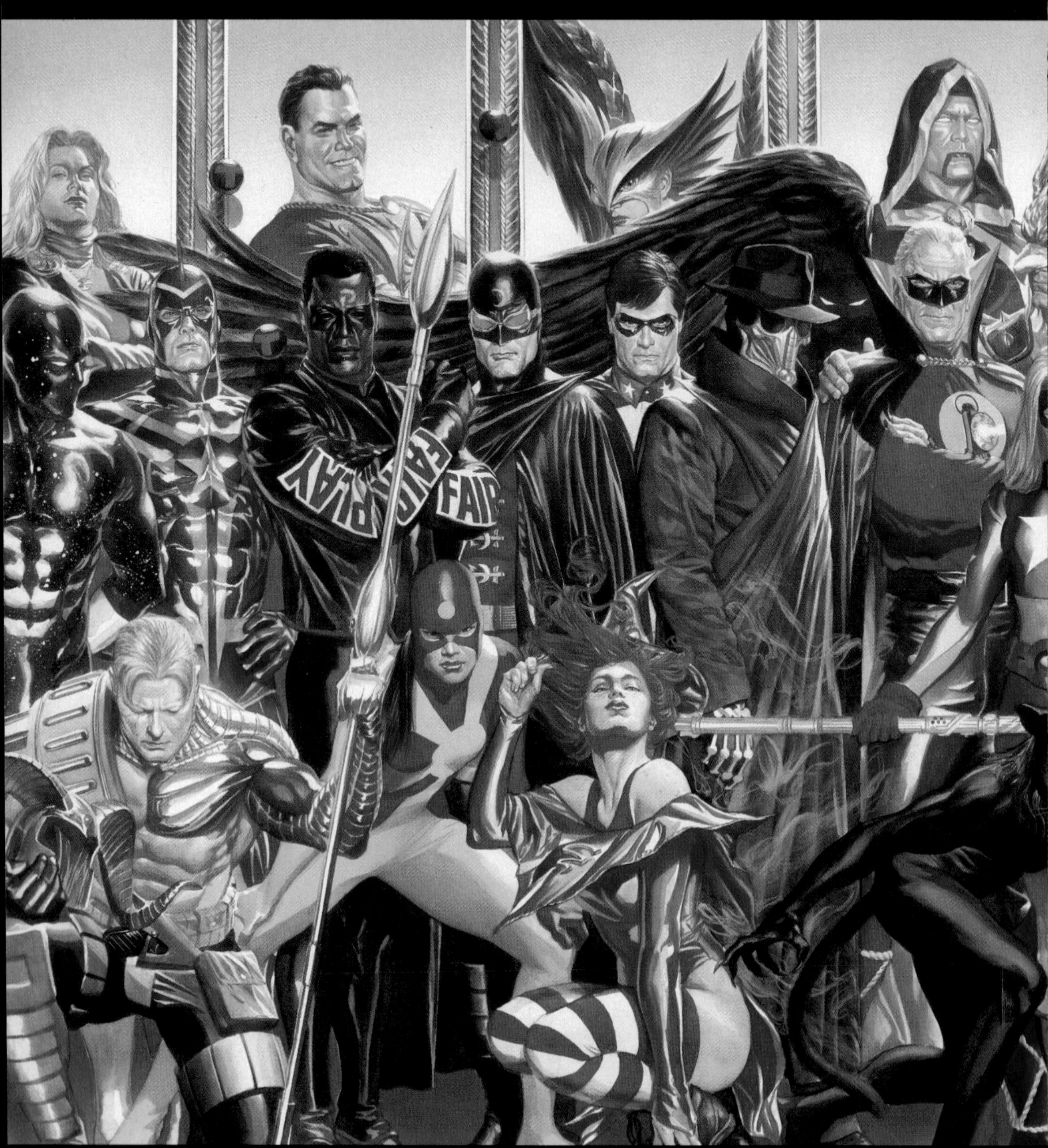
FAIR PLAY
FAIR

JUSTICE SOCIETY OF AMERICA #26 cover by Alex Ross
Interior art by Dale Eaglesham & Nathan Massengill

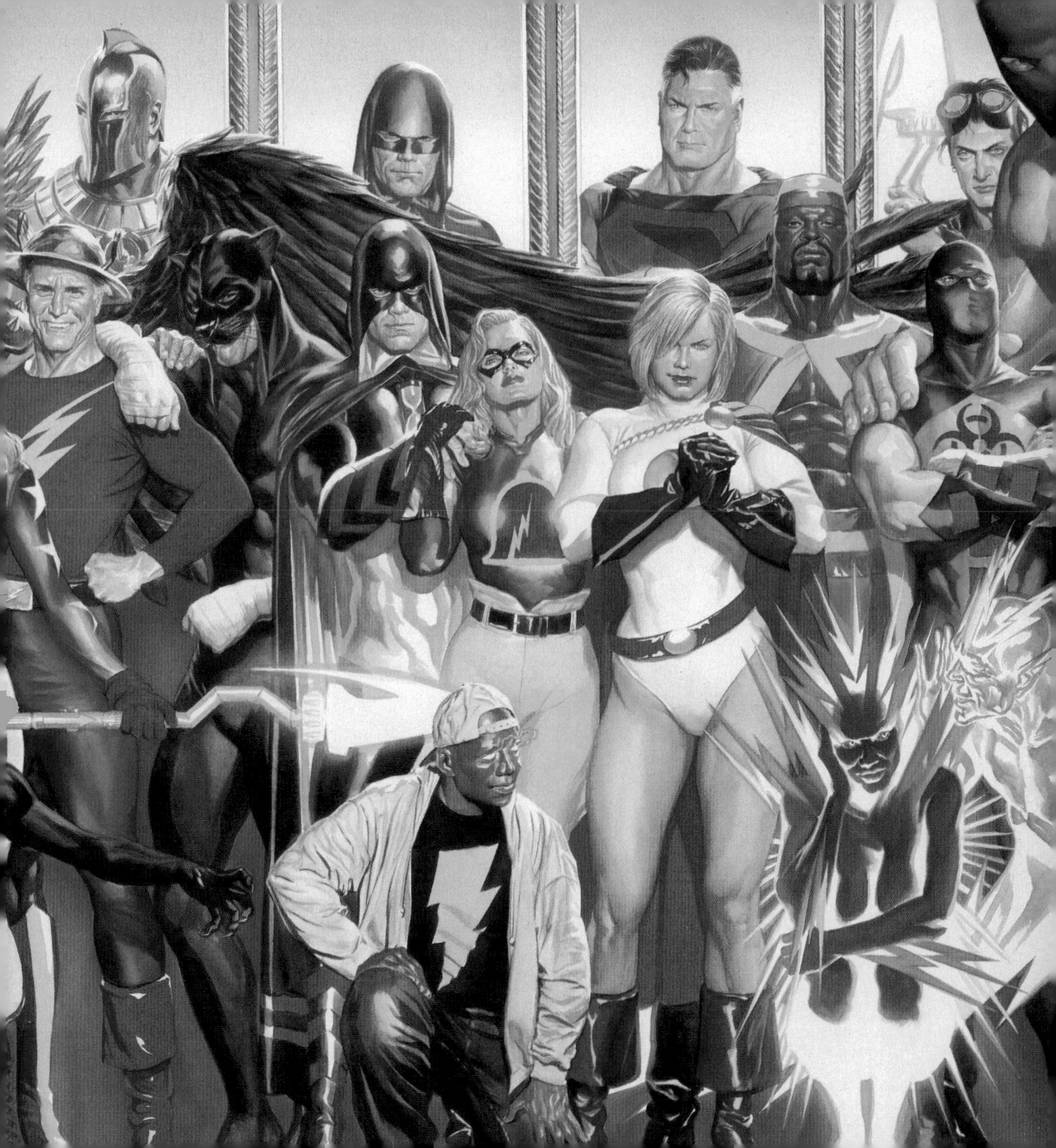

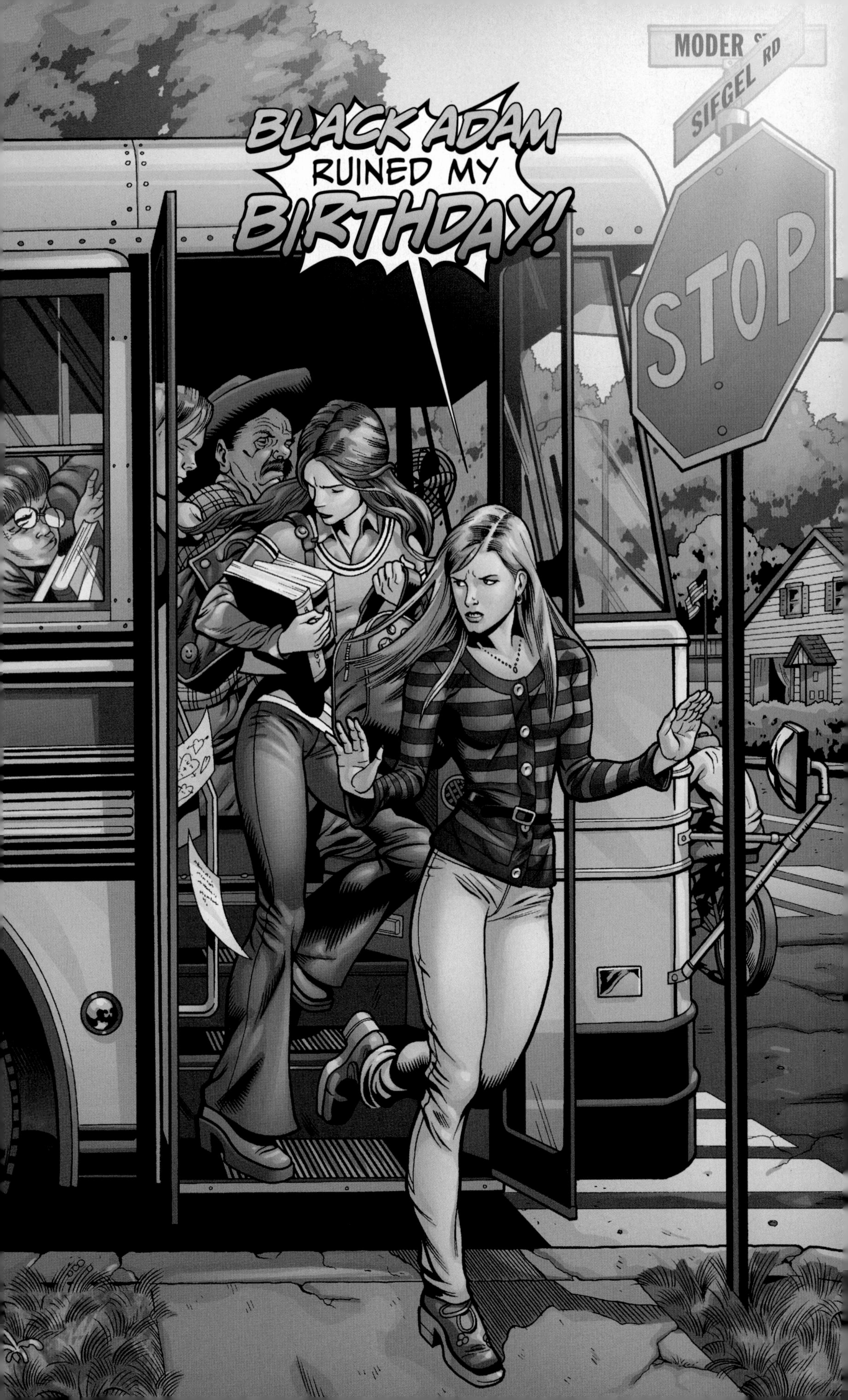
MODER ST
SIEGEL RD
BLACK ADAM RUINED MY BIRTHDAY!
STOP

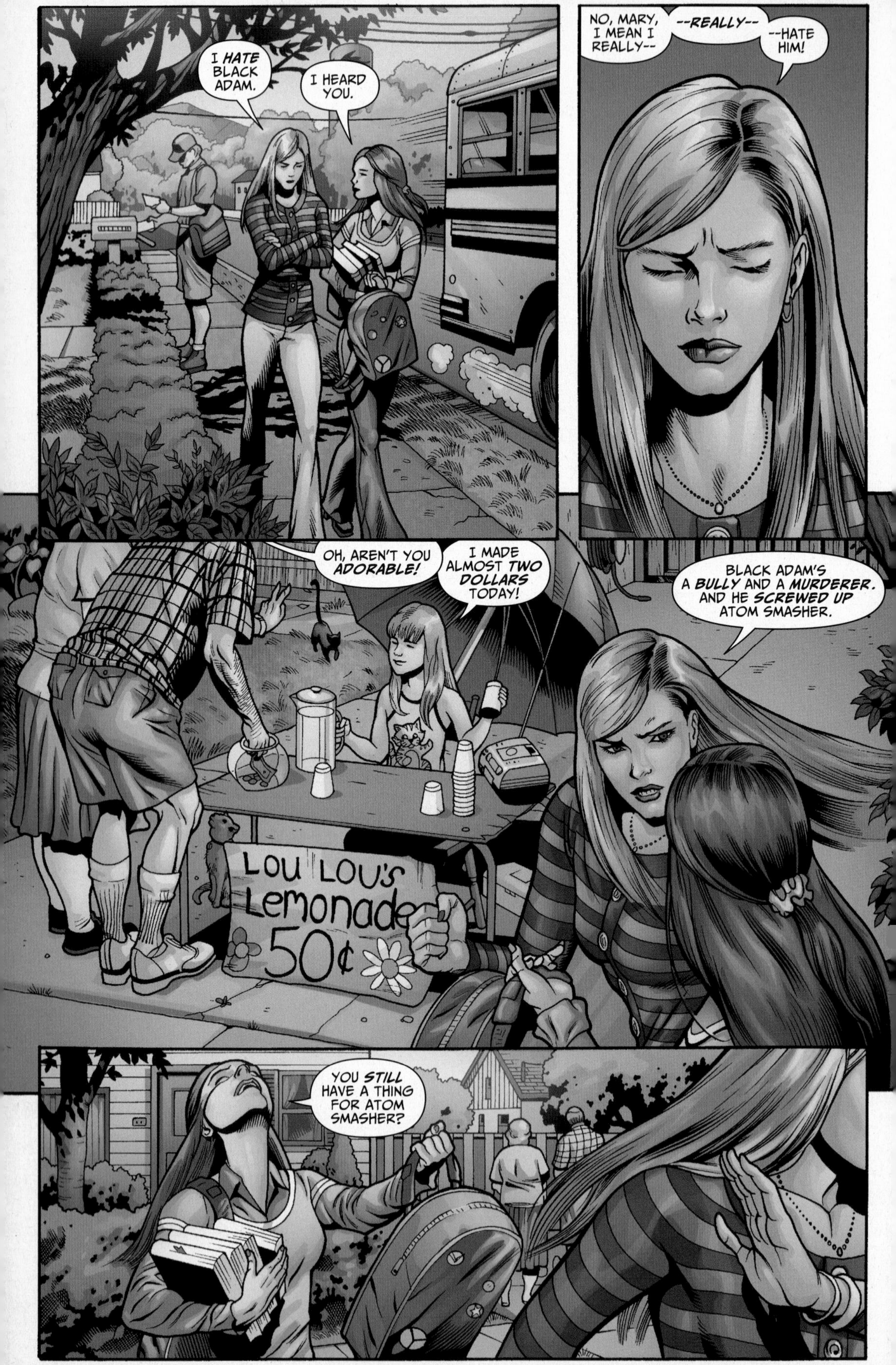
I HATE BLACK ADAM.
I HEARD YOU.
NO, MARY, I MEAN I REALLY--
--REALLY--
--HATE HIM!
OH, AREN'T YOU ADORABLE!
I MADE ALMOST TWO DOLLARS TODAY!
BLACK ADAM'S A BULLY AND A MURDERER. AND HE SCREWED UP ATOM SMASHER.
LOU LOU'S Lemonade 50¢
YOU STILL HAVE A THING FOR ATOM SMASHER?

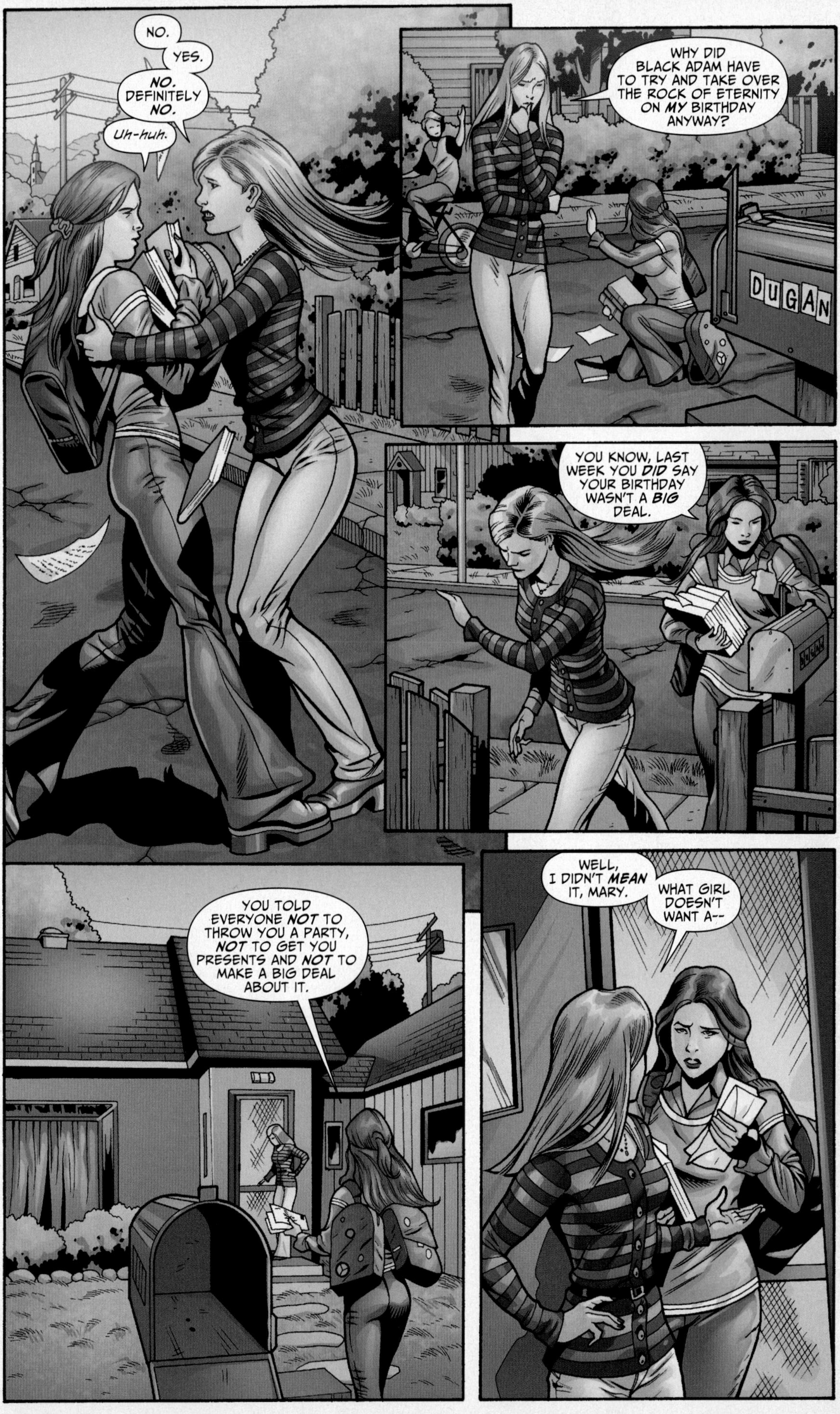
NO.
YES.
NO. DEFINITELY NO.
Uh-huh.
WHY DID BLACK ADAM HAVE TO TRY AND TAKE OVER THE ROCK OF ETERNITY ON MY BIRTHDAY ANYWAY?
DUGAN
YOU KNOW, LAST WEEK YOU DID SAY YOUR BIRTHDAY WASN'T A BIG DEAL.
YOU TOLD EVERYONE NOT TO THROW YOU A PARTY, NOT TO GET YOU PRESENTS AND NOT TO MAKE A BIG DEAL ABOUT IT.
WELL, I DIDN'T MEAN IT, MARY.
WHAT GIRL DOESN'T WANT A--

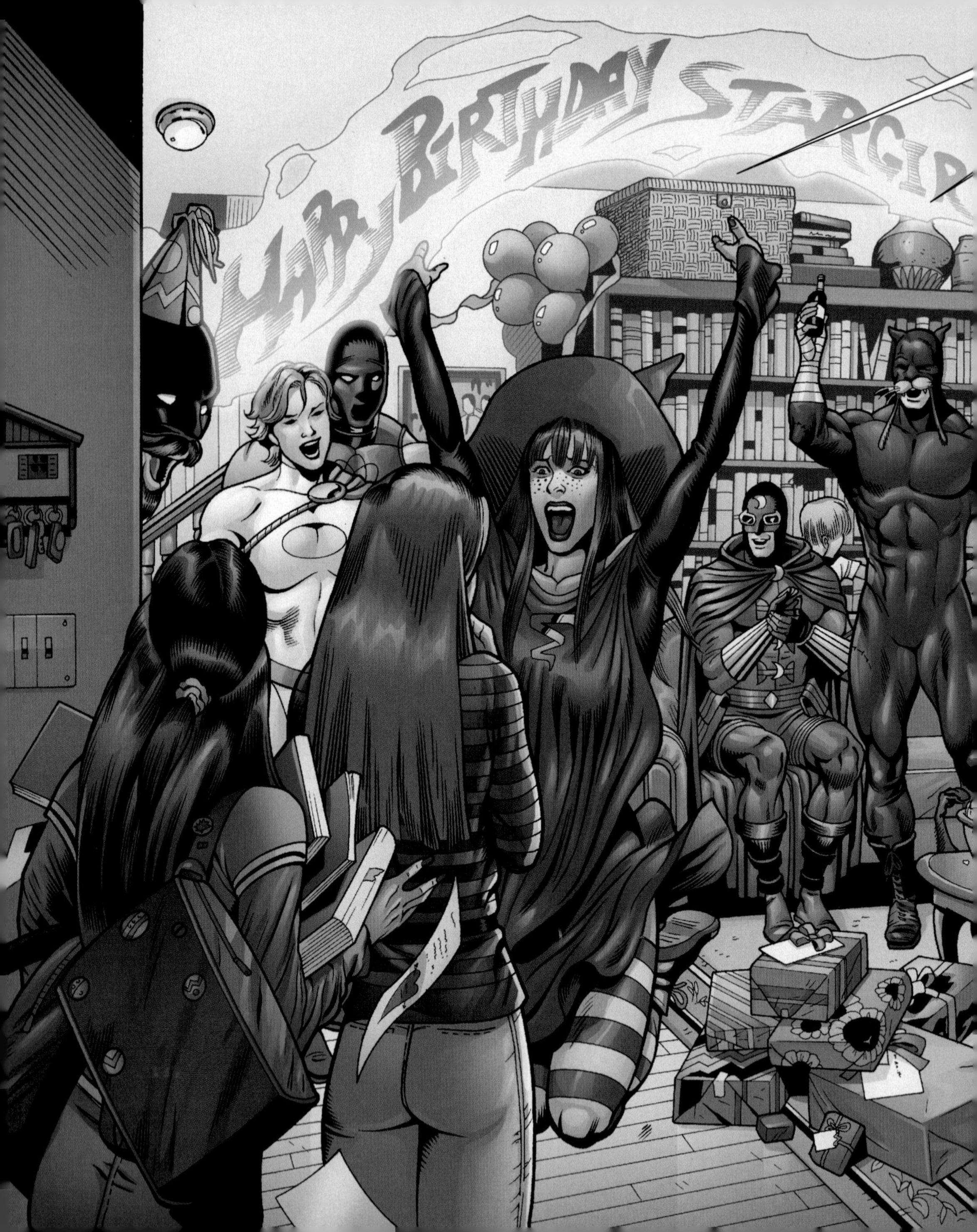
HAPPY BIRTHDAY STARGIR

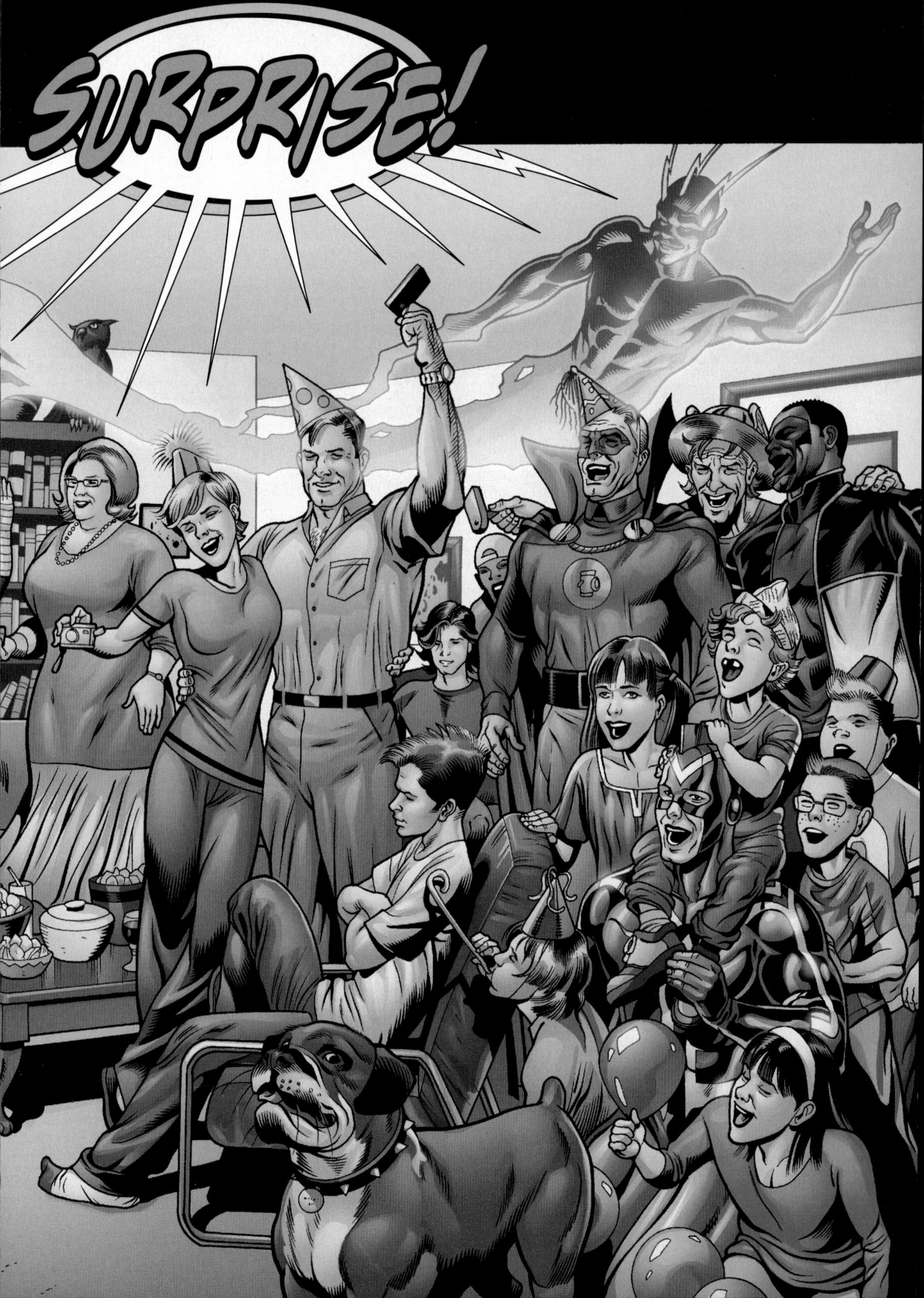
SURPRISE!

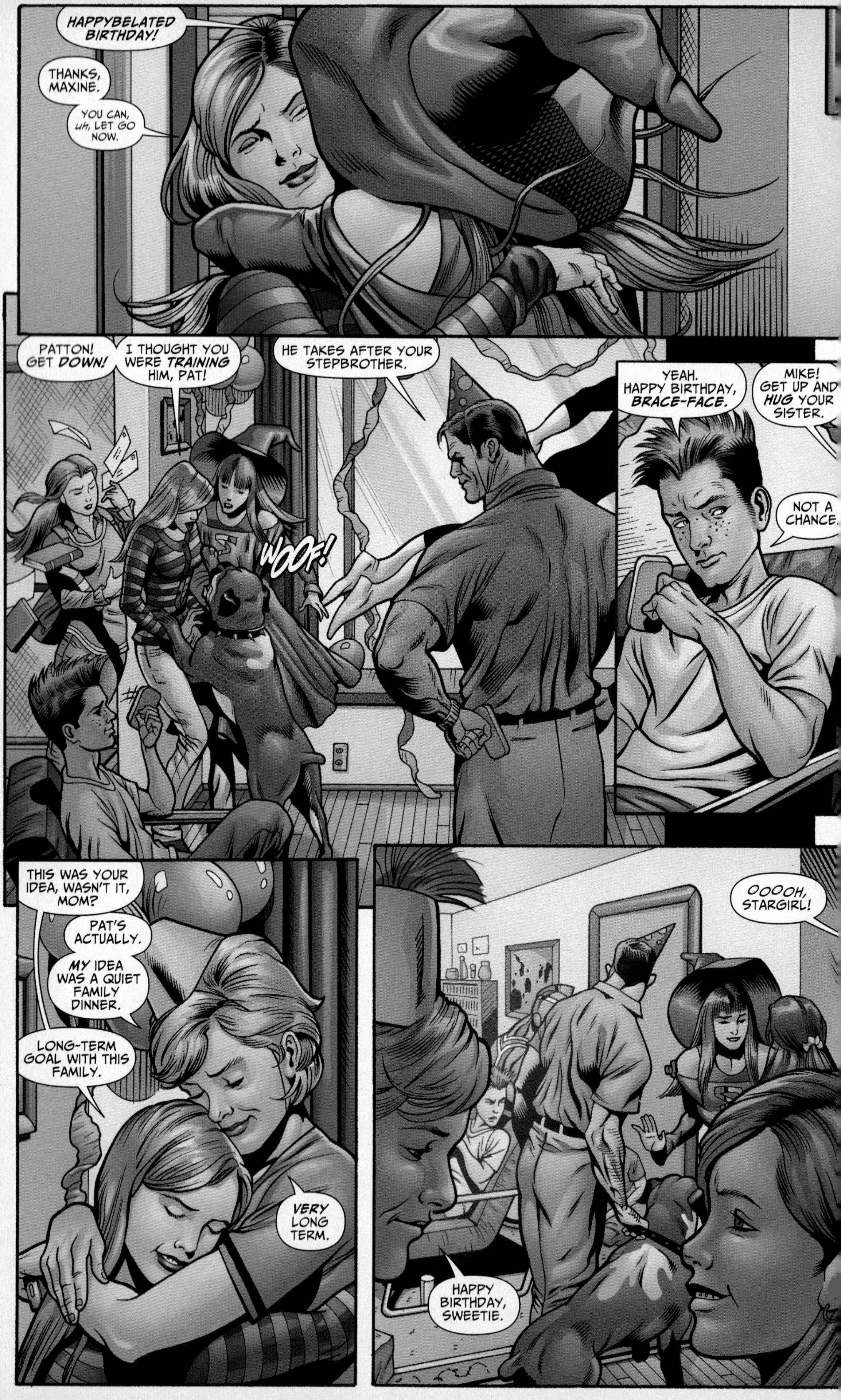
HAPPYBELATED BIRTHDAY!
THANKS, MAXINE.
YOU CAN, *uh,* LET GO NOW.
PATTON! GET *DOWN!*
I THOUGHT YOU WERE *TRAINING* HIM, PAT!
HE TAKES AFTER YOUR STEPBROTHER.
WOOF!
YEAH. HAPPY BIRTHDAY, *BRACE-FACE.*
MIKE! GET UP AND *HUG* YOUR SISTER.
NOT A CHANCE.
THIS WAS YOUR IDEA, WASN'T IT, MOM?
PAT'S ACTUALLY.
MY IDEA WAS A QUIET FAMILY DINNER.
LONG-TERM GOAL WITH THIS FAMILY.
VERY LONG TERM.
OOOOH, STARGIRL!
HAPPY BIRTHDAY, SWEETIE.

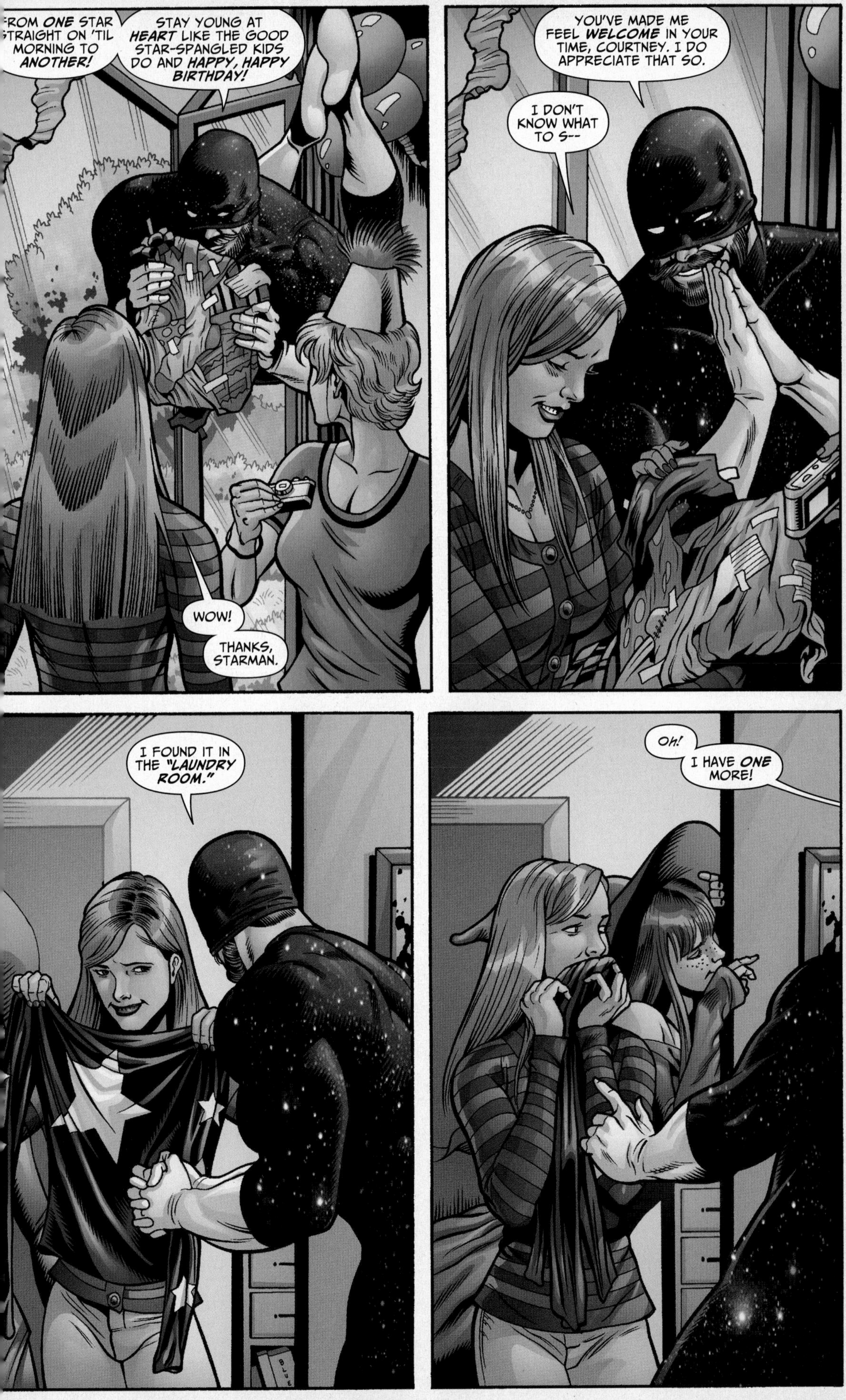
FROM ONE STAR STRAIGHT ON 'TIL MORNING TO ANOTHER!
STAY YOUNG AT HEART LIKE THE GOOD STAR-SPANGLED KIDS DO AND HAPPY, HAPPY BIRTHDAY!
WOW!
THANKS, STARMAN.
YOU'VE MADE ME FEEL WELCOME IN YOUR TIME, COURTNEY. I DO APPRECIATE THAT SO.
I DON'T KNOW WHAT TO S--
I FOUND IT IN THE "LAUNDRY ROOM."
Oh!
I HAVE ONE MORE!

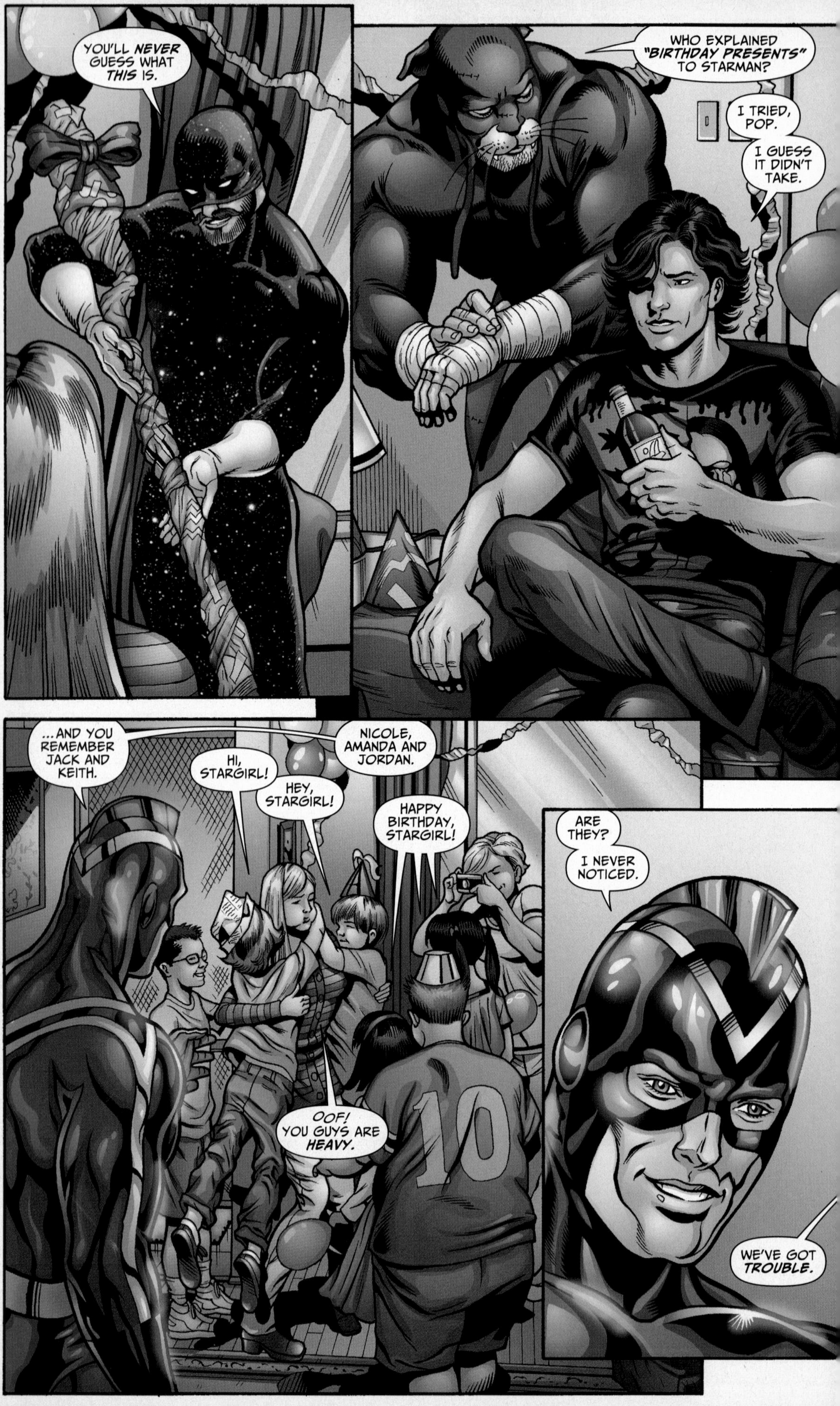
YOU'LL *NEVER* GUESS WHAT *THIS* IS.
WHO EXPLAINED *"BIRTHDAY PRESENTS"* TO STARMAN?
I TRIED, POP.
I GUESS IT DIDN'T TAKE.
...AND YOU REMEMBER JACK AND KEITH.
NICOLE, AMANDA AND JORDAN.
HI, STARGIRL!
HEY, STARGIRL!
HAPPY BIRTHDAY, STARGIRL!
OOF! YOU GUYS ARE *HEAVY.*
10
ARE THEY?
I NEVER NOTICED.
WE'VE GOT *TROUBLE.*

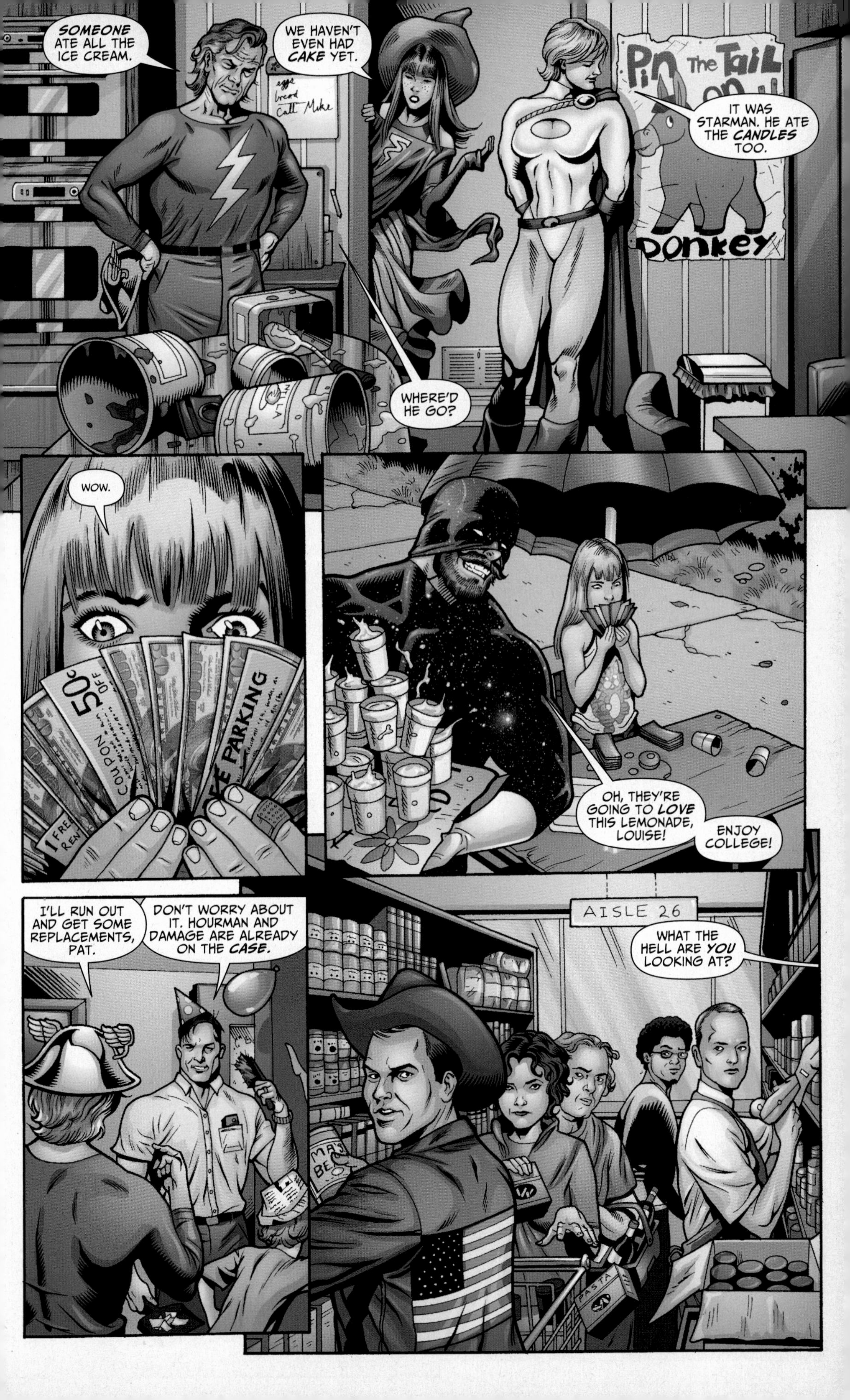
SOMEONE ATE ALL THE ICE CREAM.
WE HAVEN'T EVEN HAD CAKE YET.
eggs
bread
Call Mike
Pin The Tail
DONKEY
IT WAS STARMAN. HE ATE THE CANDLES TOO.
WHERE'D HE GO?
WOW.
OH, THEY'RE GOING TO LOVE THIS LEMONADE, LOUISE!
ENJOY COLLEGE!
I'LL RUN OUT AND GET SOME REPLACEMENTS, PAT.
DON'T WORRY ABOUT IT. HOURMAN AND DAMAGE ARE ALREADY ON THE CASE.
AISLE 26
WHAT THE HELL ARE YOU LOOKING AT?
PASTA

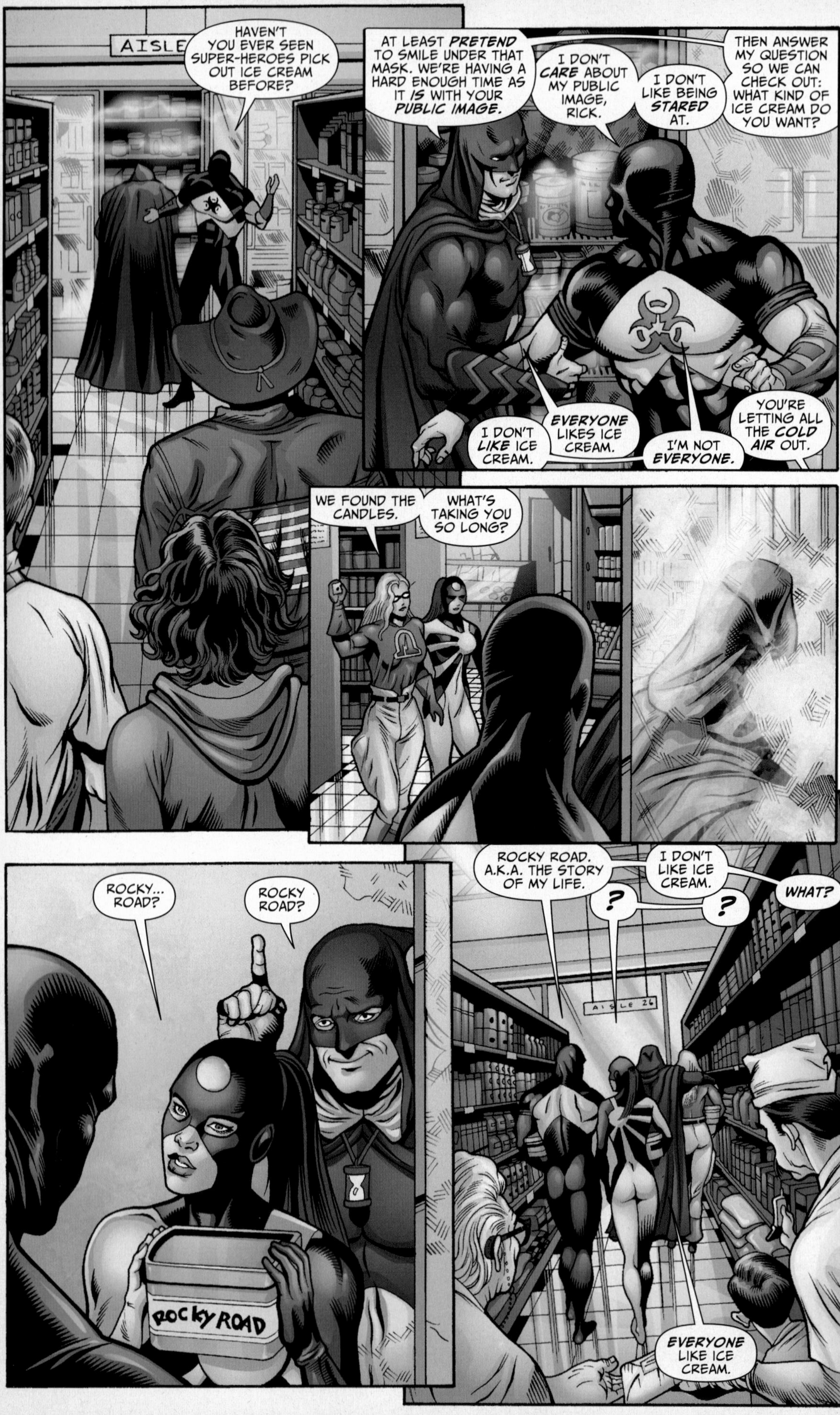
AISLE
HAVEN'T YOU EVER SEEN SUPER-HEROES PICK OUT ICE CREAM BEFORE?
AT LEAST PRETEND TO SMILE UNDER THAT MASK. WE'RE HAVING A HARD ENOUGH TIME AS IT IS WITH YOUR PUBLIC IMAGE.
I DON'T CARE ABOUT MY PUBLIC IMAGE, RICK.
I DON'T LIKE BEING STARED AT.
THEN ANSWER MY QUESTION SO WE CAN CHECK OUT: WHAT KIND OF ICE CREAM DO YOU WANT?
I DON'T LIKE ICE CREAM.
EVERYONE LIKES ICE CREAM.
I'M NOT EVERYONE.
YOU'RE LETTING ALL THE COLD AIR OUT.
WE FOUND THE CANDLES.
WHAT'S TAKING YOU SO LONG?
ROCKY... ROAD?
ROCKY ROAD?
ROCKY ROAD
ROCKY ROAD. A.K.A. THE STORY OF MY LIFE.
I DON'T LIKE ICE CREAM.
?
?
WHAT?
AISLE 26
EVERYONE LIKE ICE CREAM.

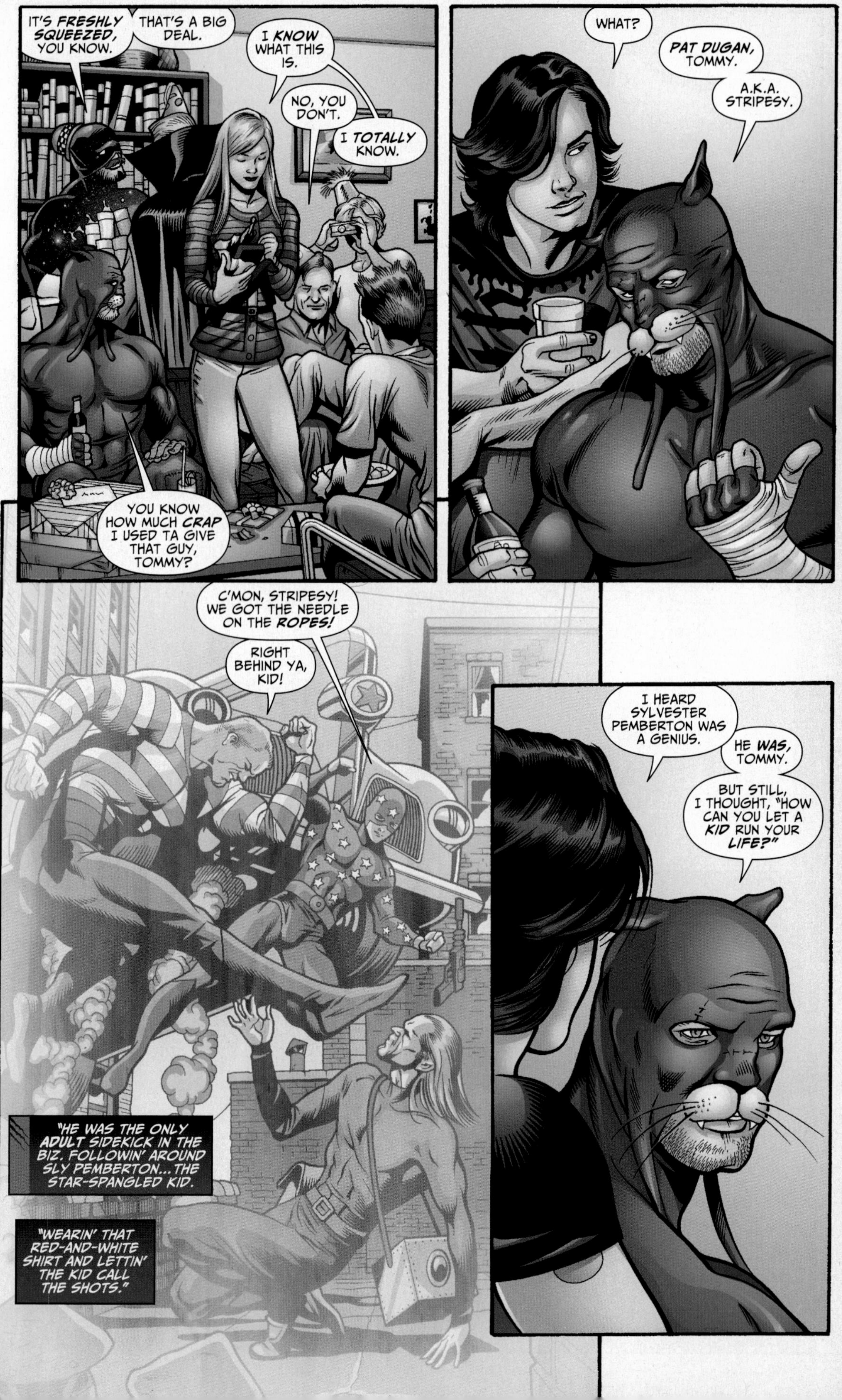
IT'S FRESHLY SQUEEZED, YOU KNOW.
THAT'S A BIG DEAL.
I KNOW WHAT THIS IS.
NO, YOU DON'T.
I TOTALLY KNOW.
YOU KNOW HOW MUCH CRAP I USED TA GIVE THAT GUY, TOMMY?
WHAT?
PAT DUGAN, TOMMY.
A.K.A. STRIPESY.
C'MON, STRIPESY! WE GOT THE NEEDLE ON THE ROPES!
RIGHT BEHIND YA, KID!
"HE WAS THE ONLY ADULT SIDEKICK IN THE BIZ. FOLLOWIN' AROUND SLY PEMBERTON...THE STAR-SPANGLED KID.
"WEARIN' THAT RED-AND-WHITE SHIRT AND LETTIN' THE KID CALL THE SHOTS."
I HEARD SYLVESTER PEMBERTON WAS A GENIUS.
HE WAS, TOMMY.
BUT STILL, I THOUGHT, "HOW CAN YOU LET A KID RUN YOUR LIFE?"

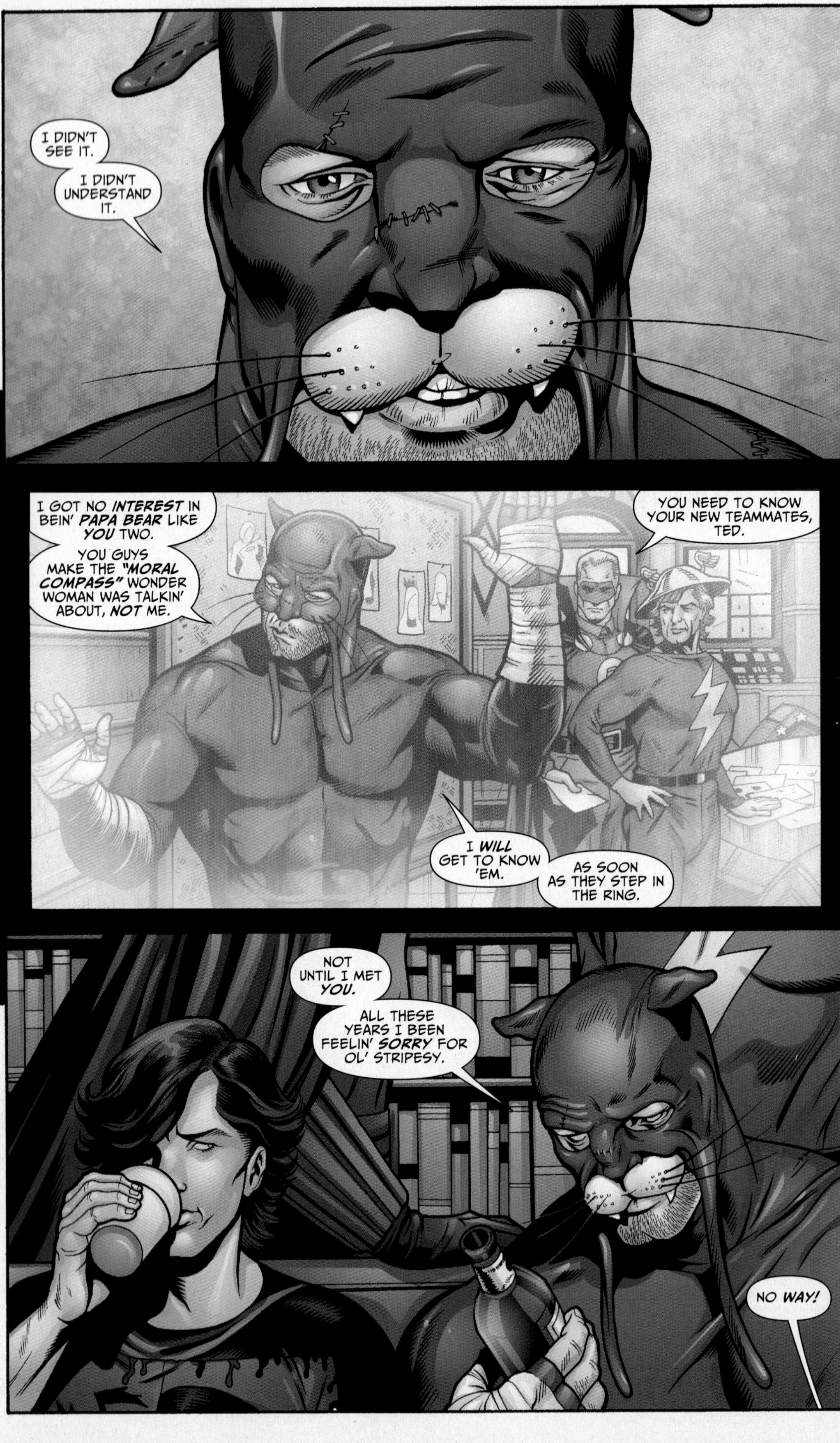
I DIDN'T SEE IT.
I DIDN'T UNDERSTAND IT.
I GOT NO INTEREST IN BEIN' PAPA BEAR LIKE YOU TWO.
YOU GUYS MAKE THE "MORAL COMPASS" WONDER WOMAN WAS TALKIN' ABOUT, NOT ME.
YOU NEED TO KNOW YOUR NEW TEAMMATES, TED.
I WILL GET TO KNOW 'EM.
AS SOON AS THEY STEP IN THE RING.
NOT UNTIL I MET YOU.
ALL THESE YEARS I BEEN FEELIN' SORRY FOR OL' STRIPESY.
NO WAY!

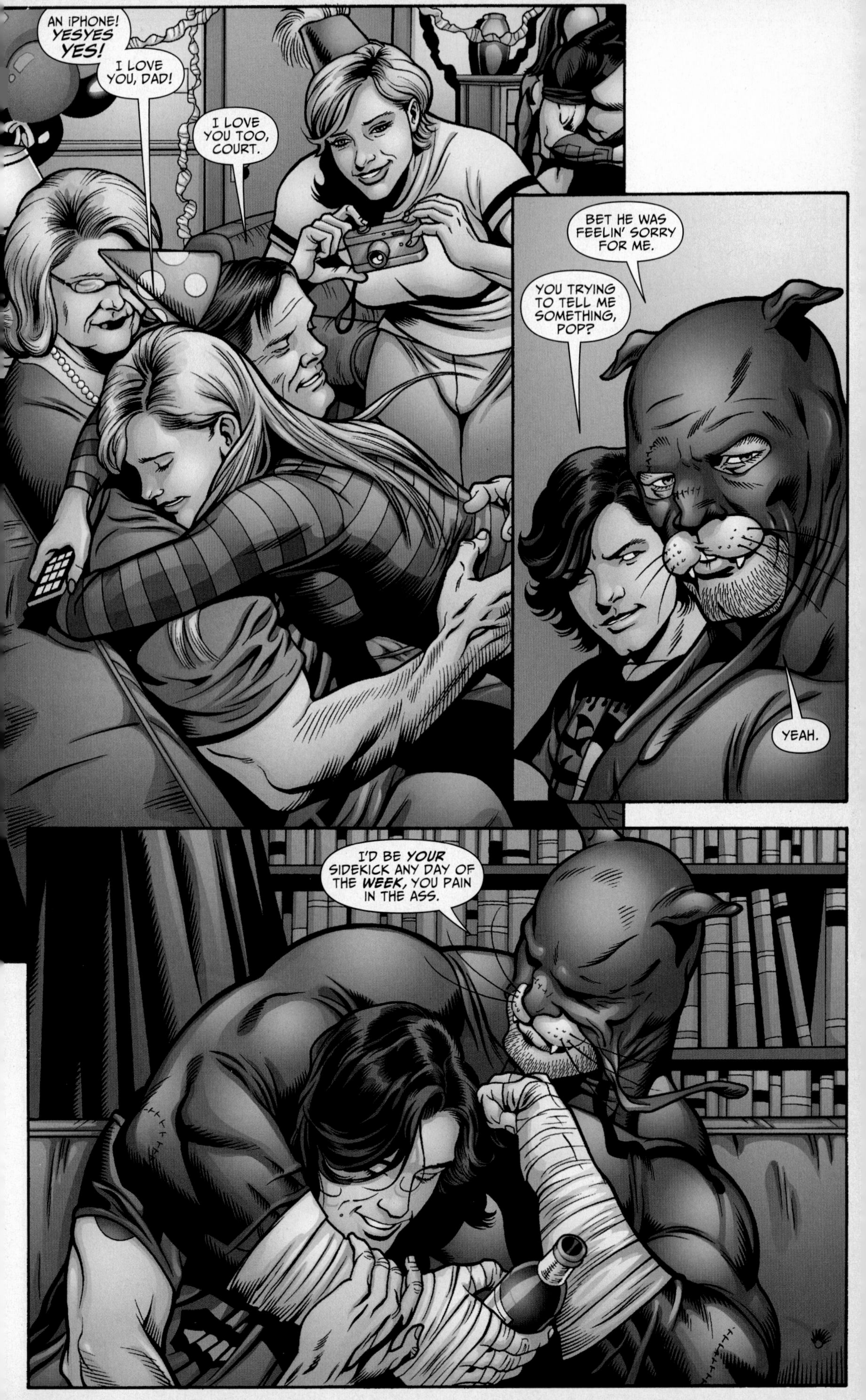
AN iPHONE! YESYES YES!
I LOVE YOU, DAD!
I LOVE YOU TOO, COURT.
BET HE WAS FEELIN' SORRY FOR ME.
YOU TRYING TO TELL ME SOMETHING, POP?
YEAH.
I'D BE YOUR SIDEKICK ANY DAY OF THE WEEK, YOU PAIN IN THE ASS.

HERE. IT'S FROM ME, CYCLONE AND THE OTHER KIDS.

Um, THANKS, JAKEEM.

YOU DIDN'T HAVE TO.

WE DID. ESPECIALLY *ME.*

WHAT ARE YOU TALKING ABOUT?

NOBODY LIKED ME WHEN I FIRST GOT THE THUNDERBOLT. ESPECIALLY YOU.

BUT YOU REMEMBER THAT HALLOWEEN? WHEN YOU AND I WERE THE ONLY ONES IN THE BROWNSTONE AND SOLOMON GRUNDY DECIDED TA *TRICK* OR *TREAT?*

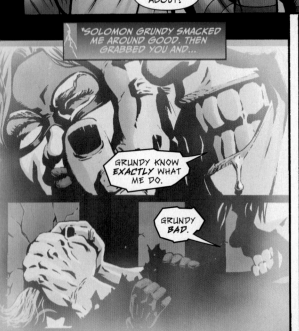

"SOLOMON GRUNDY SMACKED ME AROUND GOOD. THEN GRABBED YOU AND...

GRUNDY KNOW *EXACTLY* WHAT ME DO.

GRUNDY *BAD.*

...I ORDERED THE THUNDERBOLT TO HELP YOU. ELECTROCUTED THAT WALKING, WHITE HILLBILLY.

YO, THUNDERBOLT!

YEAH?

BURN SOLOMON GRUNDY FROM THE INSIDE OUT.

YOU GOT IT.

ARRRR

THANK YOU.

SHOULDN'T I THANK *YOU?*

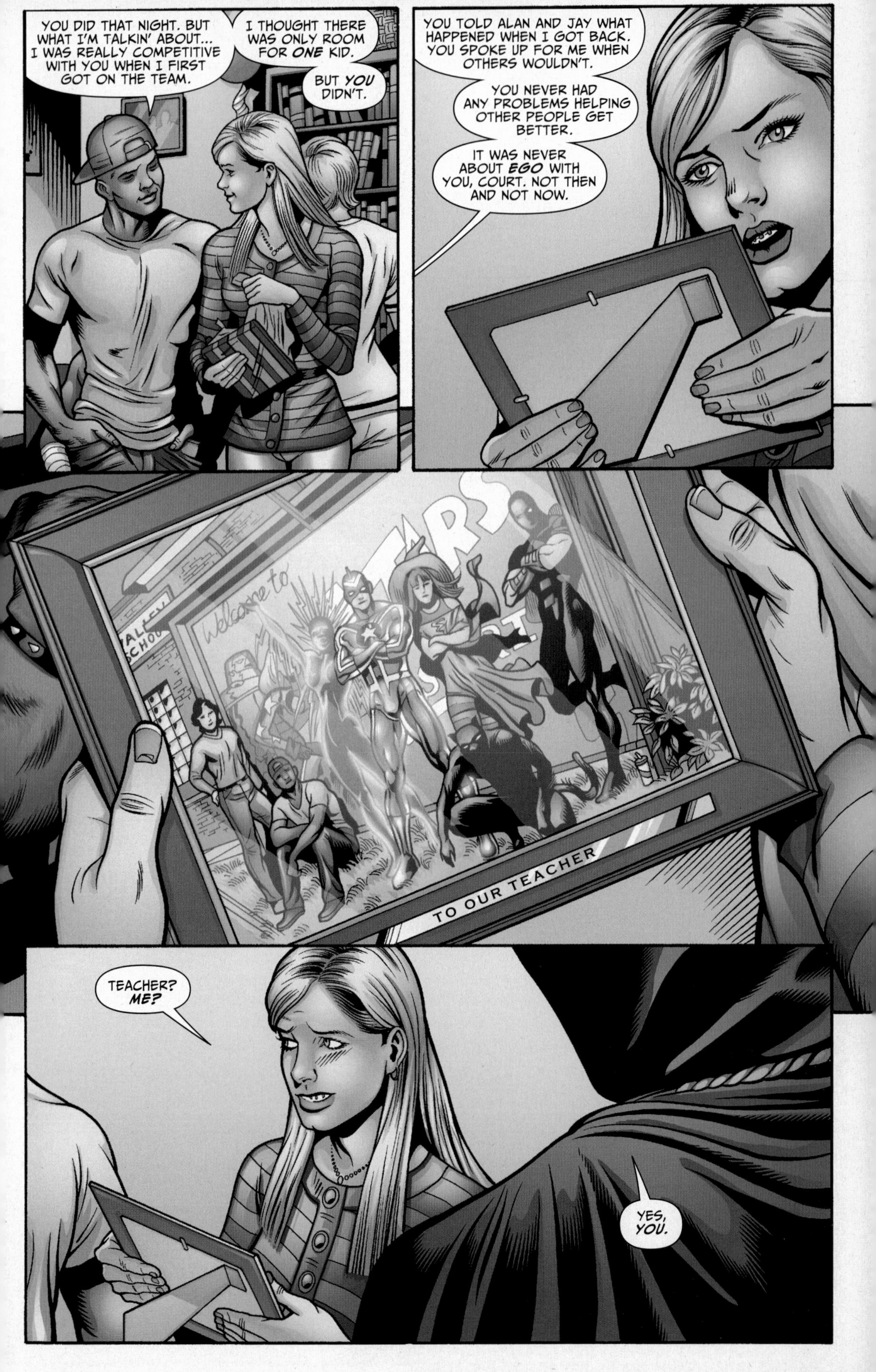
YOU DID THAT NIGHT. BUT WHAT I'M TALKIN' ABOUT... I WAS REALLY COMPETITIVE WITH YOU WHEN I FIRST GOT ON THE TEAM.
I THOUGHT THERE WAS ONLY ROOM FOR ONE KID.
BUT YOU DIDN'T.
YOU TOLD ALAN AND JAY WHAT HAPPENED WHEN I GOT BACK. YOU SPOKE UP FOR ME WHEN OTHERS WOULDN'T.
YOU NEVER HAD ANY PROBLEMS HELPING OTHER PEOPLE GET BETTER.
IT WAS NEVER ABOUT EGO WITH YOU, COURT. NOT THEN AND NOT NOW.
Welcome to
TO OUR TEACHER
TEACHER? ME?
YES, YOU.

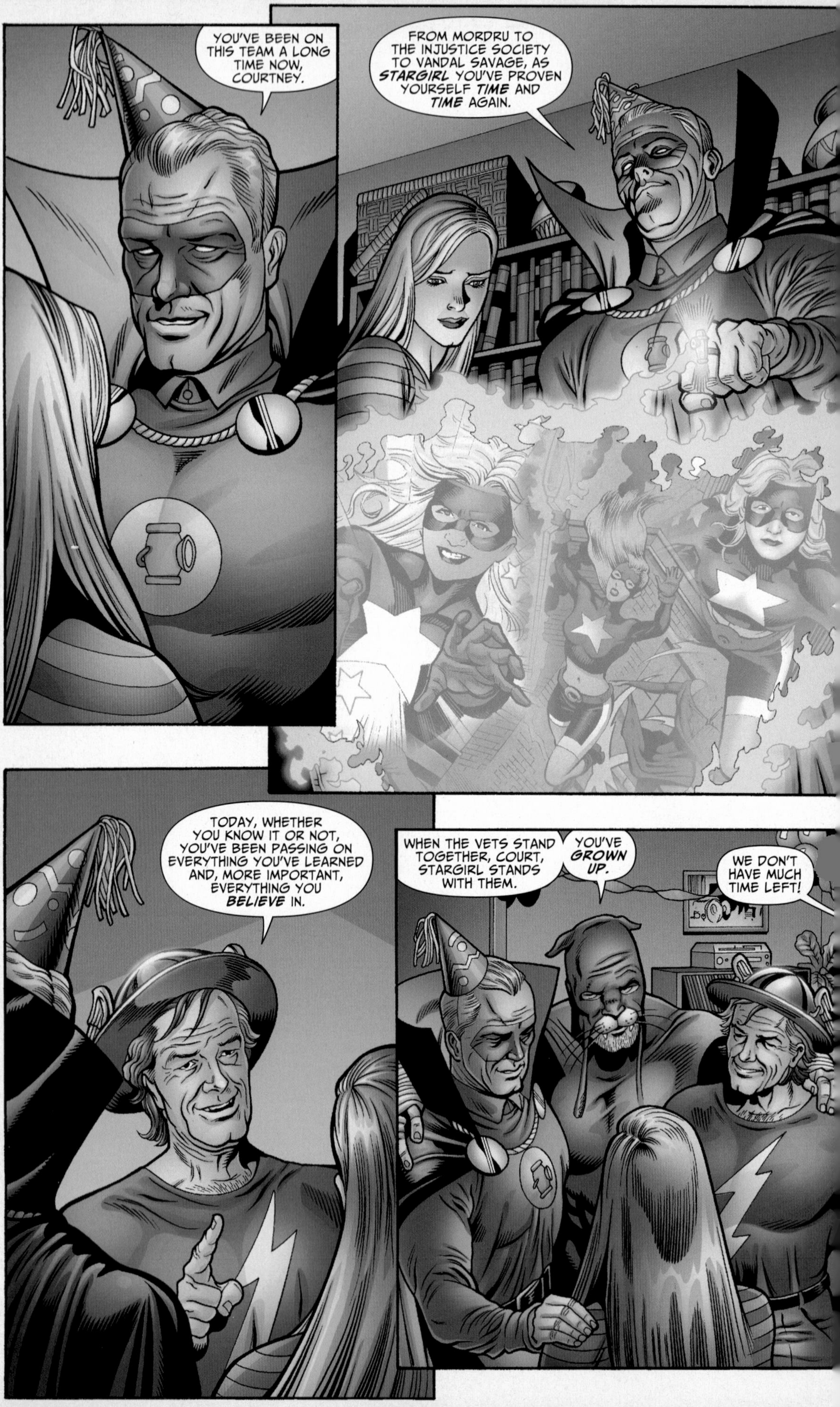
YOU'VE BEEN ON THIS TEAM A LONG TIME NOW, COURTNEY.
FROM MORDRU TO THE INJUSTICE SOCIETY TO VANDAL SAVAGE, AS STARGIRL YOU'VE PROVEN YOURSELF TIME AND TIME AGAIN.
TODAY, WHETHER YOU KNOW IT OR NOT, YOU'VE BEEN PASSING ON EVERYTHING YOU'VE LEARNED AND, MORE IMPORTANT, EVERYTHING YOU BELIEVE IN.
WHEN THE VETS STAND TOGETHER, COURT, STARGIRL STANDS WITH THEM.
YOU'VE GROWN UP.
WE DON'T HAVE MUCH TIME LEFT!

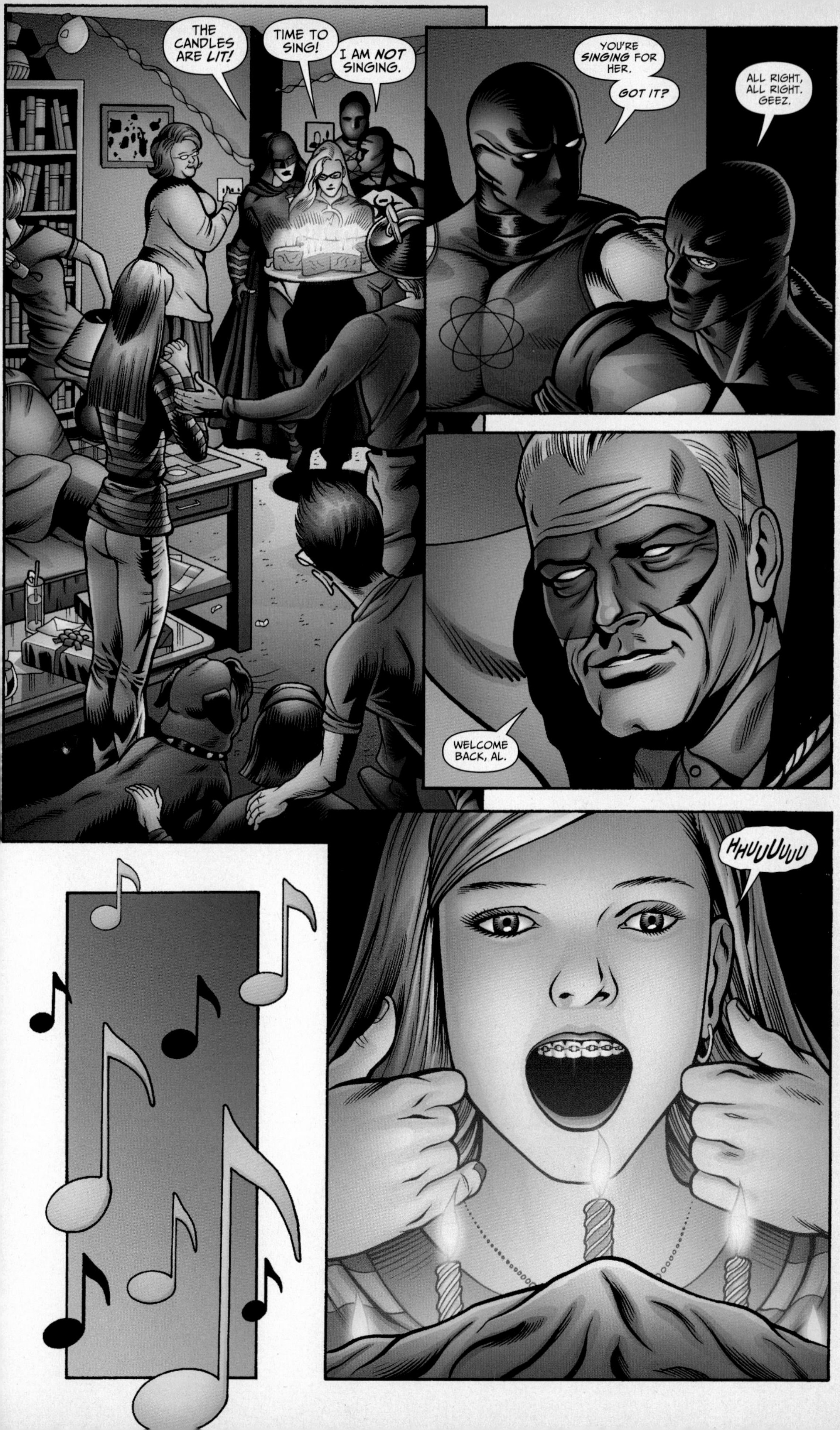
THE CANDLES ARE LIT!
TIME TO SING!
I AM NOT SINGING.
YOU'RE SINGING FOR HER.
GOT IT?
ALL RIGHT, ALL RIGHT. GEEZ.
WELCOME BACK, AL.
HHUUUUUU

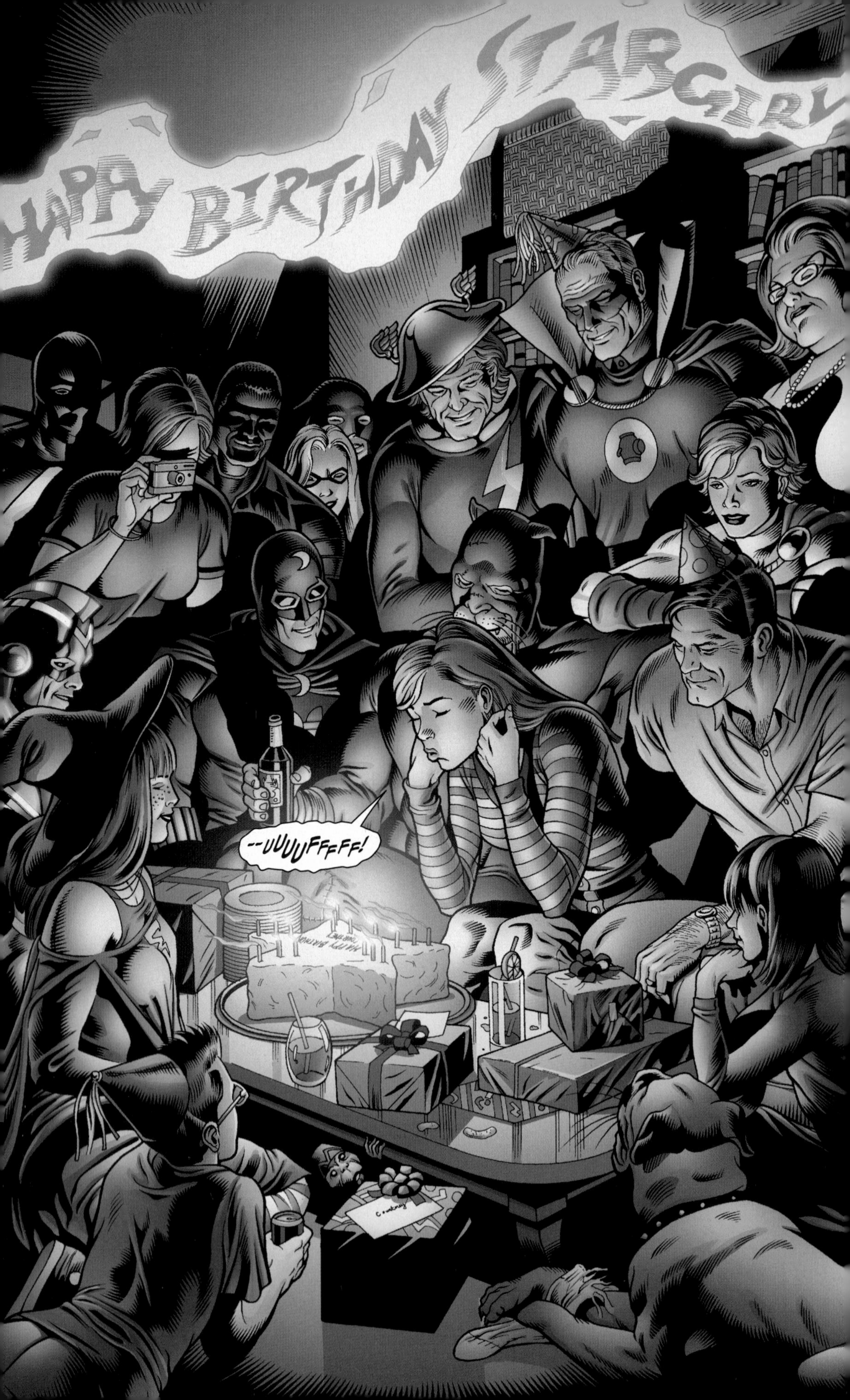
HAPPY BIRTHDAY STARGIRL
--UUUUFFFFF!

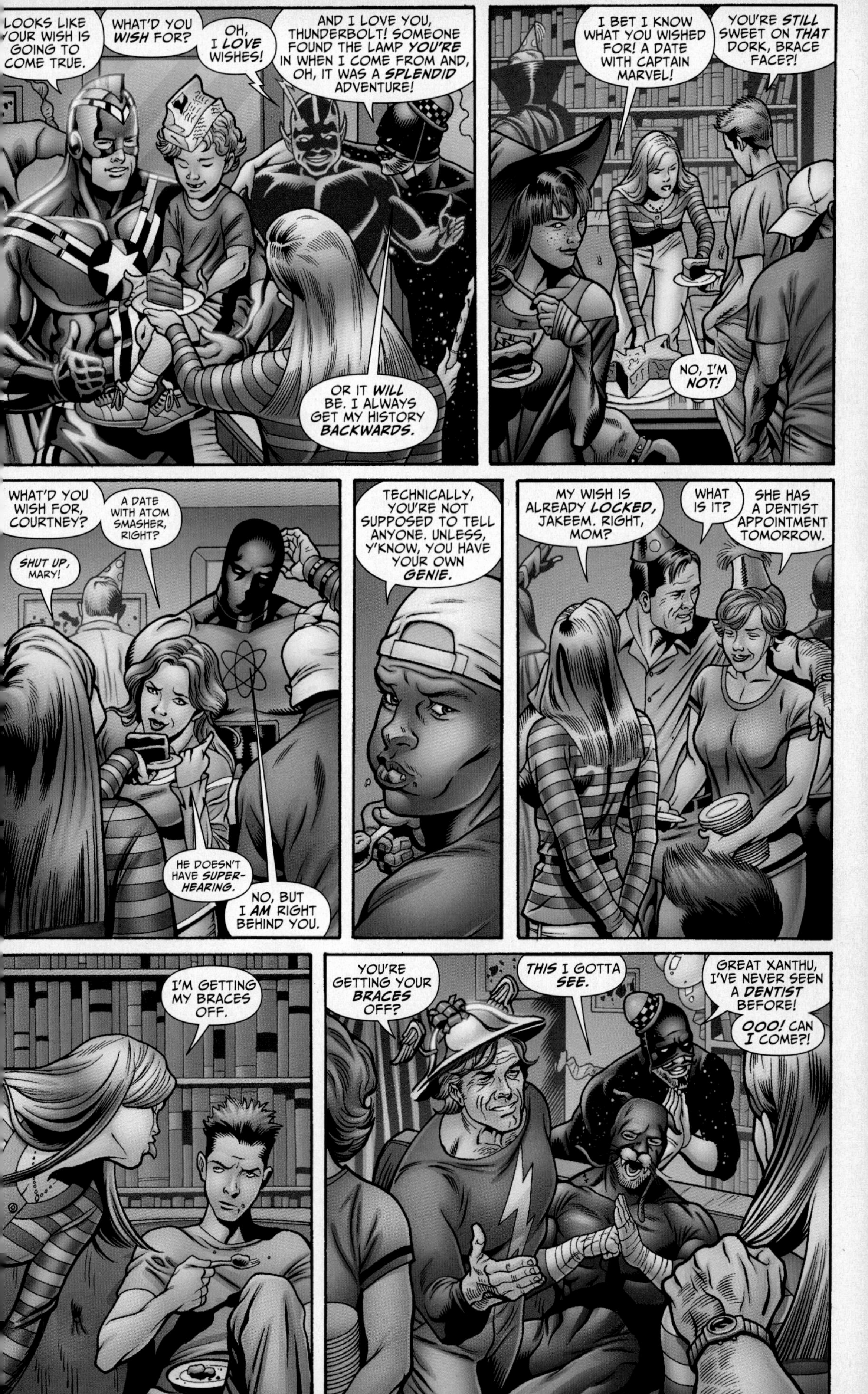
LOOKS LIKE YOUR WISH IS GOING TO COME TRUE.
WHAT'D YOU WISH FOR?
OH, I LOVE WISHES!
AND I LOVE YOU, THUNDERBOLT! SOMEONE FOUND THE LAMP YOU'RE IN WHEN I COME FROM AND, OH, IT WAS A SPLENDID ADVENTURE!
OR IT WILL BE. I ALWAYS GET MY HISTORY BACKWARDS.
I BET I KNOW WHAT YOU WISHED FOR! A DATE WITH CAPTAIN MARVEL!
YOU'RE STILL SWEET ON THAT DORK, BRACE FACE?!
NO, I'M NOT!
WHAT'D YOU WISH FOR, COURTNEY?
A DATE WITH ATOM SMASHER, RIGHT?
SHUT UP, MARY!
HE DOESN'T HAVE SUPER-HEARING.
NO, BUT I AM RIGHT BEHIND YOU.
TECHNICALLY, YOU'RE NOT SUPPOSED TO TELL ANYONE. UNLESS, Y'KNOW, YOU HAVE YOUR OWN GENIE.
MY WISH IS ALREADY LOCKED, JAKEEM. RIGHT, MOM?
WHAT IS IT?
SHE HAS A DENTIST APPOINTMENT TOMORROW.
I'M GETTING MY BRACES OFF.
YOU'RE GETTING YOUR BRACES OFF?
THIS I GOTTA SEE.
GREAT XANTHU, I'VE NEVER SEEN A DENTIST BEFORE!
OOO! CAN I COME?!

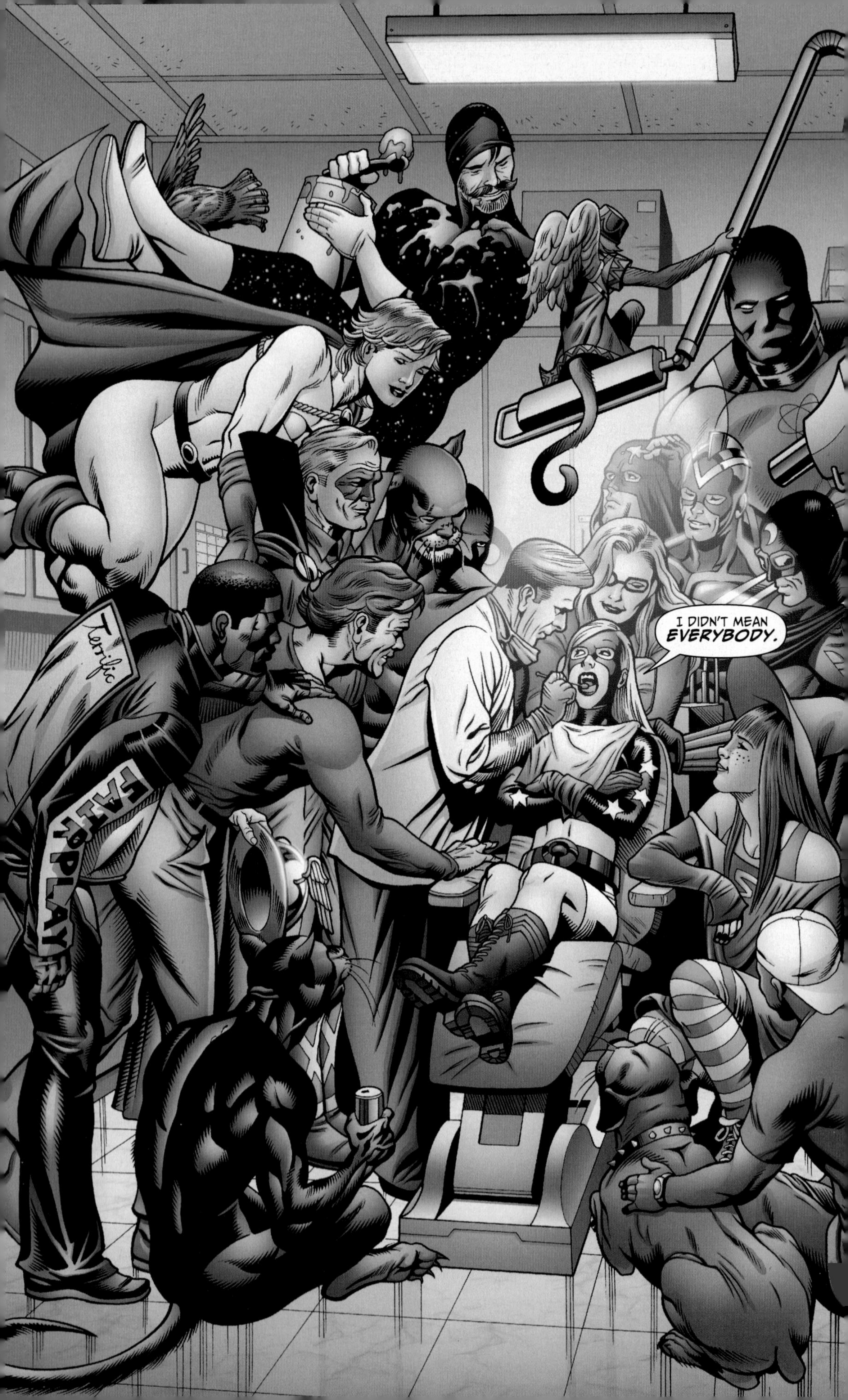
Terrific
I DIDN'T MEAN **EVERYBODY.**

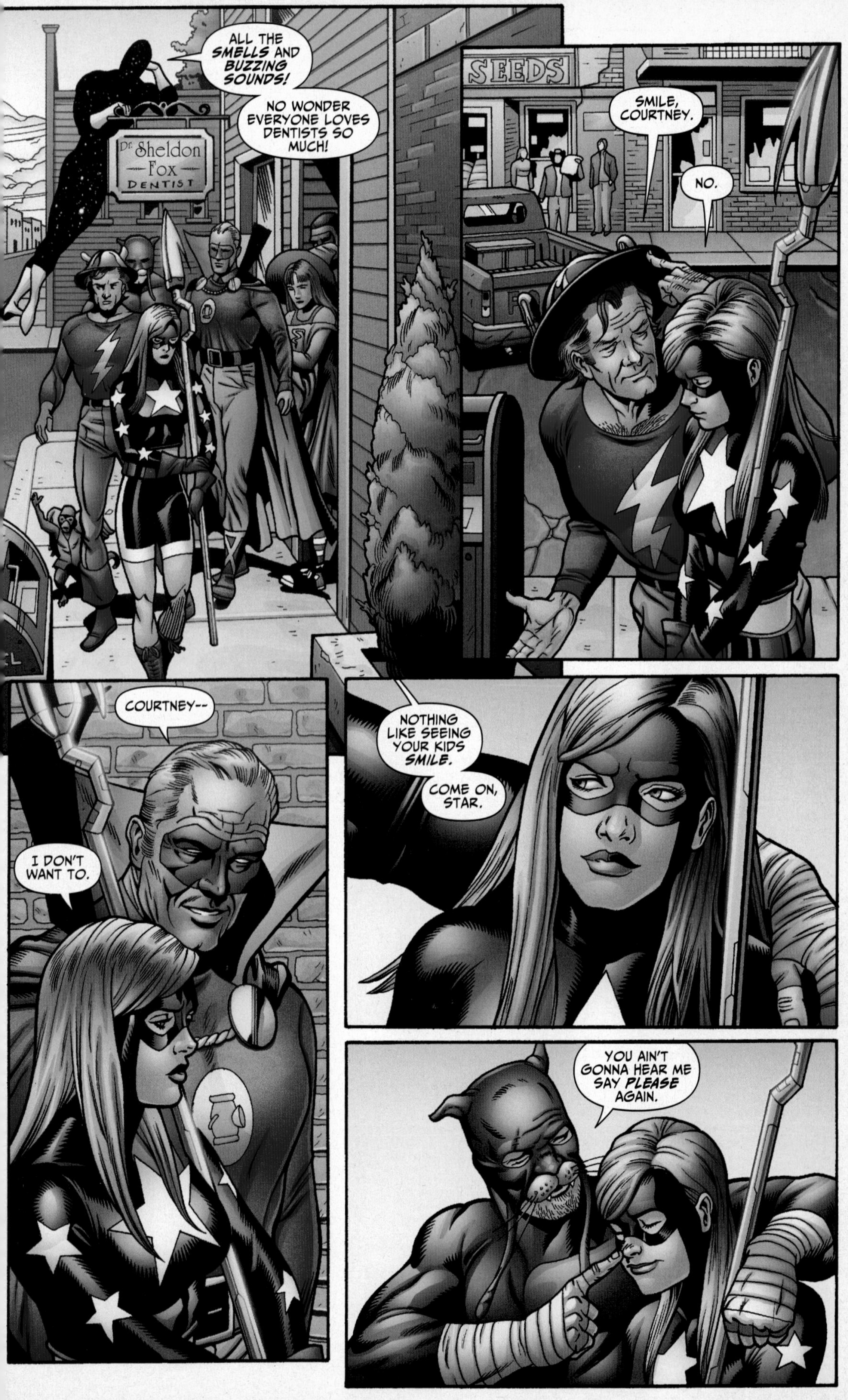
ALL THE SMELLS AND BUZZING SOUNDS!
NO WONDER EVERYONE LOVES DENTISTS SO MUCH!
Dr. Sheldon Fox DENTIST
SEEDS
SMILE, COURTNEY.
NO.
COURTNEY--
I DON'T WANT TO.
NOTHING LIKE SEEING YOUR KIDS SMILE.
COME ON, STAR.
YOU AIN'T GONNA HEAR ME SAY PLEASE AGAIN.

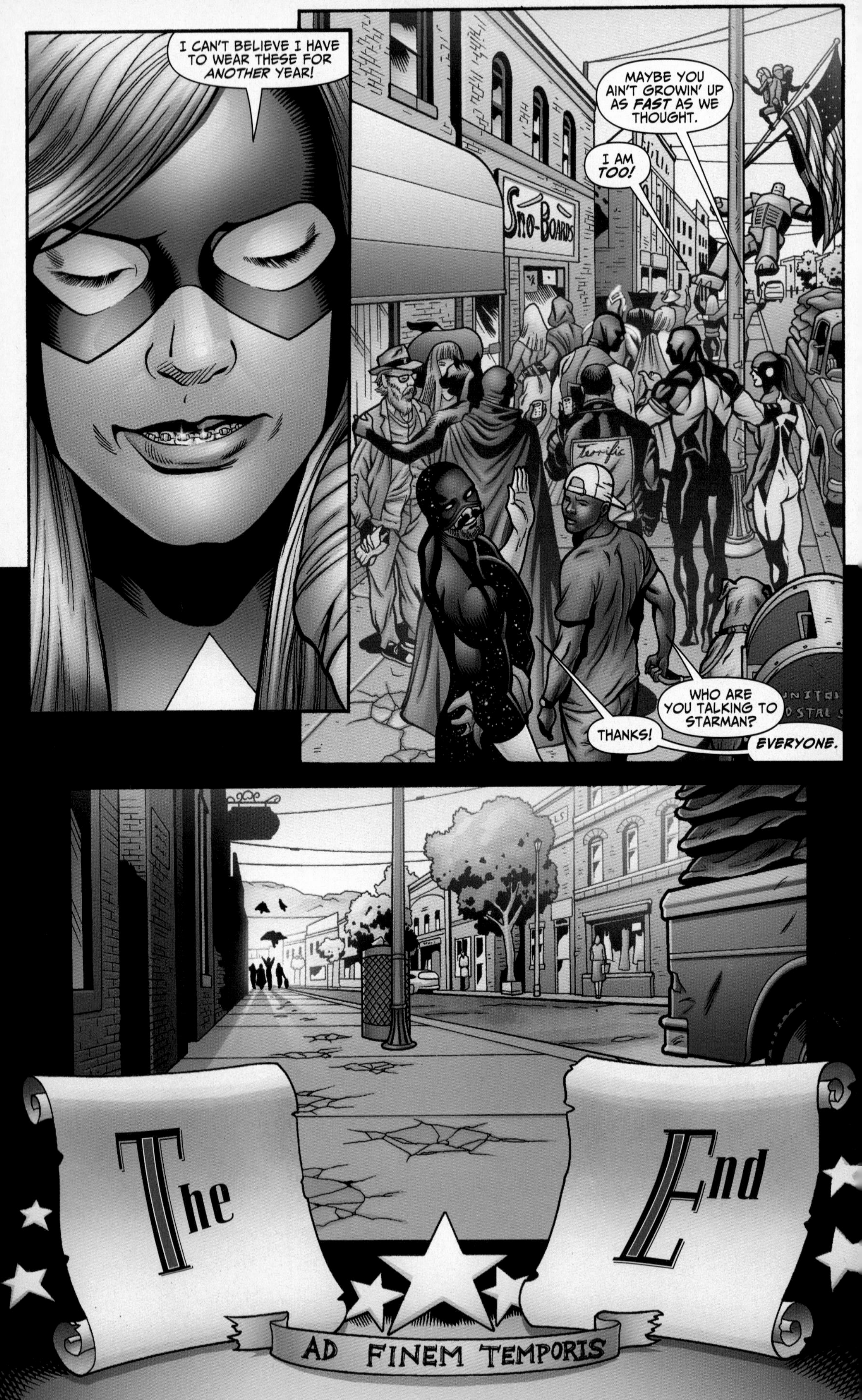
I CAN'T BELIEVE I HAVE TO WEAR THESE FOR *ANOTHER* YEAR!
MAYBE YOU AIN'T GROWIN' UP AS *FAST* AS WE THOUGHT.
I AM *TOO!*
SNO-BOARDS
Terrific
WHO ARE YOU TALKING TO STARMAN?
THANKS!
EVERYONE.
The End
AD FINEM TEMPORIS

JUSTICE SOCIETY OF AMERICA #27 cover by Jerry Ordway
Interior art by Ordway & Bob Wiacek

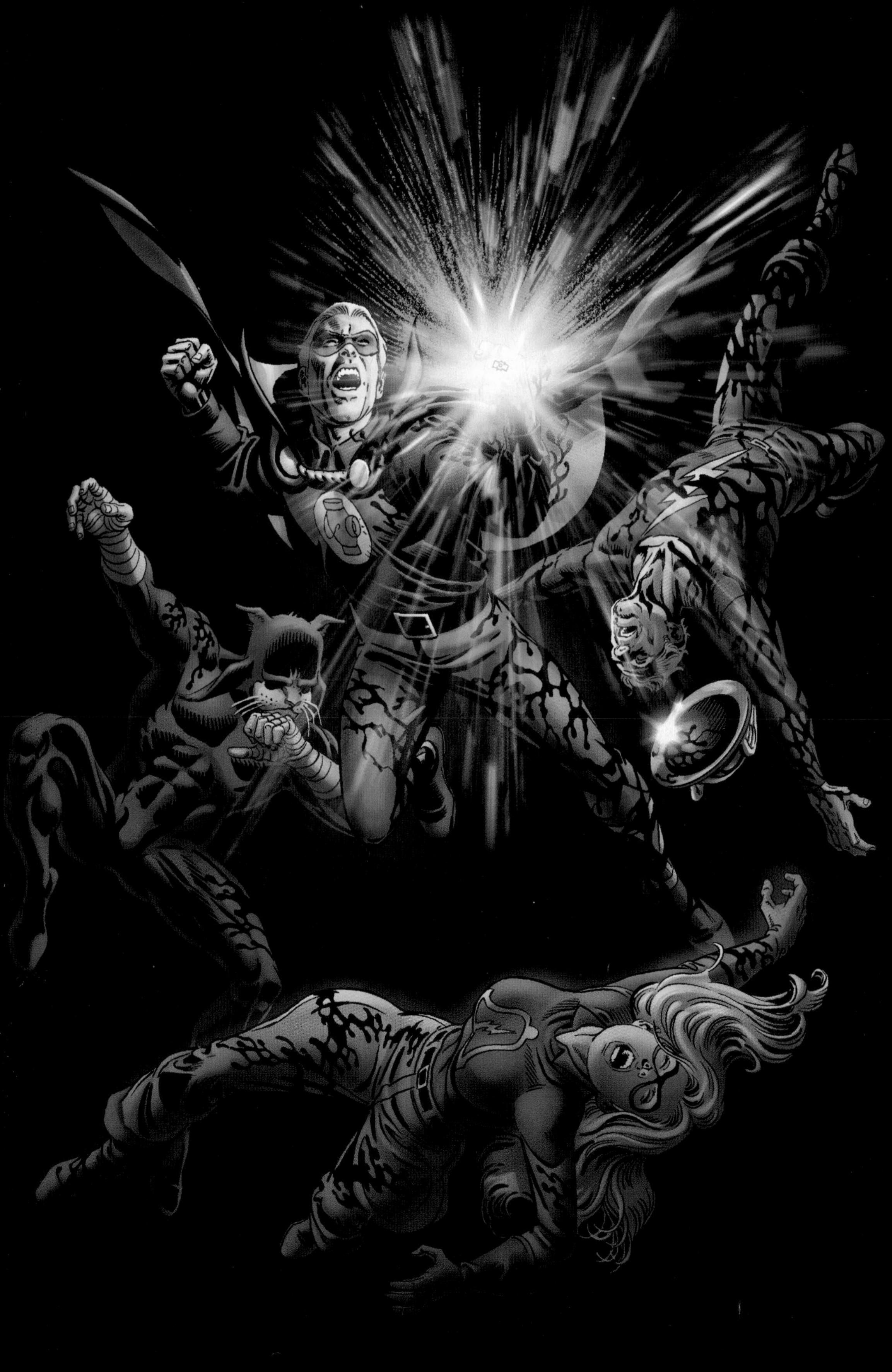

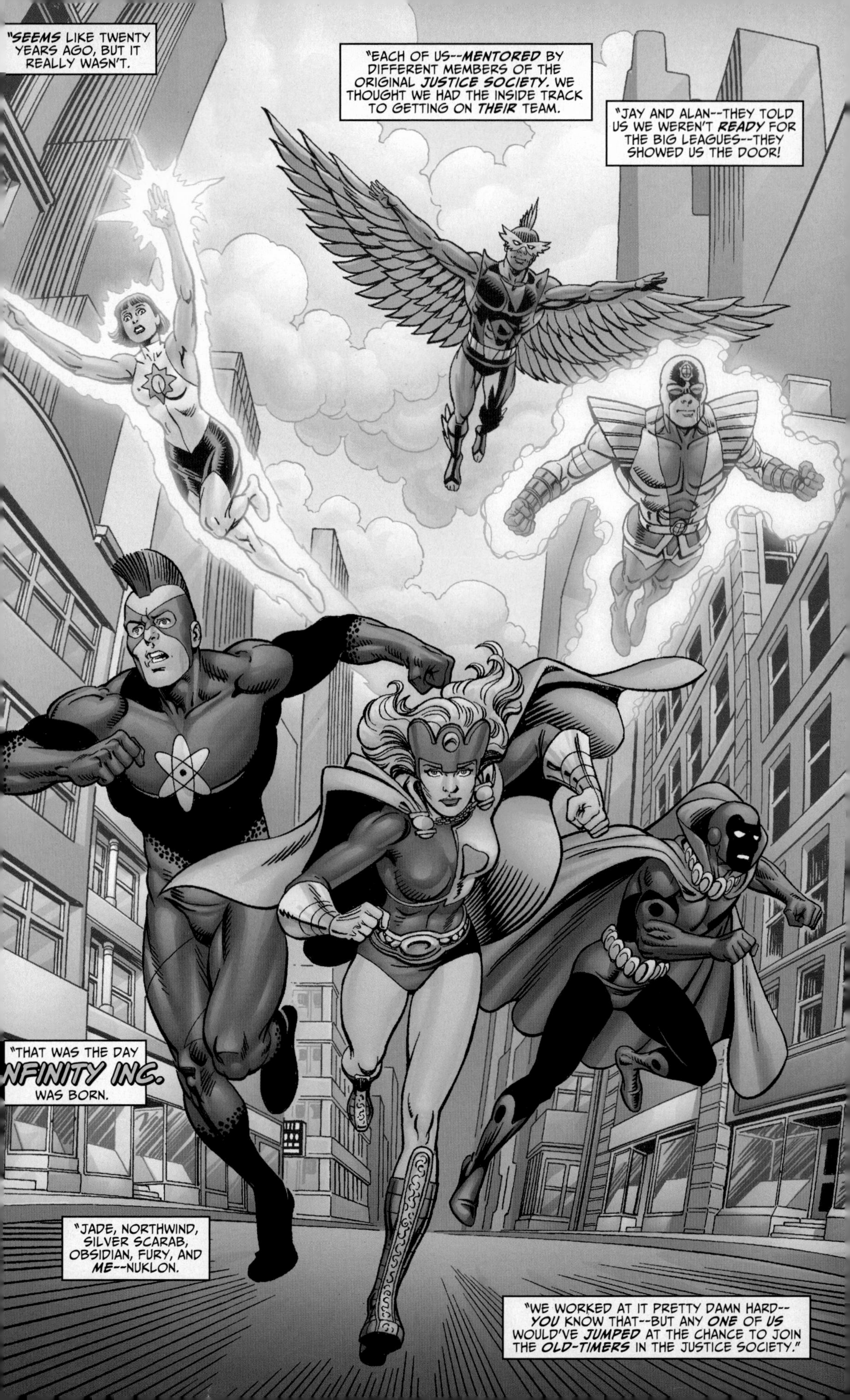

"SEEMS LIKE TWENTY YEARS AGO, BUT IT REALLY WASN'T.
"EACH OF US--MENTORED BY DIFFERENT MEMBERS OF THE ORIGINAL JUSTICE SOCIETY. WE THOUGHT WE HAD THE INSIDE TRACK TO GETTING ON THEIR TEAM.
"JAY AND ALAN--THEY TOLD US WE WEREN'T READY FOR THE BIG LEAGUES--THEY SHOWED US THE DOOR!
"THAT WAS THE DAY INFINITY INC. WAS BORN.
"JADE, NORTHWIND, SILVER SCARAB, OBSIDIAN, FURY, AND ME--NUKLON.
"WE WORKED AT IT PRETTY DAMN HARD--YOU KNOW THAT--BUT ANY ONE OF US WOULD'VE JUMPED AT THE CHANCE TO JOIN THE OLD-TIMERS IN THE JUSTICE SOCIETY."

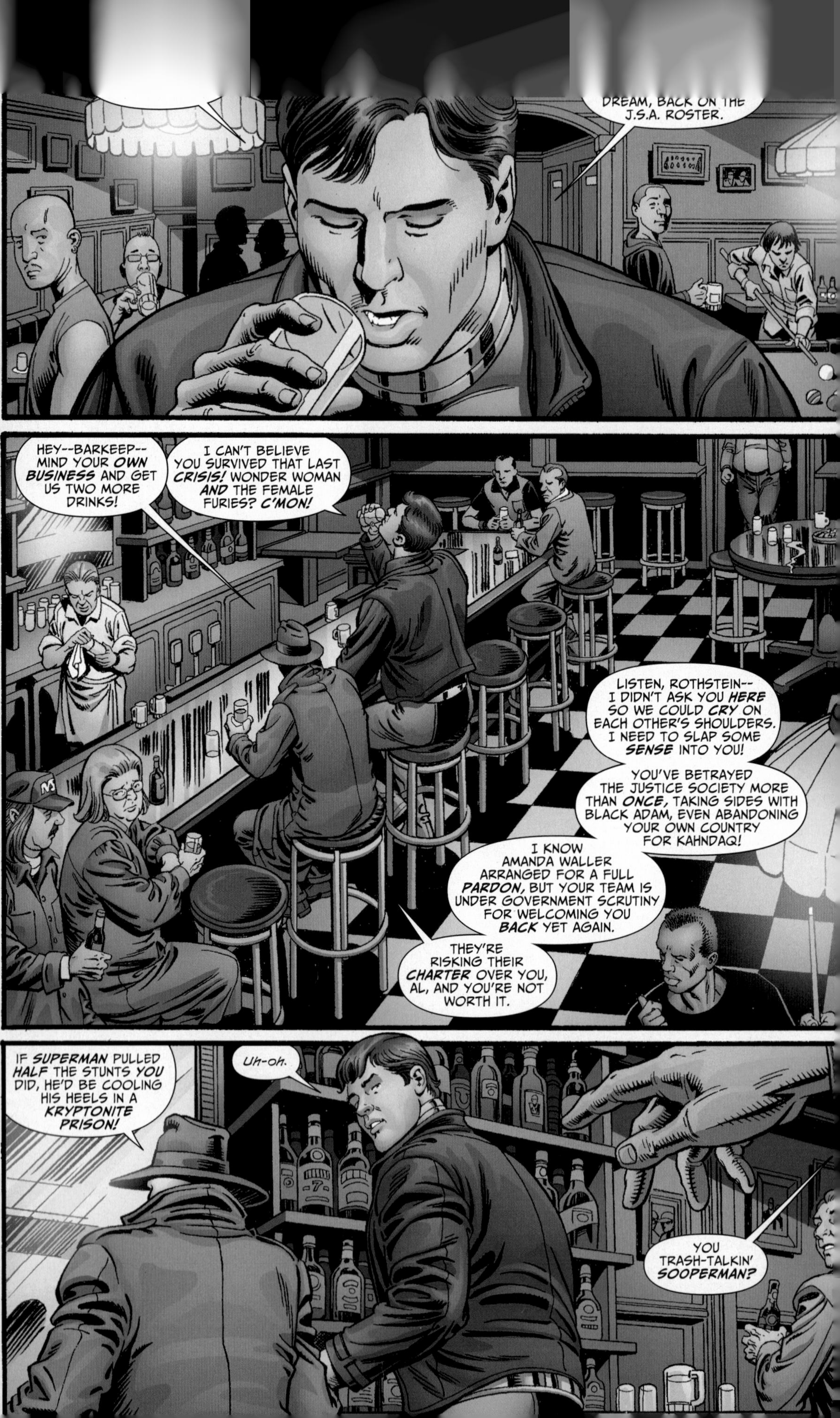

DREAM, BACK ON THE J.S.A. ROSTER.
HEY--BARKEEP--MIND YOUR OWN BUSINESS AND GET US TWO MORE DRINKS!
I CAN'T BELIEVE YOU SURVIVED THAT LAST CRISIS! WONDER WOMAN AND THE FEMALE FURIES? C'MON!
LISTEN, ROTHSTEIN--I DIDN'T ASK YOU HERE SO WE COULD CRY ON EACH OTHER'S SHOULDERS. I NEED TO SLAP SOME SENSE INTO YOU!
YOU'VE BETRAYED THE JUSTICE SOCIETY MORE THAN ONCE, TAKING SIDES WITH BLACK ADAM, EVEN ABANDONING YOUR OWN COUNTRY FOR KAHNDAQ!
I KNOW AMANDA WALLER ARRANGED FOR A FULL PARDON, BUT YOUR TEAM IS UNDER GOVERNMENT SCRUTINY FOR WELCOMING YOU BACK YET AGAIN.
THEY'RE RISKING THEIR CHARTER OVER YOU, AL, AND YOU'RE NOT WORTH IT.
IF SUPERMAN PULLED HALF THE STUNTS YOU DID, HE'D BE COOLING HIS HEELS IN A KRYPTONITE PRISON!
Uh-oh.
YOU TRASH-TALKIN' SOOPERMAN?

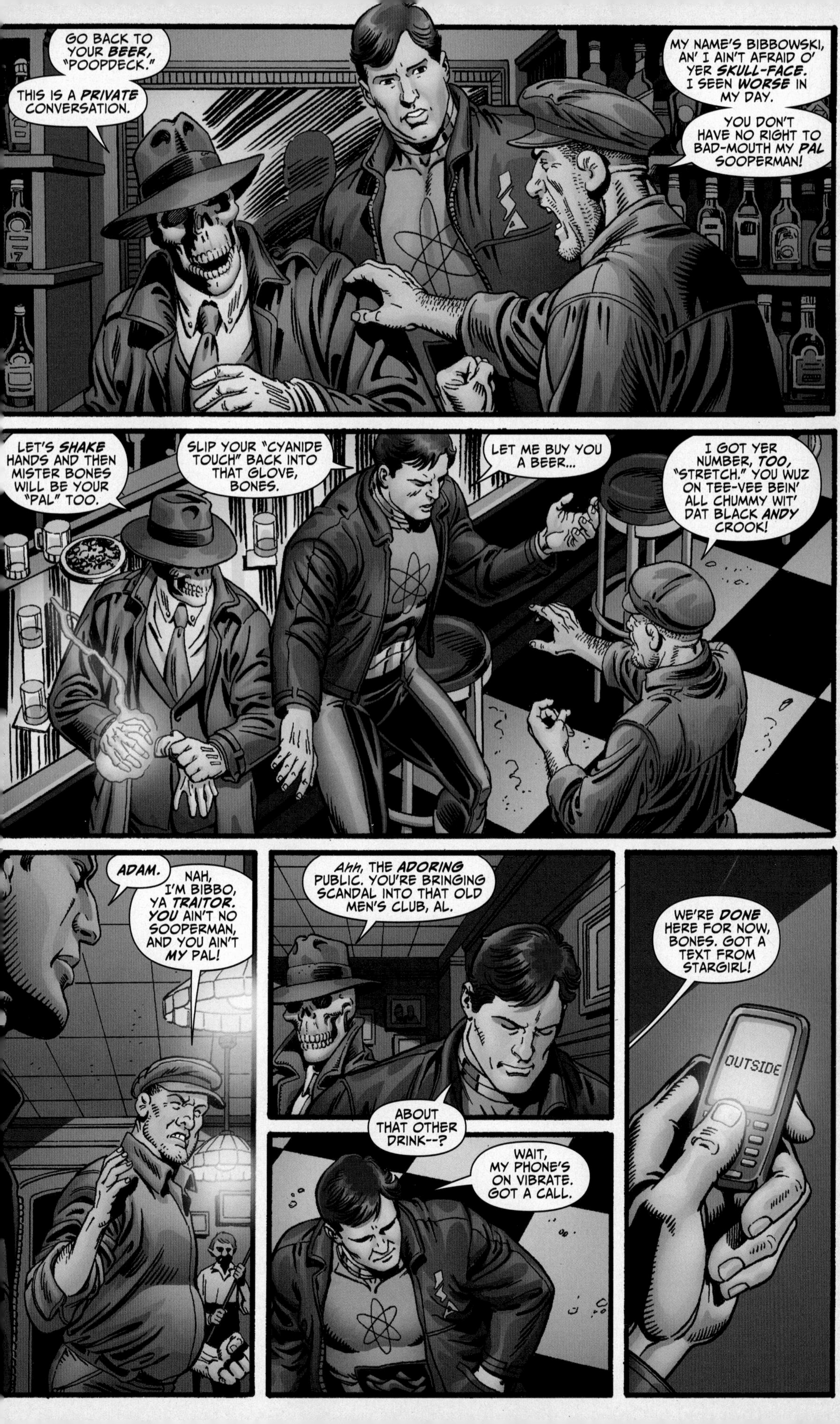
GO BACK TO YOUR *BEER*, "POOPDECK."
THIS IS A *PRIVATE* CONVERSATION.
MY NAME'S BIBBOWSKI, AN' I AIN'T AFRAID O' YER *SKULL-FACE*. I SEEN *WORSE* IN MY DAY.
YOU DON'T HAVE NO RIGHT TO BAD-MOUTH MY *PAL* SOOPERMAN!
LET'S *SHAKE* HANDS AND THEN MISTER BONES WILL BE YOUR "PAL" TOO.
SLIP YOUR "CYANIDE TOUCH" BACK INTO THAT GLOVE, BONES.
LET ME BUY YOU A BEER...
I GOT YER NUMBER, *TOO*, "STRETCH." YOU WUZ ON TEE-VEE BEIN' ALL CHUMMY WIT' DAT BLACK *ANDY* CROOK!
ADAM.
NAH, I'M BIBBO, YA *TRAITOR*. *YOU* AIN'T NO SOOPERMAN, AND YOU AIN'T *MY* PAL!
Ahh, THE *ADORING* PUBLIC. YOU'RE BRINGING SCANDAL INTO THAT OLD MEN'S CLUB, AL.
ABOUT THAT OTHER DRINK--?
WAIT, MY PHONE'S ON VIBRATE. GOT A CALL.
WE'RE *DONE* HERE FOR NOW, BONES. GOT A TEXT FROM STARGIRL!
OUTSIDE

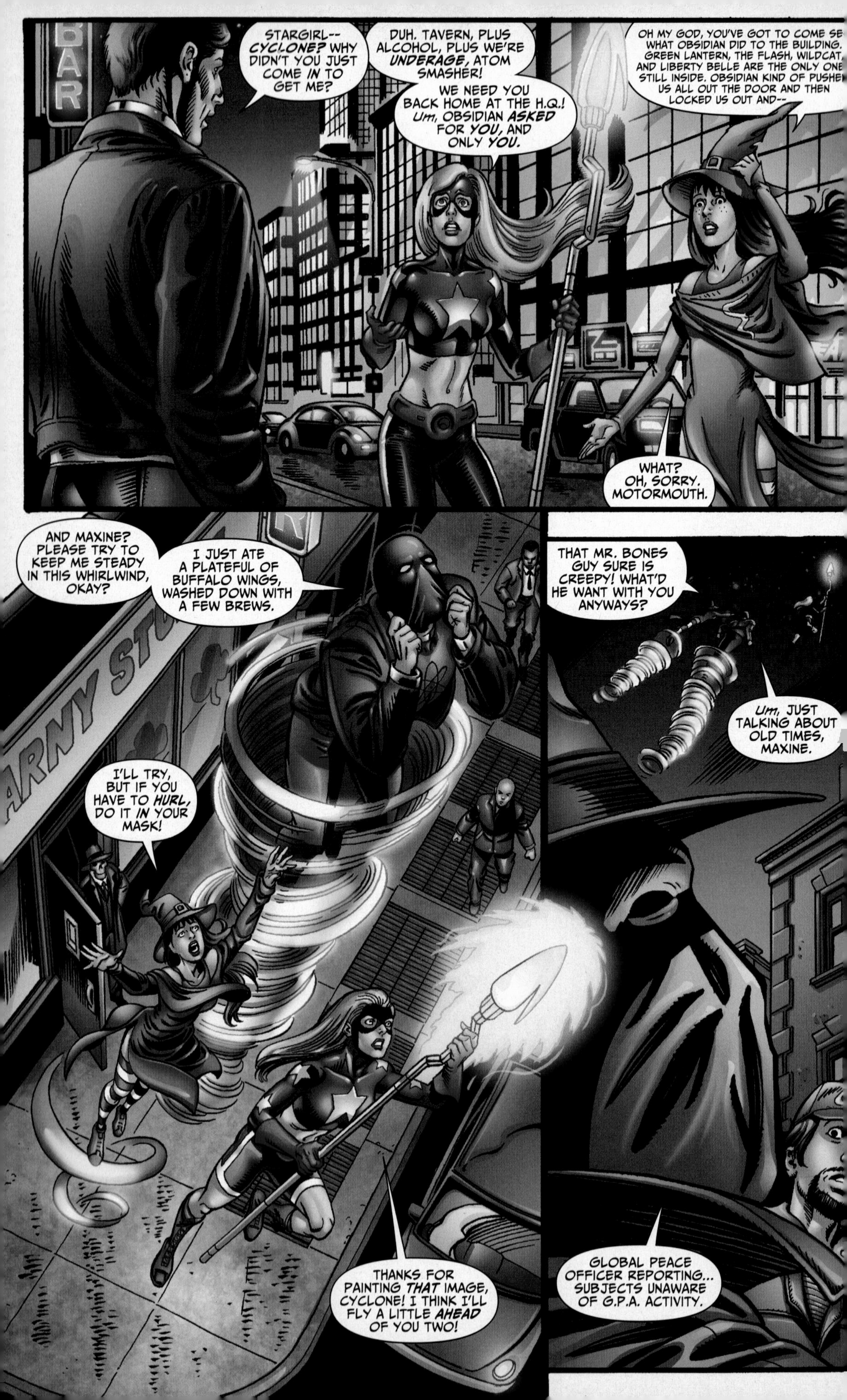
BAR
STARGIRL-- CYCLONE? WHY DIDN'T YOU JUST COME IN TO GET ME?
DUH. TAVERN, PLUS ALCOHOL, PLUS WE'RE UNDERAGE, ATOM SMASHER!
WE NEED YOU BACK HOME AT THE H.Q.! Um, OBSIDIAN ASKED FOR YOU, AND ONLY YOU.
OH MY GOD, YOU'VE GOT TO COME SE WHAT OBSIDIAN DID TO THE BUILDING. GREEN LANTERN, THE FLASH, WILDCAT, AND LIBERTY BELLE ARE THE ONLY ONE STILL INSIDE. OBSIDIAN KIND OF PUSHE US ALL OUT THE DOOR AND THEN LOCKED US OUT AND--
WHAT? OH, SORRY. MOTORMOUTH.
AND MAXINE? PLEASE TRY TO KEEP ME STEADY IN THIS WHIRLWIND, OKAY?
I JUST ATE A PLATEFUL OF BUFFALO WINGS, WASHED DOWN WITH A FEW BREWS.
I'LL TRY, BUT IF YOU HAVE TO HURL, DO IT IN YOUR MASK!
THANKS FOR PAINTING THAT IMAGE, CYCLONE! I THINK I'LL FLY A LITTLE AHEAD OF YOU TWO!
THAT MR. BONES GUY SURE IS CREEPY! WHAT'D HE WANT WITH YOU ANYWAYS?
Um, JUST TALKING ABOUT OLD TIMES, MAXINE.
GLOBAL PEACE OFFICER REPORTING... SUBJECTS UNAWARE OF G.P.A. ACTIVITY.

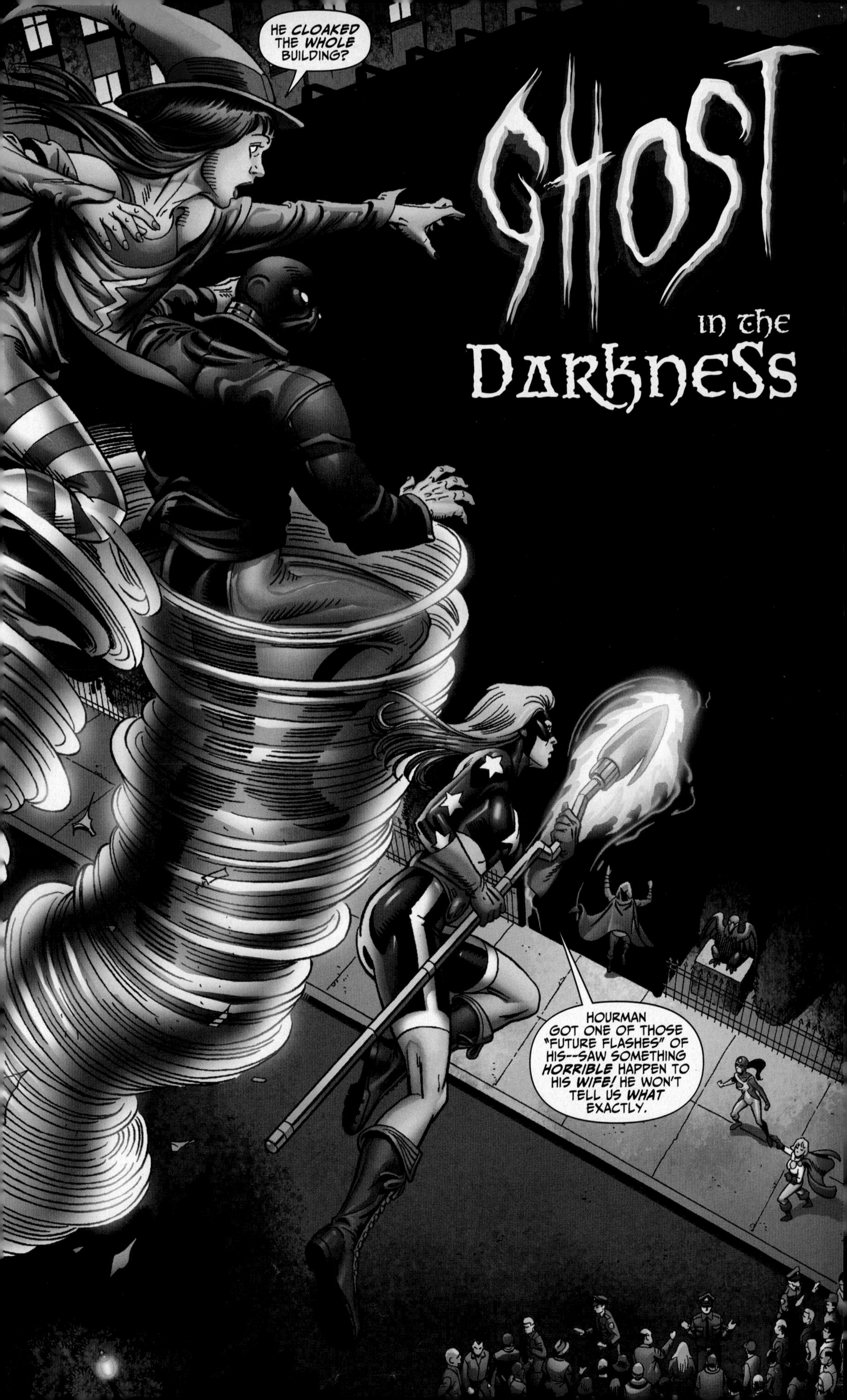

HE CLOAKED THE WHOLE BUILDING?
GHOST in the DARKNESS
HOURMAN GOT ONE OF THOSE "FUTURE FLASHES" OF HIS--SAW SOMETHING HORRIBLE HAPPEN TO HIS WIFE! HE WON'T TELL US WHAT EXACTLY.

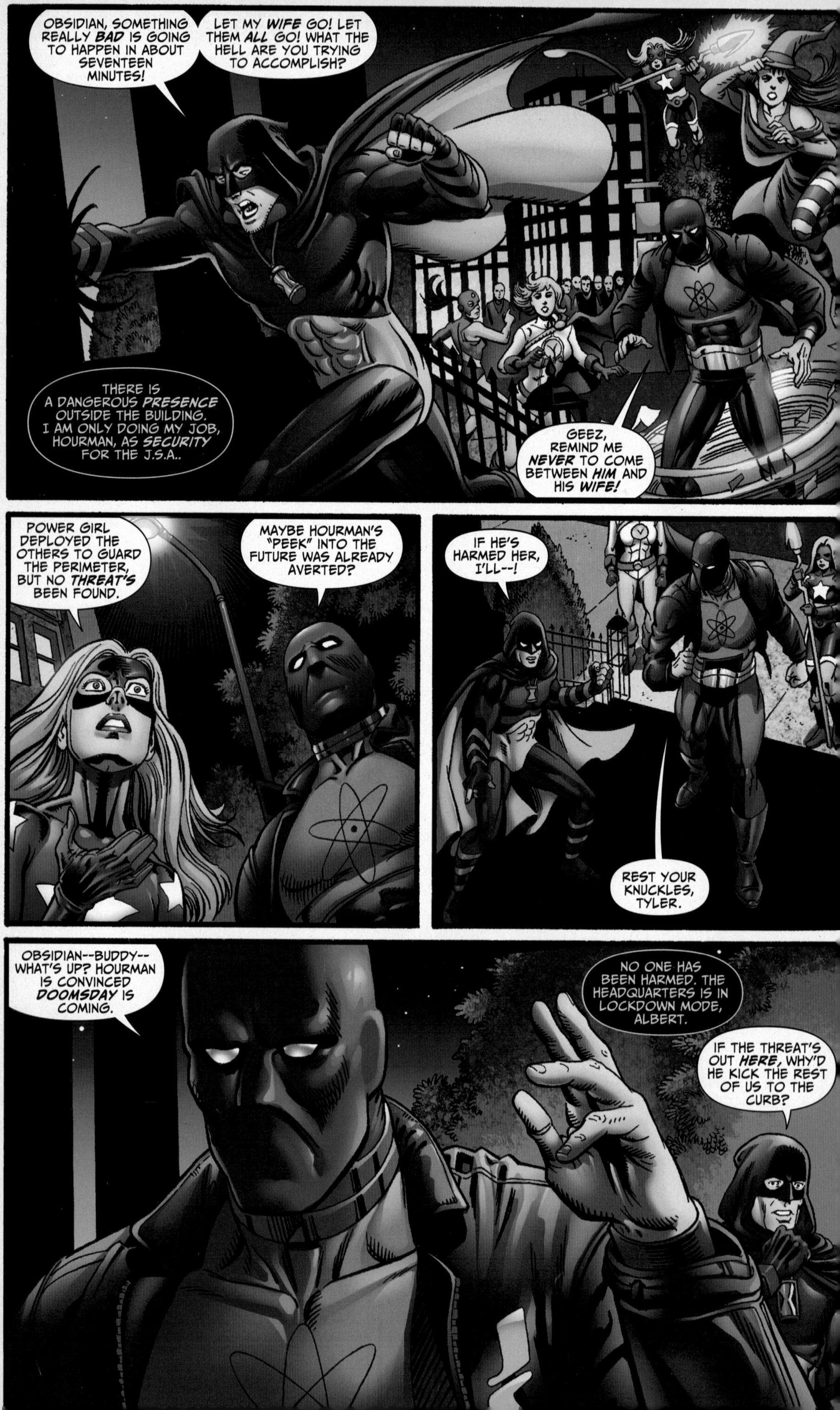
OBSIDIAN, SOMETHING REALLY BAD IS GOING TO HAPPEN IN ABOUT SEVENTEEN MINUTES!
LET MY WIFE GO! LET THEM ALL GO! WHAT THE HELL ARE YOU TRYING TO ACCOMPLISH?
THERE IS A DANGEROUS PRESENCE OUTSIDE THE BUILDING. I AM ONLY DOING MY JOB, HOURMAN, AS SECURITY FOR THE J.S.A..
GEEZ, REMIND ME NEVER TO COME BETWEEN HIM AND HIS WIFE!
POWER GIRL DEPLOYED THE OTHERS TO GUARD THE PERIMETER, BUT NO THREAT'S BEEN FOUND.
MAYBE HOURMAN'S "PEEK" INTO THE FUTURE WAS ALREADY AVERTED?
IF HE'S HARMED HER, I'LL--!
REST YOUR KNUCKLES, TYLER.
OBSIDIAN--BUDDY-- WHAT'S UP? HOURMAN IS CONVINCED DOOMSDAY IS COMING.
NO ONE HAS BEEN HARMED. THE HEADQUARTERS IS IN LOCKDOWN MODE, ALBERT.
IF THE THREAT'S OUT HERE, WHY'D HE KICK THE REST OF US TO THE CURB?

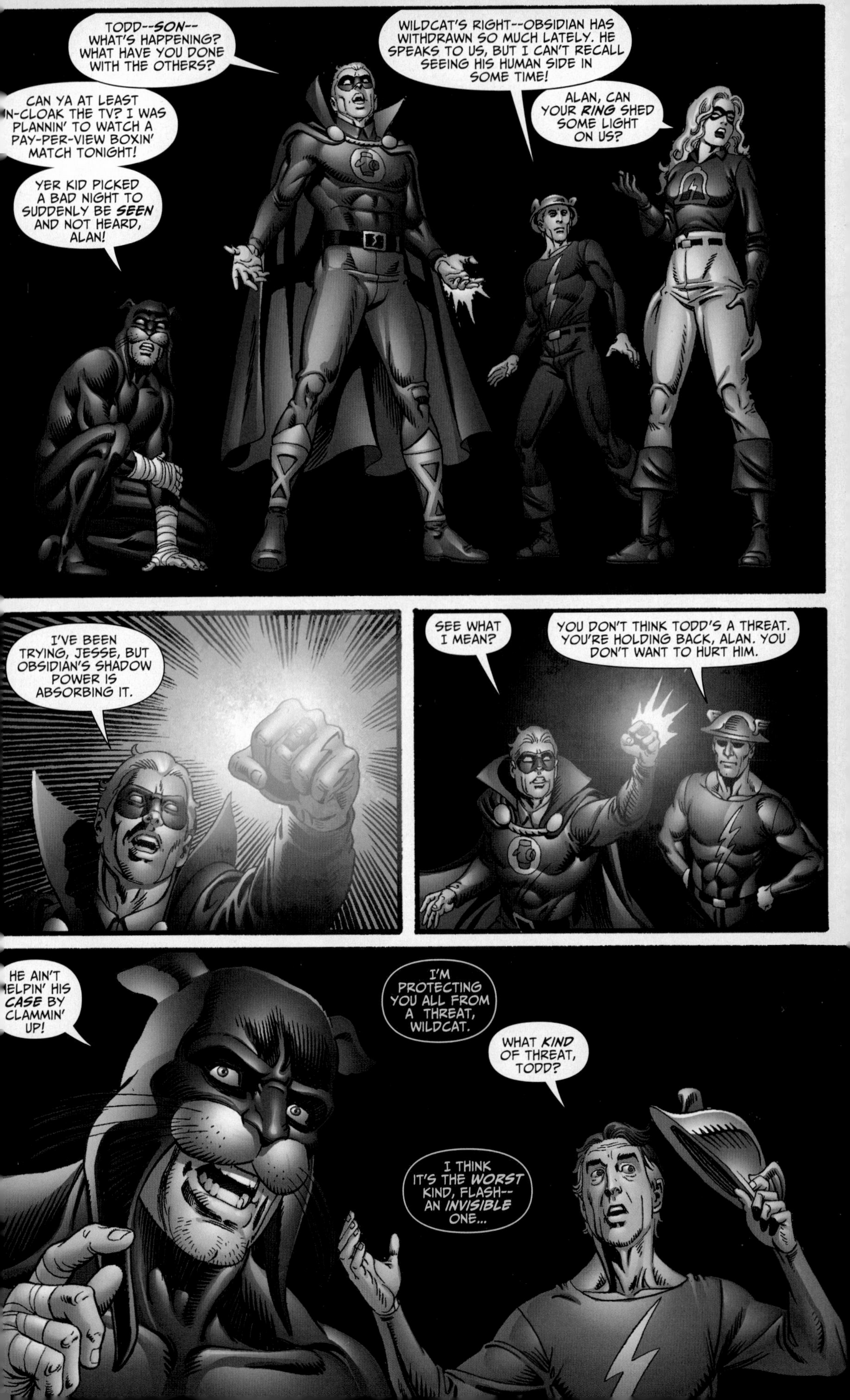
TODD--SON--
WHAT'S HAPPENING?
WHAT HAVE YOU DONE
WITH THE OTHERS?
CAN YA AT LEAST
N-CLOAK THE TV? I WAS
PLANNIN' TO WATCH A
PAY-PER-VIEW BOXIN'
MATCH TONIGHT!
YER KID PICKED
A BAD NIGHT TO
SUDDENLY BE SEEN
AND NOT HEARD,
ALAN!
WILDCAT'S RIGHT--OBSIDIAN HAS
WITHDRAWN SO MUCH LATELY. HE
SPEAKS TO US, BUT I CAN'T RECALL
SEEING HIS HUMAN SIDE IN
SOME TIME!
ALAN, CAN
YOUR RING SHED
SOME LIGHT
ON US?
I'VE BEEN
TRYING, JESSE, BUT
OBSIDIAN'S SHADOW
POWER IS
ABSORBING IT.
SEE WHAT
I MEAN?
YOU DON'T THINK TODD'S A THREAT.
YOU'RE HOLDING BACK, ALAN. YOU
DON'T WANT TO HURT HIM.
HE AIN'T
ELPIN' HIS
CASE BY
CLAMMIN'
UP!
I'M
PROTECTING
YOU ALL FROM
A THREAT,
WILDCAT.
WHAT KIND
OF THREAT,
TODD?
I THINK
IT'S THE WORST
KIND, FLASH--
AN INVISIBLE
ONE...

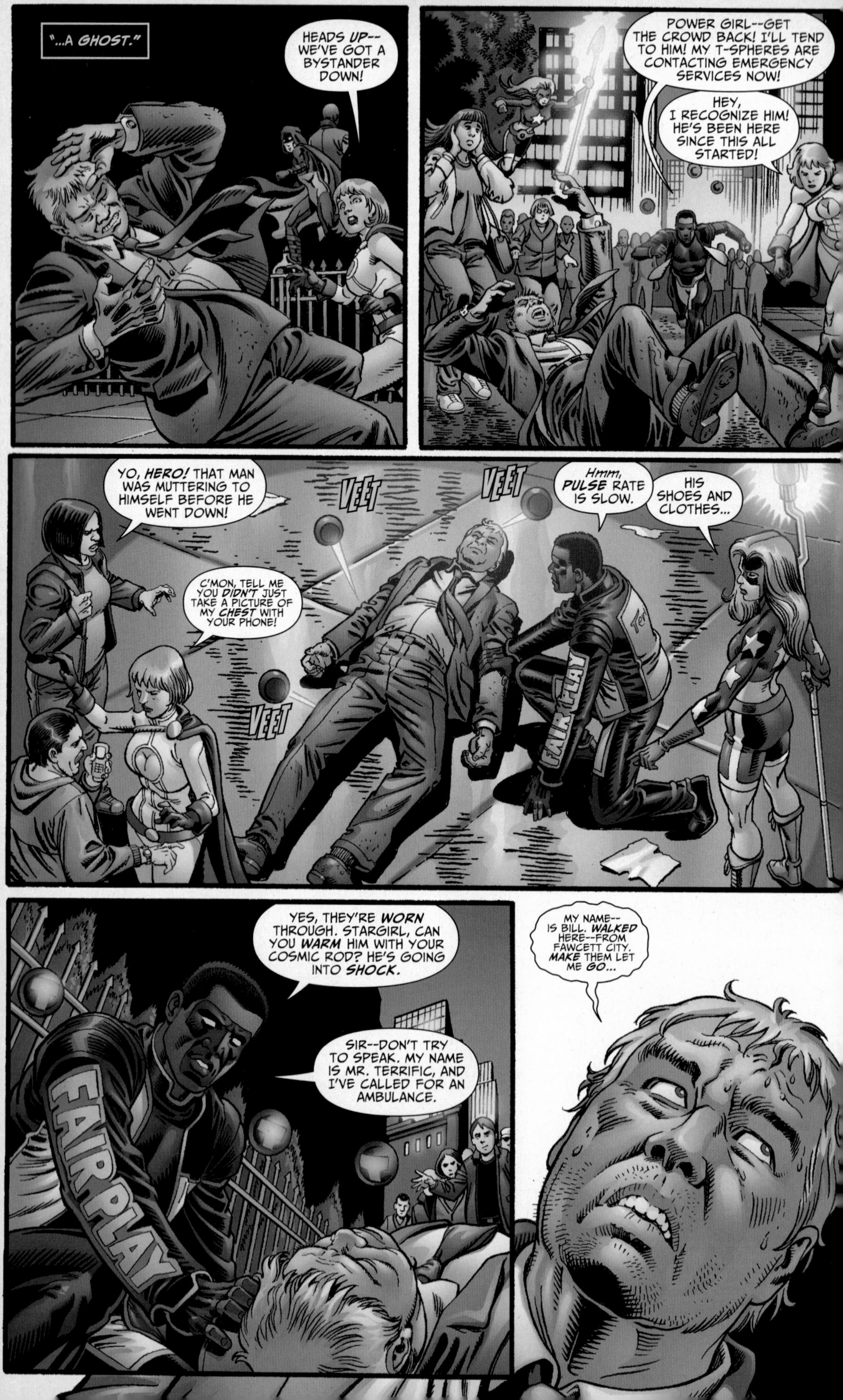
"...A GHOST."
HEADS UP--WE'VE GOT A BYSTANDER DOWN!
POWER GIRL--GET THE CROWD BACK! I'LL TEND TO HIM! MY T-SPHERES ARE CONTACTING EMERGENCY SERVICES NOW!
HEY, I RECOGNIZE HIM! HE'S BEEN HERE SINCE THIS ALL STARTED!
YO, HERO! THAT MAN WAS MUTTERING TO HIMSELF BEFORE HE WENT DOWN!
VEET
VEET
Hmm, PULSE RATE IS SLOW.
HIS SHOES AND CLOTHES...
C'MON, TELL ME YOU DIDN'T JUST TAKE A PICTURE OF MY CHEST WITH YOUR PHONE!
VEET
FAIRPLAY
YES, THEY'RE WORN THROUGH. STARGIRL, CAN YOU WARM HIM WITH YOUR COSMIC ROD? HE'S GOING INTO SHOCK.
SIR--DON'T TRY TO SPEAK. MY NAME IS MR. TERRIFIC, AND I'VE CALLED FOR AN AMBULANCE.
FAIRPLAY
MY NAME--IS BILL. WALKED HERE--FROM FAWCETT CITY. MAKE THEM LET ME GO...

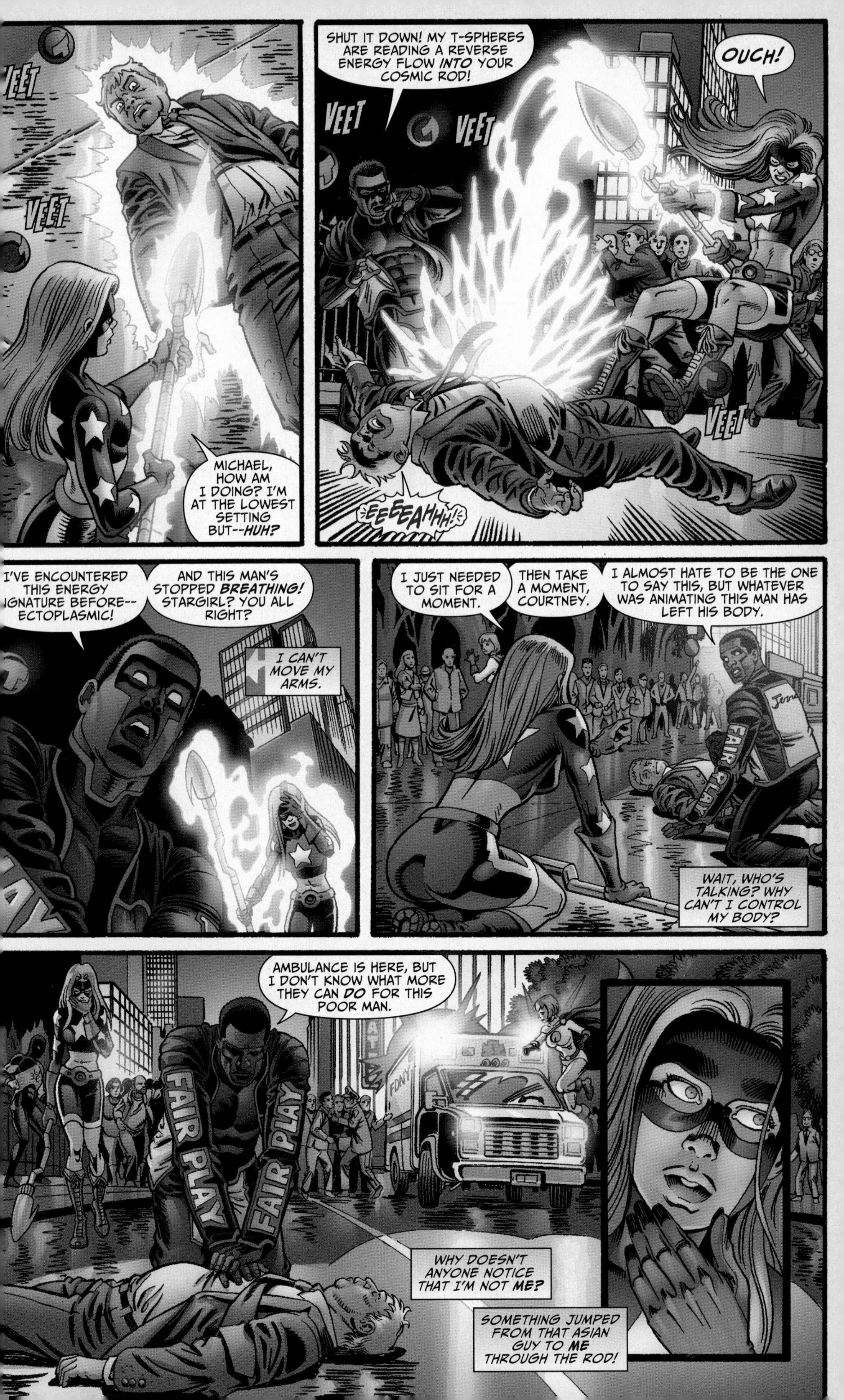
VEET
VEET
MICHAEL, HOW AM I DOING? I'M AT THE LOWEST SETTING BUT--HUH?
SHUT IT DOWN! MY T-SPHERES ARE READING A REVERSE ENERGY FLOW INTO YOUR COSMIC ROD!
VEET
VEET
OUCH!
VEET
EEEEAHHH!
I'VE ENCOUNTERED THIS ENERGY IGNATURE BEFORE-- ECTOPLASMIC!
AND THIS MAN'S STOPPED BREATHING! STARGIRL? YOU ALL RIGHT?
I CAN'T MOVE MY ARMS.
I JUST NEEDED TO SIT FOR A MOMENT.
THEN TAKE A MOMENT, COURTNEY.
I ALMOST HATE TO BE THE ONE TO SAY THIS, BUT WHATEVER WAS ANIMATING THIS MAN HAS LEFT HIS BODY.
WAIT, WHO'S TALKING? WHY CAN'T I CONTROL MY BODY?
AMBULANCE IS HERE, BUT I DON'T KNOW WHAT MORE THEY CAN DO FOR THIS POOR MAN.
FAIR PLAY
FAIR PLAY
FDNY
WHY DOESN'T ANYONE NOTICE THAT I'M NOT ME?
SOMETHING JUMPED FROM THAT ASIAN GUY TO ME THROUGH THE ROD!

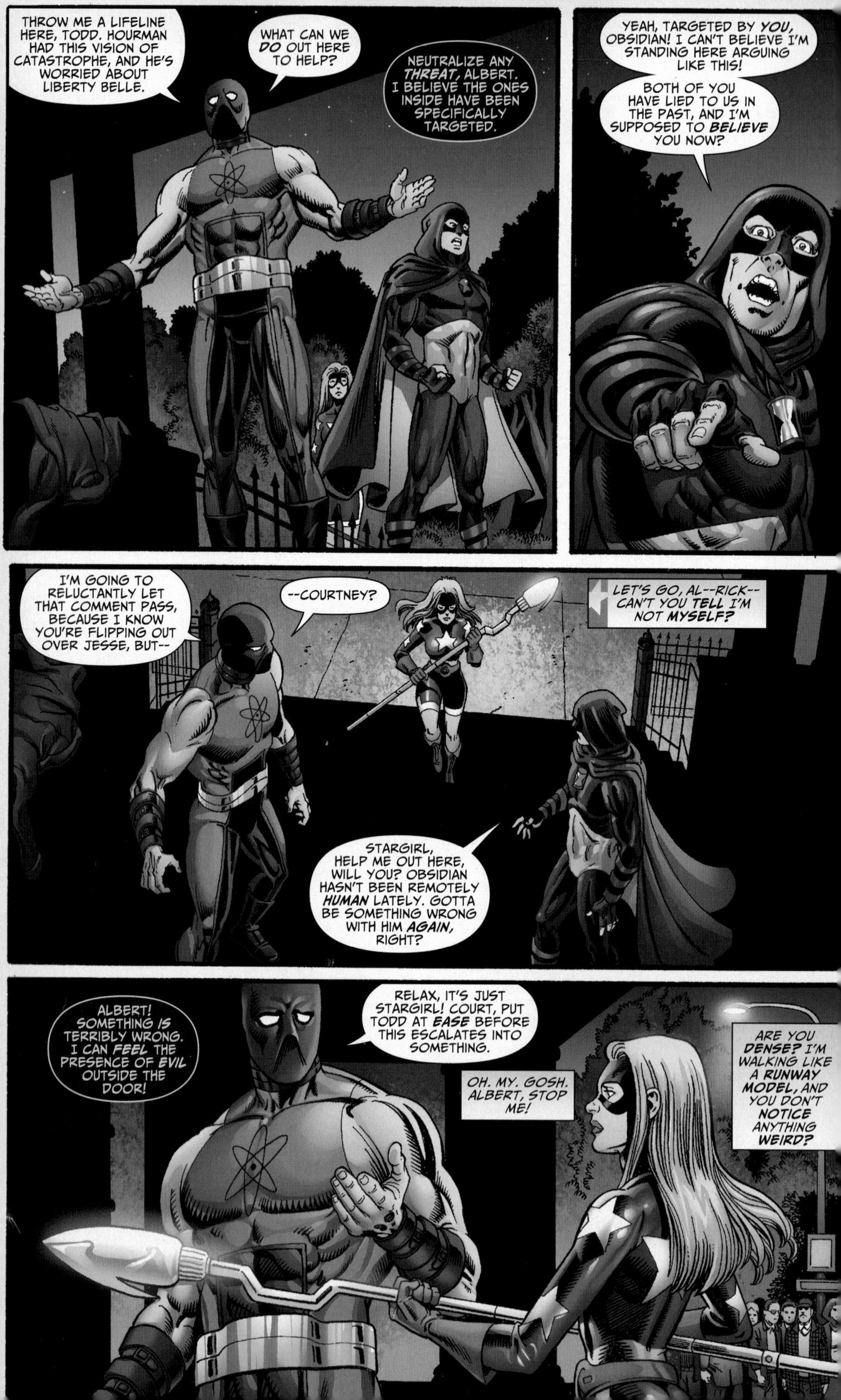

THROW ME A LIFELINE HERE, TODD. HOURMAN HAD THIS VISION OF CATASTROPHE, AND HE'S WORRIED ABOUT LIBERTY BELLE.
WHAT CAN WE DO OUT HERE TO HELP?
NEUTRALIZE ANY THREAT, ALBERT. I BELIEVE THE ONES INSIDE HAVE BEEN SPECIFICALLY TARGETED.
YEAH, TARGETED BY YOU, OBSIDIAN! I CAN'T BELIEVE I'M STANDING HERE ARGUING LIKE THIS!
BOTH OF YOU HAVE LIED TO US IN THE PAST, AND I'M SUPPOSED TO BELIEVE YOU NOW?
I'M GOING TO RELUCTANTLY LET THAT COMMENT PASS, BECAUSE I KNOW YOU'RE FLIPPING OUT OVER JESSE, BUT--
--COURTNEY?
LET'S GO, AL--RICK-- CAN'T YOU TELL I'M NOT MYSELF?
STARGIRL, HELP ME OUT HERE, WILL YOU? OBSIDIAN HASN'T BEEN REMOTELY HUMAN LATELY. GOTTA BE SOMETHING WRONG WITH HIM AGAIN, RIGHT?
ALBERT! SOMETHING IS TERRIBLY WRONG. I CAN FEEL THE PRESENCE OF EVIL OUTSIDE THE DOOR!
RELAX, IT'S JUST STARGIRL! COURT, PUT TODD AT EASE BEFORE THIS ESCALATES INTO SOMETHING.
OH. MY. GOSH. ALBERT, STOP ME!
ARE YOU DENSE? I'M WALKING LIKE A RUNWAY MODEL, AND YOU DON'T NOTICE ANYTHING WEIRD?

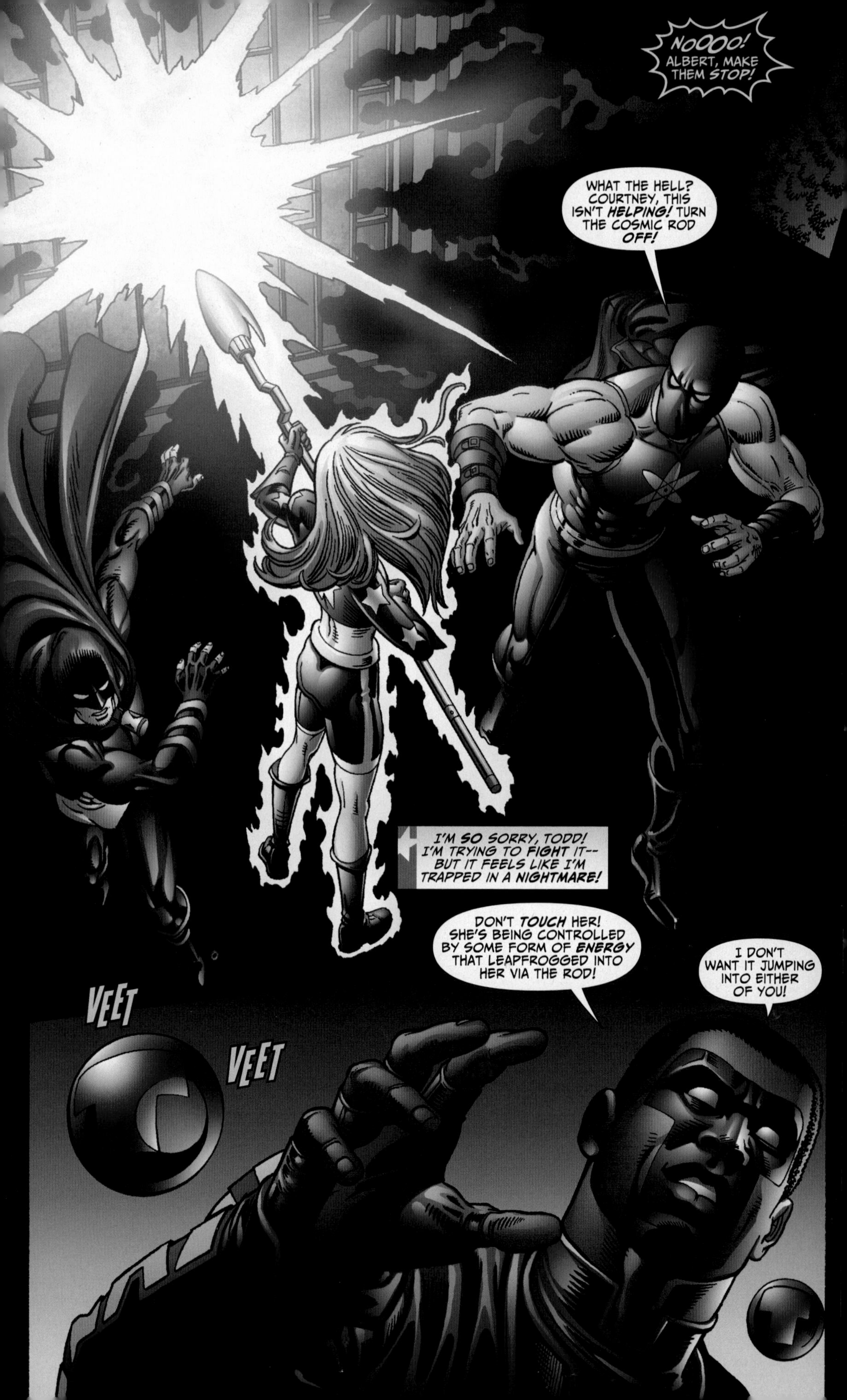
NOOOO! ALBERT, MAKE THEM STOP!
WHAT THE HELL? COURTNEY, THIS ISN'T HELPING! TURN THE COSMIC ROD OFF!
I'M SO SORRY, TODD! I'M TRYING TO FIGHT IT-- BUT IT FEELS LIKE I'M TRAPPED IN A NIGHTMARE!
DON'T TOUCH HER! SHE'S BEING CONTROLLED BY SOME FORM OF ENERGY THAT LEAPFROGGED INTO HER VIA THE ROD!
I DON'T WANT IT JUMPING INTO EITHER OF YOU!
VEET
VEET

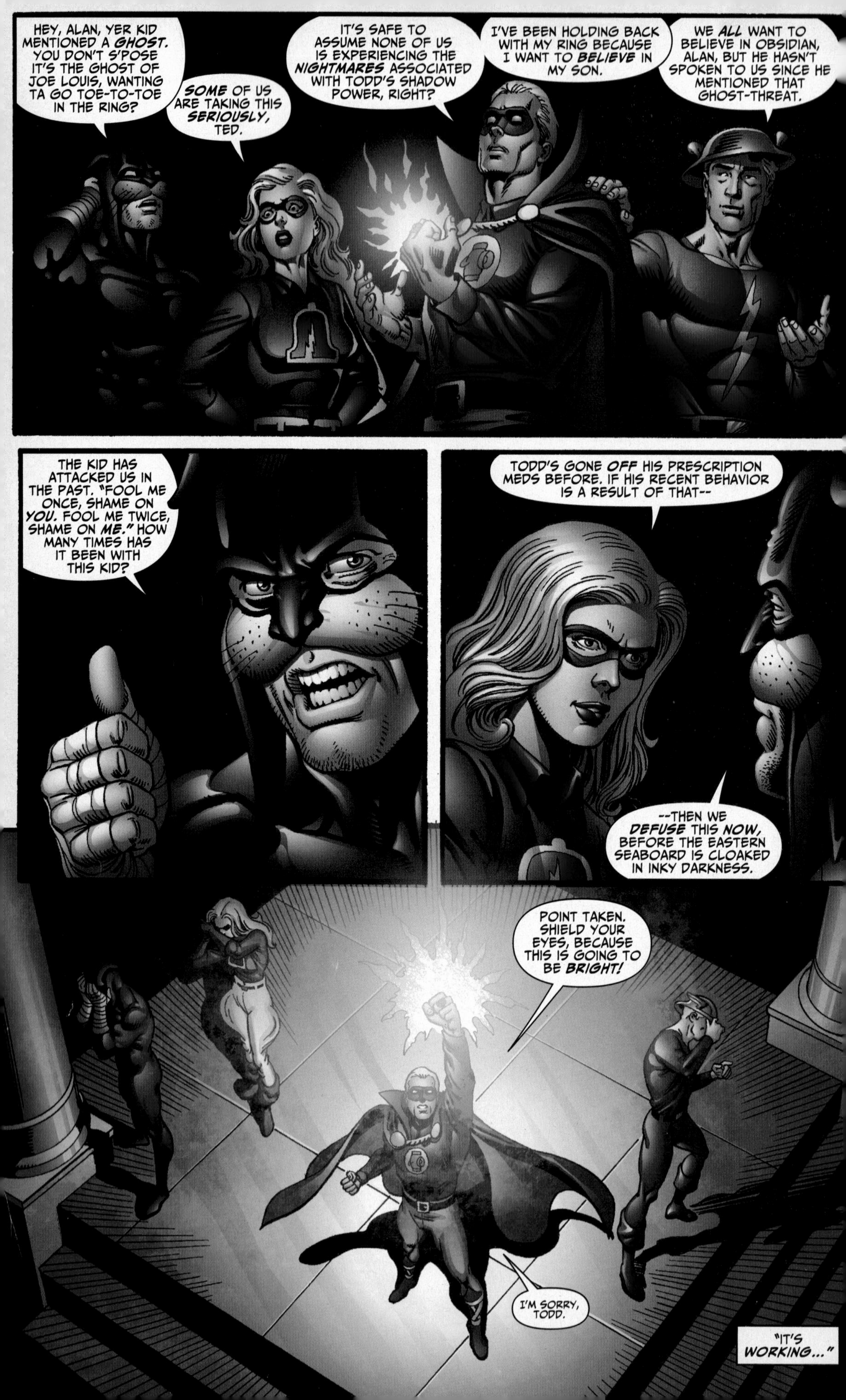
HEY, ALAN, YER KID MENTIONED A *GHOST*. YOU DON'T S'POSE IT'S THE GHOST OF JOE LOUIS, WANTING TA GO TOE-TO-TOE IN THE RING?
SOME OF US ARE TAKING THIS *SERIOUSLY*, TED.
IT'S SAFE TO ASSUME NONE OF US IS EXPERIENCING THE *NIGHTMARES* ASSOCIATED WITH TODD'S SHADOW POWER, RIGHT?
I'VE BEEN HOLDING BACK WITH MY RING BECAUSE I WANT TO *BELIEVE* IN MY SON.
WE *ALL* WANT TO BELIEVE IN OBSIDIAN, ALAN, BUT HE HASN'T SPOKEN TO US SINCE HE MENTIONED THAT GHOST-THREAT.
THE KID HAS ATTACKED US IN THE PAST. "FOOL ME ONCE, SHAME ON *YOU*. FOOL ME TWICE, SHAME ON *ME*." HOW MANY TIMES HAS IT BEEN WITH THIS KID?
TODD'S GONE *OFF* HIS PRESCRIPTION MEDS BEFORE. IF HIS RECENT BEHAVIOR IS A RESULT OF THAT--
--THEN WE *DEFUSE* THIS *NOW*, BEFORE THE EASTERN SEABOARD IS CLOAKED IN INKY DARKNESS.
POINT TAKEN. SHIELD YOUR EYES, BECAUSE THIS IS GOING TO BE *BRIGHT!*
I'M SORRY, TODD.
"IT'S *WORKING...*"

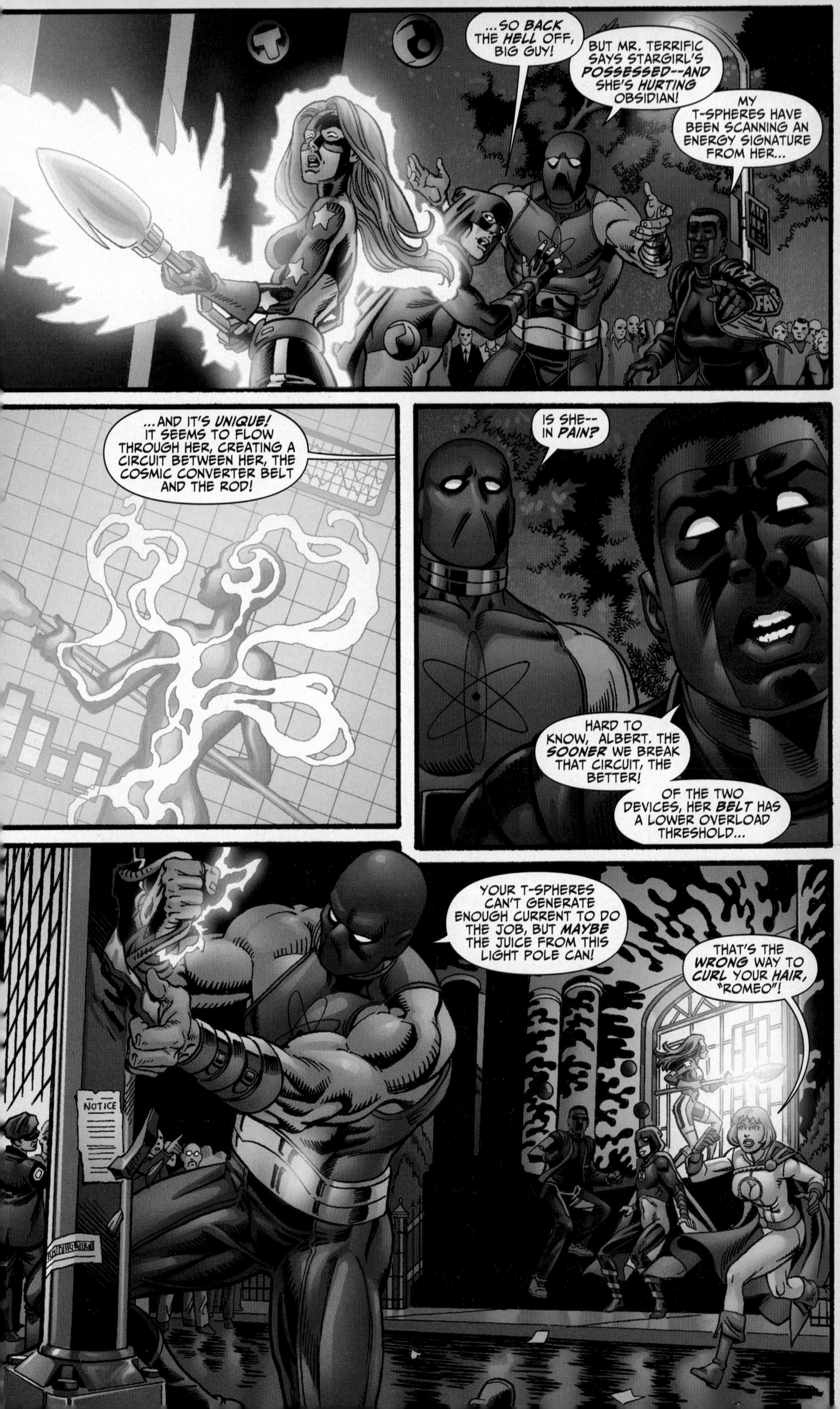
...SO BACK THE HELL OFF, BIG GUY!
BUT MR. TERRIFIC SAYS STARGIRL'S POSSESSED--AND SHE'S HURTING OBSIDIAN!
MY T-SPHERES HAVE BEEN SCANNING AN ENERGY SIGNATURE FROM HER...
...AND IT'S UNIQUE! IT SEEMS TO FLOW THROUGH HER, CREATING A CIRCUIT BETWEEN HER, THE COSMIC CONVERTER BELT AND THE ROD!
IS SHE-- IN PAIN?
HARD TO KNOW, ALBERT. THE SOONER WE BREAK THAT CIRCUIT, THE BETTER!
OF THE TWO DEVICES, HER BELT HAS A LOWER OVERLOAD THRESHOLD...
YOUR T-SPHERES CAN'T GENERATE ENOUGH CURRENT TO DO THE JOB, BUT MAYBE THE JUICE FROM THIS LIGHT POLE CAN!
THAT'S THE WRONG WAY TO CURL YOUR HAIR, "ROMEO"!
NOTICE

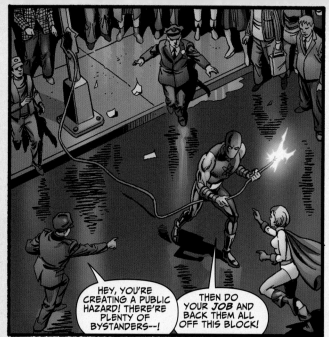

HEY, YOU'RE CREATING A PUBLIC HAZARD! THERE'RE PLENTY OF BYSTANDERS--!

THEN DO YOUR *JOB* AND BACK THEM ALL OFF THIS BLOCK!

AND WHAT'S WITH THE "ROMEO" COMMENT?

I'VE SEEN THE *WAY* YOU TWO *LOOK* AT EACH OTHER, ATOM SMASHER.

I'M BETTER EQUIPPED TO SURVIVE ELECTROCUTION. GET READY TO SWOOP IN AND CATCH YOUR FAIR MAIDEN.

THIS SHOULD TRIP THE CIRCUITS ON THE LIGHT POLE AT THE SAME TIME!

Ohhh!

ZAAMPF

I'VE GOT YOU!

THE COSMIC ROD--?

OH, ALBERT-- IT WAS HORRIBLE-- IT WAS A THOUSAND VOICES SCREAMING FOR VENGEANCE ALL AT ONCE. I WOULD HAVE GONE MAD IF YOU HADN'T STOPPED IT!

WE DIDN'T *STOP* IT...

GET READY TO CATCH IT-- THE ENERGY HAS SPREAD *OUT,* ACROSS THE BUILDING!

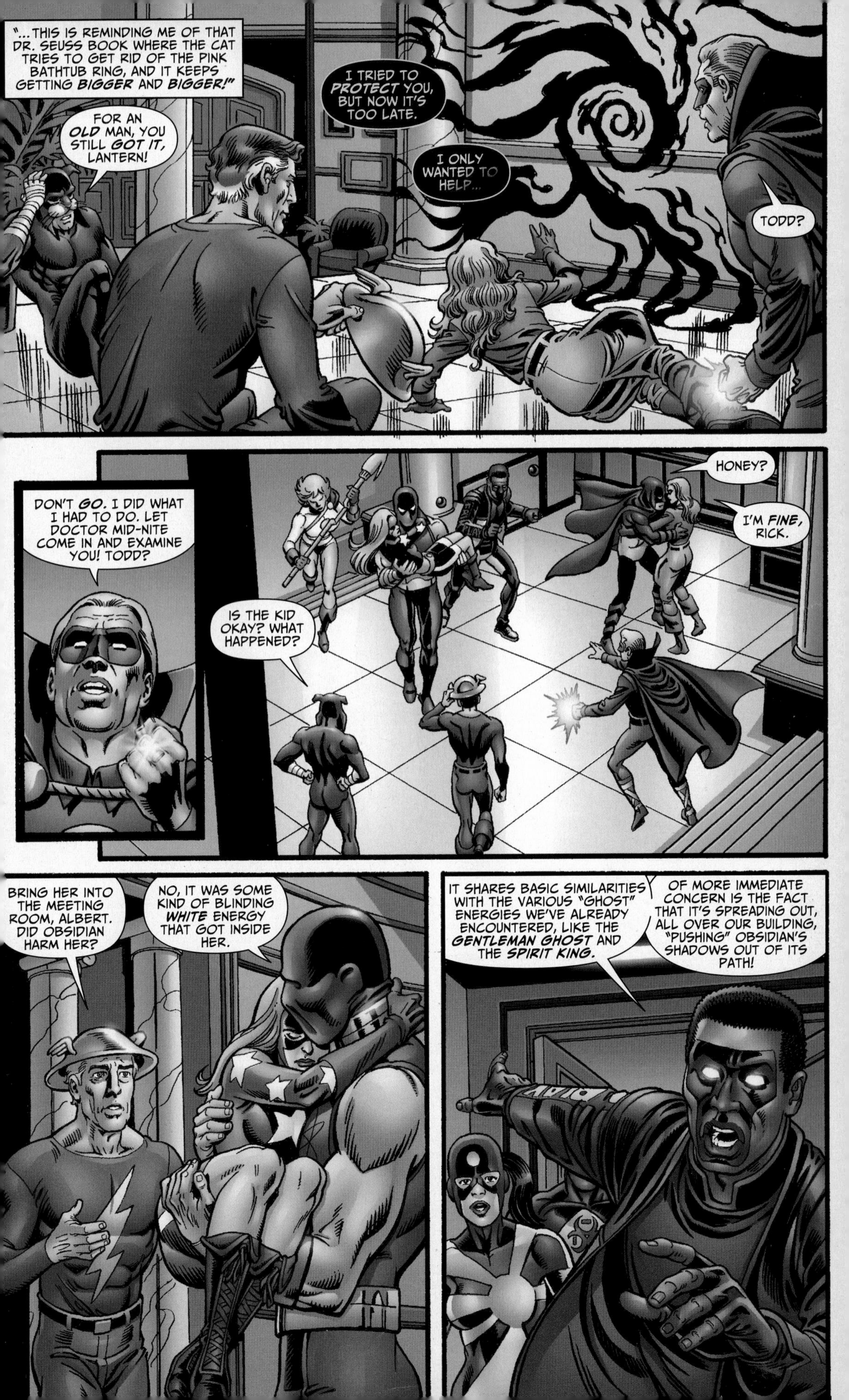
"...THIS IS REMINDING ME OF THAT DR. SEUSS BOOK WHERE THE CAT TRIES TO GET RID OF THE PINK BATHTUB RING, AND IT KEEPS GETTING BIGGER AND BIGGER!"
FOR AN OLD MAN, YOU STILL GOT IT, LANTERN!
I TRIED TO PROTECT YOU, BUT NOW IT'S TOO LATE.
I ONLY WANTED TO HELP...
TODD?
DON'T GO. I DID WHAT I HAD TO DO. LET DOCTOR MID-NITE COME IN AND EXAMINE YOU! TODD?
HONEY?
I'M FINE, RICK.
IS THE KID OKAY? WHAT HAPPENED?
BRING HER INTO THE MEETING ROOM, ALBERT. DID OBSIDIAN HARM HER?
NO, IT WAS SOME KIND OF BLINDING WHITE ENERGY THAT GOT INSIDE HER.
IT SHARES BASIC SIMILARITIES WITH THE VARIOUS "GHOST" ENERGIES WE'VE ALREADY ENCOUNTERED, LIKE THE GENTLEMAN GHOST AND THE SPIRIT KING.
OF MORE IMMEDIATE CONCERN IS THE FACT THAT IT'S SPREADING OUT, ALL OVER OUR BUILDING, "PUSHING" OBSIDIAN'S SHADOWS OUT OF ITS PATH!

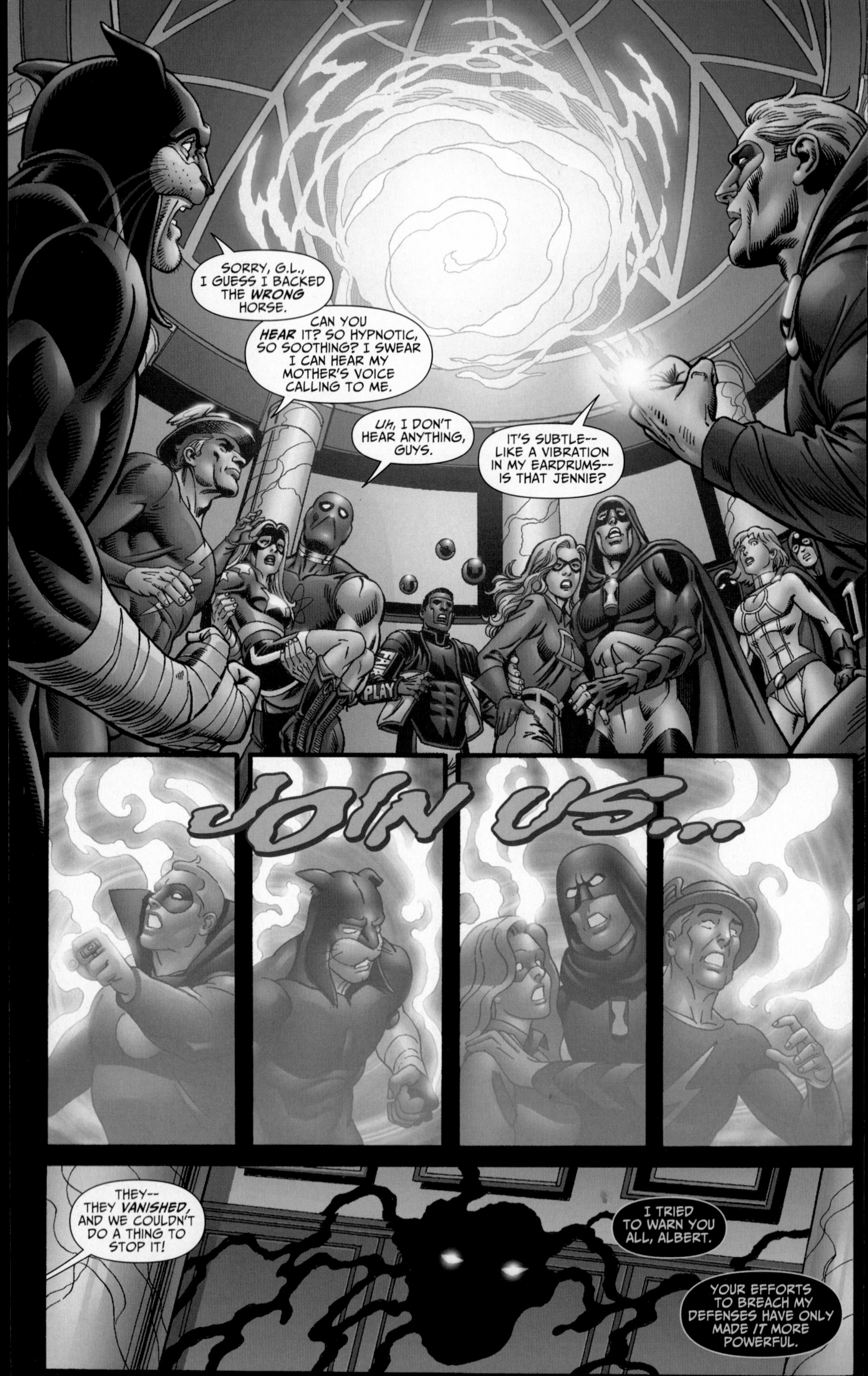
SORRY, G.L., I GUESS I BACKED THE WRONG HORSE.
CAN YOU HEAR IT? SO HYPNOTIC, SO SOOTHING? I SWEAR I CAN HEAR MY MOTHER'S VOICE CALLING TO ME.
Uh, I DON'T HEAR ANYTHING, GUYS.
IT'S SUBTLE-- LIKE A VIBRATION IN MY EARDRUMS-- IS THAT JENNIE?
FAIR PLAY
JOIN US...
THEY-- THEY VANISHED, AND WE COULDN'T DO A THING TO STOP IT!
I TRIED TO WARN YOU ALL, ALBERT.
YOUR EFFORTS TO BREACH MY DEFENSES HAVE ONLY MADE IT MORE POWERFUL.

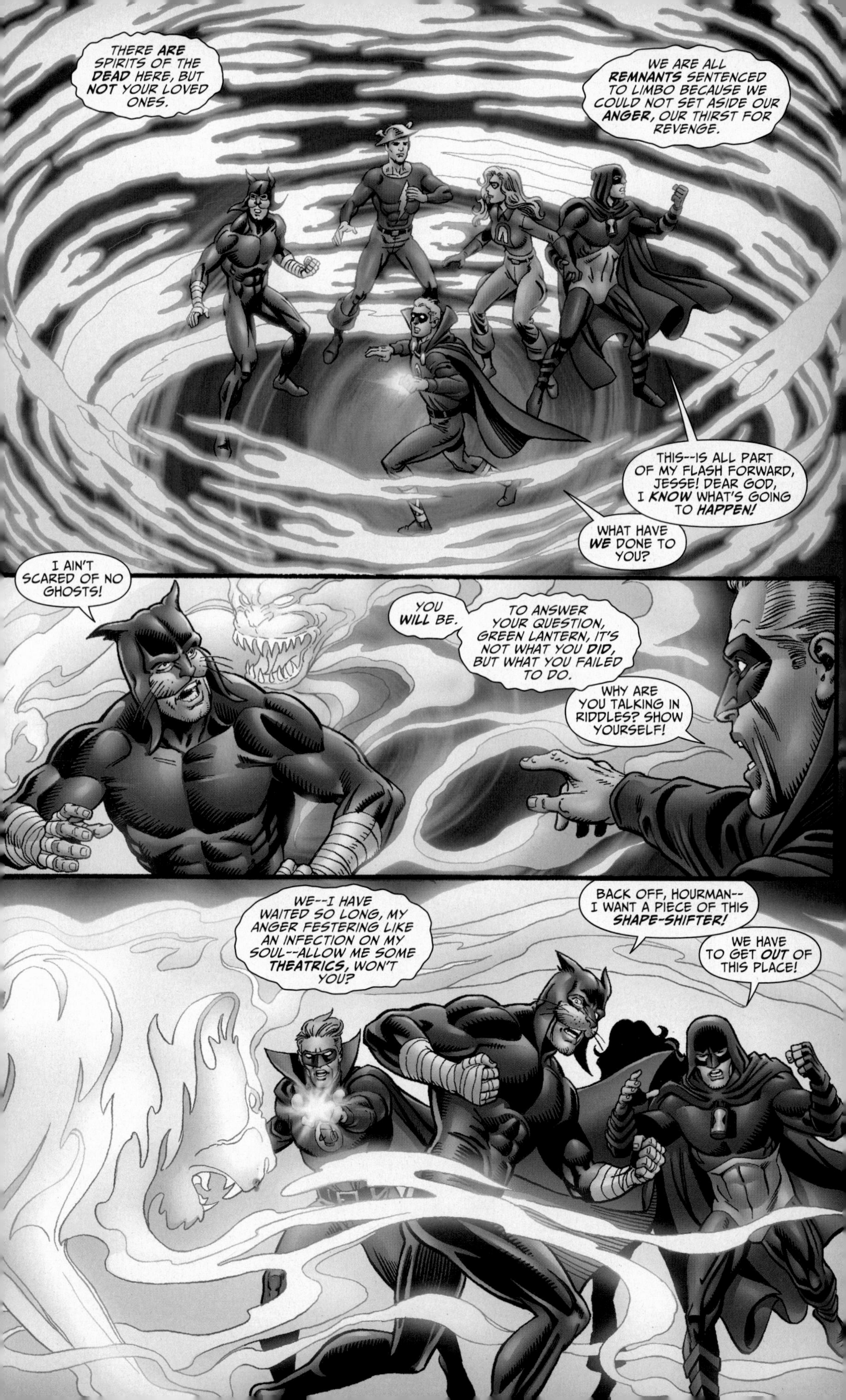
THERE ARE SPIRITS OF THE DEAD HERE, BUT NOT YOUR LOVED ONES.
WE ARE ALL REMNANTS SENTENCED TO LIMBO BECAUSE WE COULD NOT SET ASIDE OUR ANGER, OUR THIRST FOR REVENGE.
THIS--IS ALL PART OF MY FLASH FORWARD, JESSE! DEAR GOD, I KNOW WHAT'S GOING TO HAPPEN!
WHAT HAVE WE DONE TO YOU?
I AIN'T SCARED OF NO GHOSTS!
YOU WILL BE.
TO ANSWER YOUR QUESTION, GREEN LANTERN, IT'S NOT WHAT YOU DID, BUT WHAT YOU FAILED TO DO.
WHY ARE YOU TALKING IN RIDDLES? SHOW YOURSELF!
WE--I HAVE WAITED SO LONG, MY ANGER FESTERING LIKE AN INFECTION ON MY SOUL--ALLOW ME SOME THEATRICS, WON'T YOU?
BACK OFF, HOURMAN-- I WANT A PIECE OF THIS SHAPE-SHIFTER!
WE HAVE TO GET OUT OF THIS PLACE!

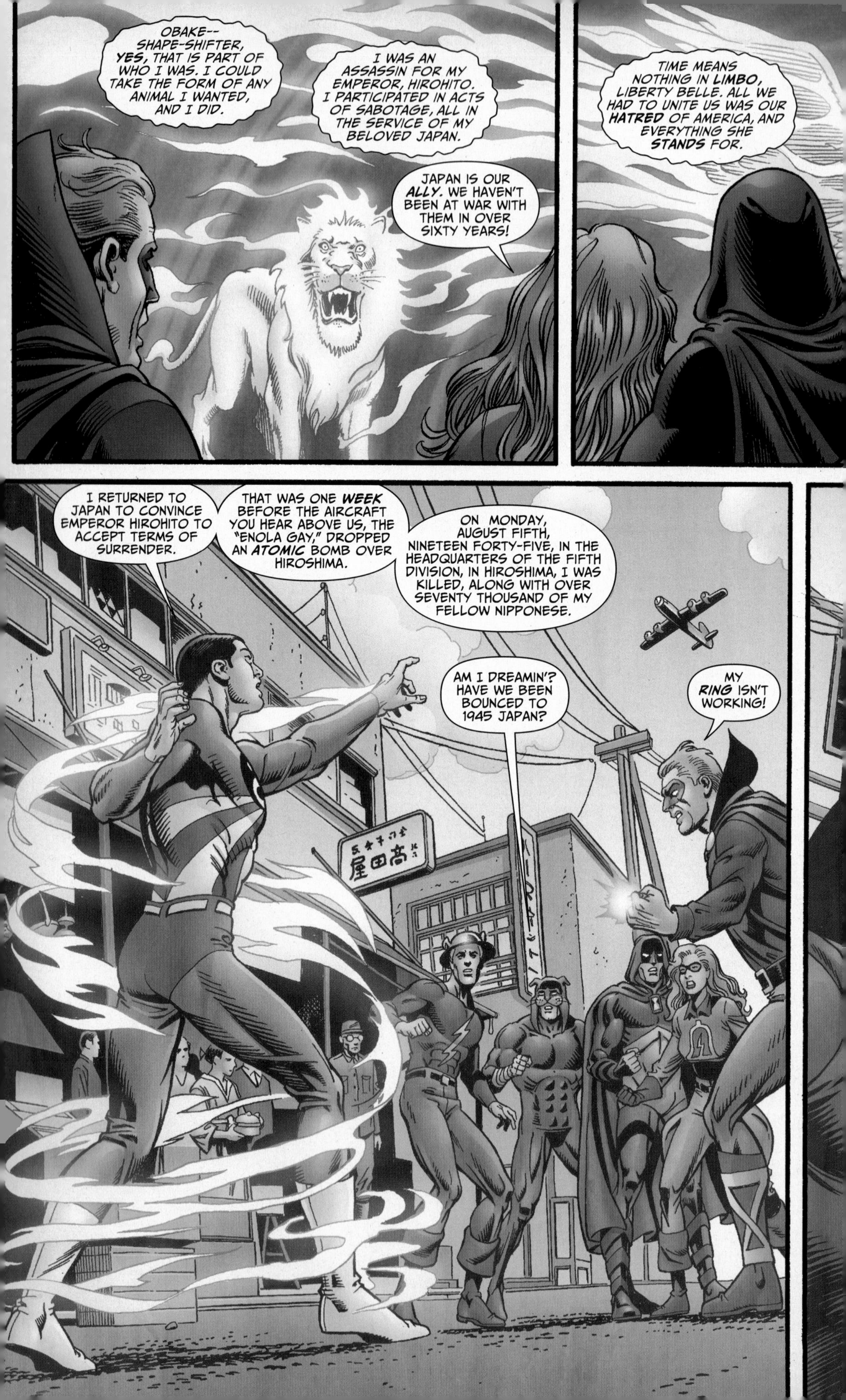
OBAKE-- SHAPE-SHIFTER, YES, THAT IS PART OF WHO I WAS. I COULD TAKE THE FORM OF ANY ANIMAL I WANTED, AND I DID.
I WAS AN ASSASSIN FOR MY EMPEROR, HIROHITO. I PARTICIPATED IN ACTS OF SABOTAGE, ALL IN THE SERVICE OF MY BELOVED JAPAN.
JAPAN IS OUR ALLY. WE HAVEN'T BEEN AT WAR WITH THEM IN OVER SIXTY YEARS!
TIME MEANS NOTHING IN LIMBO, LIBERTY BELLE. ALL WE HAD TO UNITE US WAS OUR HATRED OF AMERICA, AND EVERYTHING SHE STANDS FOR.
I RETURNED TO JAPAN TO CONVINCE EMPEROR HIROHITO TO ACCEPT TERMS OF SURRENDER.
THAT WAS ONE WEEK BEFORE THE AIRCRAFT YOU HEAR ABOVE US, THE "ENOLA GAY," DROPPED AN ATOMIC BOMB OVER HIROSHIMA.
ON MONDAY, AUGUST FIFTH, NINETEEN FORTY-FIVE, IN THE HEADQUARTERS OF THE FIFTH DIVISION, IN HIROSHIMA, I WAS KILLED, ALONG WITH OVER SEVENTY THOUSAND OF MY FELLOW NIPPONESE.
AM I DREAMIN'? HAVE WE BEEN BOUNCED TO 1945 JAPAN?
MY RING ISN'T WORKING!

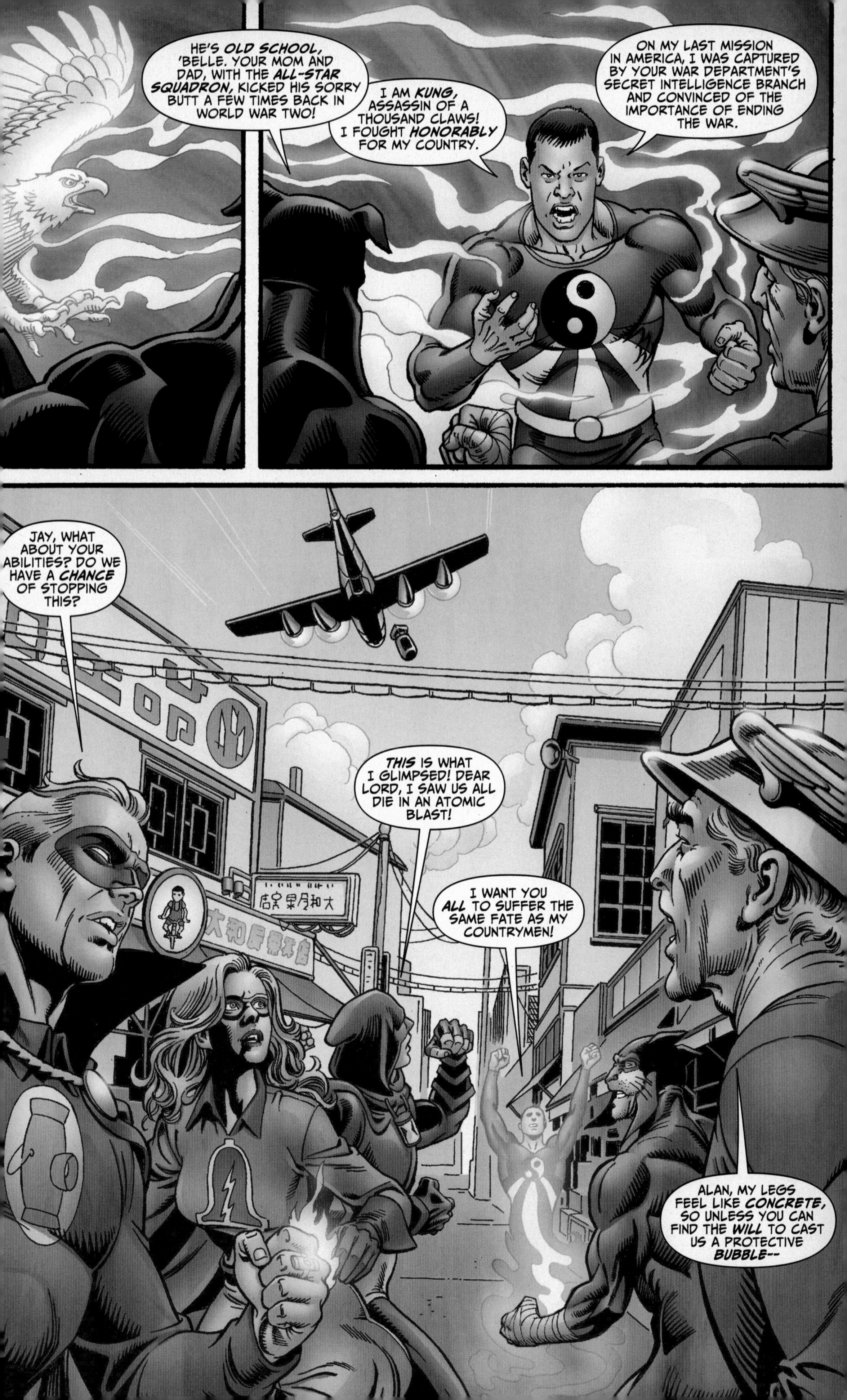
HE'S OLD SCHOOL, 'BELLE. YOUR MOM AND DAD, WITH THE ALL-STAR SQUADRON, KICKED HIS SORRY BUTT A FEW TIMES BACK IN WORLD WAR TWO!
I AM KUNG, ASSASSIN OF A THOUSAND CLAWS! I FOUGHT HONORABLY FOR MY COUNTRY.
ON MY LAST MISSION IN AMERICA, I WAS CAPTURED BY YOUR WAR DEPARTMENT'S SECRET INTELLIGENCE BRANCH AND CONVINCED OF THE IMPORTANCE OF ENDING THE WAR.
JAY, WHAT ABOUT YOUR ABILITIES? DO WE HAVE A CHANCE OF STOPPING THIS?
THIS IS WHAT I GLIMPSED! DEAR LORD, I SAW US ALL DIE IN AN ATOMIC BLAST!
I WANT YOU ALL TO SUFFER THE SAME FATE AS MY COUNTRYMEN!
ALAN, MY LEGS FEEL LIKE CONCRETE, SO UNLESS YOU CAN FIND THE WILL TO CAST US A PROTECTIVE BUBBLE--

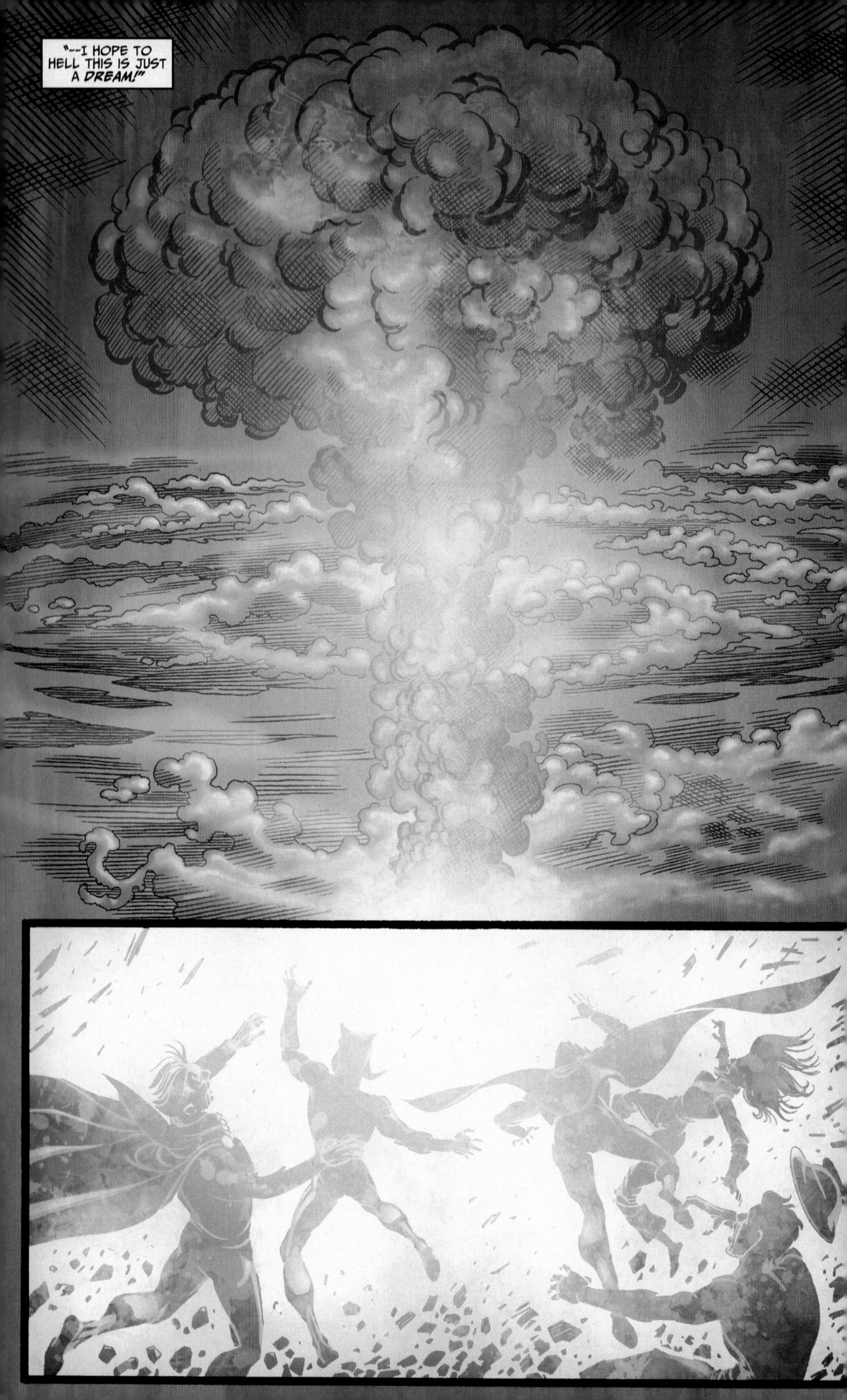
"--I HOPE TO HELL THIS IS JUST A DREAM!"

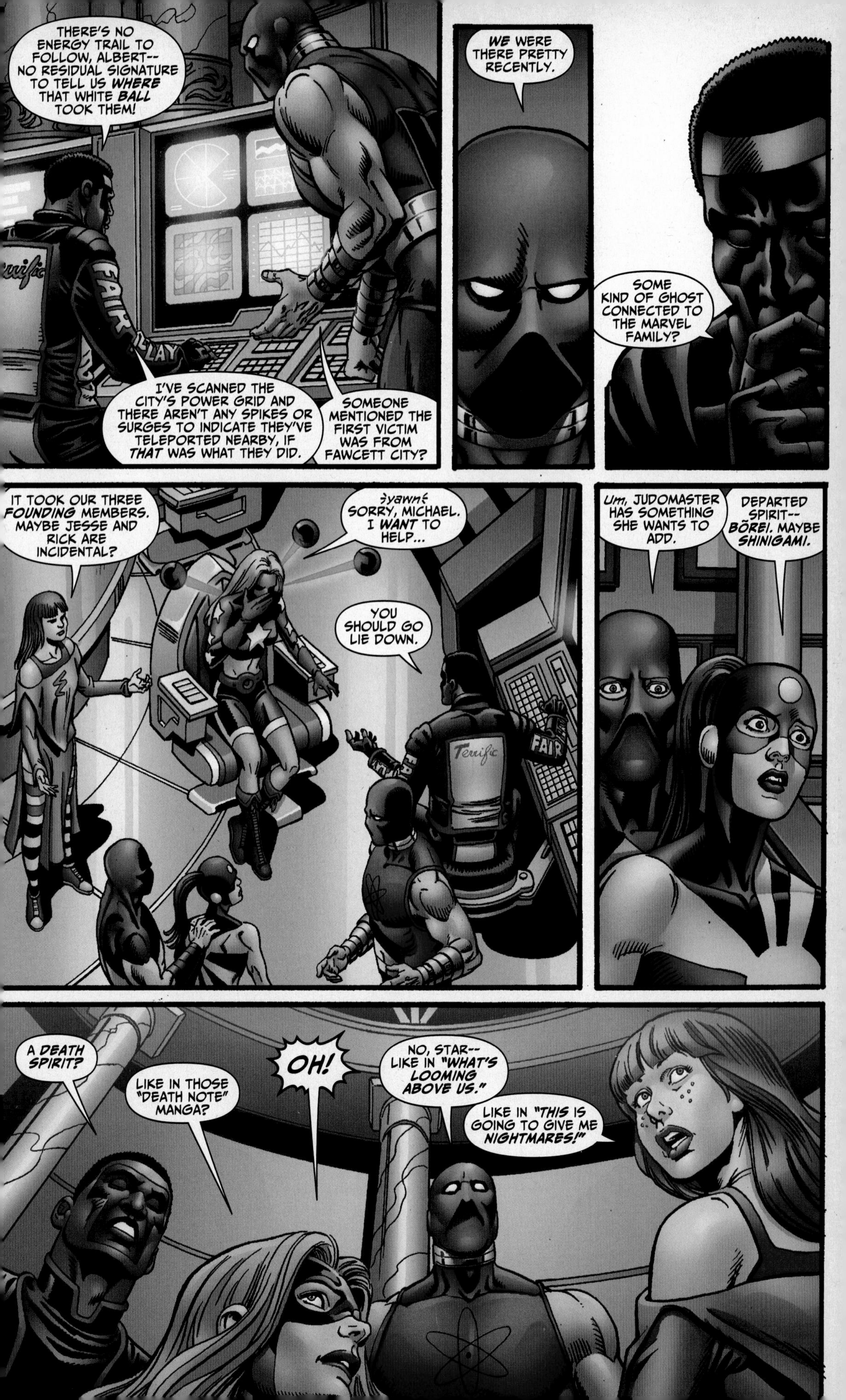
THERE'S NO ENERGY TRAIL TO FOLLOW, ALBERT-- NO RESIDUAL SIGNATURE TO TELL US WHERE THAT WHITE BALL TOOK THEM!
I'VE SCANNED THE CITY'S POWER GRID AND THERE AREN'T ANY SPIKES OR SURGES TO INDICATE THEY'VE TELEPORTED NEARBY, IF THAT WAS WHAT THEY DID.
SOMEONE MENTIONED THE FIRST VICTIM WAS FROM FAWCETT CITY?
WE WERE THERE PRETTY RECENTLY.
SOME KIND OF GHOST CONNECTED TO THE MARVEL FAMILY?
IT TOOK OUR THREE FOUNDING MEMBERS. MAYBE JESSE AND RICK ARE INCIDENTAL?
yawn SORRY, MICHAEL. I WANT TO HELP...
YOU SHOULD GO LIE DOWN.
Um, JUDOMASTER HAS SOMETHING SHE WANTS TO ADD.
DEPARTED SPIRIT-- BŌREI. MAYBE SHINIGAMI.
A DEATH SPIRIT?
LIKE IN THOSE "DEATH NOTE" MANGA?
OH!
NO, STAR-- LIKE IN "WHAT'S LOOMING ABOVE US."
LIKE IN "THIS IS GOING TO GIVE ME NIGHTMARES!"

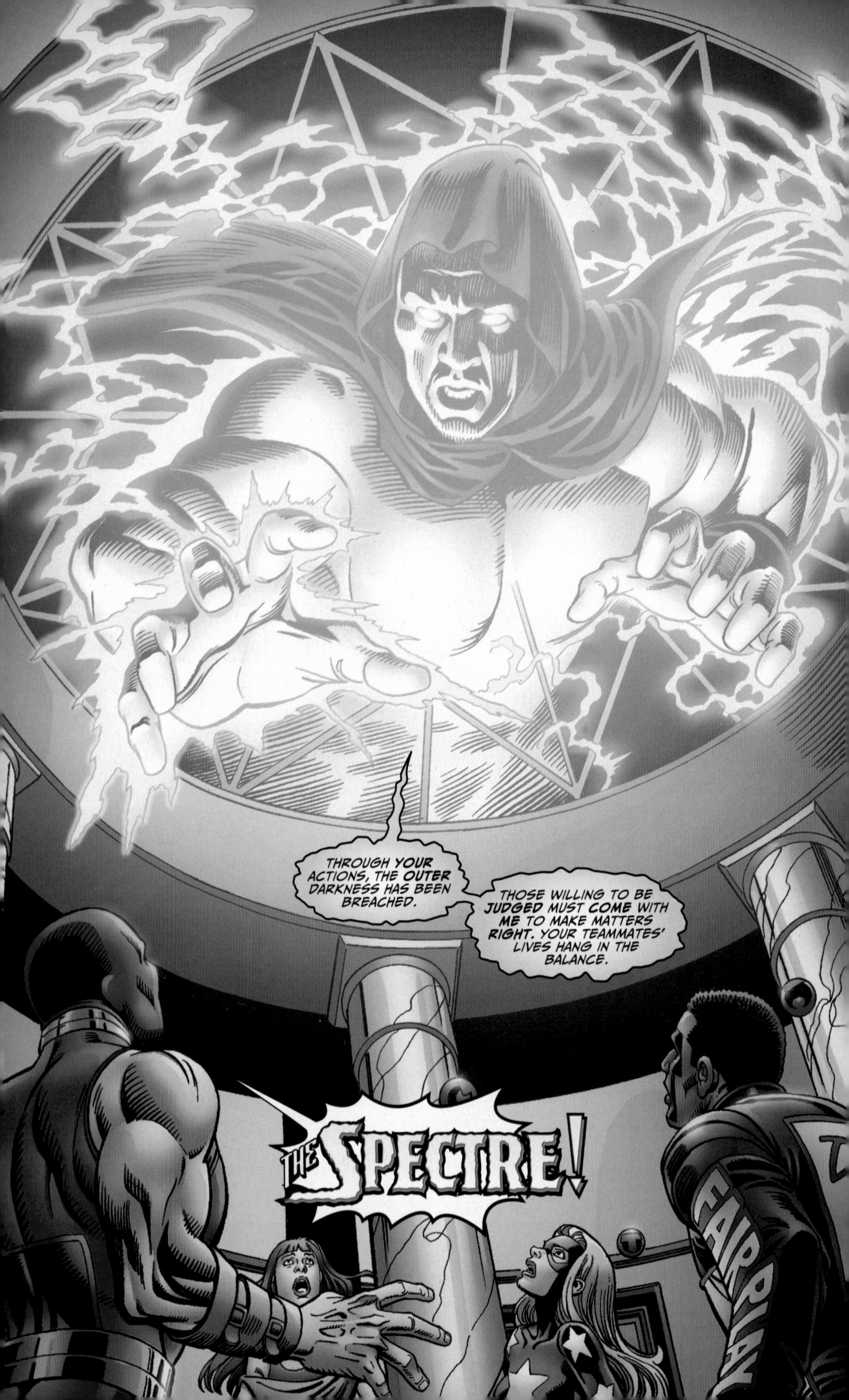
THROUGH YOUR ACTIONS, THE OUTER DARKNESS HAS BEEN BREACHED.
THOSE WILLING TO BE JUDGED MUST COME WITH ME TO MAKE MATTERS RIGHT. YOUR TEAMMATES' LIVES HANG IN THE BALANCE.
THE SPECTRE!
FAIRPLAY

JUSTICE SOCIETY OF AMERICA #28 cover by Jerry Ordway
Interior art by Ordway & Bob Wiacek

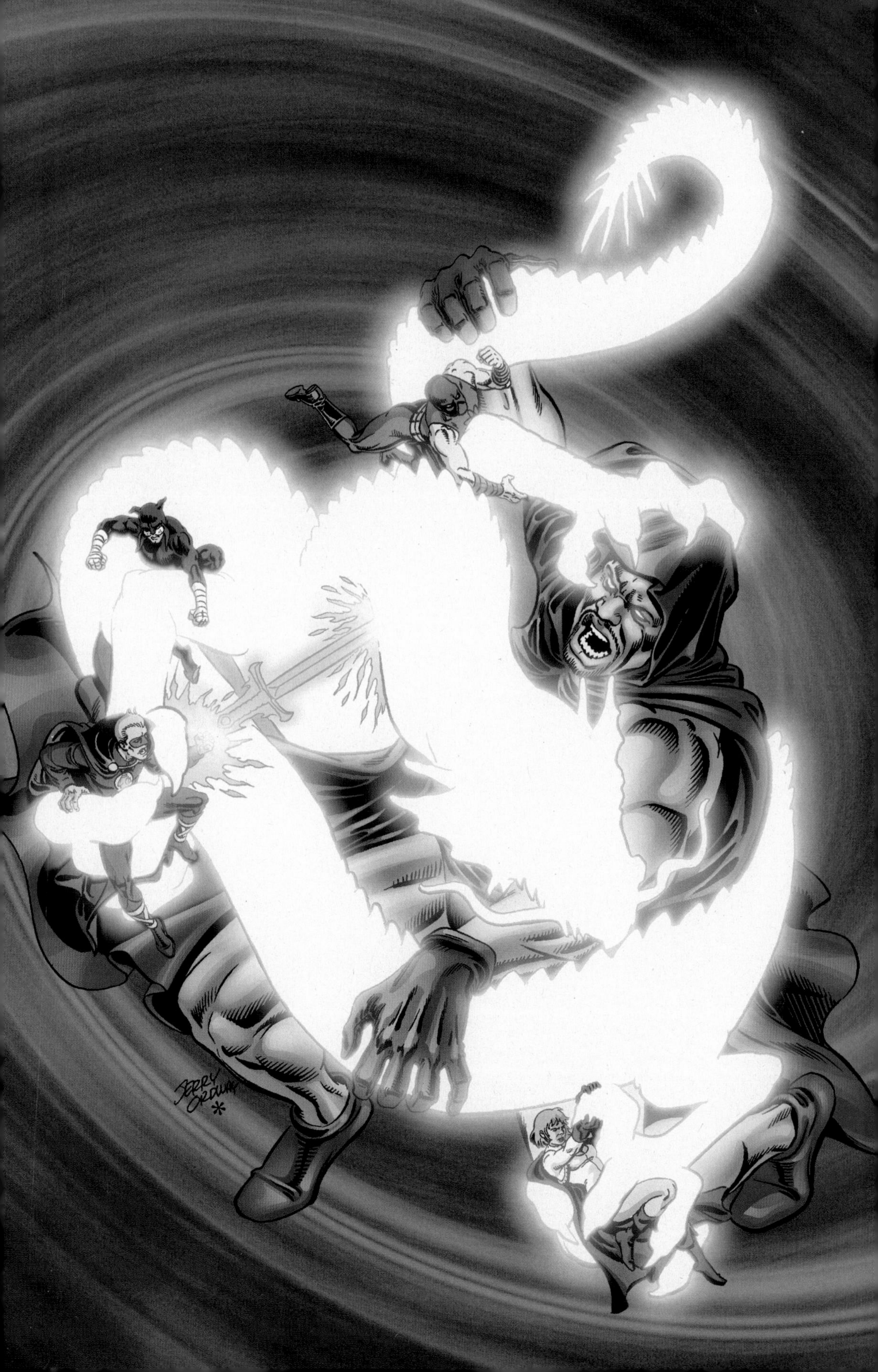
JERRY ORDWAY

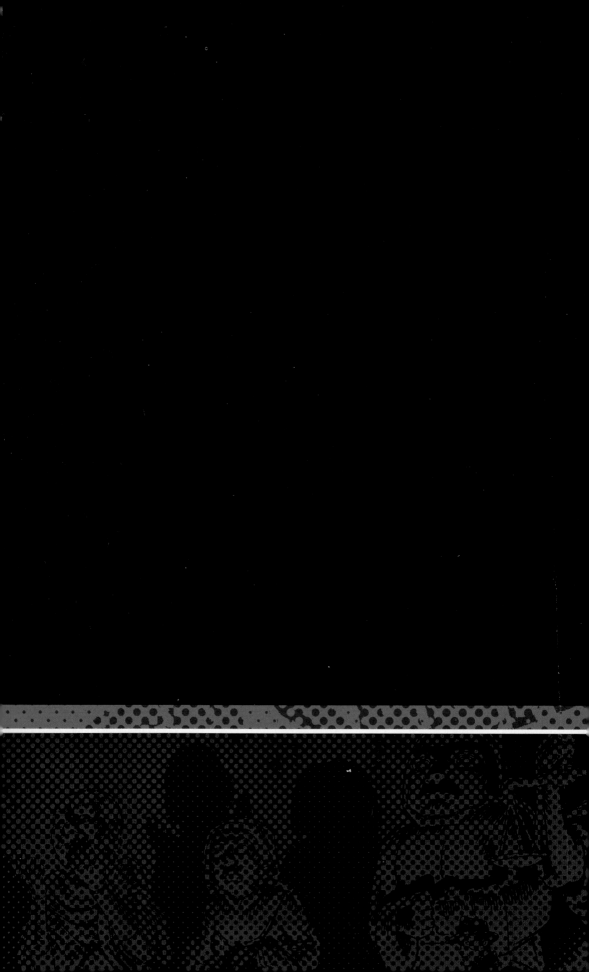

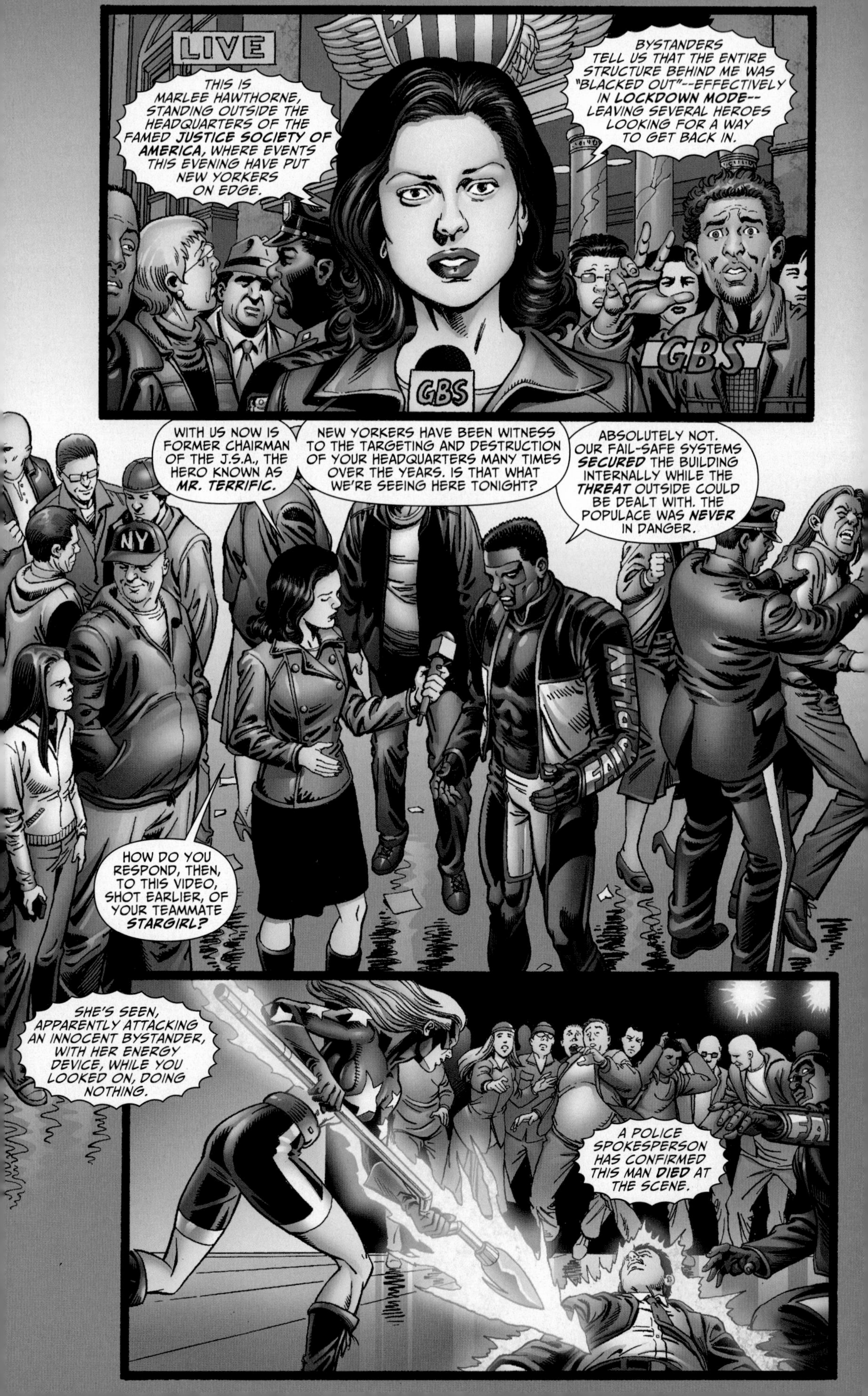
LIVE
THIS IS MARLEE HAWTHORNE, STANDING OUTSIDE THE HEADQUARTERS OF THE FAMED JUSTICE SOCIETY OF AMERICA, WHERE EVENTS THIS EVENING HAVE PUT NEW YORKERS ON EDGE.
BYSTANDERS TELL US THAT THE ENTIRE STRUCTURE BEHIND ME WAS "BLACKED OUT"--EFFECTIVELY IN LOCKDOWN MODE-- LEAVING SEVERAL HEROES LOOKING FOR A WAY TO GET BACK IN.
GBS
GBS
WITH US NOW IS FORMER CHAIRMAN OF THE J.S.A., THE HERO KNOWN AS MR. TERRIFIC.
NEW YORKERS HAVE BEEN WITNESS TO THE TARGETING AND DESTRUCTION OF YOUR HEADQUARTERS MANY TIMES OVER THE YEARS. IS THAT WHAT WE'RE SEEING HERE TONIGHT?
ABSOLUTELY NOT. OUR FAIL-SAFE SYSTEMS SECURED THE BUILDING INTERNALLY WHILE THE THREAT OUTSIDE COULD BE DEALT WITH. THE POPULACE WAS NEVER IN DANGER.
NY
FAIR PLAY
HOW DO YOU RESPOND, THEN, TO THIS VIDEO, SHOT EARLIER, OF YOUR TEAMMATE STARGIRL?
SHE'S SEEN, APPARENTLY ATTACKING AN INNOCENT BYSTANDER, WITH HER ENERGY DEVICE, WHILE YOU LOOKED ON, DOING NOTHING.
A POLICE SPOKESPERSON HAS CONFIRMED THIS MAN DIED AT THE SCENE.

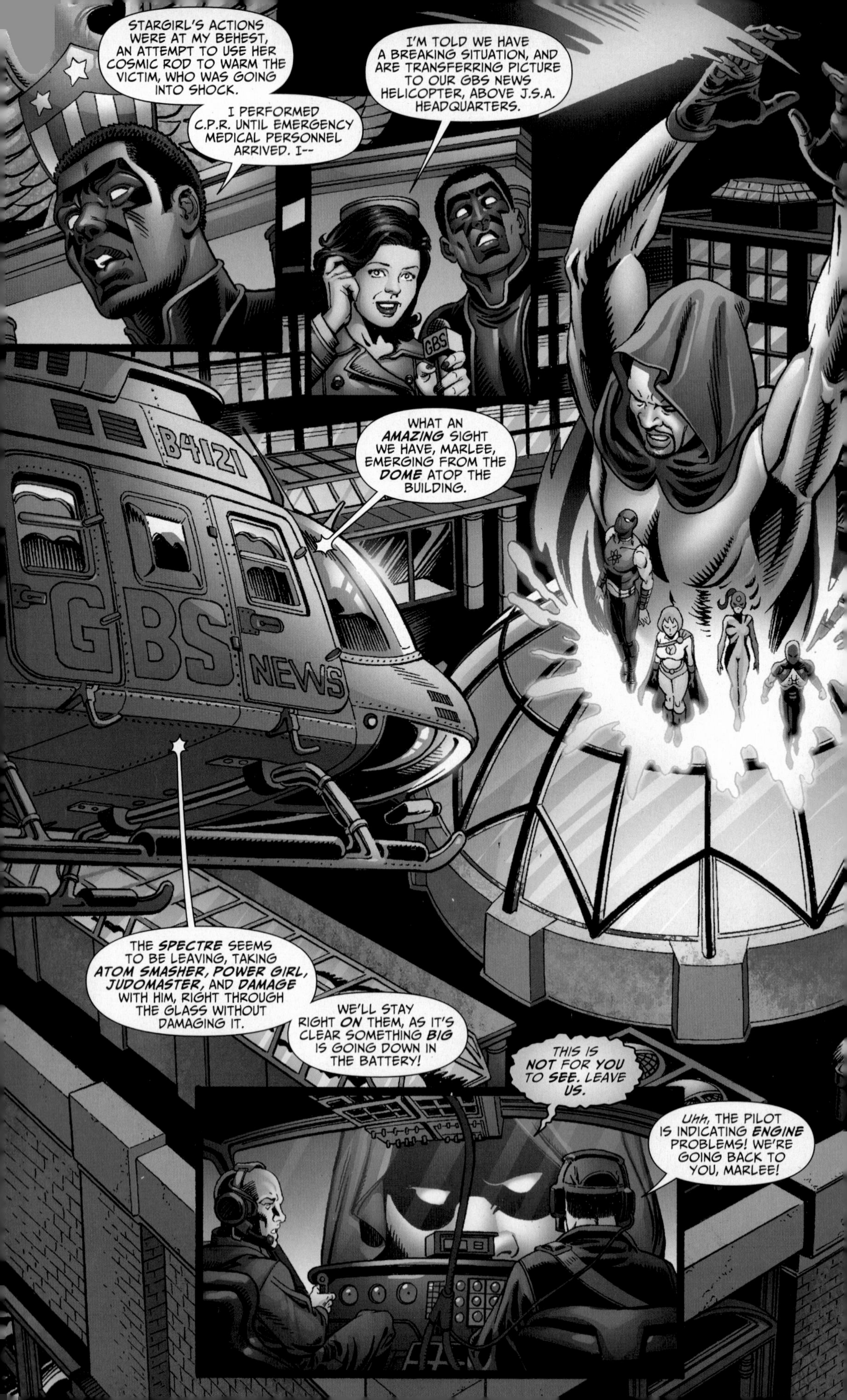
STARGIRL'S ACTIONS WERE AT MY BEHEST, AN ATTEMPT TO USE HER COSMIC ROD TO WARM THE VICTIM, WHO WAS GOING INTO SHOCK.
I PERFORMED C.P.R. UNTIL EMERGENCY MEDICAL PERSONNEL ARRIVED. I--
I'M TOLD WE HAVE A BREAKING SITUATION, AND ARE TRANSFERRING PICTURE TO OUR GBS NEWS HELICOPTER, ABOVE J.S.A. HEADQUARTERS.
GBS
B4121
GBS NEWS
WHAT AN AMAZING SIGHT WE HAVE, MARLEE, EMERGING FROM THE DOME ATOP THE BUILDING.
THE SPECTRE SEEMS TO BE LEAVING, TAKING ATOM SMASHER, POWER GIRL, JUDOMASTER, AND DAMAGE WITH HIM, RIGHT THROUGH THE GLASS WITHOUT DAMAGING IT.
WE'LL STAY RIGHT ON THEM, AS IT'S CLEAR SOMETHING BIG IS GOING DOWN IN THE BATTERY!
THIS IS NOT FOR YOU TO SEE. LEAVE US.
Uhh, THE PILOT IS INDICATING ENGINE PROBLEMS! WE'RE GOING BACK TO YOU, MARLEE!

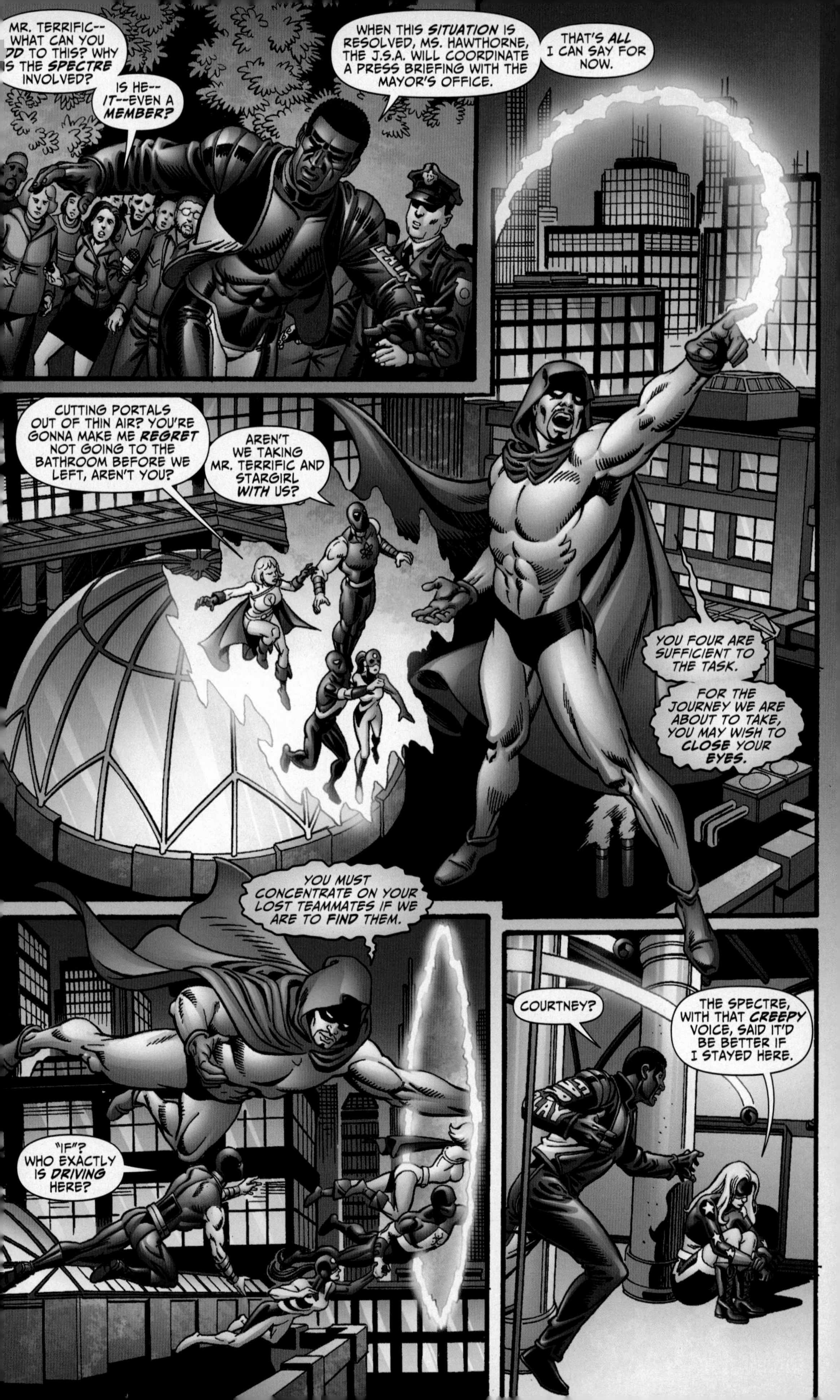
MR. TERRIFIC-- WHAT CAN YOU DD TO THIS? WHY IS THE SPECTRE INVOLVED?
IS HE-- IT--EVEN A MEMBER?
WHEN THIS SITUATION IS RESOLVED, MS. HAWTHORNE, THE J.S.A. WILL COORDINATE A PRESS BRIEFING WITH THE MAYOR'S OFFICE.
THAT'S ALL I CAN SAY FOR NOW.
CUTTING PORTALS OUT OF THIN AIR? YOU'RE GONNA MAKE ME REGRET NOT GOING TO THE BATHROOM BEFORE WE LEFT, AREN'T YOU?
AREN'T WE TAKING MR. TERRIFIC AND STARGIRL WITH US?
YOU FOUR ARE SUFFICIENT TO THE TASK.
FOR THE JOURNEY WE ARE ABOUT TO TAKE, YOU MAY WISH TO CLOSE YOUR EYES.
YOU MUST CONCENTRATE ON YOUR LOST TEAMMATES IF WE ARE TO FIND THEM.
"IF"? WHO EXACTLY IS DRIVING HERE?
COURTNEY?
THE SPECTRE, WITH THAT CREEPY VOICE, SAID IT'D BE BETTER IF I STAYED HERE.

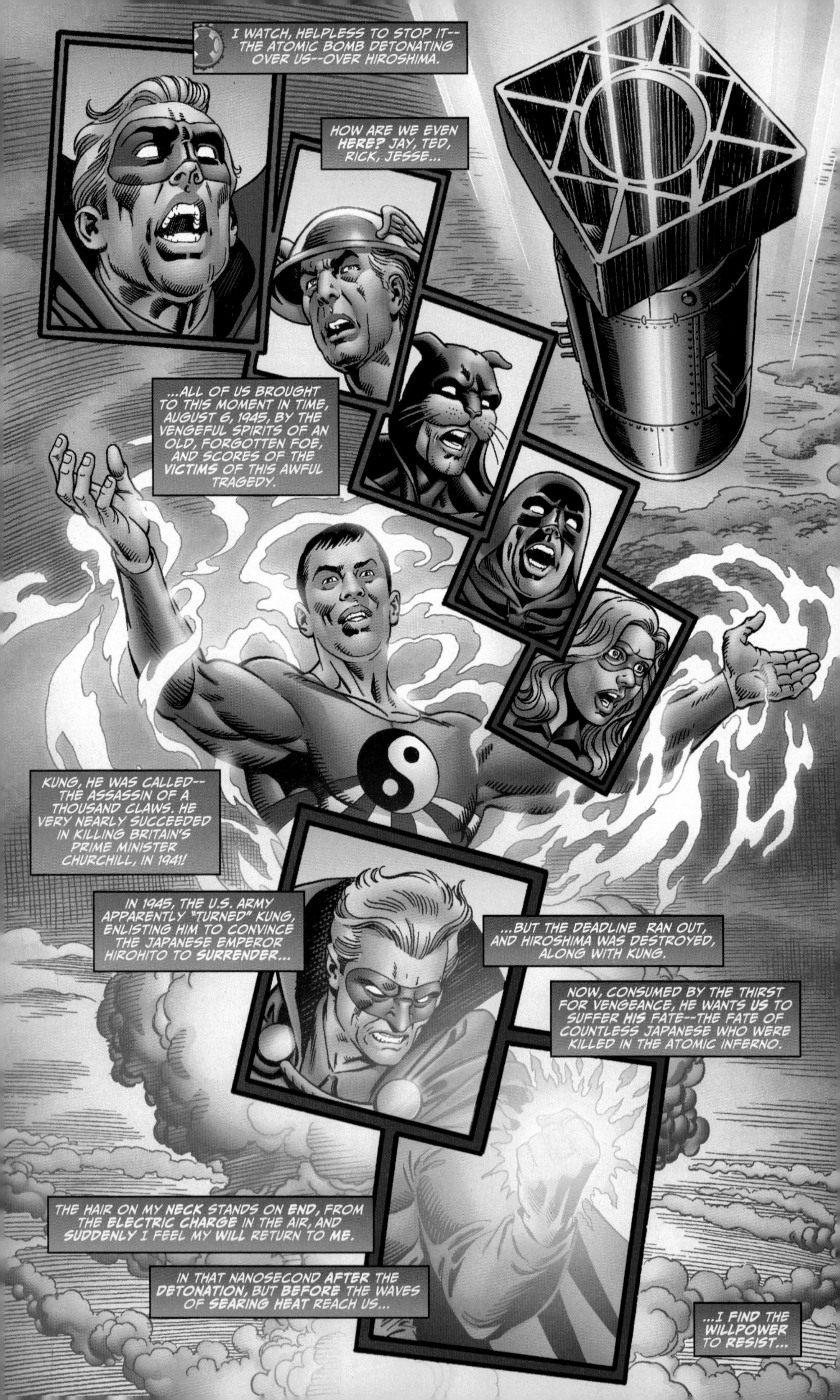

I WATCH, HELPLESS TO STOP IT-- THE ATOMIC BOMB DETONATING OVER US--OVER HIROSHIMA.
HOW ARE WE EVEN HERE? JAY, TED, RICK, JESSE...
...ALL OF US BROUGHT TO THIS MOMENT IN TIME, AUGUST 6, 1945, BY THE VENGEFUL SPIRITS OF AN OLD, FORGOTTEN FOE, AND SCORES OF THE VICTIMS OF THIS AWFUL TRAGEDY.
KUNG, HE WAS CALLED-- THE ASSASSIN OF A THOUSAND CLAWS. HE VERY NEARLY SUCCEEDED IN KILLING BRITAIN'S PRIME MINISTER CHURCHILL, IN 1941!
IN 1945, THE U.S. ARMY APPARENTLY "TURNED" KUNG, ENLISTING HIM TO CONVINCE THE JAPANESE EMPEROR HIROHITO TO SURRENDER...
...BUT THE DEADLINE RAN OUT, AND HIROSHIMA WAS DESTROYED, ALONG WITH KUNG.
NOW, CONSUMED BY THE THIRST FOR VENGEANCE, HE WANTS US TO SUFFER HIS FATE--THE FATE OF COUNTLESS JAPANESE WHO WERE KILLED IN THE ATOMIC INFERNO.
THE HAIR ON MY NECK STANDS ON END, FROM THE ELECTRIC CHARGE IN THE AIR, AND SUDDENLY I FEEL MY WILL RETURN TO ME.
IN THAT NANOSECOND AFTER THE DETONATION, BUT BEFORE THE WAVES OF SEARING HEAT REACH US...
...I FIND THE WILLPOWER TO RESIST...

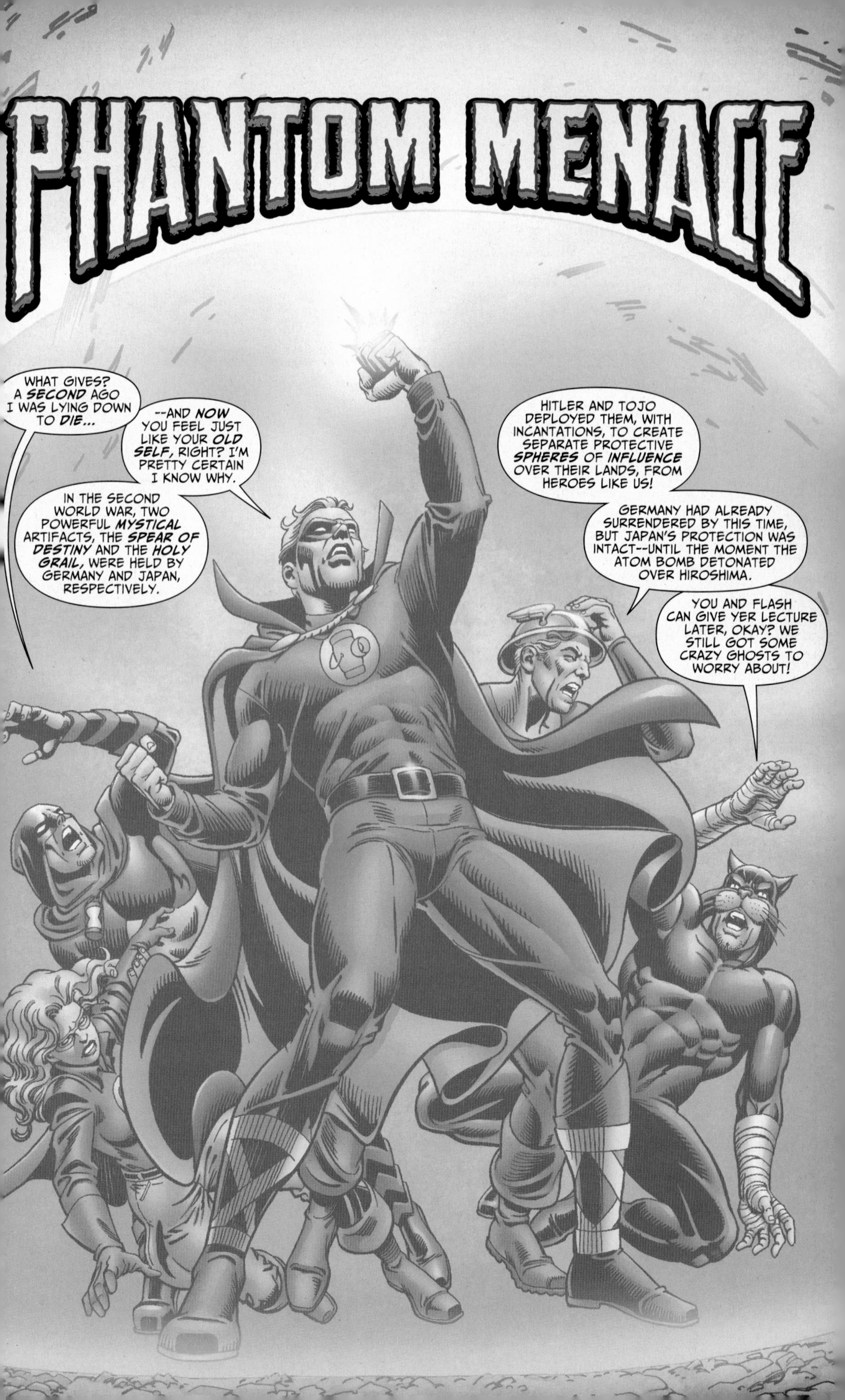
PHANTOM MENACE
WHAT GIVES? A SECOND AGO I WAS LYING DOWN TO DIE...
--AND NOW YOU FEEL JUST LIKE YOUR OLD SELF, RIGHT? I'M PRETTY CERTAIN I KNOW WHY.
IN THE SECOND WORLD WAR, TWO POWERFUL MYSTICAL ARTIFACTS, THE SPEAR OF DESTINY AND THE HOLY GRAIL, WERE HELD BY GERMANY AND JAPAN, RESPECTIVELY.
HITLER AND TOJO DEPLOYED THEM, WITH INCANTATIONS, TO CREATE SEPARATE PROTECTIVE SPHERES OF INFLUENCE OVER THEIR LANDS, FROM HEROES LIKE US!
GERMANY HAD ALREADY SURRENDERED BY THIS TIME, BUT JAPAN'S PROTECTION WAS INTACT--UNTIL THE MOMENT THE ATOM BOMB DETONATED OVER HIROSHIMA.
YOU AND FLASH CAN GIVE YER LECTURE LATER, OKAY? WE STILL GOT SOME CRAZY GHOSTS TO WORRY ABOUT!

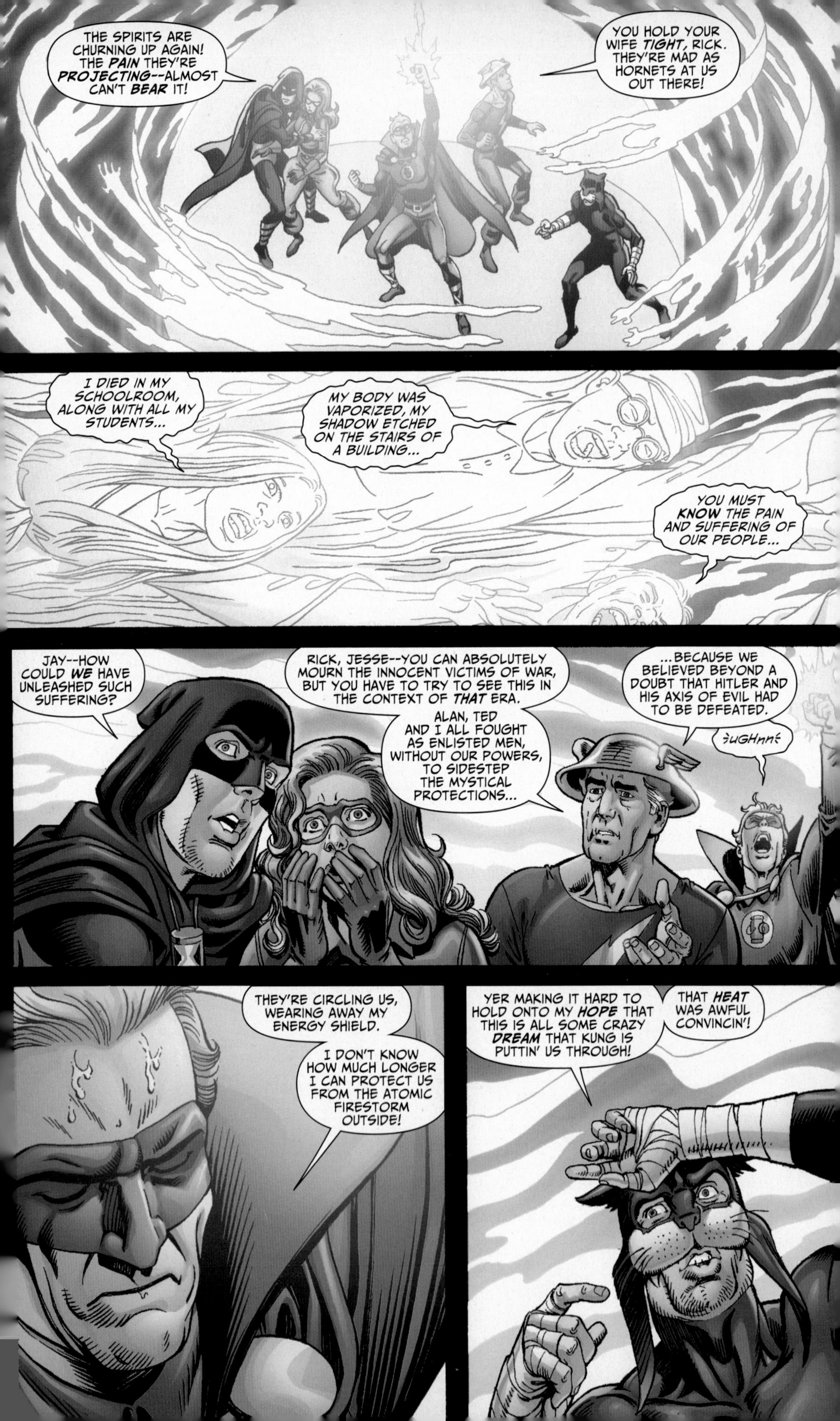
THE SPIRITS ARE CHURNING UP AGAIN! THE PAIN THEY'RE PROJECTING--ALMOST CAN'T BEAR IT!
YOU HOLD YOUR WIFE TIGHT, RICK. THEY'RE MAD AS HORNETS AT US OUT THERE!
I DIED IN MY SCHOOLROOM, ALONG WITH ALL MY STUDENTS...
MY BODY WAS VAPORIZED, MY SHADOW ETCHED ON THE STAIRS OF A BUILDING...
YOU MUST KNOW THE PAIN AND SUFFERING OF OUR PEOPLE...
JAY--HOW COULD WE HAVE UNLEASHED SUCH SUFFERING?
RICK, JESSE--YOU CAN ABSOLUTELY MOURN THE INNOCENT VICTIMS OF WAR, BUT YOU HAVE TO TRY TO SEE THIS IN THE CONTEXT OF THAT ERA.
ALAN, TED AND I ALL FOUGHT AS ENLISTED MEN, WITHOUT OUR POWERS, TO SIDESTEP THE MYSTICAL PROTECTIONS...
...BECAUSE WE BELIEVED BEYOND A DOUBT THAT HITLER AND HIS AXIS OF EVIL HAD TO BE DEFEATED.
UGHNN
THEY'RE CIRCLING US, WEARING AWAY MY ENERGY SHIELD.
I DON'T KNOW HOW MUCH LONGER I CAN PROTECT US FROM THE ATOMIC FIRESTORM OUTSIDE!
YER MAKING IT HARD TO HOLD ONTO MY HOPE THAT THIS IS ALL SOME CRAZY DREAM THAT KUNG IS PUTTIN' US THROUGH!
THAT HEAT WAS AWFUL CONVINCIN'!

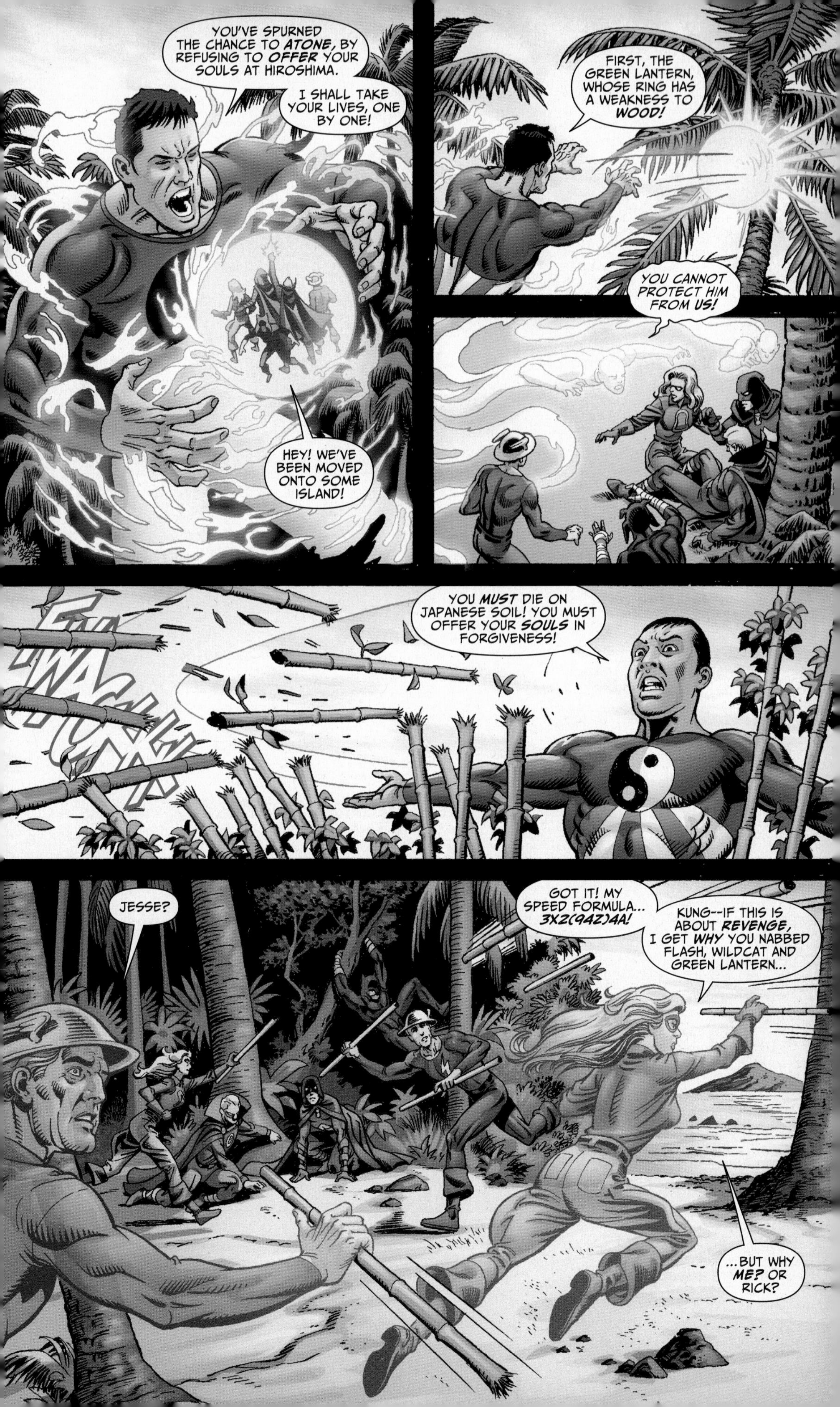
YOU'VE SPURNED THE CHANCE TO ATONE, BY REFUSING TO OFFER YOUR SOULS AT HIROSHIMA.
I SHALL TAKE YOUR LIVES, ONE BY ONE!
HEY! WE'VE BEEN MOVED ONTO SOME ISLAND!
FIRST, THE GREEN LANTERN, WHOSE RING HAS A WEAKNESS TO WOOD!
YOU CANNOT PROTECT HIM FROM US!
YOU MUST DIE ON JAPANESE SOIL! YOU MUST OFFER YOUR SOULS IN FORGIVENESS!
JESSE?
GOT IT! MY SPEED FORMULA... 3X2(9YZ)4A!
KUNG--IF THIS IS ABOUT REVENGE, I GET WHY YOU NABBED FLASH, WILDCAT AND GREEN LANTERN...
...BUT WHY ME? OR RICK?

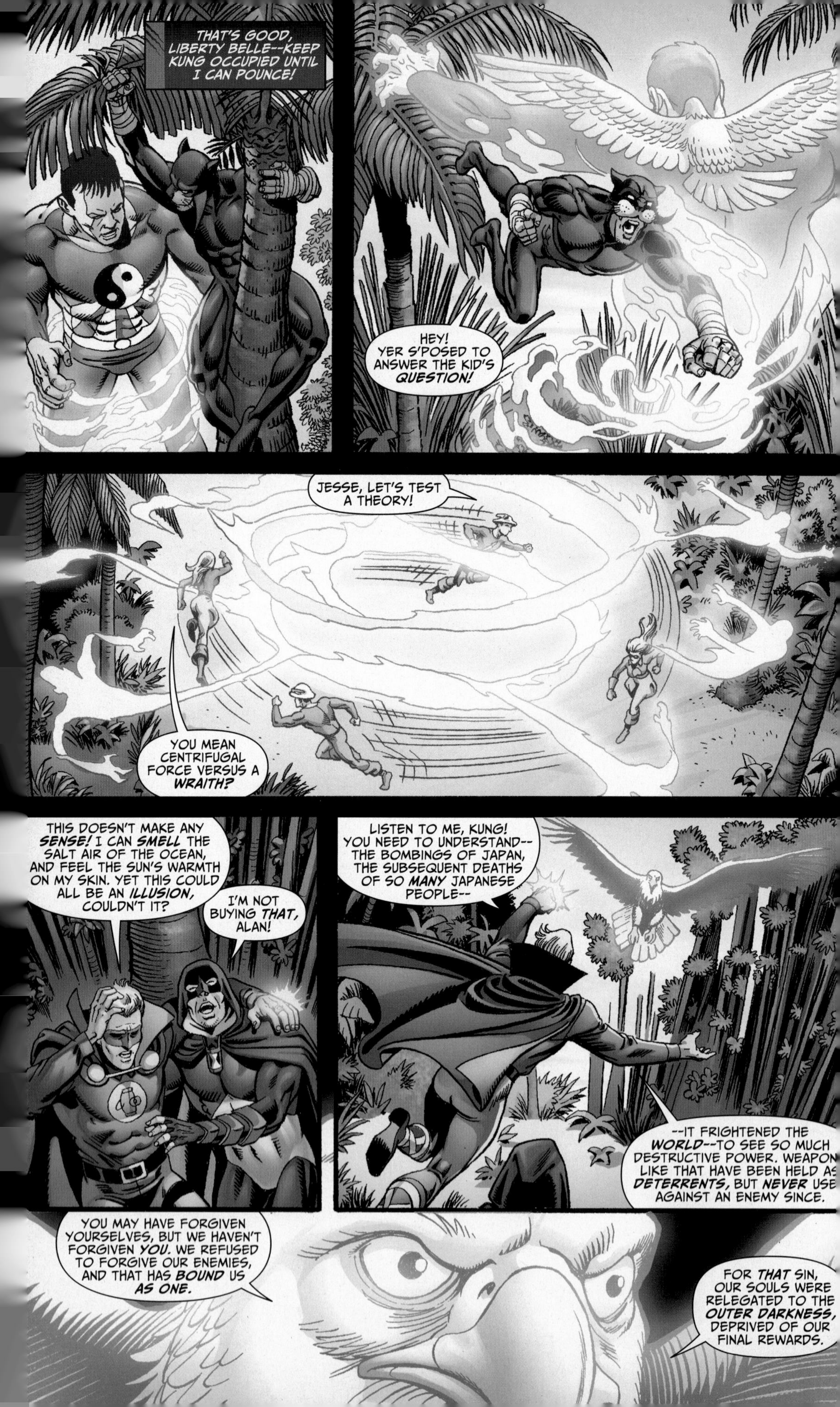

THAT'S GOOD, LIBERTY BELLE--KEEP KUNG OCCUPIED UNTIL I CAN POUNCE!
HEY! YER S'POSED TO ANSWER THE KID'S QUESTION!
JESSE, LET'S TEST A THEORY!
YOU MEAN CENTRIFUGAL FORCE VERSUS A WRAITH?
THIS DOESN'T MAKE ANY SENSE! I CAN SMELL THE SALT AIR OF THE OCEAN, AND FEEL THE SUN'S WARMTH ON MY SKIN. YET THIS COULD ALL BE AN ILLUSION, COULDN'T IT?
I'M NOT BUYING THAT, ALAN!
LISTEN TO ME, KUNG! YOU NEED TO UNDERSTAND-- THE BOMBINGS OF JAPAN, THE SUBSEQUENT DEATHS OF SO MANY JAPANESE PEOPLE--
--IT FRIGHTENED THE WORLD--TO SEE SO MUCH DESTRUCTIVE POWER. WEAPON LIKE THAT HAVE BEEN HELD AS DETERRENTS, BUT NEVER USE AGAINST AN ENEMY SINCE.
YOU MAY HAVE FORGIVEN YOURSELVES, BUT WE HAVEN'T FORGIVEN YOU. WE REFUSED TO FORGIVE OUR ENEMIES, AND THAT HAS BOUND US AS ONE.
FOR THAT SIN, OUR SOULS WERE RELEGATED TO THE OUTER DARKNESS, DEPRIVED OF OUR FINAL REWARDS.

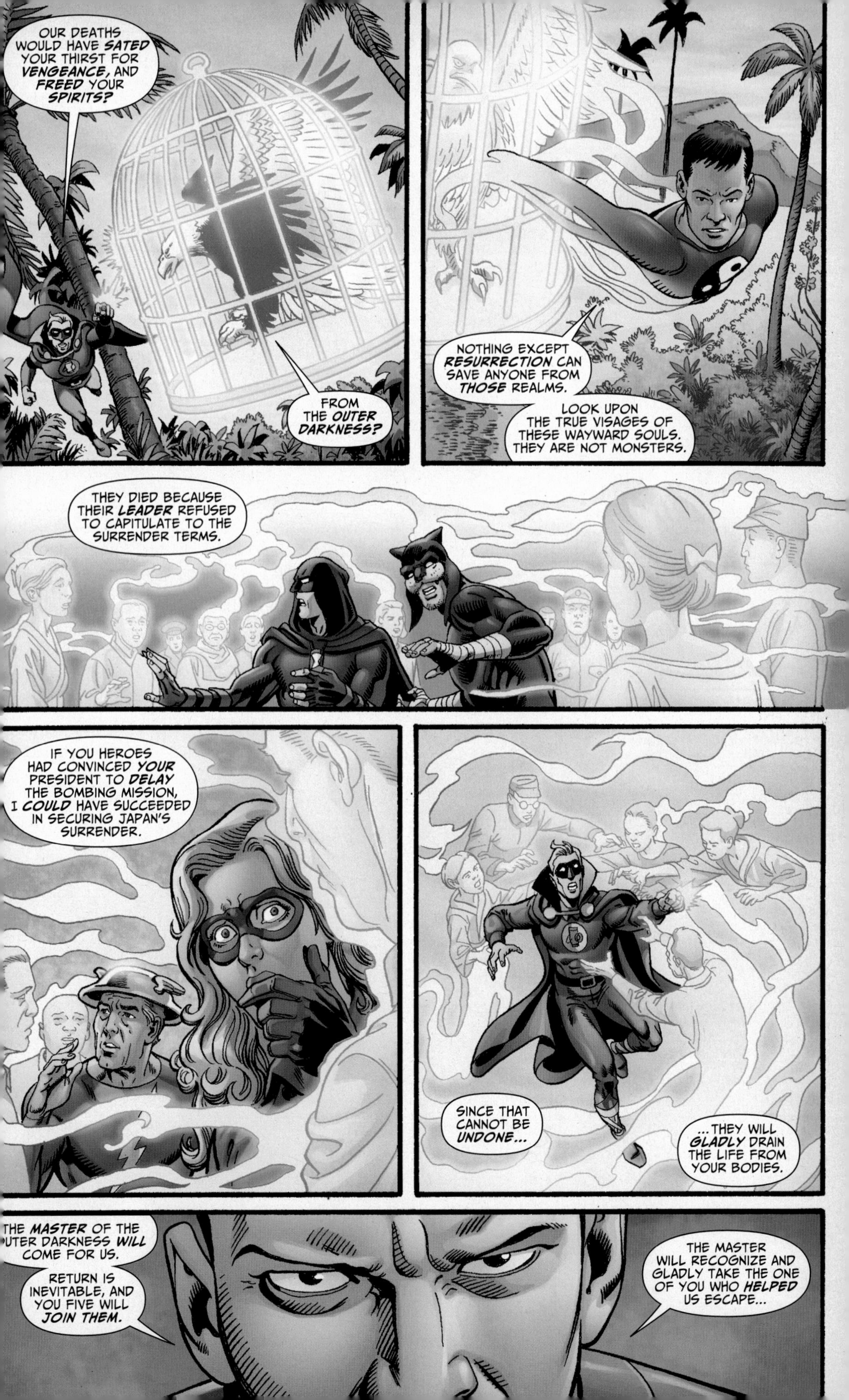
OUR DEATHS WOULD HAVE SATED YOUR THIRST FOR VENGEANCE, AND FREED YOUR SPIRITS?
FROM THE OUTER DARKNESS?
NOTHING EXCEPT RESURRECTION CAN SAVE ANYONE FROM THOSE REALMS.
LOOK UPON THE TRUE VISAGES OF THESE WAYWARD SOULS. THEY ARE NOT MONSTERS.
THEY DIED BECAUSE THEIR LEADER REFUSED TO CAPITULATE TO THE SURRENDER TERMS.
IF YOU HEROES HAD CONVINCED YOUR PRESIDENT TO DELAY THE BOMBING MISSION, I COULD HAVE SUCCEEDED IN SECURING JAPAN'S SURRENDER.
SINCE THAT CANNOT BE UNDONE...
...THEY WILL GLADLY DRAIN THE LIFE FROM YOUR BODIES.
THE MASTER OF THE OUTER DARKNESS WILL COME FOR US.
RETURN IS INEVITABLE, AND YOU FIVE WILL JOIN THEM.
THE MASTER WILL RECOGNIZE AND GLADLY TAKE THE ONE OF YOU WHO HELPED US ESCAPE...

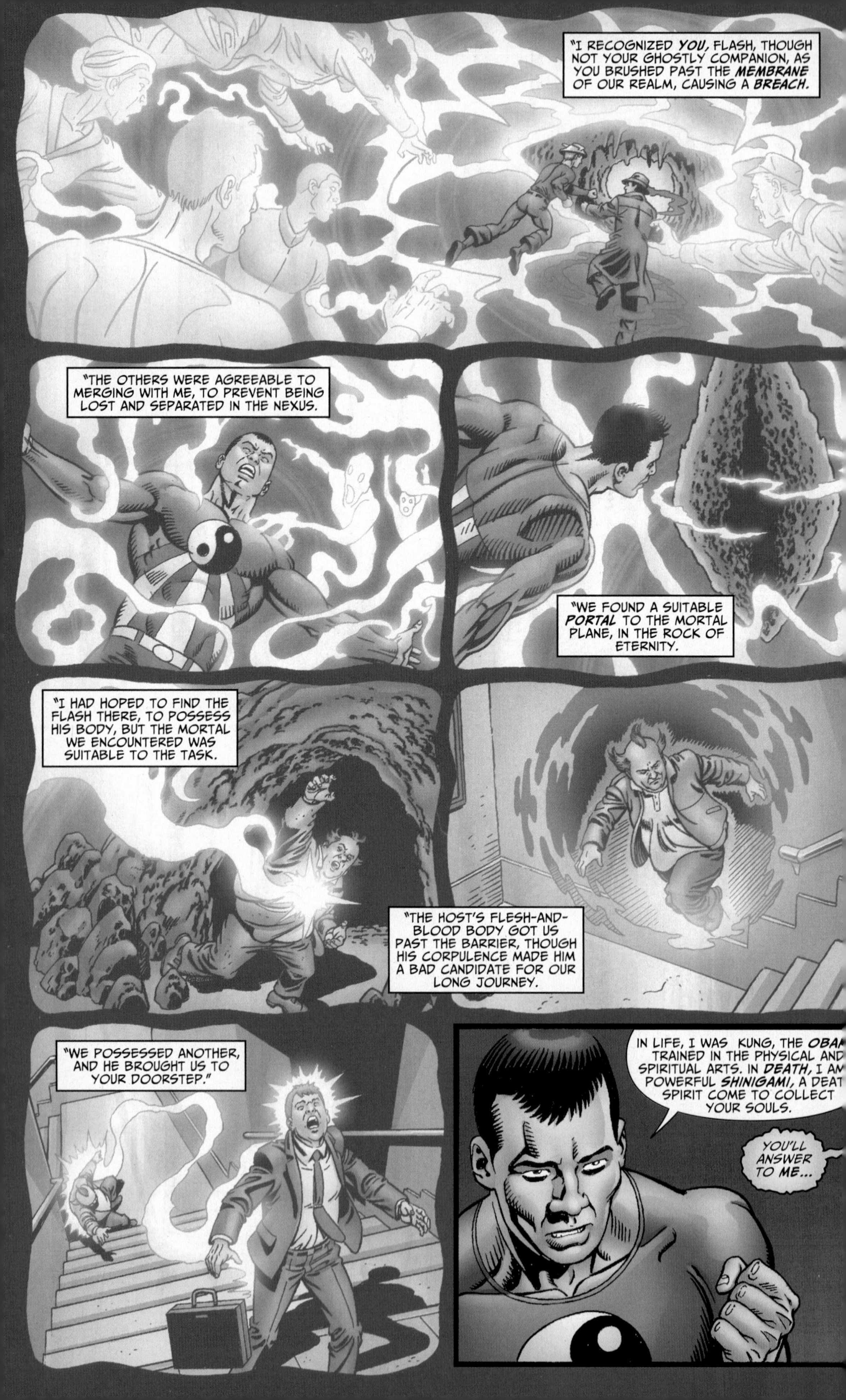
"I RECOGNIZED YOU, FLASH, THOUGH NOT YOUR GHOSTLY COMPANION, AS YOU BRUSHED PAST THE MEMBRANE OF OUR REALM, CAUSING A BREACH.
"THE OTHERS WERE AGREEABLE TO MERGING WITH ME, TO PREVENT BEING LOST AND SEPARATED IN THE NEXUS.
"WE FOUND A SUITABLE PORTAL TO THE MORTAL PLANE, IN THE ROCK OF ETERNITY.
"I HAD HOPED TO FIND THE FLASH THERE, TO POSSESS HIS BODY, BUT THE MORTAL WE ENCOUNTERED WAS SUITABLE TO THE TASK.
"THE HOST'S FLESH-AND-BLOOD BODY GOT US PAST THE BARRIER, THOUGH HIS CORPULENCE MADE HIM A BAD CANDIDATE FOR OUR LONG JOURNEY.
"WE POSSESSED ANOTHER, AND HE BROUGHT US TO YOUR DOORSTEP."
IN LIFE, I WAS KUNG, THE OBA TRAINED IN THE PHYSICAL AND SPIRITUAL ARTS. IN DEATH, I AM POWERFUL SHINIGAMI, A DEAT SPIRIT COME TO COLLECT YOUR SOULS.
YOU'LL ANSWER TO ME...

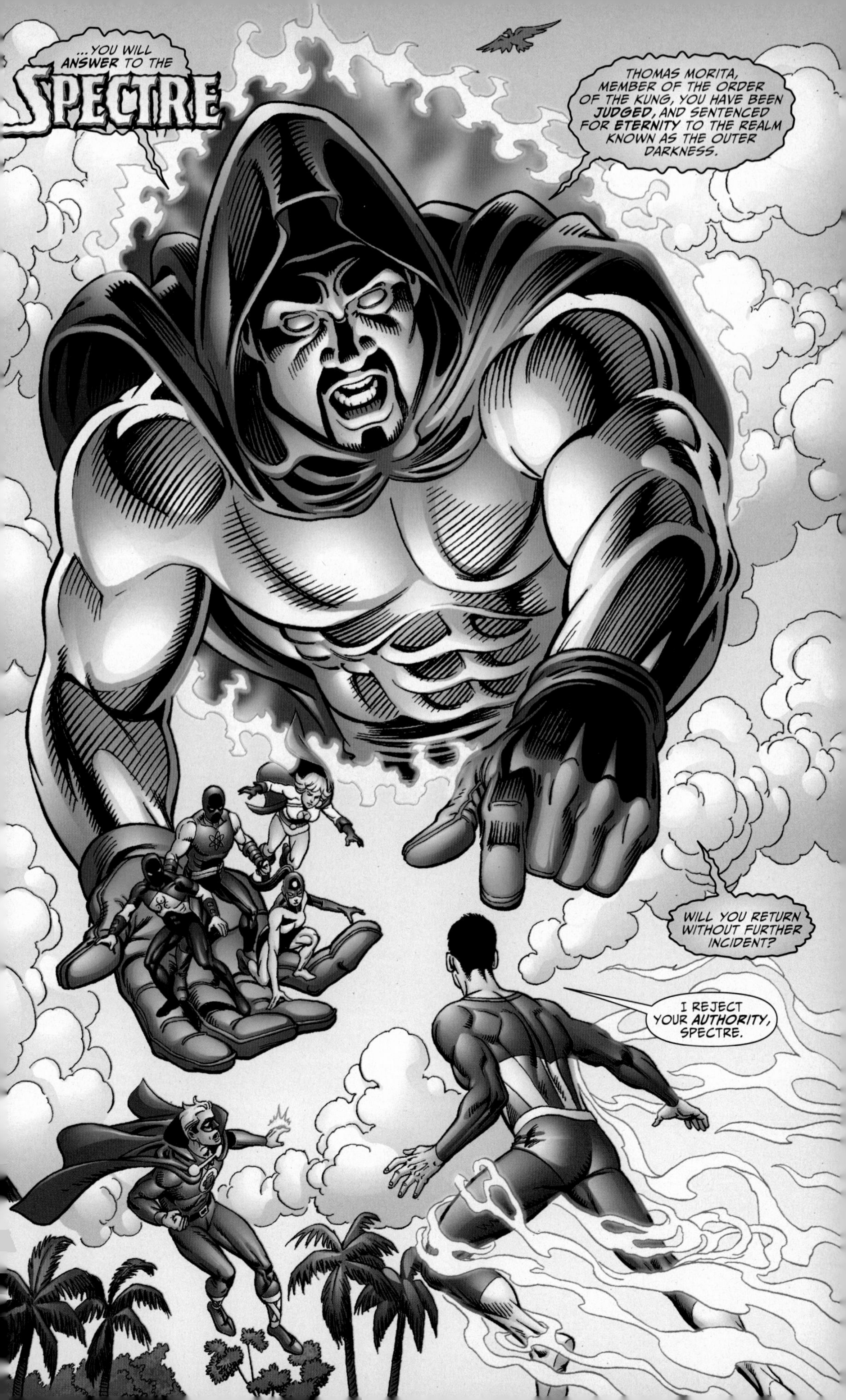

...YOU WILL ANSWER TO THE
SPECTRE
THOMAS MORITA, MEMBER OF THE ORDER OF THE KUNG, YOU HAVE BEEN JUDGED, AND SENTENCED FOR ETERNITY TO THE REALM KNOWN AS THE OUTER DARKNESS.
WILL YOU RETURN WITHOUT FURTHER INCIDENT?
I REJECT YOUR AUTHORITY, SPECTRE.

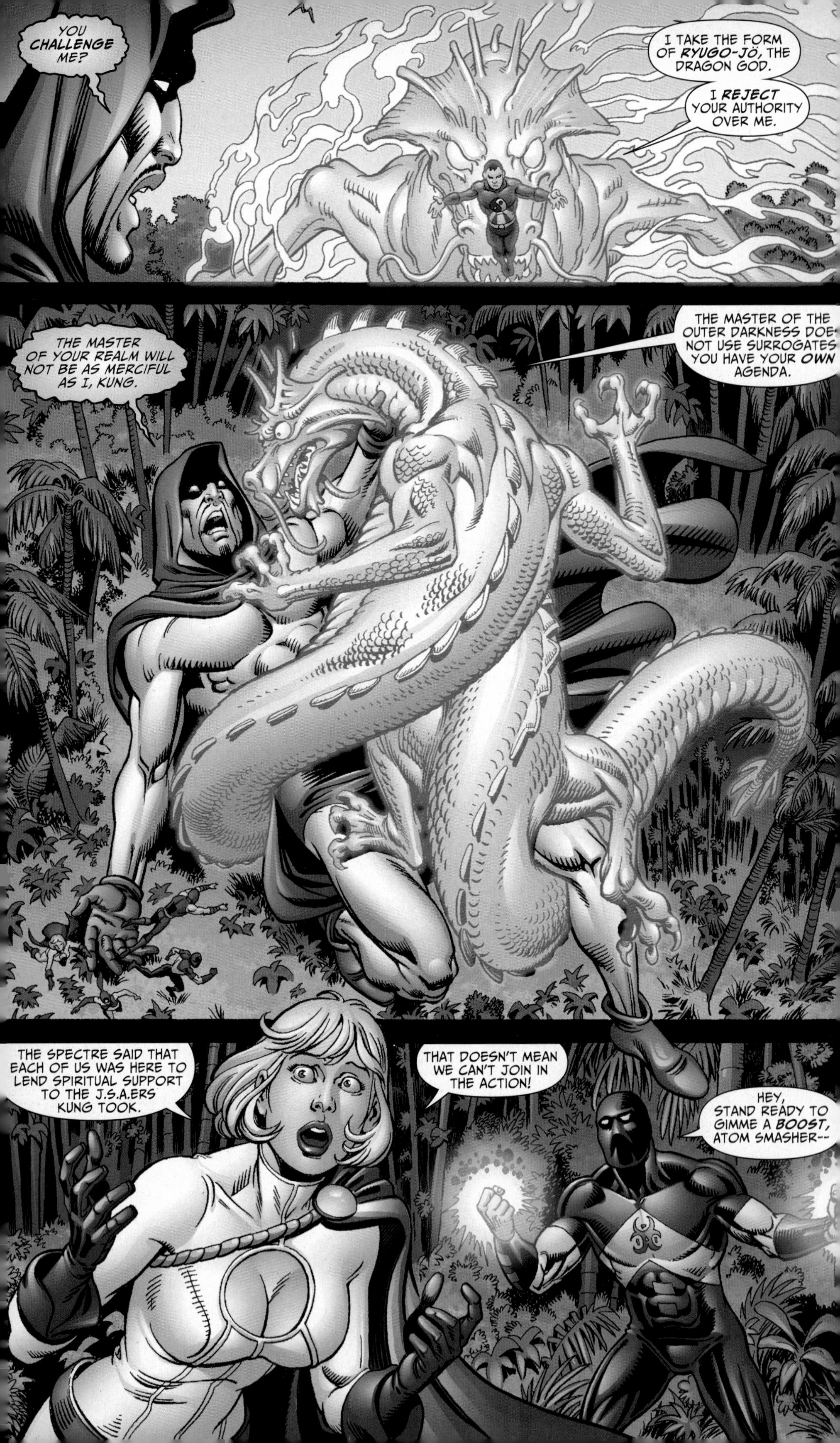
YOU CHALLENGE ME?
I TAKE THE FORM OF RYUGO-JÖ, THE DRAGON GOD.
I REJECT YOUR AUTHORITY OVER ME.
THE MASTER OF YOUR REALM WILL NOT BE AS MERCIFUL AS I, KUNG.
THE MASTER OF THE OUTER DARKNESS DOE NOT USE SURROGATES YOU HAVE YOUR OWN AGENDA.
THE SPECTRE SAID THAT EACH OF US WAS HERE TO LEND SPIRITUAL SUPPORT TO THE J.S.A.ERS KUNG TOOK.
THAT DOESN'T MEAN WE CAN'T JOIN IN THE ACTION!
HEY, STAND READY TO GIMME A BOOST, ATOM SMASHER--

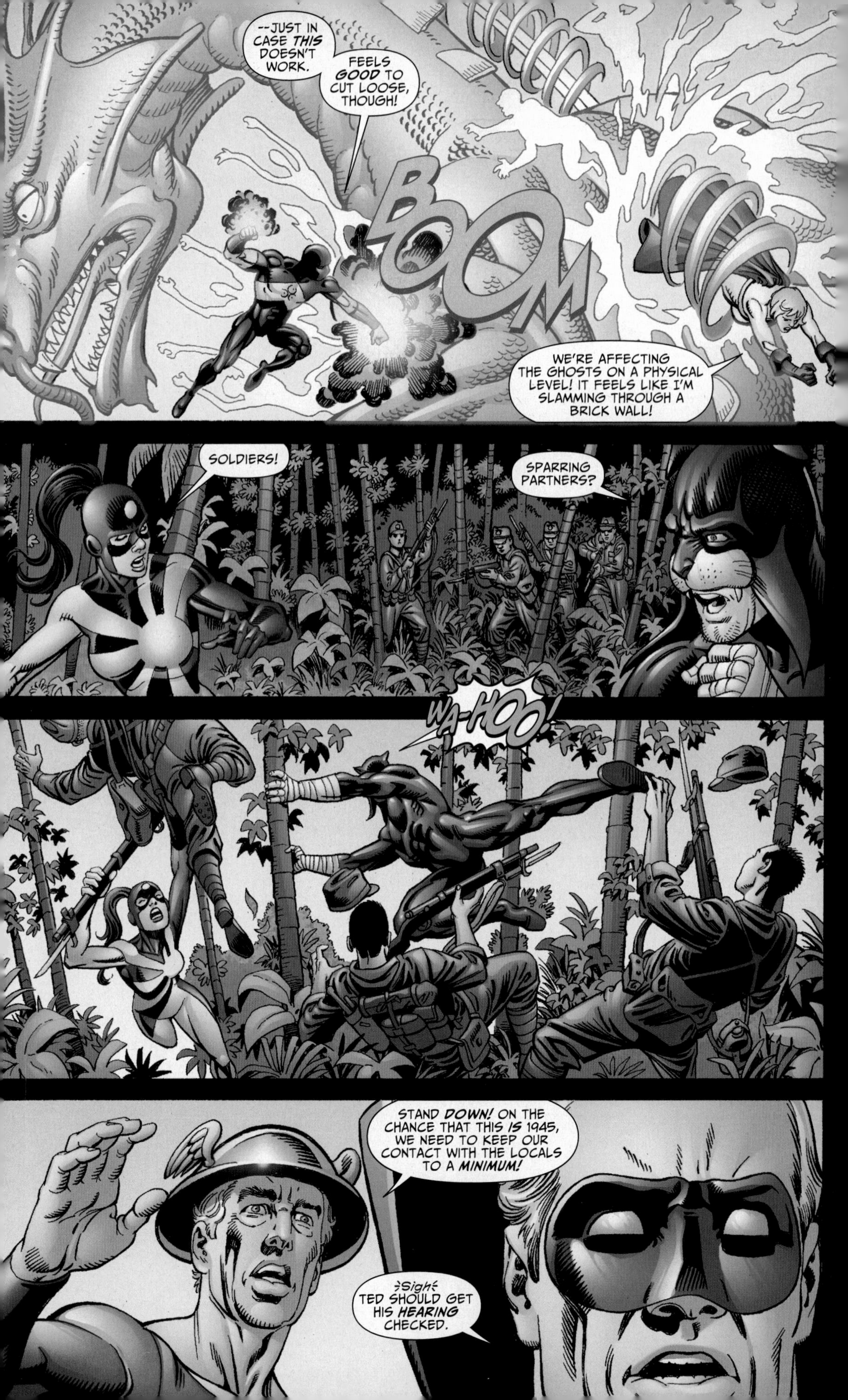
--JUST IN CASE THIS DOESN'T WORK.
FEELS GOOD TO CUT LOOSE, THOUGH!
BOOM
WE'RE AFFECTING THE GHOSTS ON A PHYSICAL LEVEL! IT FEELS LIKE I'M SLAMMING THROUGH A BRICK WALL!
SOLDIERS!
SPARRING PARTNERS?
WA-HOO!
STAND DOWN! ON THE CHANCE THAT THIS IS 1945, WE NEED TO KEEP OUR CONTACT WITH THE LOCALS TO A MINIMUM!
Sigh
TED SHOULD GET HIS HEARING CHECKED.

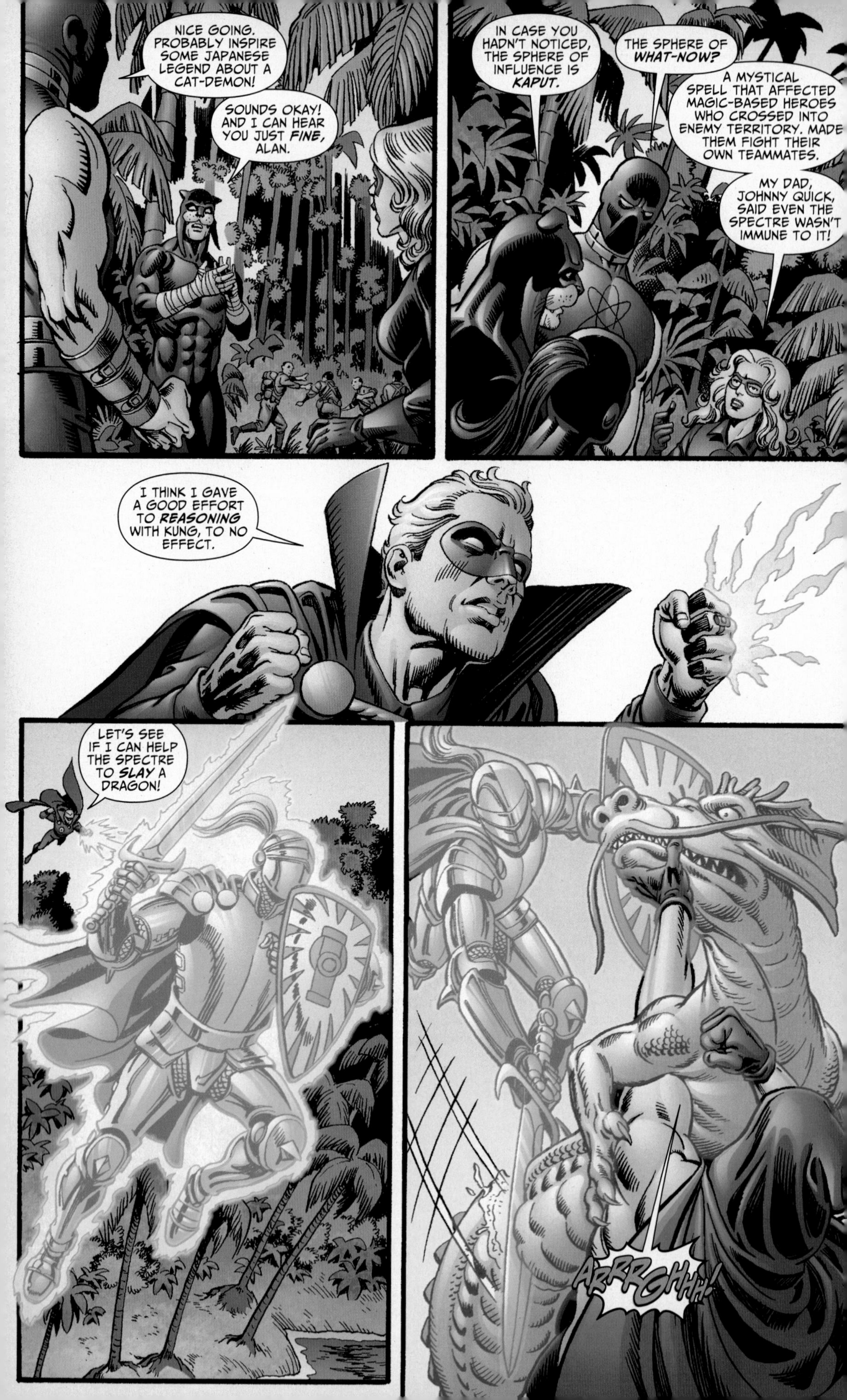
NICE GOING. PROBABLY INSPIRE SOME JAPANESE LEGEND ABOUT A CAT-DEMON!
SOUNDS OKAY! AND I CAN HEAR YOU JUST *FINE*, ALAN.
IN CASE YOU HADN'T NOTICED, THE SPHERE OF INFLUENCE IS ***KAPUT.***
THE SPHERE OF ***WHAT-NOW?***
A MYSTICAL SPELL THAT AFFECTED MAGIC-BASED HEROES WHO CROSSED INTO ENEMY TERRITORY. MADE THEM FIGHT THEIR OWN TEAMMATES.
MY DAD, JOHNNY QUICK, SAID EVEN THE SPECTRE WASN'T IMMUNE TO IT!
I THINK I GAVE A GOOD EFFORT TO ***REASONING*** WITH KUNG, TO NO EFFECT.
LET'S SEE IF I CAN HELP THE SPECTRE TO ***SLAY*** A DRAGON!
ARRRGHHH!

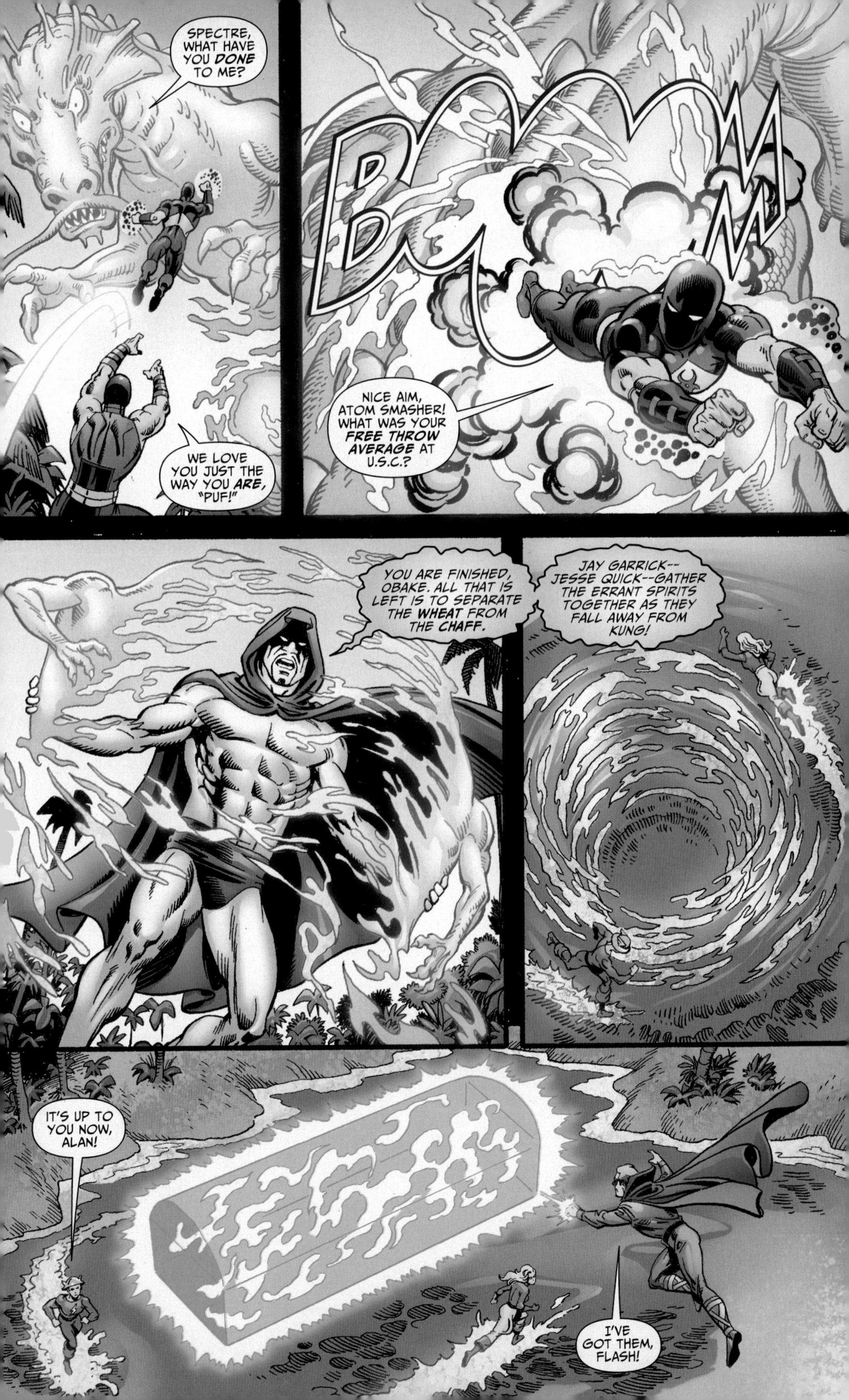
SPECTRE, WHAT HAVE YOU DONE TO ME?
WE LOVE YOU JUST THE WAY YOU ARE, "PUF!"
BOOM
NICE AIM, ATOM SMASHER! WHAT WAS YOUR FREE THROW AVERAGE AT U.S.C.?
YOU ARE FINISHED, OBAKE. ALL THAT IS LEFT IS TO SEPARATE THE WHEAT FROM THE CHAFF.
JAY GARRICK-- JESSE QUICK--GATHER THE ERRANT SPIRITS TOGETHER AS THEY FALL AWAY FROM KUNG!
IT'S UP TO YOU NOW, ALAN!
I'VE GOT THEM, FLASH!

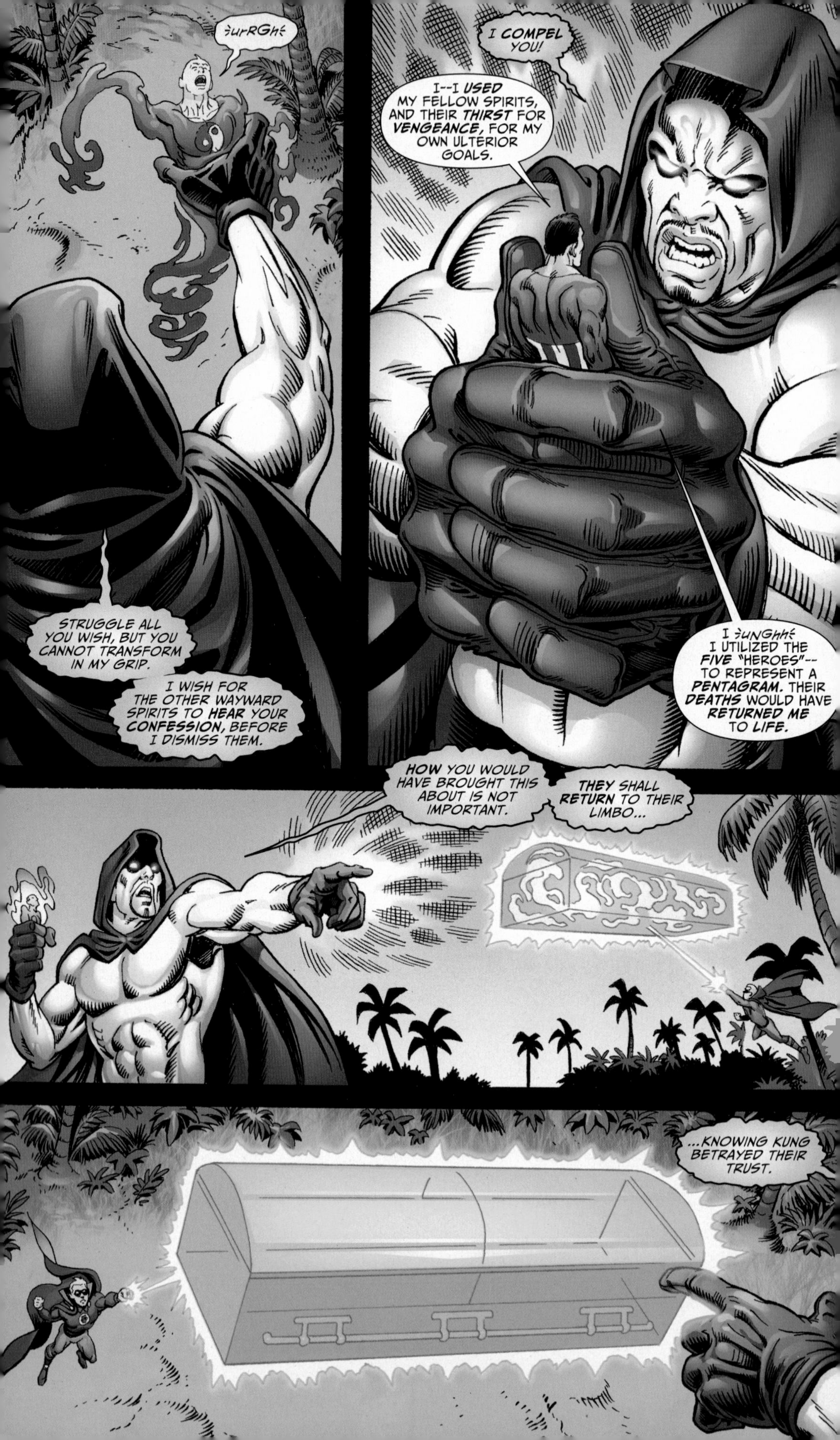
urRGh
I COMPEL YOU!
I--I USED MY FELLOW SPIRITS, AND THEIR THIRST FOR VENGEANCE, FOR MY OWN ULTERIOR GOALS.
STRUGGLE ALL YOU WISH, BUT YOU CANNOT TRANSFORM IN MY GRIP.
I WISH FOR THE OTHER WAYWARD SPIRITS TO HEAR YOUR CONFESSION, BEFORE I DISMISS THEM.
I uNGhh I UTILIZED THE FIVE "HEROES"-- TO REPRESENT A PENTAGRAM. THEIR DEATHS WOULD HAVE RETURNED ME TO LIFE.
HOW YOU WOULD HAVE BROUGHT THIS ABOUT IS NOT IMPORTANT.
THEY SHALL RETURN TO THEIR LIMBO...
...KNOWING KUNG BETRAYED THEIR TRUST.

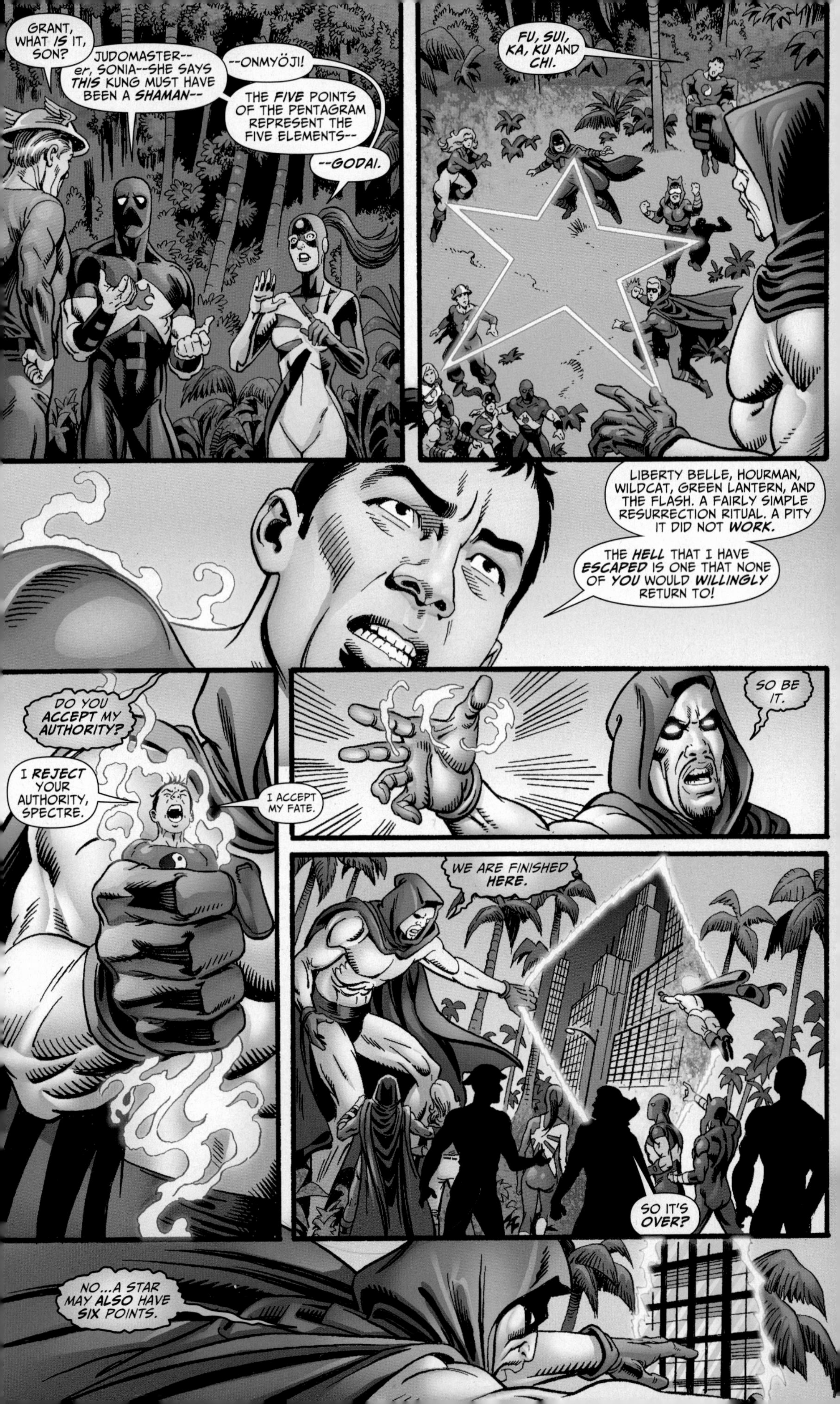

GRANT, WHAT IS IT, SON?
JUDOMASTER-- er, SONIA--SHE SAYS THIS KUNG MUST HAVE BEEN A SHAMAN--
--ONMYŌJI!
THE FIVE POINTS OF THE PENTAGRAM REPRESENT THE FIVE ELEMENTS--
--GODAI.
FU, SUI, KA, KU AND CHI.
LIBERTY BELLE, HOURMAN, WILDCAT, GREEN LANTERN, AND THE FLASH. A FAIRLY SIMPLE RESURRECTION RITUAL. A PITY IT DID NOT WORK.
THE HELL THAT I HAVE ESCAPED IS ONE THAT NONE OF YOU WOULD WILLINGLY RETURN TO!
DO YOU ACCEPT MY AUTHORITY?
I REJECT YOUR AUTHORITY, SPECTRE.
I ACCEPT MY FATE.
SO BE IT.
WE ARE FINISHED HERE.
SO IT'S OVER?
NO...A STAR MAY ALSO HAVE SIX POINTS.

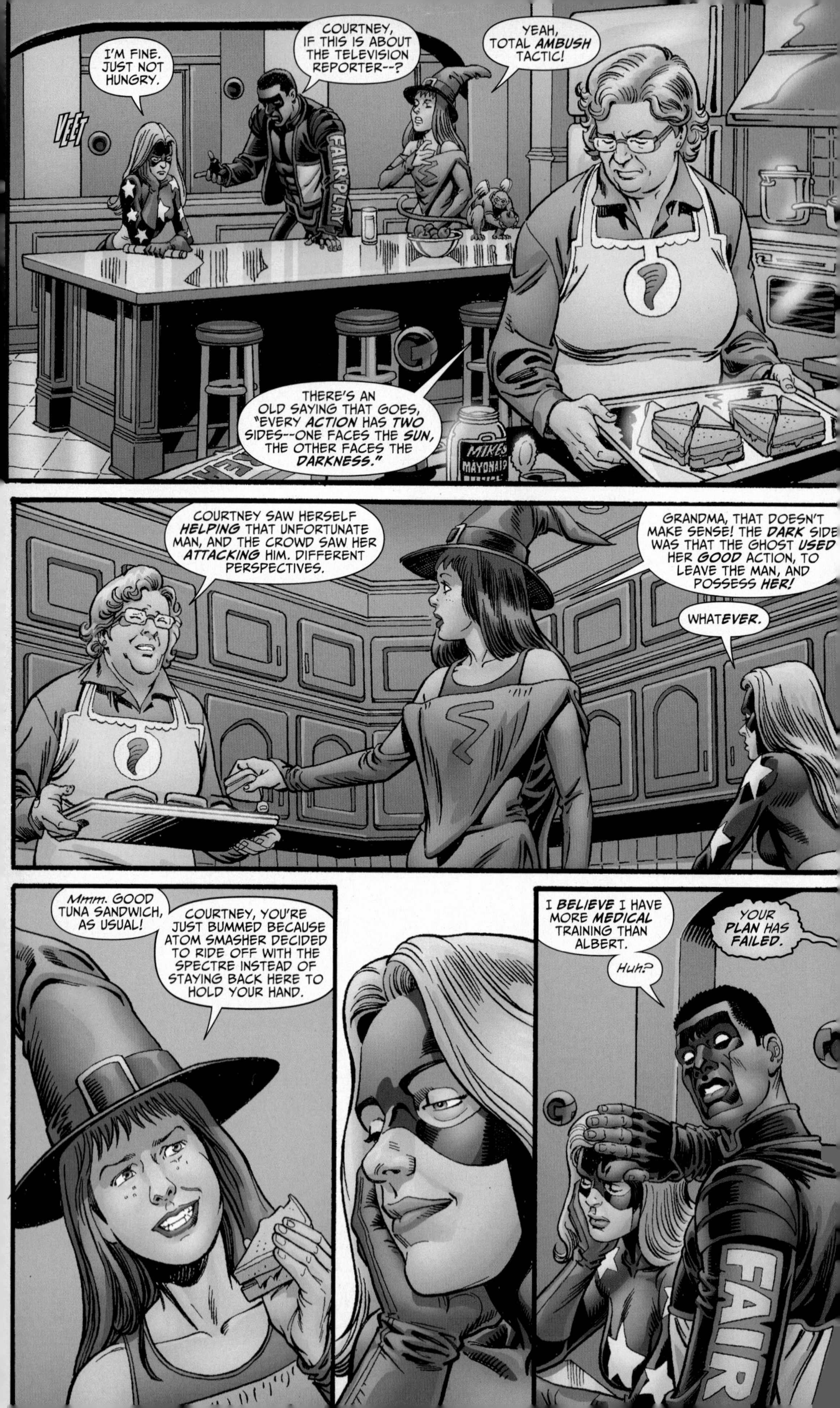
I'M FINE. JUST NOT HUNGRY.
VEET
COURTNEY, IF THIS IS ABOUT THE TELEVISION REPORTER--?
YEAH, TOTAL AMBUSH TACTIC!
FAIR PLAY
THERE'S AN OLD SAYING THAT GOES, "EVERY ACTION HAS TWO SIDES--ONE FACES THE SUN, THE OTHER FACES THE DARKNESS."
MIKE'S MAYONAI
COURTNEY SAW HERSELF HELPING THAT UNFORTUNATE MAN, AND THE CROWD SAW HER ATTACKING HIM. DIFFERENT PERSPECTIVES.
GRANDMA, THAT DOESN'T MAKE SENSE! THE DARK SIDE WAS THAT THE GHOST USED HER GOOD ACTION, TO LEAVE THE MAN, AND POSSESS HER!
WHATEVER.
Mmm. GOOD TUNA SANDWICH, AS USUAL!
COURTNEY, YOU'RE JUST BUMMED BECAUSE ATOM SMASHER DECIDED TO RIDE OFF WITH THE SPECTRE INSTEAD OF STAYING BACK HERE TO HOLD YOUR HAND.
I BELIEVE I HAVE MORE MEDICAL TRAINING THAN ALBERT.
Huh?
YOUR PLAN HAS FAILED.
FAIR

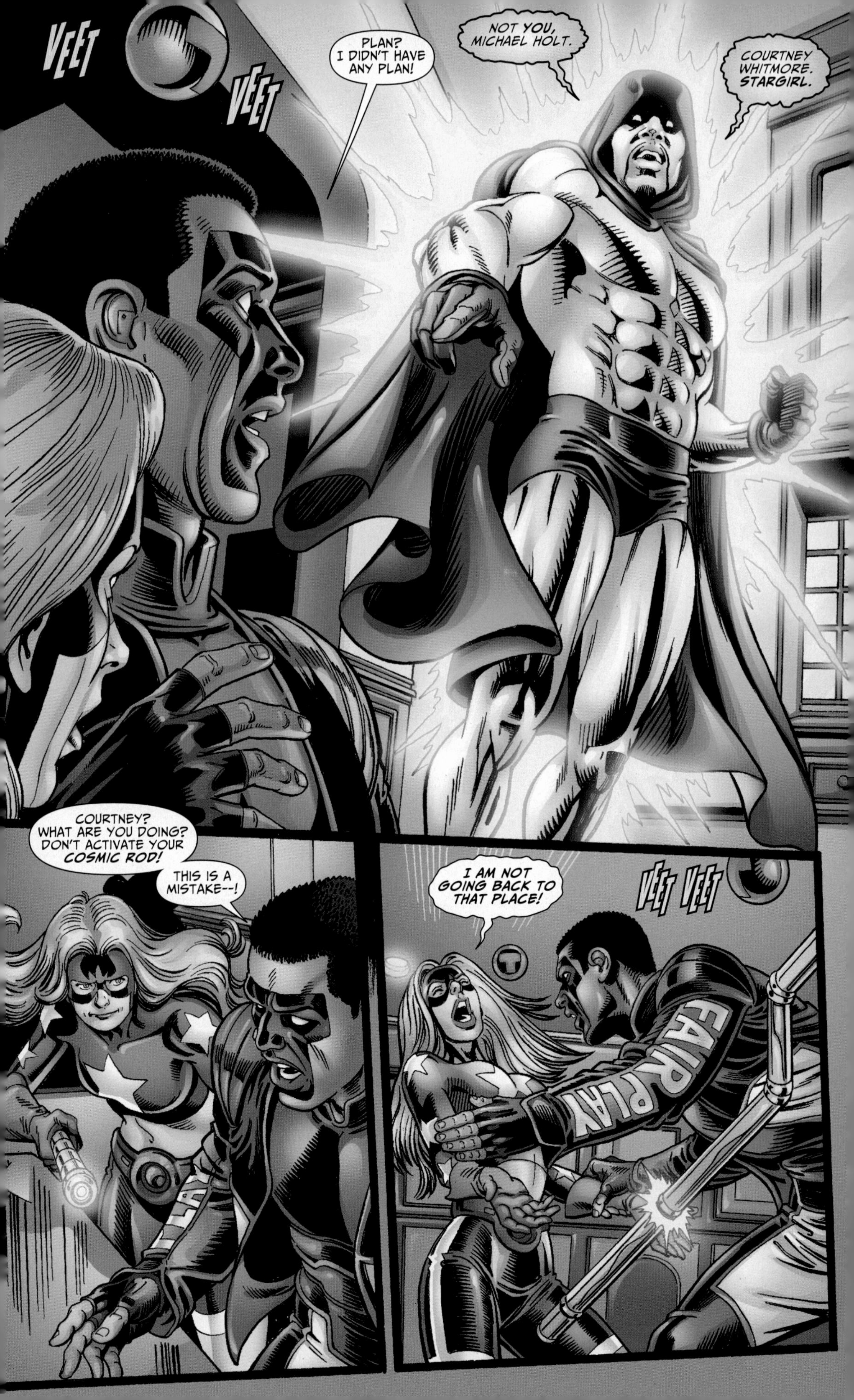
VEET
VEET
PLAN? I DIDN'T HAVE ANY PLAN!
NOT YOU, MICHAEL HOLT.
COURTNEY WHITMORE. STARGIRL.
COURTNEY? WHAT ARE YOU DOING? DON'T ACTIVATE YOUR COSMIC ROD!
THIS IS A MISTAKE--!
I AM NOT GOING BACK TO THAT PLACE!
VEET VEET
FAIR PLAY

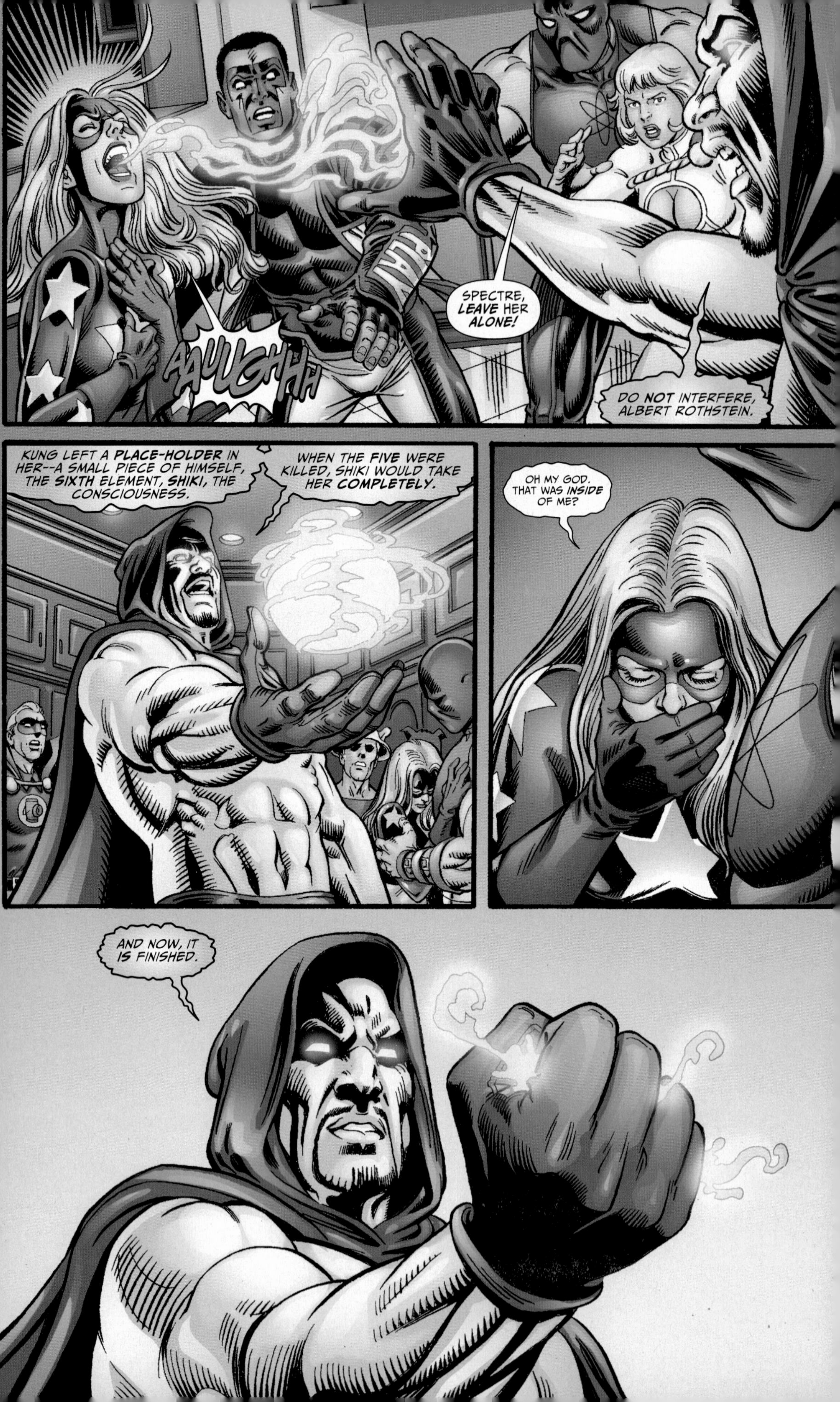

AAUUGHHH
SPECTRE, LEAVE HER ALONE!
DO NOT INTERFERE, ALBERT ROTHSTEIN.
KUNG LEFT A PLACE-HOLDER IN HER--A SMALL PIECE OF HIMSELF, THE SIXTH ELEMENT, SHIKI, THE CONSCIOUSNESS.
WHEN THE FIVE WERE KILLED, SHIKI WOULD TAKE HER COMPLETELY.
OH MY GOD. THAT WAS INSIDE OF ME?
AND NOW, IT IS FINISHED.

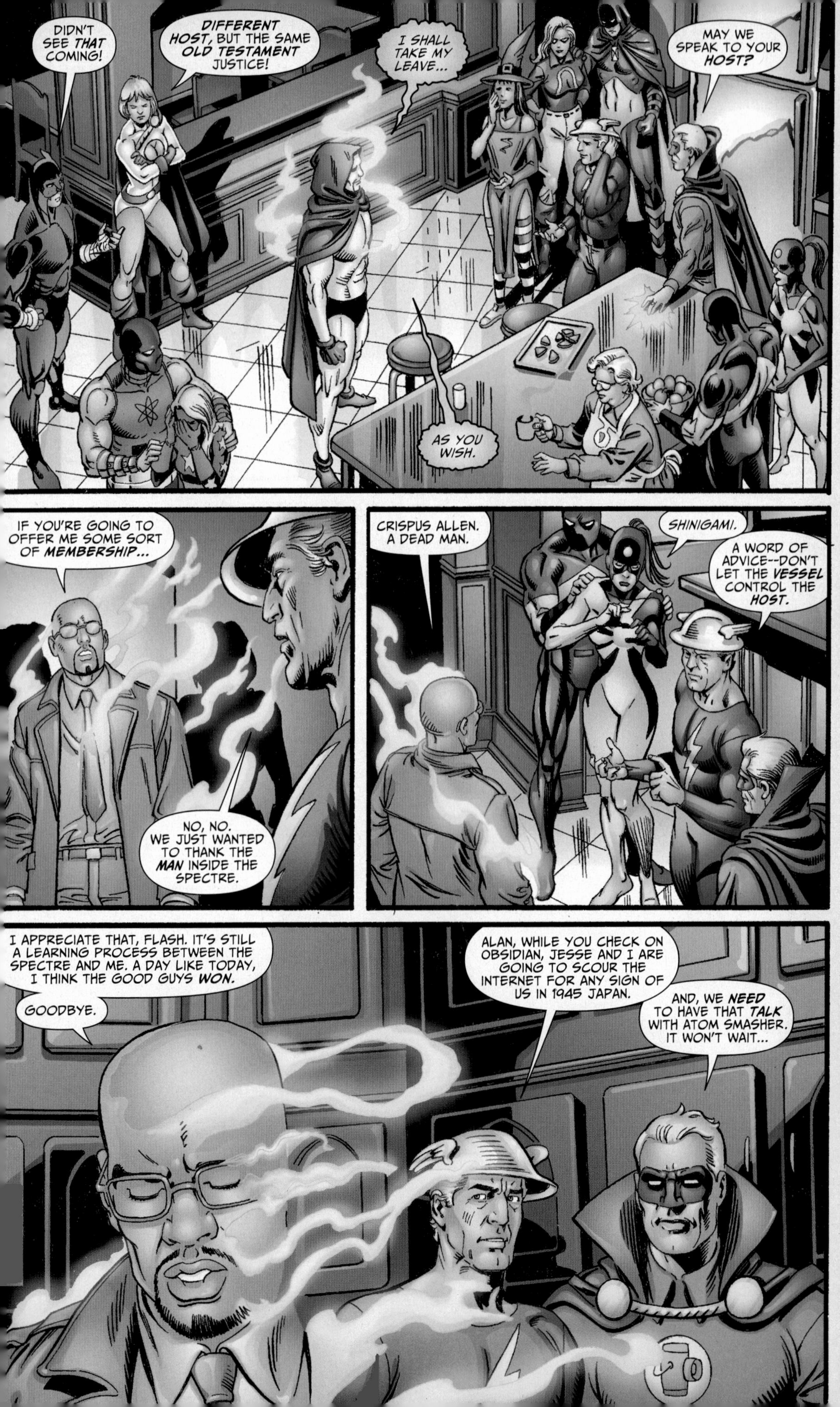
DIDN'T SEE THAT COMING!
DIFFERENT HOST, BUT THE SAME OLD TESTAMENT JUSTICE!
I SHALL TAKE MY LEAVE...
MAY WE SPEAK TO YOUR HOST?
AS YOU WISH.
IF YOU'RE GOING TO OFFER ME SOME SORT OF MEMBERSHIP...
NO, NO. WE JUST WANTED TO THANK THE MAN INSIDE THE SPECTRE.
CRISPUS ALLEN. A DEAD MAN.
SHINIGAMI.
A WORD OF ADVICE--DON'T LET THE VESSEL CONTROL THE HOST.
I APPRECIATE THAT, FLASH. IT'S STILL A LEARNING PROCESS BETWEEN THE SPECTRE AND ME. A DAY LIKE TODAY, I THINK THE GOOD GUYS WON.
GOODBYE.
ALAN, WHILE YOU CHECK ON OBSIDIAN, JESSE AND I ARE GOING TO SCOUR THE INTERNET FOR ANY SIGN OF US IN 1945 JAPAN.
AND, WE NEED TO HAVE THAT TALK WITH ATOM SMASHER. IT WON'T WAIT...

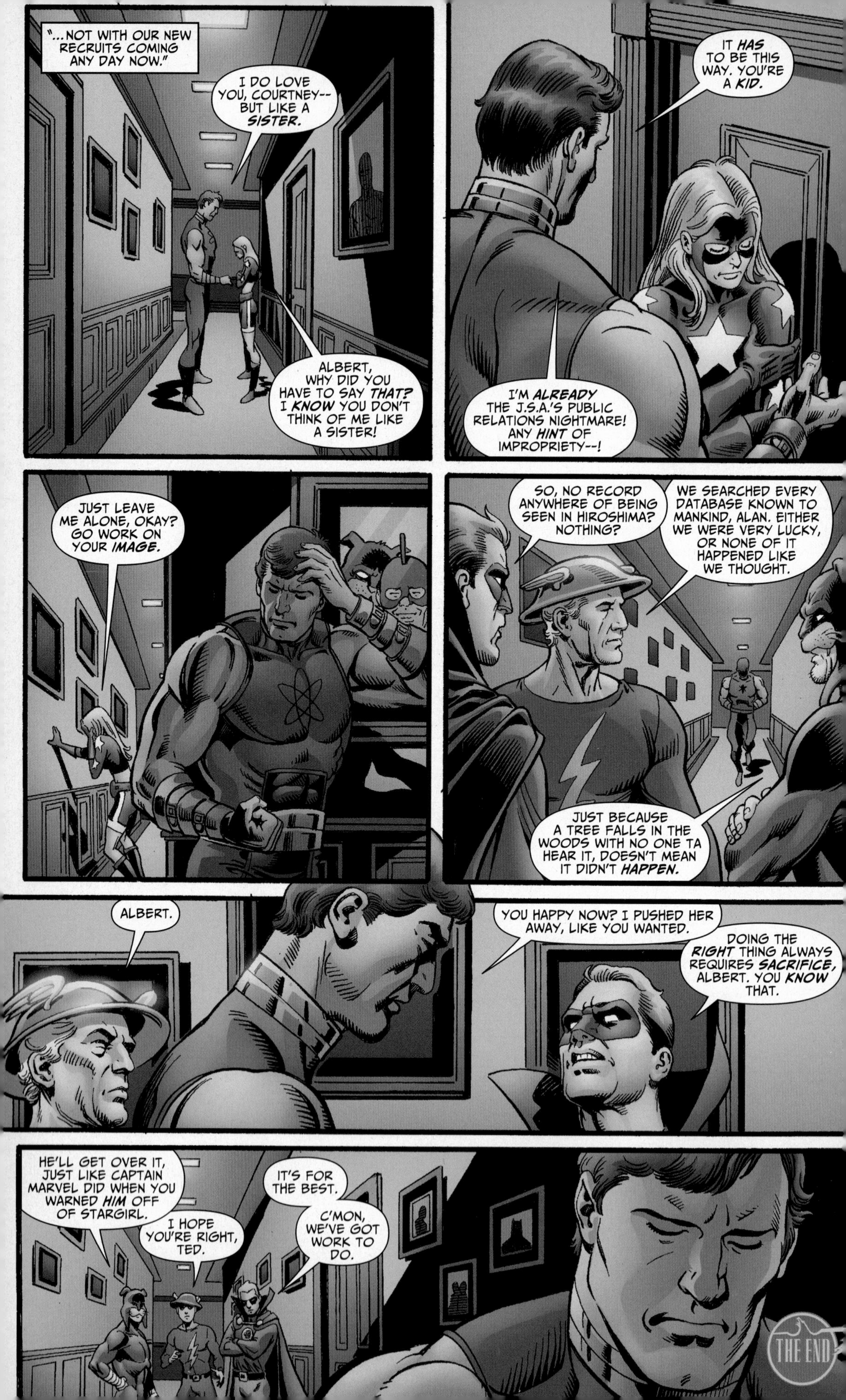
"...NOT WITH OUR NEW RECRUITS COMING ANY DAY NOW."
I DO LOVE YOU, COURTNEY-- BUT LIKE A SISTER.
ALBERT, WHY DID YOU HAVE TO SAY THAT? I KNOW YOU DON'T THINK OF ME LIKE A SISTER!
IT HAS TO BE THIS WAY. YOU'RE A KID.
I'M ALREADY THE J.S.A.'S PUBLIC RELATIONS NIGHTMARE! ANY HINT OF IMPROPRIETY--!
JUST LEAVE ME ALONE, OKAY? GO WORK ON YOUR IMAGE.
SO, NO RECORD ANYWHERE OF BEING SEEN IN HIROSHIMA? NOTHING?
WE SEARCHED EVERY DATABASE KNOWN TO MANKIND, ALAN. EITHER WE WERE VERY LUCKY, OR NONE OF IT HAPPENED LIKE WE THOUGHT.
JUST BECAUSE A TREE FALLS IN THE WOODS WITH NO ONE TA HEAR IT, DOESN'T MEAN IT DIDN'T HAPPEN.
ALBERT.
YOU HAPPY NOW? I PUSHED HER AWAY, LIKE YOU WANTED.
DOING THE RIGHT THING ALWAYS REQUIRES SACRIFICE, ALBERT. YOU KNOW THAT.
HE'LL GET OVER IT, JUST LIKE CAPTAIN MARVEL DID WHEN YOU WARNED HIM OFF OF STARGIRL.
I HOPE YOU'RE RIGHT, TED.
IT'S FOR THE BEST.
C'MON, WE'VE GOT WORK TO DO.
THE END

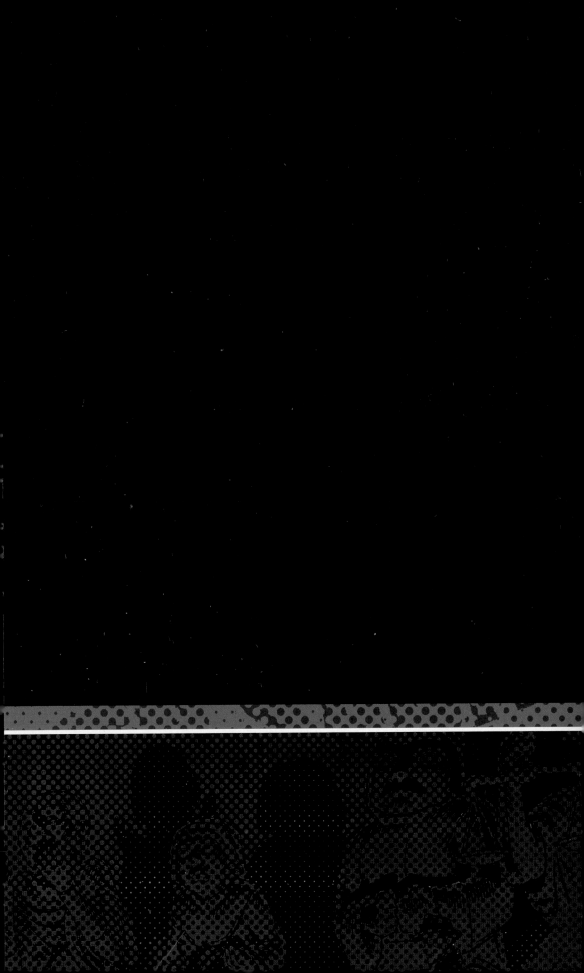

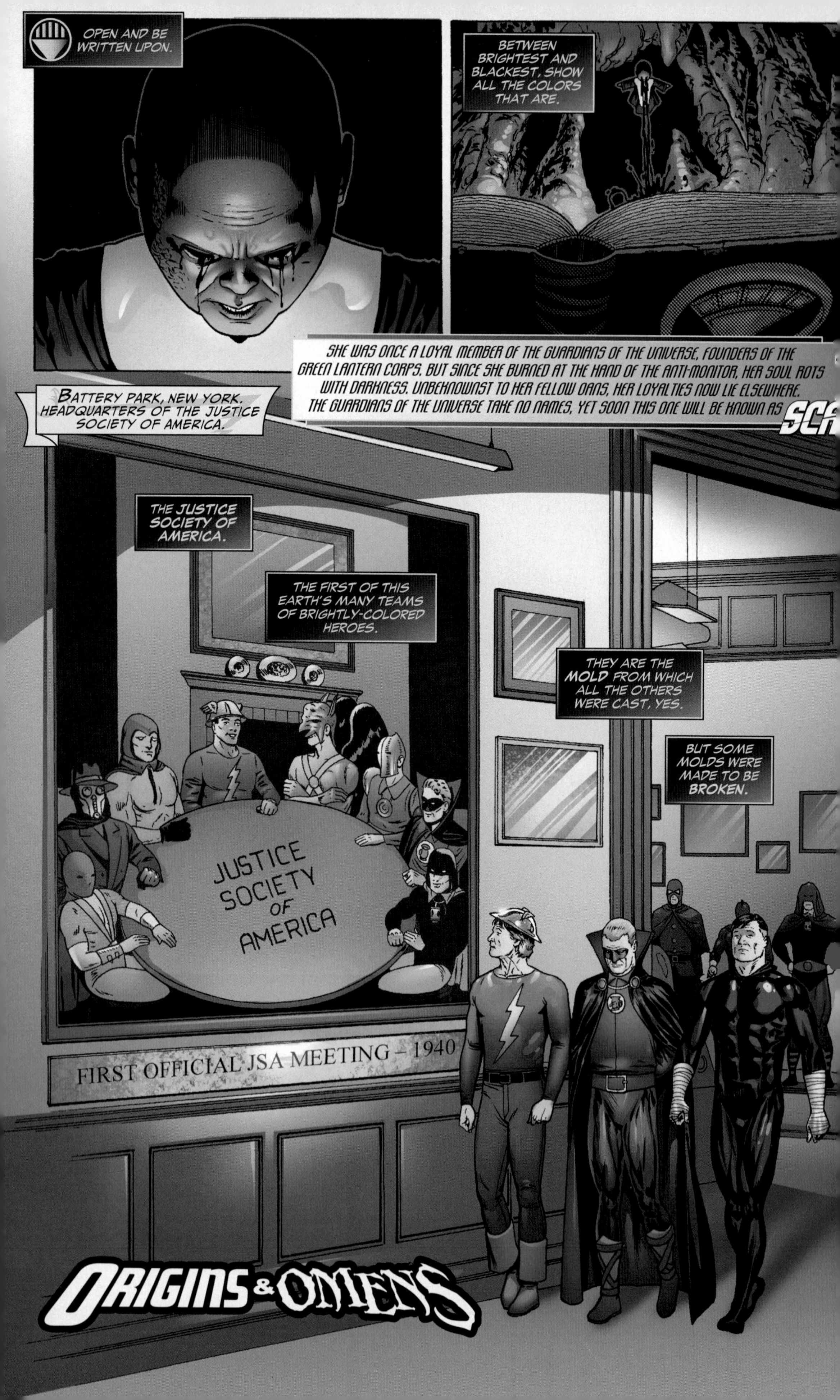
OPEN AND BE WRITTEN UPON.
BETWEEN BRIGHTEST AND BLACKEST, SHOW ALL THE COLORS THAT ARE.
SHE WAS ONCE A LOYAL MEMBER OF THE GUARDIANS OF THE UNIVERSE, FOUNDERS OF THE GREEN LANTERN CORPS. BUT SINCE SHE BURNED AT THE HAND OF THE ANTI-MONITOR, HER SOUL ROTS WITH DARKNESS. UNBEKNOWNST TO HER FELLOW OANS, HER LOYALTIES NOW LIE ELSEWHERE. THE GUARDIANS OF THE UNIVERSE TAKE NO NAMES, YET SOON THIS ONE WILL BE KNOWN AS SCA
BATTERY PARK, NEW YORK. HEADQUARTERS OF THE JUSTICE SOCIETY OF AMERICA.
THE JUSTICE SOCIETY OF AMERICA.
THE FIRST OF THIS EARTH'S MANY TEAMS OF BRIGHTLY-COLORED HEROES.
THEY ARE THE MOLD FROM WHICH ALL THE OTHERS WERE CAST, YES.
BUT SOME MOLDS WERE MADE TO BE BROKEN.
JUSTICE SOCIETY OF AMERICA
FIRST OFFICIAL JSA MEETING – 1940
ORIGINS & OMENS

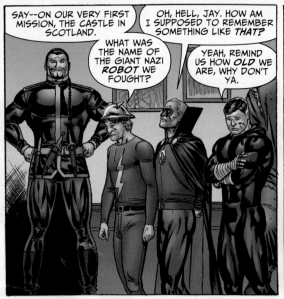

SAY--ON OUR VERY FIRST MISSION, THE CASTLE IN SCOTLAND.

WHAT WAS THE NAME OF THE GIANT NAZI *ROBOT* WE FOUGHT?

OH, HELL, JAY. HOW AM I SUPPOSED TO REMEMBER SOMETHING LIKE *THAT?*

YEAH, REMIND US HOW *OLD* WE ARE, WHY DON'T YA.

YOU FEEL OLD? I WAS TALKING TO COURTNEY THE OTHER DAY--DO YOU KNOW SHE'S NEVER EVEN *HEARD* OF TOMMY DORSEY?

THIS IS 20*09*, FLASH. SHE'S PROBABLY *NEVER* HEARD OF ELVIS.

I'M WORRIED, GUYS. THERE'S A... RIFT GROWING.

YOU TWO CAN FEEL IT, CAN'T YOU? AND NOT BECAUSE OF GOG--GOG WAS JUST A CATALYST.

YEAH. I SEEM TO RECALL THE *LAST* TIME THE JSA "RIFTED" WE ENDED UP WITH ATOM SMASHER IN JAIL AND ALEX MONTEZ SIX FEET IN THE DIRT.

IF YOU *BOYS* ARE GOING TO FRET ALOUD, YOU SHOULD DO IT IN A PLACE *WHERE* YOUR VOICES DON'T CARRY SO WELL. LITTLE EARS, YOU KNOW.

AND BY THE WAY, THE NAZI ROBOT WAS CALLED THE "MURDER MACHINE."

THAT'S IT! HOW DID YOU KNOW THAT?

BECAUSE IT'S OVER THERE SOMEWHERE. I JUST DUSTED IT THE OTHER DAY.

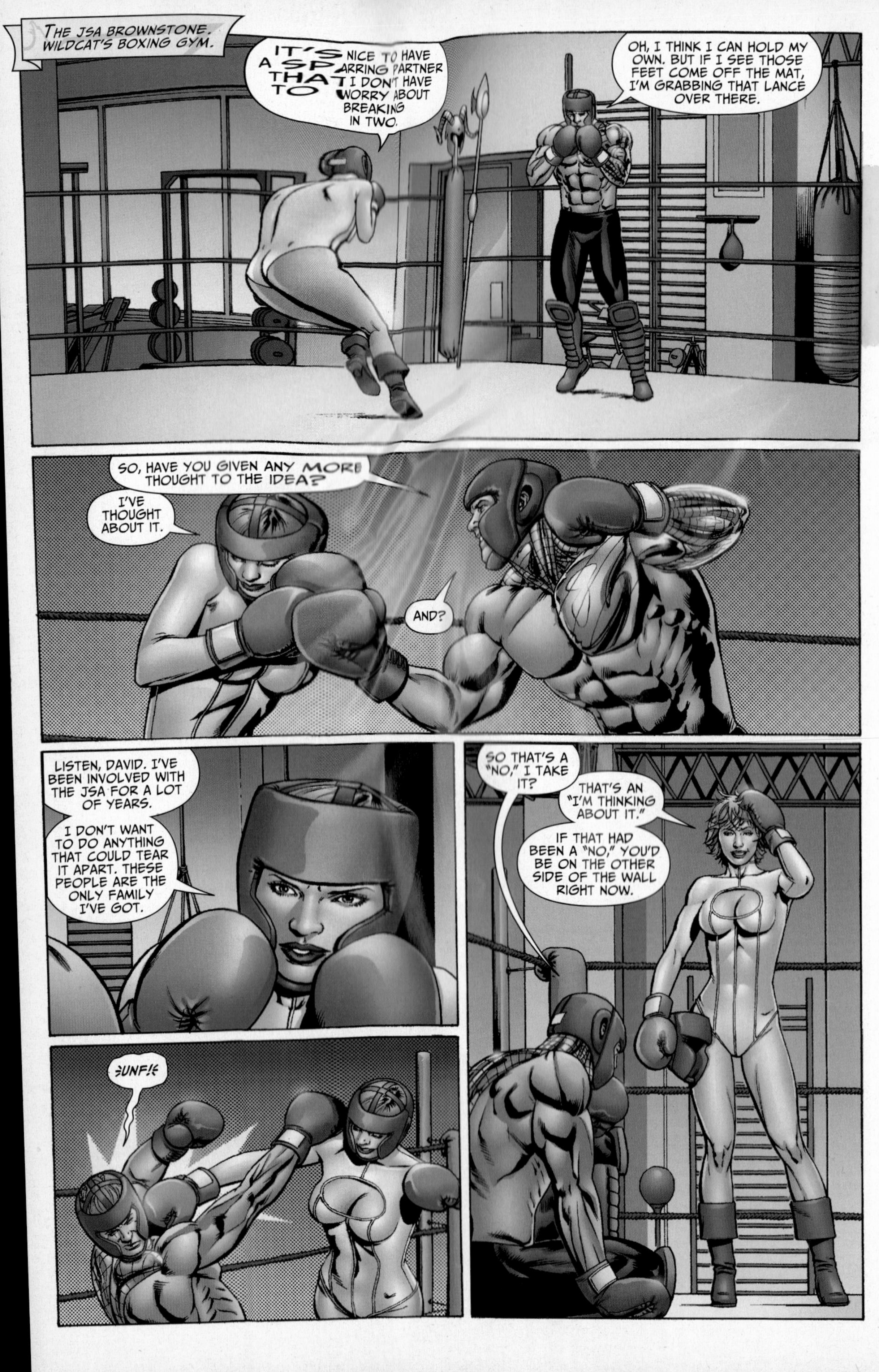

THE JSA BROWNSTONE. WILDCAT'S BOXING GYM.
IT'S NICE TO HAVE A SPARRING PARTNER THAT I DON'T HAVE TO WORRY ABOUT BREAKING IN TWO.
OH, I THINK I CAN HOLD MY OWN. BUT IF I SEE THOSE FEET COME OFF THE MAT, I'M GRABBING THAT LANCE OVER THERE.
SO, HAVE YOU GIVEN ANY MORE THOUGHT TO THE IDEA?
I'VE THOUGHT ABOUT IT.
AND?
LISTEN, DAVID. I'VE BEEN INVOLVED WITH THE JSA FOR A LOT OF YEARS.
I DON'T WANT TO DO ANYTHING THAT COULD TEAR IT APART. THESE PEOPLE ARE THE ONLY FAMILY I'VE GOT.
UNF!
SO THAT'S A "NO," I TAKE IT?
THAT'S AN "I'M THINKING ABOUT IT."
IF THAT HAD BEEN A "NO," YOU'D BE ON THE OTHER SIDE OF THE WALL RIGHT NOW.

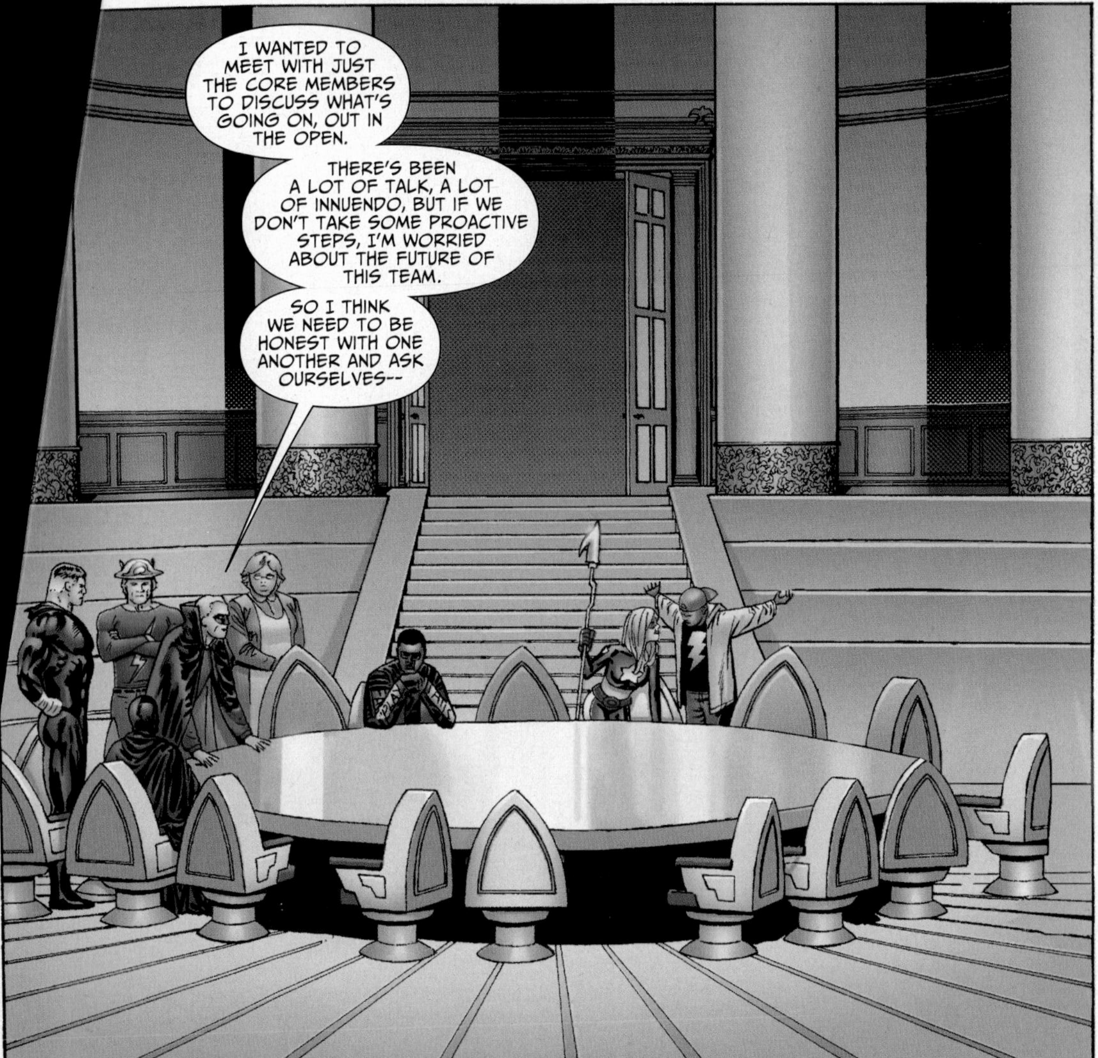
I WANTED TO MEET WITH JUST THE CORE MEMBERS TO DISCUSS WHAT'S GOING ON, OUT IN THE OPEN.
THERE'S BEEN A LOT OF TALK, A LOT OF INNUENDO, BUT IF WE DON'T TAKE SOME PROACTIVE STEPS, I'M WORRIED ABOUT THE FUTURE OF THIS TEAM.
SO I THINK WE NEED TO BE HONEST WITH ONE ANOTHER AND ASK OURSELVES--

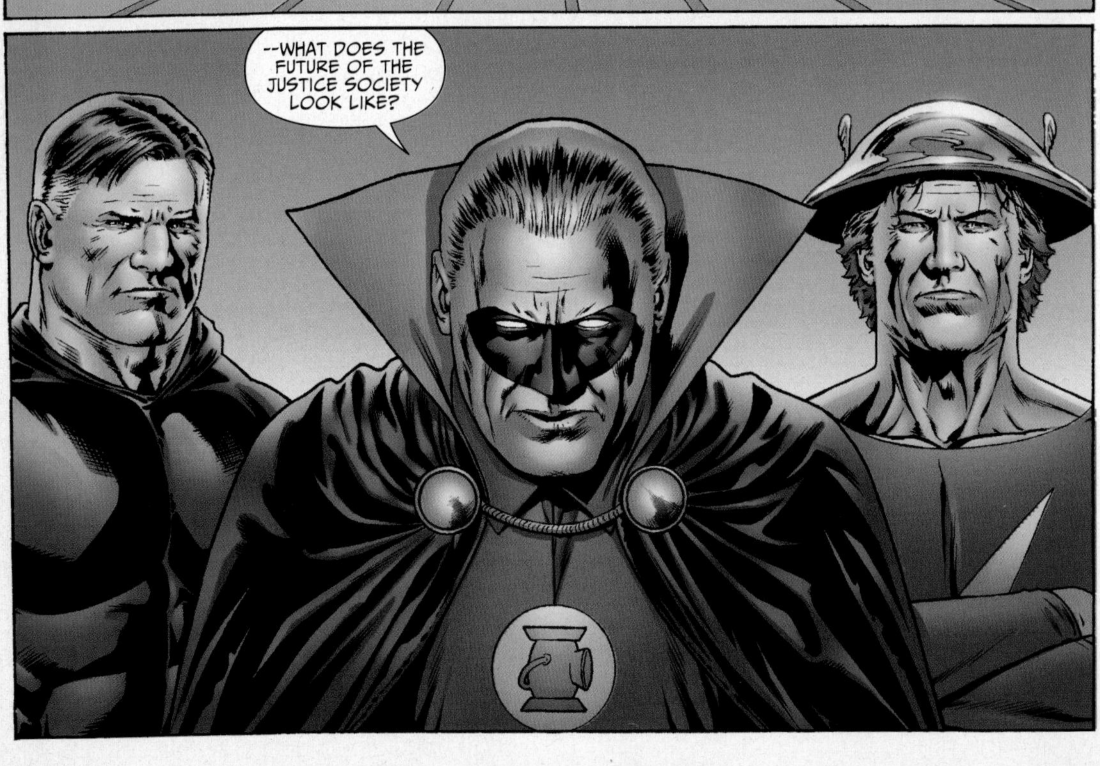
--WHAT DOES THE FUTURE OF THE JUSTICE SOCIETY LOOK LIKE?

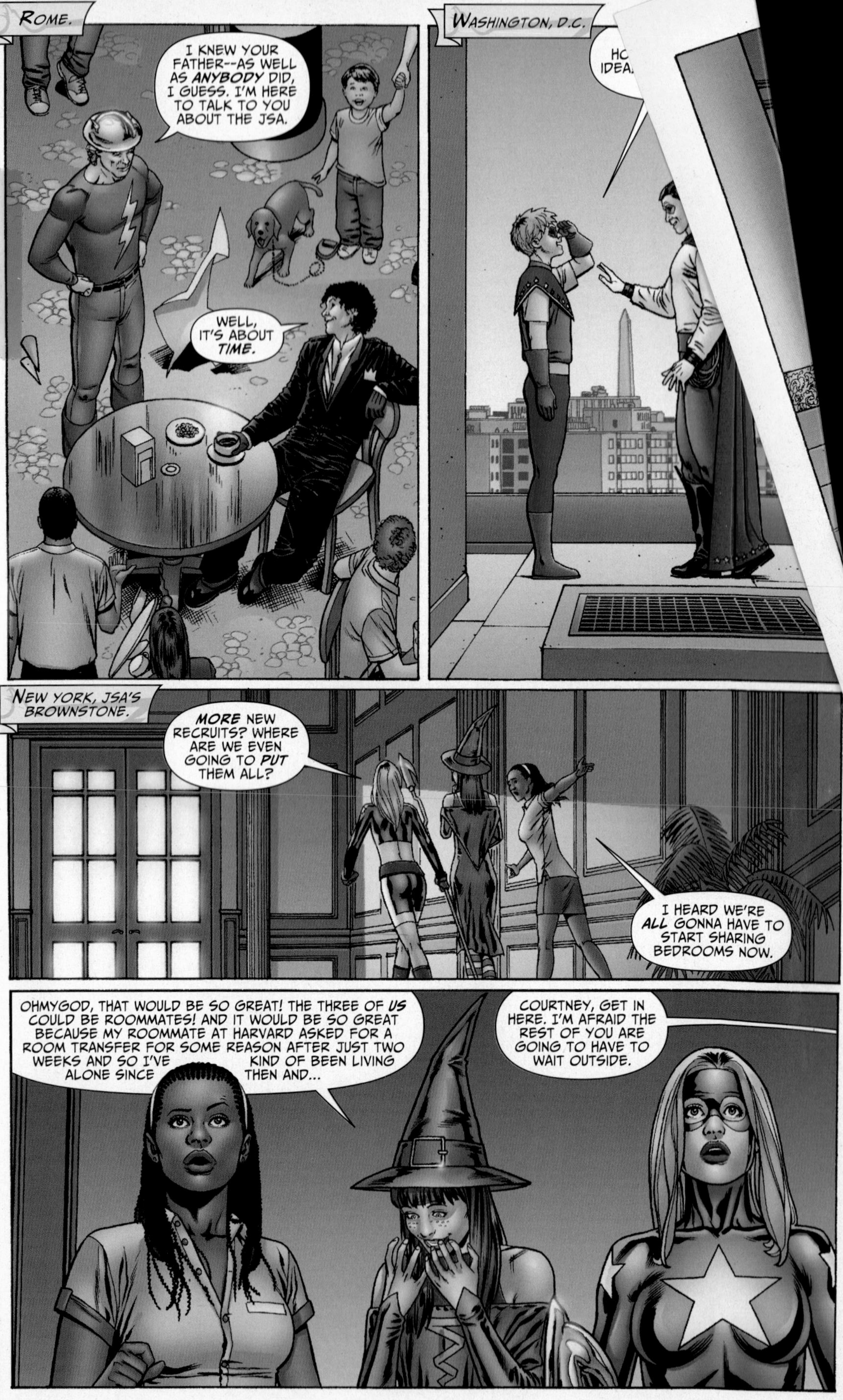
ROME.
I KNEW YOUR FATHER--AS WELL AS ANYBODY DID, I GUESS. I'M HERE TO TALK TO YOU ABOUT THE JSA.
WELL, IT'S ABOUT TIME.
WASHINGTON, D.C.
NEW YORK, JSA'S BROWNSTONE.
MORE NEW RECRUITS? WHERE ARE WE EVEN GOING TO PUT THEM ALL?
I HEARD WE'RE ALL GONNA HAVE TO START SHARING BEDROOMS NOW.
OHMYGOD, THAT WOULD BE SO GREAT! THE THREE OF US COULD BE ROOMMATES! AND IT WOULD BE SO GREAT BECAUSE MY ROOMMATE AT HARVARD ASKED FOR A ROOM TRANSFER FOR SOME REASON AFTER JUST TWO WEEKS AND SO I'VE KIND OF BEEN LIVING ALONE SINCE THEN AND...
COURTNEY, GET IN HERE. I'M AFRAID THE REST OF YOU ARE GOING TO HAVE TO WAIT OUTSIDE.

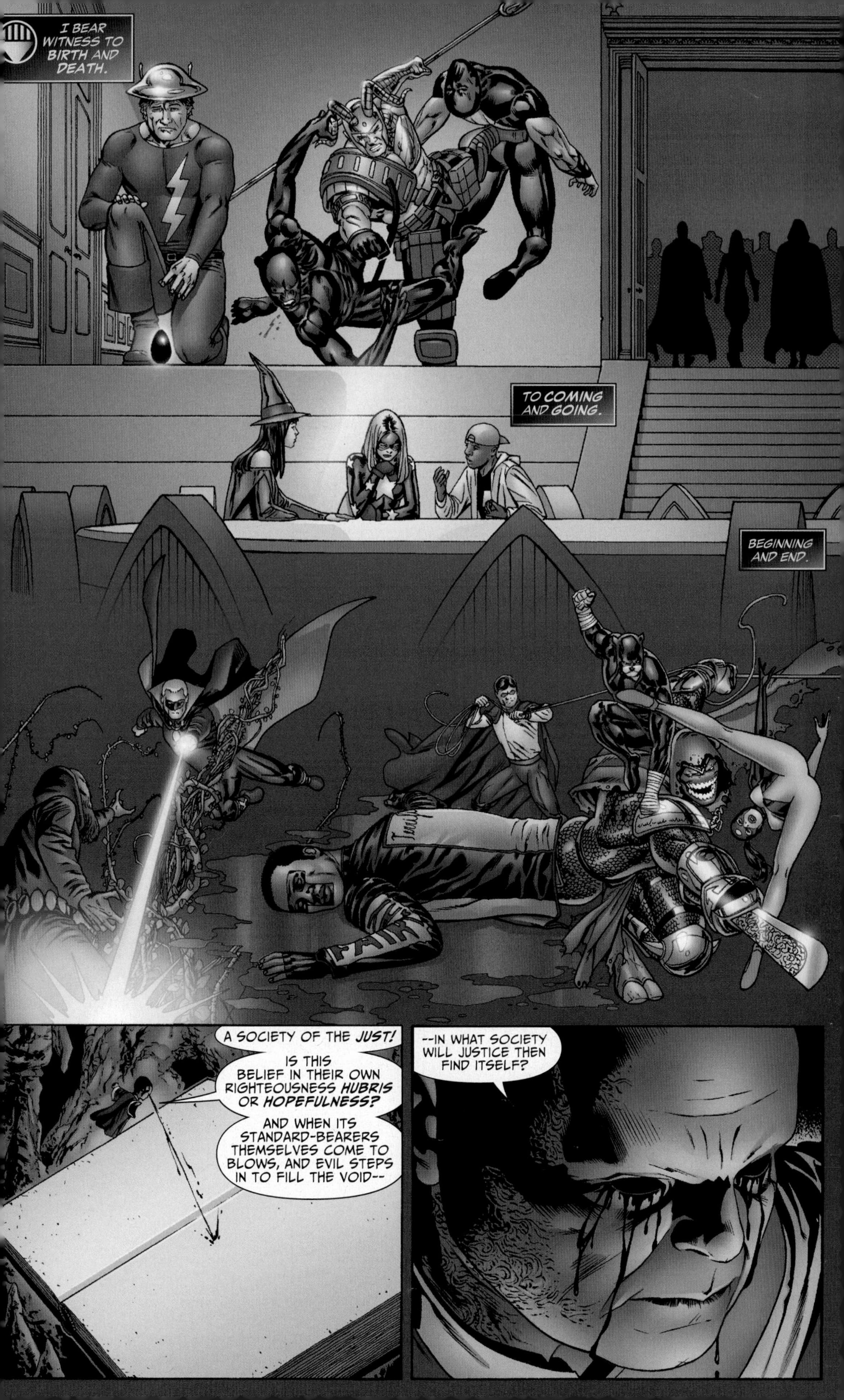
I BEAR WITNESS TO BIRTH AND DEATH.
TO COMING AND GOING.
BEGINNING AND END.
A SOCIETY OF THE JUST!
IS THIS BELIEF IN THEIR OWN RIGHTEOUSNESS HUBRIS OR HOPEFULNESS?
AND WHEN ITS STANDARD-BEARERS THEMSELVES COME TO BLOWS, AND EVIL STEPS IN TO FILL THE VOID--
--IN WHAT SOCIETY WILL JUSTICE THEN FIND ITSELF?

JUSTICE SOCIETY OF AMERICA #24 cover B by Jerry Ordway

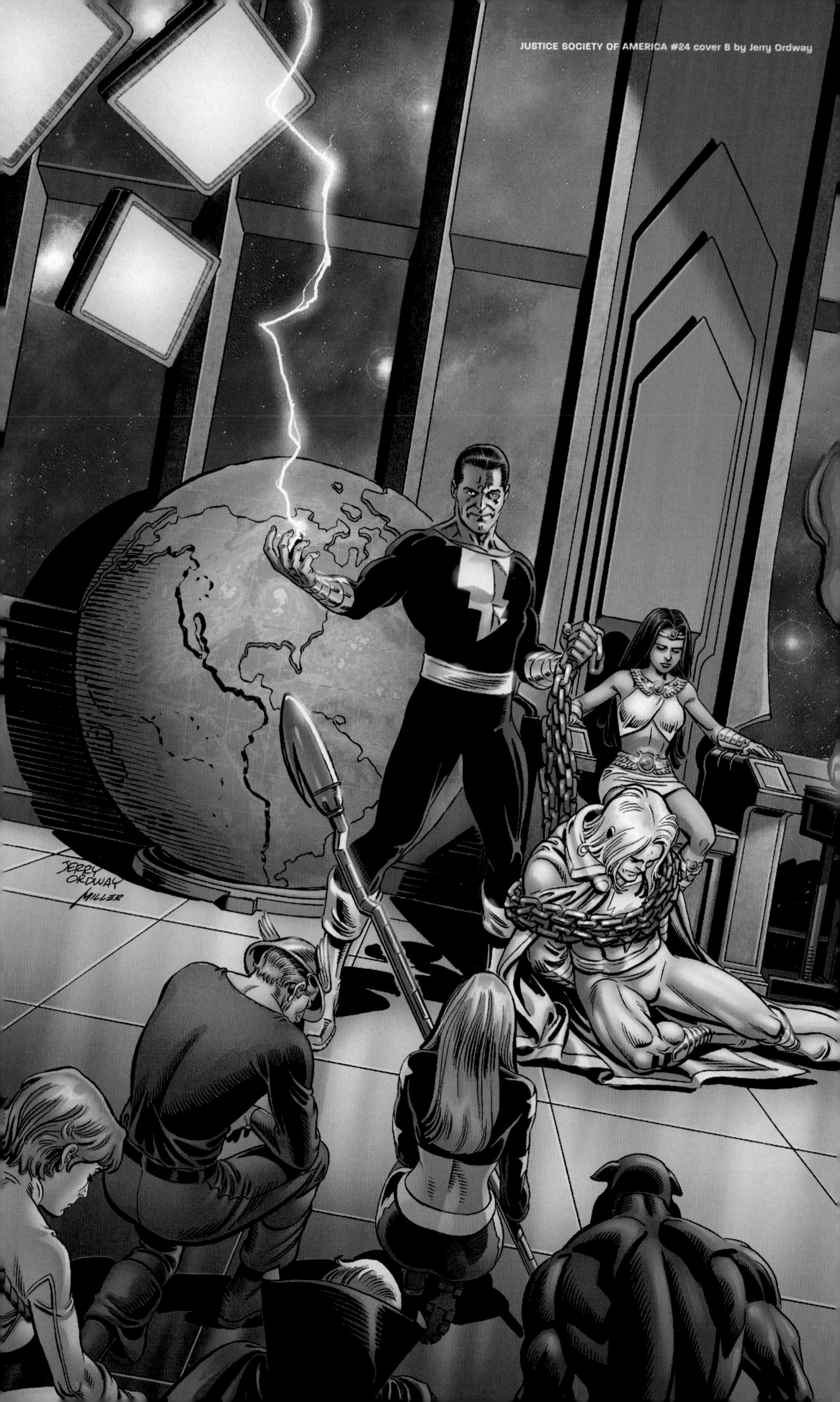
JERRY ORDWAY
MILLER

JUSTICE SOCIETY OF AMERICA #25 cover B by Jerry Ordway

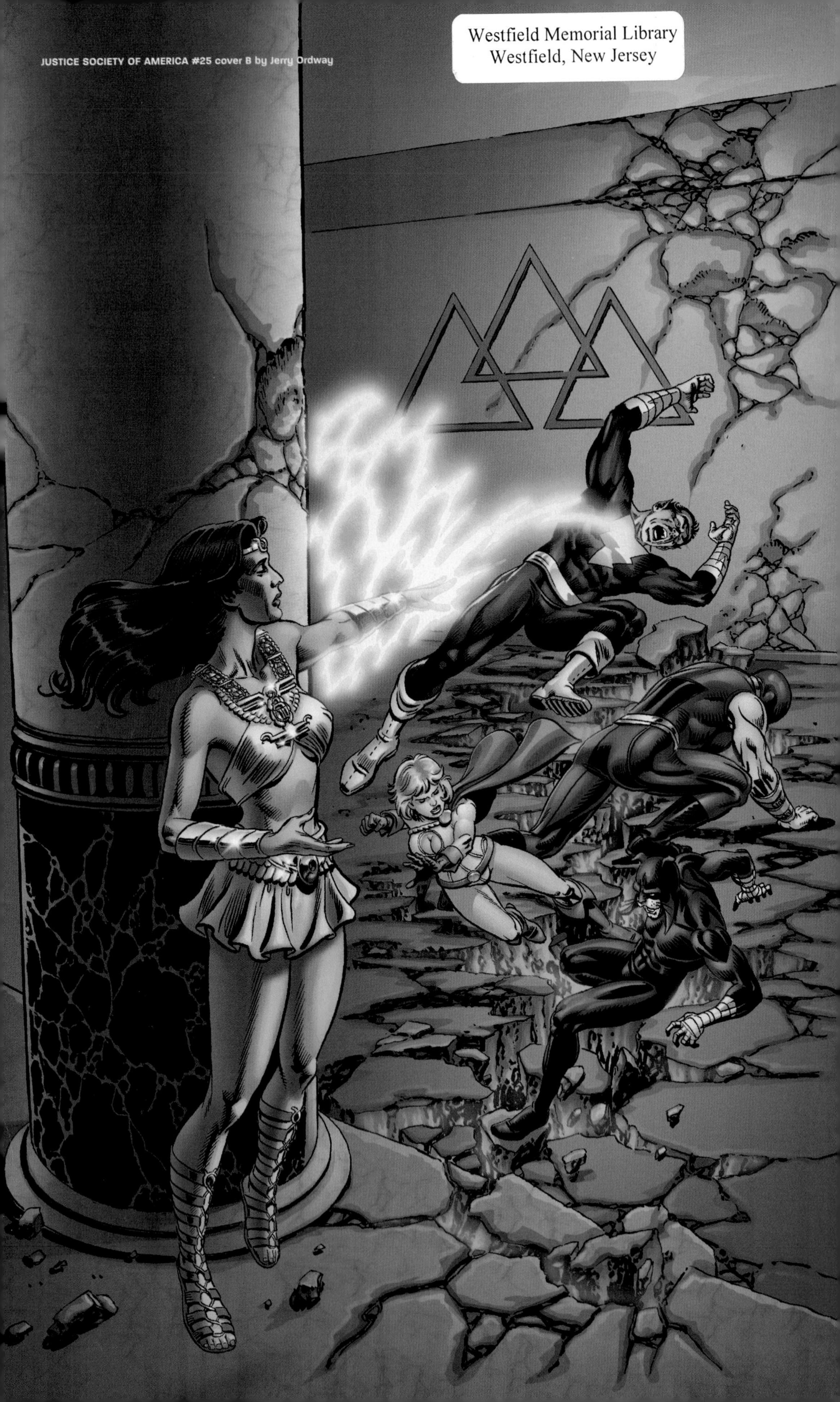

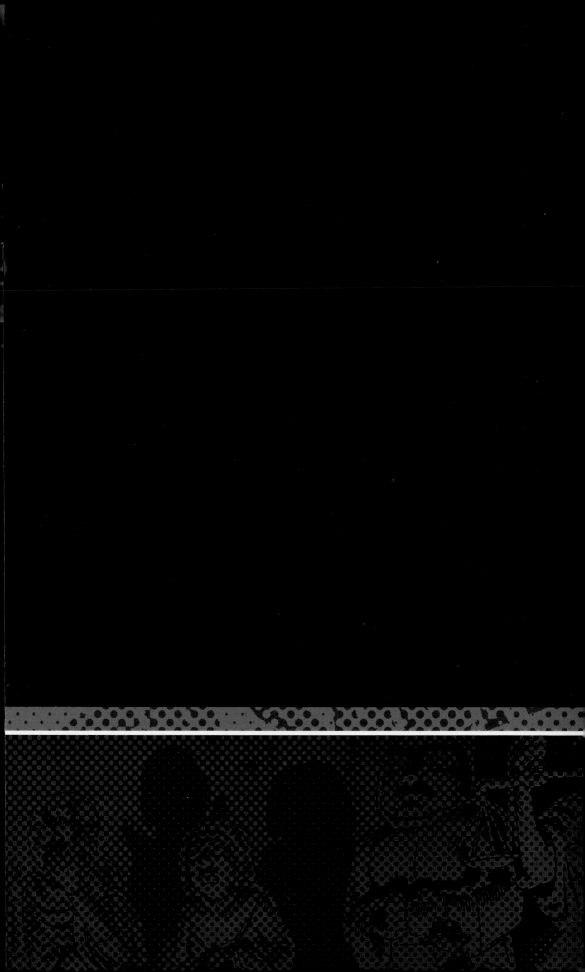

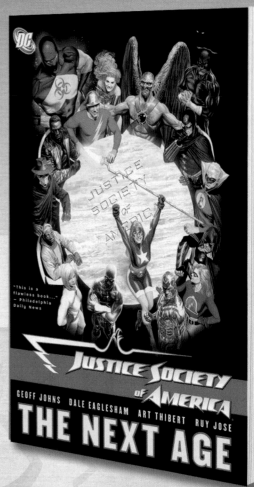

FROM THE WRITER OF
GREEN LANTERN *AND* **JSA**

GEOFF JOHNS

Witness the gathering of a new team of
Teen Titans and their initial battle against
an old, familiar foe: the most lethal
mercenary on earth, Deathstroke!

with **MIKE McKONE**

VOL. 1: A KID'S GAME

VOL. 2: FAMILY LOST

VOL. 3: BEAST BOYS AND GIRLS

VOL. 4: THE FUTURE IS NOW

VOL. 5: LIFE AND DEATH

VOL. 6: TITANS AROUND THE WORLD

TEEN TITANS / OUTSIDERS: THE INSIDERS

TEEN TITANS VOL. 2:
FAMILY LOST

with
MIKE McKONE

TEEN TITANS VOL. 4:
THE FUTURE IS NOW

with
MIKE McKONE

TEEN TITANS VOL. 5
LIFE AND DEATH

with
VARIOUS ARTISTS

SEARCH THE GRAPHIC NOVELS SECTION OF
DCCOMICS.COM
FOR ART AND INFORMATION ON ALL OF OUR BOOKS!